EDUCATING HARLEM

Contents

Acknowledgments   ix
Abbreviations   xi

Introduction   1
Ansley T. Erickson and Ernest Morrell

PART I   Debating What and How Harlem Students Learn
in the Renaissance and Beyond

1   Schooling the New Negro: Progressive Education,
Black Modernity, and the Long Harlem Renaissance
Daniel Perlstein   31

2   "A Serious Pedagogical Situation": Diverging School
Reform Priorities in Depression-Era Harlem
Thomas Harbison   55

3   Wadleigh High School: The Price of Segregation
Kimberley Johnson   77

PART II   Organizing, Writing, and Teaching for Reform
in the 1930s Through the 1950s

4   Cinema for Social Change: The Human Relations Film Series
of the Harlem Committee of the Teachers Union, 1936–1950
Lisa Rabin and Craig Kridel   103

5   Bringing Harlem to the Schools: Langston Hughes's
The First Book of Negroes and Crafting a Juvenile Readership
Jonna Perrillo   119

6   Harlem Schools and the New York City Teachers Union
Clarence Taylor   138

PART III   Divergent Educational Visions in the Activist
1960s and 1970s

7   HARYOU: An Apprenticeship for Young Leaders
Ansley T. Erickson   161

8   Intermediate School 201: Race, Space, and Modern
Architecture in Harlem
Marta Gutman   183

9   Black Power as Educational Renaissance: The Harlem Landscape
Russell Rickford   210

10   "Harlem Sophistication": Community-Based Paraprofessional
Educators in Central Harlem and East Harlem
Nick Juravich   234

PART IV   Post–Civil Rights Setbacks and Structural Alternatives

11   Harlem Schools in the Fiscal Crisis
Kim Phillips-Fein and Esther Cyna   257

12   Pursuing "Real Power to Parents": Babette Edwards's Activism
      from Community Control to Charter Schools
                Brittney Lewer   276

13   Teaching Harlem: Black Teachers and the Changing Educational
      Landscape of Twenty-First-Century Central Harlem
            Bethany L. Rogers and Terrenda C. White   298

                      Conclusion
       Ernest Morrell and Ansley T. Erickson   328

                  Contributors   339
                    Index   343

Acknowledgments

This book began in a conversation among a few colleagues in the spring of 2012, but it would not have come to fruition without the support and critical engagement of countless people. We would like to thank Teachers College provost Thomas James, who provided initial funding for this collaboration and what has become the Harlem Education History Project. We also appreciated Khalil Muhammad's early support and engagement with our work during his service as director of the Schomburg Center for Research in Black Culture. From the start, the team at the Columbia Libraries Digital Humanities Center developed the tools that enabled collaboration among authors and that host the book in its open-access form at harlemeducationhistory.library.columbia.edu.

The subsequent conversations that guided this project have taken many forms. Charles Payne, Monica Miller, Tracy Steffes, Kimberley Johnson, Johanna Fernandez, Vanessa Siddle Walker, and Dionne Danns provided feedback as discussants in internal and public conference presentations and helped shape the chapters in their developmental stages. Small and large conversations with Samuel K. Roberts Jr., Jeanne Theoharis, Deirdre Hollman, Joe Rogers Jr., Matthew Delmont, Jack Dougherty, Erica Walker, John Rogers, Paul McIntosh, Deborah Lucas Davis, Karen Taylor, and Terri Watson helped inform us as historians and storytellers. Veronica Holly at the Institute for Urban and Minority Education helped facilitate our work while also sharing her own Harlem history.

Ansley would like especially to thank her Schomburg Center 2017–18 fellowship cohort under the steady leadership of Brent Hayes Edwards. Ernest would like to thank his former staff at the Institute for Urban and Minority Education for their commitment to this project from the outset.

Our work benefited from a tremendous team of doctoral students in the Program in History and Education at Teachers College, who contributed to this work at various and in some cases multiple stages. We appreciate Antonia Abram Smith, Barry Goldenberg, Viola Huang, Jean Park, Esther Cyna, Deidre Flowers, and Rachel Klepper. Esther Cyna helped steer many aspects of the work, and it is all the more pleasing that she appears in the list of contributors as well. Alongside these young scholars, dozens of Teachers College students helped discuss and refine ideas that appear in this volume.

Most of all, we wish to thank the contributors. Together they represent fourteen different institutions, thirteen different kinds of disciplinary homes in the academy. Along with Heather Lewis, they have been wonderful collaborators, willing to join in summer reading groups and online draft comment sessions, game to learn from one another and helpful in articulating from their various perspectives the need for these histories to be in the world.

None of the contributors would have been able to assemble their work without the numerous archivists and librarians who helped curate and preserve the materials that are the grist for our investigations. We would like to thank especially the teams at the Municipal Archives of the City of New York and the Schomburg Center for Research in Black Culture, whose work can be found on each page of this book.

Despite this abundance of support, any errors remain ours alone.

As an editorial team, although we came from different starting points, we were both new to Harlem and its history. Through the process that yielded this book, and through ongoing work, we have been honored to share the accounts gathered here and look forward to the further historical investigations that Harlem's educational history deserves.

Ansley T. Erickson
New York, New York

Ernest Morrell
South Bend, Indiana

Abbreviations

BOE—Board of Education of the City of New York Collection
MA—New York City Municipal Archives
MSRC—Moorland-Spingarn Research Center, Howard University
NYCBOE—New York City Board of Education
NYCIBO—New York City Independent Budget Office
NYCPC—New York City Planning Commission
NYSDOE—New York State Department of Education
Schomburg—Schomburg Center for Research in Black Culture, New York Public Library
Tamiment—Tamiment Library and Robert F. Wagner Labor Archives, New York University
UFT—United Federation of Teachers
USNY—University of the State of New York

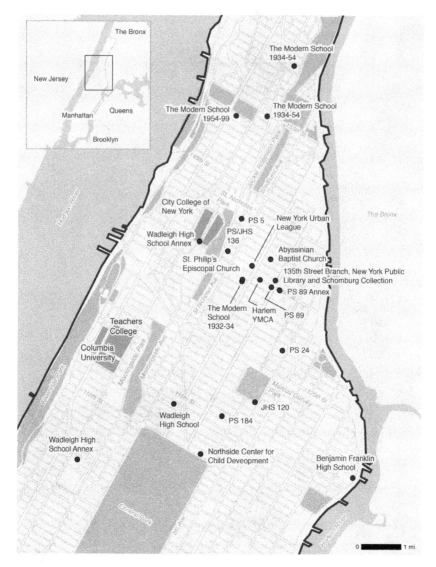

Please note that these maps to do not offer a comprehensive portrayal of Harlem's educational landscape. They show those sites that receive substantial discussion in the chapters in this volume.

Map design by Rachael Dottle. Map research by Rachel Klepper. Map layers from: Department of Information Technology and Telecommunications, Department of Urban Planning, City of New York; Atlas of the city of New York, borough of Manhattan. From actual surveys and official plans / by George W. and Walter S. Bromley,

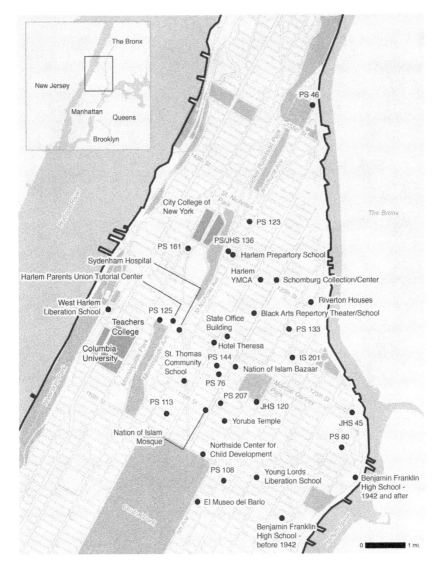

The Bronx

New Jersey

Manhattan

Queens

Brooklyn

PS 46

City College of
New York

PS 123

The Bronx

PS 161

PS/JHS 136

Harlem Preparatory School

Sydenham Hospital

Harlem Parents Union Tutorial Center

Harlem
YMCA

Schomburg Collection/Center

West Harlem
Liberation School

PS 125

Riverton Houses

Teachers
College

State Office
Building

Black Arts Repertory Theater/School

PS 133

Columbia
University

Hotel Theresa

St. Thomas
Community
School

PS 144

IS 201

Nation of Islam Bazaar

PS 76

PS 113

PS 207

JHS 120

Yoruba Temple

JHS 45

Nation of Islam
Mosque

Northside Center for
Child Development

PS 80

PS 108

Young Lords
Liberation School

Benjamin Franklin
High School -
1942 and after

El Museo del Bario

Benjamin Franklin
High School -
before 1942

0   1 mi.

New York Public Library Map Warper: http://maps.nypl.org/warper/layers/871; Manhattan Land book of the City of New York. Desk and Library ed. [1956]; New York Public Library Map Warper: http://maps.nypl.org/warper/layers/1453#Metadata _tab; and State of New Jersey GIS: https://www.state.nj.us/dep/gis/stateshp.html. Point locations from: School Directories, New York City Board of Education, *New York Amsterdam News* via ProQuest Historical Newspapers, and multiple archival sources cited in relevant chapters.

EDUCATING HARLEM

Introduction

ANSLEY T. ERICKSON AND ERNEST MORRELL

The speakers' corner at 135th and Lenox Avenue in Harlem drew radicals and revolutionaries, tellers of tales and teachers of the public. In a white stone-fronted building only yards away, a noted novelist worked as a librarian, fostering a refuge for children and adult readers. A few long avenues to the west on Edgecombe Avenue, and a few decades later, mothers risked jail to press for better facilities and qualified educators for their children at Junior High School 136. At the same junior high school and others not far away, teenagers gathered to ride buses downtown to City Hall to press the city to fund new youth programs. From the first signs of their concerted migration in 1899 through the end of the twentieth century, people of African descent labored, organized, imagined, and built Harlem.[1]

But they did not build from scratch, nor in a landscape entirely under their own control. In 1811, the Commissioner's Plan for New York City carved most of Manhattan into a regimented grid of north–south avenues plotted 920 feet apart, crossed by east–west streets spaced 200 feet apart. Designed by a politician, a surveyor, and a lawyer, the street grid facilitated the sale and development of land, the conversion of soil into cash.[2] These wealthy and powerful white men drew the grid that helped parcel out Harlem, an area that had been farmland tilled in part by enslaved Africans, into a new and profitable residential district. The first sales targets were middle-class white New Yorkers, often of Jewish and European heritage. But not long after, Black residents began to arrive from farther south in Manhattan, where hostile neighbors pushed them out, or from southern states, where Jim Crow sought to hold them in place, or from the West Indies. In Harlem, African American migrants and West Indian immigrants found a landscape of new opportunities. But they also found well-worn pathways of racism, economic exploitation, and political oppression. Like the street grid, these realities formed Harlem's sightlines and rhythms. Street speakers and librarians and youth organizers imagined their Harlem, striving to build a place that would recognize their full humanity, a place to learn and teach and thrive. But to do so, they had to confront a world very much not of their own making.

Harlem has long been an idea as much as a place, both for its residents and for those looking on from outside.[3] The creative efflorescence of the Harlem Renaissance made the place a synonym for literature, music, and art, and Marcus Garvey's Universal Negro Improvement Association based there stood for pan-African nationalism and autonomous development.[4] In 1935, amid the Depression's strong grip on Harlem, and again in 1943, with Black soldiers seeing the contradictions between oppression at home and the fight for liberation abroad, Harlem stood also for a place of protest against racism in its northern, urban form.[5] The need for that protest only intensified as the era of mass white suburbanization drew resources away from Harlem, and barriers to justice—in education, employment, housing, and political representation—remained high. From a base in Harlem, James Baldwin wrote powerfully in 1963 of the "fire next time," and Malcolm X addressed street crowds and galvanized a new phase of Black protest.[6] By the early 1990s, signs of economic revitalization appeared, and quickly Harlem stood for the reclaiming of the U.S. city by (often white) capital, the radical transformations of gentrification.[7]

Harlem was a nationally powerful symbol or totem, but at the same time it remained the terrain of families' and individuals' intimate lives. Not only did quotidian life often challenge the iconic representations of Harlem, but it proved the falsehood of any idea of a single Harlem story or unification of Harlem voices into a single community. The years of Harlem Renaissance artists and Jazz Age nightlife were also years of steady tenant and labor organizing.[8] Images of Harlem as an all-Black space missed the presence and the power of white people who moved through the neighborhood daily as teachers, police officers, or drivers who traversed Harlem streets en route downtown.[9] Vibrant protests for Black and Latinx community control of schools gained national attention in the 1960s and 1970s, but these did not wholly displace integrationist efforts, which at times contained their own commitments to democratic governance.[10] And even if Harlem seemed constant in one respect—it remained a center of Black life and Black residence—Harlem residents diverged in the ways they constructed their ideas of Blackness, their thinking about race in relationship to gender and class and culture and nation.[11] Despite the power of Harlem Renaissance or protest or urban-crisis Harlem, no monolithic Harlem existed. Many experiences of difference, identity, politics, and expression divided Harlem into many stories and many communities.

Harlem schools sat at the juncture of Harlem as a symbol and Harlem as a daily reality. The quest for educational opportunity denied in the South helped propel Black migrants northward. From their arrival, residents pursued a range of innovating educational visions. To do so they worked against overcrowding and understaffing caused by systematic neglect by the city system; school resources and curricula that paid little heed to the stories and perspectives of people of African descent; policies that subtly or overtly encouraged segregation; and teaching methods that denied students' and community members' humanity rather than celebrating it.[12] Educational activists in Harlem took up a variety of strategies, from leading youth to become educators about African and African American history to organizing parent boycotts to opening pathways for Black and Puerto Rican mothers to become licensed teachers.[13]

This book is the first volume wholly dedicated to documenting primary and secondary education in Harlem as it evolved across the twentieth century. Across thirteen chapters that narrate Harlem's educational history from the 1920s through the 2010s, two key themes emerge. First, educational struggle was an ever-present reality in Harlem. Most accounts of urban school systems have emphasized a rise-and-fall trajectory that celebrated early twentieth-century accomplishment as contrasted with a post–World War II decline. But the narrative looks different from the perspective of an African American neighborhood. Black urban dwellers did not enjoy a "rise" in which city schools expanded access and excelled in creating new mobility. And although city schools, like many other aspects of urban infrastructure, faced new challenges in the post–World War II decades, their fall was never so great as to end community investment and striving via education. The variety and endurance of this struggle reveal themselves best when, as this volume does, the work of women, children and youth, and activists across a variety of ideological positions receives the historical attention it merits.

Second, the diversity of Harlem's community—political, ideological, economical, and cultural—was matched by the diversity of Harlem's educational visions and strategies for securing them. Just as no single label or image—of literary renaissance or urban crisis, nationalist politics or integrationist protest—could capture the range of experiences of Harlem life and politics, no single educational approach ever did.[14] Like the diversity of political approaches that flowered in Harlem, from Garveyite pan-African nationalism to interracial communism to pressures for middle-class respectability, educational approaches ranged from moderate reformism to profound reinvention. To speak again in terms of the street grid, some educational leaders wanted to create safe passage through Harlem's rectilinear streets; others wanted to excavate the grid and put something new and organic in its place. Harlem's educational visions were not only varied, but often became national exemplars. The field of Black history had its roots in Harlem's Schomburg Collection library.[15] Kenneth and Mamie Clark pioneered educational practices that informed later "compensatory education."[16] In East Harlem Deborah Meier conceptualized a small-school approach that spread nationally, and Geoffrey Canada imagined community-wide educational transformation through Promise Zones, a model later adopted by federal policy makers under President Obama, to cite only a few examples among many.[17] Harlem proved key terrain in which to define what it meant to go to school as a Black person in twentieth-century urban America.

One of the benefits of an edited volume is the opportunity to draw together scholars with a range of disciplinary and methodological angles to consider a common topic. The chapters that follow are written by scholars with expertise in political science, sociology, and film studies, as well as many historians. And among the historians, the range of methodological approaches and source material is wide. The architectural historian Marta Gutman reads the Intermediate School (IS) 201 building itself, and its architectural drawings, as a source, and Daniel Perlstein sees literature as a window into educational thought. Oral-history interviews inform multiple chapters as well. This is far from all that could be done, and we hope this range of sources will remind readers and scholars of the breadth of the historical record and the multiplicity of angles from which historians can explore the educational past.

Although the volume enjoys this interdisciplinary and methodological breadth, it also has some limitations that are important to recognize. Harlem's geographic as well as conceptual boundaries have shifted over time. The chapters that follow focus most intensively on what, by the mid-1960s, was known as Central Harlem—the streets north of 110th and south of 155th, on the flats that stretched east of Morningside, St. Nicholas, and Colonial (later Jackie Robinson) Parks to Fifth Avenue. From the 1930s through the remainder of the twentieth century, the overwhelming majority of residents in this area were African American or West Indian. Many Harlemites who identified as Black also had Latinx roots, with connections especially to Puerto Rico. And by the 1950s Puerto Rican New Yorkers made up a majority of East Harlem's population, the area north of Ninety-Sixth Street and east of Fifth Avenue to the Harlem River. This volume gives its most intense attention to Black Americans who were long-term New Yorkers, recent arrivals from the U.S. South, or immigrants from the Anglophone Caribbean. These are certainly not the only Harlem stories to be told, but they merit the sustained focus and investigation we undertake here.

Education at times became the terrain of shared struggle for Harlem's African American and Puerto Rican communities. We follow African American individuals and organizations into their interaction with sites and struggles in East Harlem, including at Benjamin Franklin High School and IS 201, with many Puerto Rican New Yorkers. However, the volume does not offer a comprehensive view of Harlem's Latinx educational history. Fortunately, in addition to the existing contributions of scholars Lorrin Thomas, Vanessa Valdez, Sonia Song-ha Lee, and Adina Back, new work in this field is under way.[18]

Harlem residents participated in and made their mark on higher education—as professors, students, and activists.[19] This volume, however, prioritizes public education at the primary and secondary levels. Perhaps some readers will perceive this absence as somewhat ironic, given the editors' current or recent affiliations with Columbia University and this volume's placement at Columbia University Press. Columbia has not only been a figure in Harlem's history, but at times an active agent of oppression.[20] In the conclusion we consider the meaning of trying to produce new knowledge about Harlem's schools in light of this history.

Not Rise-and-Fall but Persistent Struggle

Perhaps the most familiar way to tell the story of urban education in the United States over the twentieth century is to speak of a rise and a fall. U.S. urban school districts rose in the first three or four or six decades of the century, the narrative goes. They became relatively highly resourced and bureaucratically elaborate systems that contributed to significant economic and social mobility for poor and working-class European immigrants streaming into cities. Relative to the educational opportunities available in the rural South, they marked an improvement—if much less than full equality—for Black migrants to northern cities. But then they fell. Exactly when their fates shifted varies by location and interpretation: deindustrialization increased poverty, which in turn generated greater student need while shrinking available resources; supportive political coalitions fractured; educators sought "life adjustment" for students rather than challenging academics.[21] (A sloppy and at times racist shadow assumption blames the "fall" on the arrival of majority-Black student populations and fails to identify the actions of neglect and divestment by white-dominated state power that accompanied this transition.)[22]

Like all historical accounts, the rise-and-fall narrative is a creature of the time in which it was crafted as much as it is a depiction of a time in the past. The rise-and-fall story developed amid the intellectual trends and pressures of the Cold War. Much sociology of the late 1950s and early 1960s looked at U.S. cities and communities and saw "the ghetto," a location of "social disorganization" and a "culture of poverty." The "urban crisis" was born, and many historians' energy shifted to understanding the forces of racism and capitalism that constrained and undermined U.S. cities. Less attention went to how African American urbanites defined their own lives and communities. The U.S. metropolitan landscape saw major changes—from the shrinking and suburbanization of industrial work to the boom in white homeownership and wealth accumulation alongside the concentration of poor renters of color in cities.[23] Dominant white social scientists of the period paid less attention to broad economic shifts and political choices and focused instead on the culture and predilections of poor people residing in cities, whose children brought this "cultural deprivation" into school.[24] Schools "fell" as cities "fell" in the crisis years.

The rise-and-fall framework adopted by many historians in the 1980s and 1990s allowed them to interrogate what political alliances dissolved, what community conditions grew in ways that created new challenges for educators. It also allowed them to move beyond earlier narratives that either celebrated schools as engines of mobility or condemned them as mechanisms of class reproduction. At various moments, elements of each of those interpretations was true.[25]

The rise-and-fall narrative fits best at the scale of a whole city—Detroit, New York City, Atlanta, or San Francisco. In the early twentieth century, urban municipalities like New York invested in education by building schools to serve student populations that were expanding rapidly both in number and in the extent of schooling that students achieved. Attending high school at the turn of the century marked a person as part of an educational elite; by midcentury, doing so was a normative experience for U.S. adolescents. In this context of growing educational demand, city school systems also supported an increasingly professionalized teaching and administrative workforce, and an extensive educational bureaucracy.[26]

But a neighborhood's story can diverge from a city's story. By focusing not on a city or school district as a whole, but on a single Black neighborhood, this volume explores the trajectory of urban education from a new angle.[27] Resources in expanding urban school systems flowed unequally. Even during the "rise," some areas of the city lacked new facilities, new programs, and newly trained and credentialed teachers as others took these features for granted across the twentieth century. Harlem—alongside growing Black neighborhoods in Brooklyn—experienced segregation that exacerbated overcrowding, and district choices led to fewer trained and experienced teachers and fewer new educational facilities than in other city neighborhoods.[28] There was no early twentieth-century "rise," no time when investment matched what students needed or deserved, in Harlem.

Moving away from the rise-and-fall framework helps illuminate the forces that constrained Harlem schooling in the early part of the twentieth century, but also makes space for those efforts to support and improve it. Whereas early historical works on Harlem, most notably Gilbert Osofsky's *Harlem: The Making of a Ghetto* (1966), devoted much of their energy to the disinvestment and abandonment of the area by white residents, new scholarship on Harlem identifies the persistent efforts to build and sustain Black community despite structural and political obstacles.[29] Later scholarship recognized the severity of privation in Harlem and the forms of resistance that Harlem residents deployed. Cheryl Greenberg's *"Or Does It Explode?"* links a careful analysis of Great Depression–era unemployment to the political organizing that Harlemites depended on to survive those especially hard years. More recently, Shannon King's *Whose Harlem Is This, Anyway?* reinterprets the earliest decades of Black Harlem by tracing the way working-class Harlem men and women forged alliances around labor, housing, policing, and safety in search of "community rights." Kevin McGruder complements this view by tracing the way Harlem residents made physical spaces for the learning and leisure of local children. Through McGruder's and King's work, we see that Harlem never existed without organized community-focused Black activism reflecting a variety of strategic and ideological orientations.[30]

Education was a major focus of organizing, imagining, and building in Harlem. Just as the lack of sufficient or equitably provided educational facilities and resources undermines the idea of a "rise," Harlem defies the idea of a "fall" as well. Surely, high and rising levels of poverty in the community in the 1960s, and resource cuts that accompanied the fiscal crisis of the 1970s, all within the intensifying drug economy of these decades, sharpened Harlem's educational challenges. Yet even as economic changes in the neighborhood and the city brought straitened times, educational activism continued apace, in varied voices and with varied targets. And in some contexts, educational innovation and even striking success developed. The forces of "ghettoization," disinvestment, and decline shaped Harlem—but so did persistent struggle and constant contestation. Just as we reject the notion of a rise because of its message of generalized prosperity and investment when Harlem saw no such thing, we refute the idea of a fall. Such a framing obscures the continued existence of educational success alongside educational challenge and minimizes persistent educational striving.[31] This volume works toward the unsilencing of these narratives.[32]

Many Voices in Harlem's Black Freedom Struggle for Education

The most often told element of Harlem's educational history is the IS 201 struggle.[33] Black and Puerto Rican parents, long frustrated at overcrowded and aged facilities, pressed for a new intermediate (or middle-grades) school. In keeping with the long tradition of activism against segregation in Harlem, they wanted it to serve Black, white, and Puerto Rican students. The school system provided a new building that opened in 1966, but it displayed old patterns of segregation. IS 201 represented the city's deep resistance to desegregation, and for many advocates the experience became a turning point. If desegregation was impossible, more assertive local democratic control—or "community control" of education was even more necessary. IS 201 became one focal point in a national effort for community control of urban schools.

The IS 201 story neatly aligned with earlier and popular views of civil rights movement history: a nonviolent integrationist movement led by Martin Luther King Jr. gave way to a more militant and separatist Black Power struggle with Malcolm X and Stokely Carmichael leading. And when community control in practice faced struggles and challenges, those difficulties only seemed to reinforce the view that the "Martin to Malcolm X" narrative was not a story only of change, but of decline. But as Heather Lewis has shown, community control opened opportunities for educational innovation as well. What mattered at IS 201 and other sites in the New York City community control experiment was not only what political figureheads said, but what teachers, mothers, and community members imagined and achieved.[34] Russell Rickford also reinterprets the community-control struggle by shifting away from a binary view of integrationism versus community control to recognize that, again with attention to a wider range of actors than the movement's more famous voices, strains of integrationism and striving for local democratic power over schooling ran inseparably through decades of Black educational activism.[35]

As have Rickford and Lewis, this volume consciously pursues the variety of educational visions that were shaped in Harlem, not only in the years of the IS 201 struggle but earlier and later. Earlier scholarship on Harlem pushed civil rights history to recognize the presence of women and grassroots activists, alongside celebrated male leaders in courtroom fights and national marches.[36] We contribute to this effort with a particular focus on education, seeking out the work and visions of parents, young people, aspiring teachers, artists, and many others.

Out of this effort comes the second major theme of this book: that Harlem's educational visions were as diverse, as varied, at times as contradictory as Harlem residents. Integrationist efforts coexisted and were in conversation with communist organizing, efforts at participatory democracy and liberatory pedagogy. The sweeping range of Harlem political visions—from pan-Africanism to middle-class striving to interracial communism to capitalist entrepreneurism to Black Arts nationalism—all had educational implications, and often explicitly pursued educational visions. And all operated inseparably from the ongoing effort to define Black identity and gender identity in the context of broader structures of racism and sexism.

In Harlem's history overall, scholars have found new interpretations by consciously broadening their scope of inquiry—to seek new voices and to credit the ideas that these new voices offered. Continuing to do so here helps offer a robust sense of the dynamic, varied, and consequential range of educational imagining under way over the course of twentieth-century Harlem. We seek not only to recognize this variety, to make the important if often strikingly absent point that a range of Harlem residents cared about and acted on their schools. We seek also to follow the best of recent scholarship not only in acknowledging this range of actors but also in honoring them with the respect that is full historical analysis. Advocates' work in Harlem, as everywhere, was at once bold, principled, compromised, and flawed. It was a historical force of its own and a window into the shape and limits of contemporary thought.[37]

The story of Harlem schools aligns with neither an image of an educational "rise" in the first decades of the twentieth century nor an educational decline in the latter decades. At no point in the twentieth century did a majority of Black Harlem residents enjoy confidence that their children would receive decent, sufficient, and equitable schooling. But many Harlem community members from diverse identity and ideological positions labored, theorized, imagined, organized, and built toward this goal. Their efforts, alongside local, citywide, and national networks of allies, were constant and varied in both strategy and imagined outcome. And they were highly consequential even if not fully successful.[38] Recognizing their work and the contexts against which they labored offers scholars of Black life and education a new view of education in the urban United States.

Before Our Story Begins: Schools and the Making of a Black Mecca, 1890 to 1915

The thirteen chapters in this volume explore the past one hundred years—roughly 1919 to the present. Harlem's history as an African American community began a few decades earlier, and so we offer a summary of that historical preface to our work.

With its only partially developed street grid, open lots sitting beside strings of three or four brownstones, Harlem in 1905 looked very little like the densely populated and renowned center of Black life in the United States that it would soon become. But in the early years, the basic contours of later struggles over decent housing, decent jobs, and just education were evident—and so were the sources of power from which Harlem residents would draw: collective organizing, political engagement, and cultural expression to understand and transform their community.

When real estate developers remade Harlem from farmland to New York's next subway-linked residential neighborhood, beginning in the 1890s, they drew middle-class families, with children in tow. Demand for schooling followed, and twenty-five New York City public schools served the blocks between 110th and 155th Streets, from the Hudson River to the East River, as of 1910. In the last decade of the nineteenth century, Black residents composed roughly 5 percent of Harlem's population and were scattered broadly but thinly across the neighborhood as in the city overall. The majority of the initial population consisted of middle-class white residents. They came to Harlem, but in numbers lower than developers anticipated, in part because they had their choice of many portions of the expanding city and its nascent suburbs.[39]

By 1910, Harlem had a small but growing center of Black settlement. New York's residential geography pressed Black residents seeking to escape cramped and substandard housing and hostile neighbors in other Manhattan neighborhoods toward Harlem as apartments became available there. The Great Migration brought streams of African American southerners northward as they ran from Jim Crow violence and privation and toward jobs made available when white workers headed to World War I and toward schoolrooms that were overcrowded and under-resourced, but more accessible and extensive than what Black communities and educators had eked out in the hostile South. Railroad lines carried former sharecroppers and laborers, alongside teachers and doctors straining against the confines of segregation and oppression, north to Detroit or Chicago, Philadelphia or New York City.[40] Coming from the West Indies, as did nearly 40,000 Harlem residents between 1900 and 1930, some Harlem residents drew on generations-long experience with formal education; many southern migrants, by contrast, had experienced only limited formal schooling in a public school system that had been systematically underfunded by local white officials and was often hard to reach in a dispersed rural landscape.[41]

Whether coming from inside the city, up from the South, or out of the Caribbean, migrants to Harlem carried the hope that Harlem would be the soil in which dreams for themselves, their families, and their communities would flourish. It was at times rocky and resistant soil, as the story of housing in Harlem well attests. Migrants to Harlem often found better housing stock but still-strong lines of segregation. In the first decades of the twentieth century, Black individuals and families took up residence near 135th Street and Lenox Avenue and then expanded block by block outward, via home purchases and renting. Areas of Black settlement at times opened via negotiation, as white landlords were desperate for tenants as supply temporarily exceeded demand. Black landlords saw a profitable new market as well. White resistance came alongside demand for Black residents' dollars, though. There was some physical violence, but more frequently white homeowners used paper weapons. They banded together in restrictive covenant agreements (even though New York State court ruled these illegal) that prevented ownership or rental to Black families. These mechanisms proved less strong than did the combination of profit seeking and white racist fear: more and more white residents left Harlem, and landlords rented apartments in tenement buildings on side streets, larger apartments on the avenues, and subdivided or let out whole brownstones to Black tenants who had few options in the broader New York City housing market. In Harlem, as in city neighborhoods around the United States, segregation inflated demand, allowing landlords to press rents ever higher. Working-class families responded by taking in boarders and doubling up within apartments, turning Harlem into one of the most densely populated areas of Manhattan.[42]

New York City stopped formally segregating students along color lines in 1883, but school zone lines reinforced housing patterns that concentrated Black families in some of Harlem's schools and away from other parts of the city. By 1913, Black students constituted more than a third of the student populations at three Harlem elementary schools; another four Harlem schools served between 12 percent and 15 percent African American students. For the very small number of Black teachers who found employment in New York's public schools, most found positions in Harlem schools—as at Public School (PS) 89, where 21 percent of the faculty was Black.[43]

Jacob Theobald became principal of PS 89 in 1906, as a growing number of Black students attended the school. It sat closest to Harlem's initial Black residential core around Lenox Avenue and 135th Street. Theobald celebrated the great effort that Harlem families made to encourage schooling: "There is not another [part of the city] where so much is sacrificed and even want is endured . . . to keep the boy in school." Theobald connected his school to the lives of Harlem adults as well as children. Opening the Lenox Community Center in the 1910s enabled public lectures, like those offered by the Harlem orator and socialist Hubert Harrison, as well as clubs, classes, and other community events. Theobald's efforts added to those already undertaken by networks of Harlem men and women, and youth, who created spaces for recreation and learning when Black Harlem residents were still denied access to Manhattan's equivalent spaces for white teens and children. PS 89 was a center of community activity and an overcrowded and underfunded institution.[44] This duality of limitations and persistent ambition continued through the next century.

Overview of the Book

This volume traces the story of schooling in Harlem through thirteen chronologically organized chapters, as follows.

Part I: Debating What and How Harlem Students Learn in the Renaissance Years and Beyond

The literature and art and sparkling jazz-club nightlife that emerged in the Harlem Renaissance long drew historians' attention, but a steady, quiet movement pressed forward among lesser known Harlem residents as well. Harlem's tenants and laborers campaigned against the material oppressions that at times informed and at times diverged from the images Harlem artists offered up. Harlem residents' efforts to create educational spaces, both formal and informal, for their children aligned with the activism and organizing under way simultaneously in other aspects of Harlem life, in housing, labor, and political participation.[45] Educational efforts broadly defined—from creating a space for boys to play basketball to forming study circles on African and African American history—represented one way in which Harlemites pursued ideas of self and community advancement.

In the first decades of the twentieth century, well before James Weldon Johnson, Alain Locke, and other celebrated voices of the Black intellectual elite declared Harlem the "Mecca of the New Negro," Black men and women showed through their collective efforts and their individual commitments that they placed great value on the safety and education of their children.[46] They pushed to make good use of the resources the city offered, but did not hesitate to point out the ways these were strained and insufficient. There was no universal agreement on what education should mean for Harlem's children, nor was there easy access to what was needed. But a range of Harlem actors made it clear that schooling would be a central concern in the making of their communities as well as in how they understood themselves as Black Americans. This section explores that concern from three vantage points: the work of Harlem Renaissance writers, community leaders' debates about the curriculum in Harlem schools, and the trajectory of Harlem's Wadleigh High School for Girls.

The most publicly celebrated representations of Harlem life in the early twentieth century came from Harlem Renaissance artists, who crafted new U.S. art—in jazz and poetry and literature and visual art—out of an interracial network of creativity. They were criticized by some as naive about the political power of their medium or as insufficiently engaged with the daily lives of their Harlem neighbors.[47] But they saw in the oppressions and opportunities of New York and Harlem grist for work that expressed Black humanity with fullness and complexity, and broadcast this vision to the world.

As Daniel Perlstein shows in chapter 1, New Negro and Renaissance writers and thinkers of the early 1920s were education thinkers. Drawing on New Negro thought from the 1920s as well as (primarily white) progressive education discourse in the same years, Harlem writers made schools, schooling, and teaching central in their writing. They incorporated progressive educational ideas to critique dehumanizing schooling practices and craft a view of education for Black students that would foster their own sense of humanity amid the oppressive U.S. racial, political, and economic order. Daniel Perlstein uncovers a Renaissance educational discourse that was not previously appreciated by historians or literary scholars. The writers Jean Toomer and Nella Larsen (the latter a Harlem branch librarian for the New York Public Library) have written about how Black humanity and oppressive southern Jim Crow schooling were irreconcilable.[48]

Against this literary backdrop, innovating Black women educators working in both public and private schools in Harlem in the 1930s sought to create spaces for Black children's self-directed activity while fostering alternatives to the identities a racist world had assigned them. Perlstein shows how, at Gertrude Ayer's PS 24 just south of Mount Morris Park and at The Modern School led by James Weldon Johnson's niece Mildred Johnson Edwards, Harlem educators worked to bring these ideas explored in literature into the school lives of children and teachers.

Harlem school administrators took up another strain of progressivism, one focused more on sorting and categorizing students in the name of aid and efficiency. As Thomas Harbison details in chapter 2, the schools' leadership in the 1910s and 1920s responded to the growing presence of Black southern and West Indian students by encouraging separate educational experiences for them. In doing so, white Harlem school leaders, like many New York City educators before them in earlier waves of student population growth and immigration, judged that the existing curriculum was inappropriate for the needs of new arrivals and emphasized separate, specialized approaches. Established Black leaders in Harlem, many of them middle-class men who thought migrants needed to assimilate to new cultural and class norms and to use vocational education to prepare entry into low-skilled but available work, saw schools' emphasis on adjustment as congruent with their own philosophy.

As the Great Depression tightened its grip on Harlem, a street uprising was triggered in 1935 by perceived mistreatment of a youngster by a storeowner. The subsequent local investigations of the Harlem uprising of 1935 and the conditions that helped feed it provided an opportunity for Harlem residents, teachers, and leaders to name the conditions they faced in their schools. The Board of Education's earlier emphasis on character education and vocational education, especially for Black students recently arrived from the South, seemed to many in Harlem like just another mode of educational neglect, an attempt to "segregate the Negro educationally."[49] Parent leaders, civic leaders, and some teachers spoke against the Board of Education's continued assertions that "adjustment" to the unequal world was enough educational ambition. As Harlem residents organized "Don't Buy Where You Can't Work" protests against racist hiring and mobilized against Met Life's construction of segregated housing in Manhattan, an education that accommodated itself to inequality appeared especially insufficient.[50] In 1930, roughly a third of a million people of African descent lived in Harlem, where an area of roughly six square miles or four hundred city blocks formed one of the largest and most recognized Black urban settlements in the United States, and one of its densest residential areas anywhere. By the 1930s, thirteen of Harlem's fourteen elementary schools enrolled almost exclusively Black students. The cumulative effect of overcrowding and underinvestment in the 1920s meant that even before poverty rates rose and realities such as worsening child hunger and housing insecurity made their mark on classrooms, Harlem schools were struggling. Harlem came to symbolize urban educational neglect for African Americans, and debate about how to contest this neglect and refashion schools revealed the diversity of thought within Harlem's many communities.

In chapter 3, Kimberley Johnson explores how individual white resistance, demographic changes in Harlem, and segregationist school zoning policy produced the closure of Harlem's Wadleigh High School for Girls. Opened in Harlem in 1902 as a flagship academic school for a predominantly white population, Wadleigh's Black population grew gradually over the 1920s and 1930s. Many of the educators and community leaders who knew the school well faced two competing realities: they recognized the racist tracking that consigned many Black students to the school's under-resourced vocational courses, but they also hoped that the school could continue serving a diverse population of girls of European, Caribbean, and African descent. Their hope for an integrated school faced resistance from white parents who withdrew their daughters.

By 1945, there were almost no white students at Wadleigh. The Board of Education agreed to sustain Wadleigh after plans for closure generated organized protest from teachers and leaders at the school. The school remained open, but as Johnson writes, "The New York City Board of Education proved unwilling to support a well-resourced majority-Black school or to desegregate the school." In the 1920s, 1930s, and 1940s, as in later phases of Harlem's educational history, advocates struggled to choose the most effective routes to navigate the narrow straits left by official neglect and white resistance to strong Black schools in Harlem.

By the 1930s Harlem coalesced as a leading center of Black life in the United States, one that demonstrated powerfully the multiple forms of oppression that Black urban communities faced. Simultaneously, though, Harlem's educational landscape illustrated the breadth of responses to this oppression. Not only did Harlem residents take varied strategic or philosophical approaches but they also worked in varied networks and groups—from working-class consumers to elite ministers, interracial teachers' networks to students in junior high school classes—in the search for equal and just schooling.

Some Harlem educational advocates pursued their work with a focus on the curriculum—some rooted in the interracialism of the 1930s and 1940s, others like Langston Hughes interested in addressing the absence of African American history in many New York classrooms. These efforts at times depended on interracial networks of teacher labor activists, often with organizational ties to the Communist Party. The Teachers Union, a city-wide organization also tied to the Communist Party, fostered an interracial network of activist teachers in Harlem. They spoke out in the 1935 postriot investigations and worked inside their schools and beyond for more just education for Harlem students.[51]

Chapter 4, by Lisa Rabin and Craig Kridel, examines the work of the Teachers Union's Harlem Committee and its effort to use film to encourage classroom conversation about racism and injustice. In East Harlem's Benjamin Franklin High School, and later in Central Harlem's James Fenimore Cooper Junior High School, teachers used clips of Hollywood films of the era to launch critical discussions of racism in the United States. Their intervention in the curriculum was more modest than that of The Modern School educators described in chapter 1, but they sought to ensure that school spaces in Harlem linked to nationally pressing issues including lynching. In the process, Black students voiced their developing awareness of the politics of representation in mass media.

The Harlem Committee did not speak for all New York City or all Harlem teachers, the vast majority of whom were white and lived well outside of Harlem's neighborhoods.[52] The divide between local educational leadership—including Board of Education officials, local principals, and some teachers—and community leaders, parents, and activists was on sharpest display in a 1937 mock trial of a principal. Illustrating the importance of Harlem's churches as civic and political infrastructure, Adam Clayton Powell Jr.'s Abyssinian Baptist Church hosted the two-thousand-person event in which PS 5 principal Gustav Shoenchen was "tried," in absentia, for the alleged beating of a fourteen-year-old student. With the Board of Education refusing to act, Harlem religious, civic, and political leaders united in their condemnation of Shoenchen and his seeming indifference to the needs and humanity of Black students and parents. The Teachers Union stood with Harlem leaders and firmly condemned Shoenchen, but the more recently formed Teachers Guild aligned itself with the Board of Education, signaling its acquiescence in an educational system that persistently underserved Black students.

Not all Harlem educators were school teachers, however. As Jonna Perillo shows in chapter 5, the poet Langston Hughes decided to address the persistent absence of African and African American history in school curricula. Hughes drew on his skill as a writer to create a textbook, *The First Book of Negroes*, and then visited schools in Harlem and beyond to read for students and encourage classroom use. Despite his fame, Hughes was motivated by more than a desire to intervene favorably in the lives of Harlem youngsters. He also needed the income that book sales offered.

Over the immediate post–World War II years, Harlem suffered the same systematic disinvestment, via shifts in public expenditure and private markets, as did cities around the country. Although industrial production was never the prime source of employment for Harlem workers, the decline in shipping and light manufacturing, from Brooklyn to the Bronx as well as closer to home, made finding work harder and stripped away the possibility of picking up additional shifts or work to fill employment gaps on the docks.

The public policy incentives of mass white suburbanization continued to make their mark on Harlem in the 1940s and beyond, even though "white flight" had been visible from the 1910s. Few white families resided in the core central Harlem blocks from 110th through 155th Streets in the 1950s, but white outmigration from other parts of the city created new kinds of movement in Harlem. Many aspiring middle-class Harlemites looked outside of Manhattan, to Queens or Bronx neighborhoods that had previously been segregated white but that now opened to Black people as white residents sought to move farther out, beyond the city line to the county suburbs. This movement created two distinctly postwar U.S. residential forms—the expansive new and almost exclusively white developments of the Levittowns and beyond, and the consciously middle-class Black developments of St. Albans and Hollis or East Elmhurst in Queens and similar areas in the Bronx. Moving out of Harlem became a part of the story for Black residents as it had been for white residents earlier.

Opportunities for landownership and homeownership pulled Black families to Queens, but so did concern about the ways Harlem was changing. By the late 1950s, the heroin trade made an increasingly profound mark on Harlem. Harlem was New York City's heroin marketplace, a geographically concentrated distribution center that felt the impact of the trade far out of proportion to its size. Harlem was doing New York City's drug work. For many Harlem families with the option to do so, rising concern about drug-related violence and nuisances proved a push to leave the area. The combined effects of deindustrialization, growing poverty, and middle-class outmigration made Harlem a more solidly poor and working-class community by the 1960s. It was by no means economically homogeneous, but many of the middle-class Black families who had lived close by and sent their children to some, if not all, of Harlem's public schools were shifting away.

The post–World War II years were also times of transition for New York City's teachers. Cold War pressures and targeting of teachers with communist affiliations weakened the Teachers Union, which had been a consistent voice in favor of better curricula and resources for Harlem students. The Teachers Guild, rising in influence in the same years, made less effort to connect itself to local school and community issues and emphasized teacher job security and compensation. The transition from the Teachers Union to the Teachers Guild left Harlem parents and students feeling more divided from teachers than united with them in their educational struggles. This division only reinforced the sharpening class divisions between increasingly poor Harlemites and middle-class (and predominantly white) New York City teachers living farther and farther from Harlem. The new United Federation of Teachers, recognized with collective bargaining rights in 1961, followed the Teachers Guild's model. As Clarence Taylor details in chapter 6, transitions in Harlem teachers union politics helped set the stage for later fissures between teachers unions and community members in New York and beyond.

In the 1950s and 1960s Harlem moved from being a community segregated by race to one increasingly segregated by both race and class. This transition was fueled in part by growing opportunities for middle- and working-class Black people in other areas of the city previously closed to them. In 1970, Harlem tracts had between 21 percent and 40 percent of individuals living in poverty; by 1980, those living in poverty now represented 36–50 percent of those tracts' population. By contrast, the national poverty rate hovered between 11 percent and 15 percent.[53] Private and government investment declined as community need increased, and the ripples of Cold War politics narrowed the ways in which Black activists could contest these conditions.

Part III: Divergent Educational Visions in the Activist 1960s and 1970s

Recollecting his Harlem childhood, Walter Dean Myers wrote about the magic of its streets and his affection for them. By the early 1960s, fewer Harlemites spoke so confidently, with more expressing worry over the corrosive influence of the heroin trade and continually neglected housing in a community that had lost much of its economic diversity.[54] Harlem's school buildings showed the wear of decades with little new construction. Citywide policies that reinforced segregation (through school zoning) and inequality (as in high rates of unlicensed or temporary teachers in Harlem) worsened the conditions that Harlem students found in classrooms each morning.[55]

The essays in this section reinterpret educational activism in 1960s Harlem from new angles. They illustrate the tremendous strategic and imaginative range of Harlem educational activists, and the regenerative energy that created novel educational spaces and transformed existing ones with new meanings.

In early 1960s Harlem, a network of social scientists and social work professionals decided to make youth perspectives and youth leadership central to their effort to understand Harlem's needs and propose a youth program for the neighborhood. As Ansley T. Erickson shows in chapter 7, HARYOU (or Harlem Youth Opportunities Unlimited), developed by Kenneth Clark and colleagues, became a space where Harlem youth from fourteen to twenty-one years of age debated and investigated their Harlem and tried to imagine its future. Represented in other scholarship as an illustration of the vulnerabilities of the War on Poverty Community Action programs it helped inspire, HARYOU's work reveals a commitment to young people as experts on their own lives and communities. HARYOU countered the language of cultural deficit and pathology then taking hold—including in the work of Clark. HARYOU students worked as researchers, teachers, community organizers, and artists whose words spoke to the world they knew.

HARYOU shared some ideas about local knowledge and self-determination with the community control activism taking form in the same years in East Harlem. East Harlem and Central Harlem residents worked to shape one of the Ford Foundation–supported "demonstration districts" around the planned Intermediate School 201 on 128th Street and Madison Avenue.

In chapter 8, Marta Gutman uses the tools of architectural history to yield a new interpretation of IS 201's creation and operation. Gutman recognizes the building's contemporary impact as a symbol of continued segregation after official promises that it would be otherwise. Gutman sees in its design not only a problematic separation from the local landscape—as many contemporary observers noted—but an effort to compensate for segregation with fine finishes and modern design. In this way the school's opening in 1966 Harlem harked back to the 1940s and 1950s "equalization" efforts in which segregationist southerners tried to weaken calls for desegregation by building new facilities.

Gutman's analysis continues into the years after the opening and initial protests, when IS 201 functioned as a local middle school. Working in the tradition of Henri Lefebvre and his understanding of the multiple processes through which spaces come to have social meanings, Gutman explores the ways teachers and community members in the school redefined its classrooms, hallways, and auditoriums with opportunities for community building and learning in the tradition of the African diaspora.

Russell Rickford's chapter 9 shows that the search for autonomous Black educational spaces extended well beyond IS 201. As Daniel Perlstein demonstrated with an earlier generation of Renaissance art in Harlem, Rickford shows that "Black Power in Harlem was in many respects a renaissance of educational thought and practice." Tracing small organizations— some fleeting, some more enduring—in the 1960s and 1970s shows that Harlem was the home of myriad ways of translating Black Power thought into educational practice. Some new educational spaces aligned with contemporary efforts to improve public schools—as in the West Harlem Liberation School that operated during a 1968 teachers' strike, the Congress of Racial Equality's proposal for a Harlem-only public school district, or organizing for a new high school rather than the state office building slated for the storied corner of 125th Street and Seventh Avenue. Others created intentionally autonomous, consciously oppositional educational institutions—such as the Nation of Islam's primary and secondary schools. And yet others, such as the summer program imagined by Queen Mother Audley Moore, sought to carry Black children away from Harlem, if briefly, to a farm in Upstate New York.

Both the volume and the range of these educational visions and the institutions they generated matter. In their number, they attest again to the ways Harlem residents persistently marshaled resources to the education of their children. And in their variation, they show the centrality of educational theory and practice to all political endeavors to reimagine Black life. Even as many Harlem residents decried their local schools as oppressive engines of control and neglect, they found hope and power in schooling and school-building.

Many of the important examples of 1960s and 1970s educational imagining in Harlem proved ephemeral. Freedom schools lasted a few weeks, and HARYOU programs foundered in political controversy. But as Nick Juravich shows in chapter 10, Harlem birthed enduring educational innovations as well. Now a common feature of U.S. schools, paraprofessional jobs were the invention of the 1960s. The paraprofessional educator sat at the nexus of 1960s job-creation programs and school-improvement efforts focused on closing the cultural divide between a predominantly white and middle-class teaching force and local Black and Latinx students. Black and Puerto Rican women, many of them mothers of children who attended the schools in which they worked, gained employment and access to college courses through the first forms of the paraprofessional program. They filled a wide range of roles as classroom and student aides, translators and curriculum developers, and through their presence, they linked the local community with the inside of the school building.

In the midst of intense conflict for community control between a majority-white teachers union and majority–Black and Latinx communities, which produced the massive and long 1968 teachers' strike, the United Federation of Teachers won the support of paraprofessionals in its search for labor representation. Once unionized, paraprofessionals saw their compensation improve, but earlier efforts to create a pathway for working-class women of color into the teaching profession diminished in the context of austerity and shifting educational priorities.

Harlem faced several fundamental challenges in the 1960s and 1970s—products of the reorganization of metropolitan space occurring across the United States and of the particular dynamics of divestment and segregation in New York City. Those conditions never squelched the varied, persistent work of Harlem educators, community organizers, parents, and youth to understand their community's challenges and develop ideas and institutions to pursue empowering education. Some of those ideas, like paraprofessionals, took hold across the nation and continue to do so at present; others, like freedom schools or youth research programs, still echo in work with children today. Whether permanent or ephemeral, the educational visions described in these chapters show that even in the hard years of the 1960s and 1970s, Harlem was far from a place of crisis or despair alone. It was also a space of intensive educational imagining, of reconceptualizing what schooling and learning could mean in Black America.

Part IV: Post–Civil Rights Setbacks and Structural Alternatives

Continuing the historical inquiry of the previous sections, each chapter in part IV also offers a look at the past that can shed light on questions of the present.

In 1975, New York City faced a massive financial crisis that sent city leaders to Washington seeking, unsuccessfully, a federal bailout. In chapter 11, Kim Phillips-Fein and Esther Cyna show that the consequences of the crisis were especially visible in Harlem—with cutbacks in school facilities and programs occurring more there than in other areas of the city. As at each phase of Harlem's educational history, however, Harlem community members contested this unfairness and the results not of the fiscal crisis but of the city's decision to respond to it with austerity.

Like many U.S. urban school systems in the early twenty-first century, New York has experimented over the past few decades with new forms of school design, organization, and governance. Harlem has been a particularly intense locus of these changes, with a large concentration of charter schools operating in the neighborhood today. As Brittney Lewer shows in chapter 12, charter school policy in Harlem has roots that reach back to the 1960s community-control effort. By tracing the work of the education activist Babette Edwards over decades, Lewer recognizes how the multiple phases of Harlem parent- and community-led school-improvement efforts flowed together and diverged.

Edwards pushed hard for community control of schools in the mid-1960s, and served as a member of the IS 201 governing board until 1971. She became frustrated with the limits of local democratic control under New York City's decentralization structure and the constraints on school change created, in her view, by teachers union power. She turned to new approaches that she felt would place more power directly in the hands of Harlem parents directly. Her support for public school improvement continued, but she also became one of the early Black advocates for vouchers and, later, the head of a team seeking to build a community-focused charter school in Harlem. Through her own intellectual and political trajectory, Edwards bridges what are sometimes conceived of as separate or even conflicting educational efforts in Harlem.

The composition of Harlem's teaching force has also undergone dramatic changes over the past few decades. As the historian Bethany L. Rogers and the sociologist Terrenda C. White show in chapter 13, the gradual increase in the presence of Black and Latinx teachers in Harlem over the 1970s, 1980s, and 1990s reversed in the twenty-first century. Proportionally fewer teachers of color teach in Harlem's District 5 today than did previously. In their preliminary analysis, Rogers and White see multiple causal factors for this increase and then subsequent decline—from a confluence of policies in teacher assignment as well as preparation and evaluation alongside high turnover and the emergence of school choice in Harlem. Rogers and White recognize both the immediate and historical significance of the presence of Black teachers for their students as well as communities.

Through these thirteen chapters, this volume demonstrates the persistence of educational commitment and imagining on the part of Harlem children, parents, and educators. These visions faced steep obstacles woven from a variety of sources on the common warp of racism and white supremacy.

Consciously or otherwise, ideas of the past inform approaches to the present. Today, Harlem residents continue to face massive challenges in securing just and powerful education for their children. We hope that this focused, nuanced, and humane attention to the area and its schools, recognizing interconnections with as well as distinctions from the broader New York City story, offers one source of support for their efforts.

Notes

1. Manning Marable, *Malcolm X: A Life of Reinvention* (New York: Viking, 2011); Jeffrey Perry, *Hubert Harrison: The Voice of Harlem Radicalism, 1883–1918* (New York: Columbia University Press, 2008); Adina Back, "Exposing the 'Whole Segregation Myth': The Harlem Nine and New York City's School Desegregation Battles," in *Freedom North: Black Freedom Struggles Outside the South, 1940–1980*, ed. Jeanne Theoharis and Komozi Woodard (New York: Palgrave Macmillan, 2003), 65–91; "Memo to the Thousands of Supporters of Harlem Youth Day," April 9, 1963, Library of Congress, Kenneth Clark Papers, box 50, file 2, attached to Minutes of the Meeting of the Board of Directors, April 11, 1963; and Shannon King, *Whose Harlem Is This Anyway? Community Politics and Grassroots Activism During the New Negro Era* (New York: New York University Press, 2015).
2. Edward K. Spann, "Grid Plan," in *Encyclopedia of New York City*, ed. Kenneth Jackson (New Haven, Conn.: Yale University Press, 2010), 558.
3. This duality animates Andrew Fearney and Daniel Matlin, eds., *Race Capital? Harlem as Setting and Symbol* (New York: Columbia University Press, 2018).
4. On urban space as both idea and reality, see Robert A. Orsi, *The Madonna of 115th Street: Faith and Community in Italian Harlem, 1880–1950* (New Haven, Conn.: Yale University Press, 1985); and Fearney and Matlin, *Race Capital?* On the Renaissance, see David Levering Lewis, *When Harlem Was in Vogue* (New York: Penguin Books, 1997); and Ann Douglas, *Terrible Honesty: Mongrel Manhattan in the 1920s* (New York: Farrar, Straus and Giroux, 1996).
5. Cheryl Lynn Greenberg, *"Or Does It Explode?": Black Harlem in the Great Depression* (New York: Oxford University Press, 1991); and Martha Biondi, *To Stand and Fight: The Struggle for Civil Rights in Postwar New York City* (Cambridge, Mass.: Harvard University Press, 2003).
6. James Baldwin, *The Fire Next Time* (New York: Vintage, 1992 [1963]); Marable, *Malcolm X*.
7. Brian Goldstein, *The Roots of Urban Renaissance* (Cambridge, Mass.: Harvard University Press, 2016); Sharon Zukin, *The Naked City: The Death of Authentic Urban Places* (New York: Oxford University Press, 2011); and Lance Freeman, *There Goes the 'Hood: Views of Gentrification from the Ground Up* (Philadelphia: Temple University Press, 2006).
8. King, *Whose Harlem Is This?*; and Greenberg, *"Or Does It Explode?"*
9. Stephen Robertson, Shane White, and Stephen Garton, "Harlem in Black and White: Mapping Race and Place in the 1920s," *Journal of Urban History* 39, no. 5 (March 2013): 864–80.
10. Russell Rickford, "Integration, Black Nationalism, and Radical Democratic Transformation in African American Philosophies of Education, 1965–1974," in *The New Black History: Revisiting the Second Reconstruction*, ed. Manning Marable and Elizabeth Kai Hinton (New York: Palgrave Macmillan, 2011), 287–317.
11. Clare Corbould, *Becoming African Americans: Black Public Life in Harlem, 1919–1939* (Cambridge, Mass.: Harvard University Press, 2009); Barbara Ransby, *Ella Baker and the Black Freedom Movement: A Radical Democratic Vision* (Chapel Hill: University of North Carolina Press, 2003); Ransby, *Eslanda: The Large and Unconventional Life of Mrs. Paul Robeson* (New Haven, Conn.: Yale University Press, 2014); Farah Jasmine Griffin, *Harlem Nocturne: Women Artists and Progressive Politics During World War II* (New York: Basic Civitas, 2013); Nikhil Pal Singh, *Black Is a Country: Race and the Unfinished Struggle for Democracy* (Cambridge, Mass.: Harvard University Press,

2005); and Ashley Farmer, *Remaking Black Power: How Black Women Transformed an Era* (Chapel Hill: University of North Carolina Press, 2017).

12. Jonna Perrillo, *Uncivil Rights: Teachers, Unions, and Race in the Battle for School Equity* (Chicago: University of Chicago Press, 2012); Back, "Exposing 'the Whole Segregation Myth'"; Matthew Delmont, *Why Busing Failed: Race, Media, and the National Resistance to School Desegregation* (Oakland: University of California Press, 2016); Heather Lewis, *New York City Public Schools from Brownsville to Bloomberg: Community Control and Its Legacy* (New York: Teachers College Press, 2013); James Haskins, *Diary of a Harlem Schoolteacher* (New York: New Press, 2008 [1969]); and Clarence Taylor, *Knocking at Our Own Door: Milton A. Galamison and the Struggle for School Integration in New York City* (New York: Columbia University Press, 1997).

13. Corbould, *Becoming African American*; Martha Biondi, *Black Revolution on Campus* (Oakland: University of California Press, 2012); and chapter 10 in this volume.

14. Biondi, *To Stand and Fight*; Singh, *Black Is a Country*; King, *Whose Harlem Is This?*; and Mark Naison, *Communists in Harlem During the Depression*, new ed. (Urbana-Champaign: University of Illinois Press, 2004).

15. Corbould, *Becoming African American*; and Biondi, *Black Revolution*.

16. Gerald E. Markowitz and David Rosner, *Children, Race, and Power: Kenneth and Mamie Clark's Northside Center* (New York: Routledge, 2000).

17. Seymour Fliegel, *Miracle in East Harlem: The Fight for Choice in Public Education* (New York: Random House, 1993); Deborah Meier, *The Power of Their Ideas: Lessons for America from a Small School in Harlem* (Boston: Beacon Press, 1995); and Paul Tough, *Whatever It Takes: Geoffrey Canada's Quest to Change Harlem and America* (New York: Mariner Books, 2009).

18. Lorrin Thomas, *Puerto Rican Citizen: History and Political Identity in Twentieth-Century New York and Chicago* (Chicago: University of Chicago Press, 2010); Sonia Song-Ha Lee, *Building a Latino Civil Rights Movement: Puerto Ricans, African Americans, and the Pursuit of Racial Justice in New York City* (Chapel Hill: University of North Carolina Press, 2014); Adina Back, "'Parent Power': Evelina López Antonetty, the United Bronx Parents, and the War on Poverty," in *The War on Poverty: A New Grassroots History, 1964–1980*, ed. Annelise Orleck and Lisa Hizirjian (Athens: University of Georgia Press, 2010), 184–208; and Lauren Lefty, "Seize the Schools, Que Viva Puerto Rico Libre: Cold War Education Politics in New York and San Juan, 1948–1975" (PhD diss., New York University, 2019).

19. Biondi, *Black Revolution*, chap. 4; Stefan Bradley, "'Gym Crow Must Go!' Black Student Activism at Columbia University, 1967–1968," *Journal of African American History* 88, no. 2 (Spring 2003): 163–81; and *Harlem vs. Columbia University: Black Student Power in the Late 1960s* (Urbana: University of Illinois Press, 2009).

20. Bradley, "'Gym Crow Must Go!'"; Michael Carriere, "Fighting the War Against Blight: Columbia University, Morningside Heights, Inc., and Counterinsurgent Urban Renewal," *Journal of Planning History* 10, no. 1 (2011): 5–29; and LaDale Winling, *Building the Ivory Tower: Universities and Metropolitan Development in the Twentieth Century* (Philadelphia: University of Pennsylvania Press, 2017).

21. Jean Anyon, *Ghetto Schooling: A Political Economy of Urban Educational Reform* (New York: Teachers College Press, 1997); Jeffrey Mirel, *The Rise and Fall of an Urban School System: Detroit, 1907–1981* (Ann Arbor: University of Michigan Press, 1993); and Diane Ravitch, *The Troubled Crusade: American Education, 1945–1980* (New York: Basic Books, 1983).

22. For an overview of the historiography of urban education, see Ansley T. Erickson, "Schools in U.S. Cities," *Oxford Research Encyclopedia of American History*, Octo-

ber 2018, https://oxfordre.com/americanhistory/view/10.1093/acrefore/9780199329175
.001.0001/acrefore-9780199329175-e-128, accessed June 10, 2019.

23. Gilbert Osofsky, *Harlem: The Making of a Ghetto: Negro New York, 1890–1930*, 1st ed. (New York: Harper and Row, 1966); Kenneth T. Jackson, *Crabgrass Frontier: The Suburbanization of the United States* (New York: Oxford University Press, 1985); Arnold R. Hirsch, *Making the Second Ghetto: Race and Housing in Chicago, 1940–1960* (New York: Cambridge University Press, 1983); and Thomas J. Sugrue, *The Origins of the Urban Crisis: Race and Inequality in Postwar Detroit* (Princeton, N.J.: Princeton University Press, 1996).

24. Mitchell Duneier, *Ghetto: The Invention of a Place, the History of an Idea* (New York: Farrar, Straus and Giroux, 2016); and Alice O'Connor, *Poverty Knowledge: Social Science, Social Policy, and the Poor in Twentieth-Century U.S. History* (Princeton, N.J.: Princeton University Press, 2002).

25. Thanks to Daniel Amsterdam for remarks that helped refine this point.

26. David B. Tyack, *The One Best System: A History of American Urban Education* (Cambridge, Mass.: Harvard University Press, 1974).

27. Examples of other urban histories that operate at the neighborhood level: George J. Sanchez, *Becoming Mexican American: Ethnicity, Culture, and Identity in Chicano Los Angeles, 1900–1945* (New York: Oxford University Press, 1995); Orsi, *Madonna of 115th Street*; Michael Woodsworth, *The Battle for Bed-Stuy: The Long War on Poverty in New York City* (Cambridge, Mass.: Harvard University Press, 2016); Wendell E. Pritchett, *Brownsville, Brooklyn: Blacks, Jews, and the Changing Face of the Ghetto* (Chicago: University of Chicago Press, 2002); and Erica Kitzmiller, "The Roots of Educational Inequality: Germantown High School, 1907–1968" (PhD diss., University of Pennsylvania, 2012).

28. The difference between city-level and neighborhood-level stories is highlighted as well by Jack Dougherty, *More than One Struggle: The Evolution of Black School Reform in Milwaukee* (Chapel Hill: University of North Carolina Press, 2004); and V. P. Franklin, *The Education of Black Philadelphia: The Social and Educational History of a Minority Community, 1900–1950* (Philadelphia: University of Pennsylvania Press, 1979).

29. Osofsky, *Harlem: Making of a Ghetto*. Joe Trotter, *Black Milwaukee: The Making of an Industrial Proletariat, 1915–1945*, 2nd ed. (Urbana-Champaign: University of Illinois Press, 2007) launched the critique of the "ghettoization" books and helped point later scholars to accounts of Black urban communities that recognized the constraints of structure and Black agency.

30. King, *Whose Harlem Is This?*; and Kevin McGruder, *Race and Real Estate: Conflict and Cooperation in Harlem, 1890–1920* (New York: Columbia University Press, 2015); Greenberg, *"Or Does It Explode?"*

31. In insisting on attention to these narratives we share the perspective of Ira Katznelson and Margaret Weir, *Schooling for All: Class, Race, and the Decline of the Democratic Ideal* (New York: Basic Books, 1985).

32. This term is inspired by Michel-Rolph Trouillot, *Silencing the Past: Power and the Production of History* (Boston: Beacon Press, 1995).

33. Diane Ravitch, *The Great School Wars, New York City, 1805–1973: A History of the Public Schools as Battlefield of Social Change* (New York: Basic Books, 1974).

34. Lewis, *New York City Public Schools*.

35. Rickford, "Integration, Black Nationalism."

36. Back, "Exposing 'the Whole Segregation Myth.'" Kindred efforts in educational history include Lee, *Building a Latino Civil Rights Movement* and Dougherty, *More than One Struggle*, as well as Elizabeth Todd-Breland, *A Political Education: Black Politics and Education Reform in Chicago Since the 1960s* (Chapel Hill: University of North Carolina Press,

2018), which recognizes the need to redefine the term "education reformer" to credit the ideas, labor, and impact of local Black women organizers.

37. Russell Rickford, *We Are an African People: Independent Education, Black Power, and the Radical Imagination* (New York: Oxford University Press, 2016) is an inspiring model.

38. On "freedom dreams" achieved or not, see Robin Kelley, *Freedom Dreams: The Black Radical Imagination* (Boston: Beacon Press, 2003).

39. McGruder, *Race and Real Estate.*

40. McGruder; King, *Whose Harlem Is This?* On the Great Migration, see James N. Gregory, *The Southern Diaspora: How the Great Migrations of Black and White Southerners Transformed America* (Chapel Hill: University of North Carolina Press, 2005); and Isabel Wilkerson, *The Warmth of Other Suns: The Epic Story of America's Great Migration* (New York: Vintage, 2011).

41. Irma Watkins-Owens, *Blood Relations: Caribbean Immigrants and the Harlem Community, 1900–1930* (Bloomington: Indiana University Press, 1996); and James Anderson, *The Education of Blacks in the South, 1865–1930* (Chapel Hill: University of North Carolina Press, 1988).

42. McGruder, *Race and Real Estate*; and King, *Whose Harlem Is This?*

43. McGruder, *Race and Real Estate*, chap. 5.

44. McGruder, chap. 5.

45. King, *Whose Harlem Is This?*; and McGruder, *Race and Real Estate.*

46. "Harlem: Mecca of the New Negro," *Survey Graphic*, March 1925.

47. Lewis, *When Harlem Was in Vogue.*

48. Jean Toomer, *Cane* (New York: Boni and Liveright, 1923); and Nella Larsen, *Quicksand* (New York: Knopf, 1928).

49. George S. Schuyler, "N.Y. School Jim Crow Menace Arouses Parents," *Pittsburgh Courier*, December 22, 1934.

50. Greenberg, *"Or Does It Explode?"*; and Biondi, *To Stand and Fight.*

51. Lauri Johnson, "A Generation of Women Activists: African American Female Educators in Harlem, 1930–1950," *Journal of African American History* 89, no. 3 (July 2004): 223–40.

52. Christina Collins, *"Ethnically Qualified": Race, Merit, and the Selection of Urban Teachers, 1920–1980* (New York: Teachers College Press, 2011).

53. U.S. Census Bureau, *Poverty Status of Unrelated Individuals 14 Years Old and Older (1970)*, and *Poverty Status, 1979 (1980)*, prepared by Social Explorer, www.socialexplorer.com, accessed June 8, 2019.

54. Walter Dean Myers, *Bad Boy: A Memoir* (New York: Amistad, 2001).

55. HARYOU, *Youth in the Ghetto: A Study of the Consequences of Powerlessness and a Blueprint for Change* (New York: HARYOU, 1964).

PART ONE

Debating What and How Harlem Students Learn in the Renaissance and Beyond

Schooling the New Negro

Progressive Education, Black Modernity,
and the Long Harlem Renaissance

DANIEL PERLSTEIN

One afternoon in the early 1930s, young Jimmy Baldwin was asked by his mother if his teacher at Harlem's Public School (PS) 24 was colored or white. "I said she was a little bit colored and a little bit white," Baldwin would recall years later in a conversation with psychologist Kenneth Clark. "That's part of the dilemma of being an American Negro; that one is a little bit colored and a little bit white, and not only in physical terms but in the head and in the heart. . . . How precisely are you going to reconcile yourself to your situation?"[1]

Baldwin's teacher—Principal Gertrude Ayer—had long been a fixture of Harlem's leading social, intellectual, and political circles. She contributed a landmark essay on Black women to the celebrated 1925 *New Negro* anthology that announced the Harlem Renaissance and she was a featured speaker at the 1927 opening of the Schomburg Collection at Harlem's 135th Street Library. But as Baldwin sensed, Ayer's understanding of the multiple demands and educational tasks facing African Americans was complex. To enable students to make sense of and navigate that complexity, Ayer, as the *Pittsburgh Courier* reported, was "a specialist in progressive education." Her "pupils are encouraged to think [their] own problems out."[2]

Not far from Gertrude Ayer's 128th Street school, another Black Harlem educator was developing a different version of progressive education, but one that was also "a little bit colored and a little bit white." In 1934, Mildred Johnson opened The Modern School at St. Philip's Episcopal

Church on 134th Street. One cloudy November morning, Johnson discovered a Con Edison worker at the door, there to turn off the power because St. Philip's had been unable to pay its utility bill. "We [are] going to spend a day like the pioneer children," Johnson recalled telling her young students. "We talked about the hard times people had before electricity was put into houses. We made up stories and poems about pioneer times . . . [and] ate by candlelight. . . . We discussed the making of candles and remade one from an old candle we found."[3]

The Modern School's goal, Johnson proclaimed, was "to develop the full child and make him aware of his responsibilities and opportunities in the world around him. . . . Classroom methods are progressive." John Dewey and other white progressives had long hailed the pioneer homestead as foreshadowing their pedagogical ideal (as well as the exceptional promise of individual autonomy and opportunity in the United States), and pioneer reenactments were a common means of learning by doing in white progressive classrooms. Black students, however, faced the contradictory task of escaping their brutalizing experience and environment as well as constructing meaning out of them; Johnson transmitted to her students an ideology and identity that challenged the pervasive racism of U.S. life. "Every Modern School child," she promised, "is indoctrinated with the fact that he must be well poised and be capable of doing everything that he is expected to do just a bit better than his competitor. He must understand his background and be proud of his heritage."[4]

Two schools, one public and serving Harlem's poor, one private and serving its elite, both pedagogically progressive, both headed by educators with stronger ties to the Harlem Renaissance/New Negro era of the 1920s than to Harlem's radical school organizing of the 1930s. By highlighting the educational concerns at the center of the Harlem Renaissance, we can broaden our understanding of the history of race and education and provide an expansive vision of education for children seeking to construct a meaningful life upon what Ralph Ellison called "the horns of the white man's dilemma."[5] To do so, the chapter situates Gertrude Ayer and Mildred Johnson's Black progressive educational visions and practice in the New Negro understandings of race, education, and modern life that emerged in Harlem and that were expressed in celebrated literary works that helped define the Harlem Renaissance.

Historical studies of Harlem and the Harlem Renaissance were forged by Gilbert Osofsky, Nathan Huggins, and David Levering Lewis. Huggins

argued that in their efforts to articulate a distinctly Black voice and identity, Renaissance writers lacked individual artistry; Lewis portrayed the
same artists as insufficiently connected to actual Harlem life; Osofsky suggested that Harlem's celebrated writers and literary life masked the then
emerging Harlem ghetto. This scholarship invited contrasting naively optimistic Renaissance cultural activities with radical organizing to confront
ghetto conditions in the 1930s.[6]

More recent scholarship has viewed the Renaissance more favorably, situating literary production within the broader patterns of Black life and
thought (not only within the United States but across the globe), discovering nuanced Renaissance understandings of the intersections of Black with
white and of race with class, gender, and sexuality. Scholars such as Houston Baker Jr. and James de Jongh analyze Renaissance Era Black thought
in relation to literary modernism.[7] George Hutchinson and Ann Douglas
reveal Renaissance intellectuals' engagement with white thinkers such as
John Dewey, challenge notions of autonomous Black or white cultures, and
demonstrate the interplay of elite, avant-garde literature and popular culture.[8] Finally, historians have illuminated Harlem's emergence as a both
real and imagined space, which James de Jongh has called a "landscape and
dreamscape," neither of which can be understood without the other.[9]

This more recent scholarship, highlighting interracial meaning–making
and notions of identity that extend beyond and problematize racial categories, is vast, but virtually none of it examines the Renaissance as an educational phenomenon. Moreover, this scholarship has had little influence
on educational history, which has focused far more on the 1930s and grassroots activism than on elite Black intellectual activity and the questions of
epistemology and ontology raised by Black modernists. Building on the
more recent Renaissance scholarship, this chapter examines the interplay
of Black modernism and progressive education in Renaissance thought and
schooling.

Education and the New Negro

The New Negro artists, activists, educators, and intellectuals who fash-
ioned the Harlem Renaissance lived in contradiction. They simultaneously
echoed and disavowed what the historian Evelyn Brooks Higginbotham has
labeled the "politics of respectability," as well as vindicationist campaigns

to counter allegations of Black inferiority with accounts of Black achievement. They both embraced calls for Black self-direction and highlighted the centrality of interracial activity. They expressed a growing cultural self-confidence even as they accommodated white patrons. They announced a new racial pride even as they challenged racial essentialism.[10]

In the first decades of the twentieth century, especially in the urban North, Black people increasingly participated in the broad currents of modern U.S. life. The Great Migration from the Jim Crow South to northern cities, the commercialized economy migrants found there, together with Black political, economic, and cultural activity, transformed African American life. Black artists, activists, intellectuals, and educators were well aware of the enduring power of racism in U.S. society (in the North as well as the South) but also of the ways modern life was reshaping African America and allowing African Americans to reshape themselves.[11]

"I am not a race problem," Alain Locke wrote to his mother (and implicitly to W. E. B. Du Bois as well) on becoming the first African American Rhodes Scholar. "I am Alain LeRoy Locke." (Even in the statement of his name, Locke highlighted the new opportunity for Black people to transcend the limitations that had been placed on them and to redefine themselves. The name his parents gave Locke was Arthur. Alain was his invention.)[12]

In the new world of the mid-1920s, Locke argued, African Americans were for the first time free to express their full humanity, to represent universal human concerns within the particularities of African American life. Whereas previously, Black writers "spoke to others and tried to interpret, they now speak to their own and try to express." And Locke was not alone in his view. "I will not allow one prejudiced person or one million or one hundred million to blight my life," James Weldon Johnson claimed. "My inner life is mine."[13]

Although scholars debate the exact contours of the Harlem Renaissance and the New Negro movement it epitomized, one can roughly characterize it as the African American strand of modernism. Modernists expressed the consciousness of the individual in a society marked by fragmentation, fluidity, and uncertainty. New Negro modernists, as Daphne Lamothe argues, challenged "representations of African Americans as subhuman" but also commonsense notions of identity, authenticity, and truth. Rather than seeking to re-create the segregated Black communities of the South, they explored Blackness and its instability at "the borders of American interracial and cross-cultural encounters." They "were modernists," Lamothe concludes, "because of their willingness to grapple with the uncertainty of knowing and to use this in self-reflection" and the construction of meaning. "Harlem" emerged as Black modernism's most important locale and as its symbol for African Americans everywhere. It was both a neighborhood and an ideal to be envisioned and realized. In the words of Alain Locke, it "is—or promises at least to be—a race capital." For the writer Arna Bontemps, it offered a "foretaste of paradise."[14]

Renaissance Literature and Progressive Pedagogy

Like the New Negro construction of meaning and identity amid uncertainty and flux, progressive education's focus on the meaning-making of learners in a changing environment constituted an expression of modernism. Even though white U.S. progressive educators did little to challenge racial inequality in schooling, New Negro educational ideas had much in common with and owed much to the white mainstream of progressive education.

"Rules . . . precedents . . . [and] knowledge received at second hand," claimed the teacher and future *Crisis* literary editor Jessie Fauset in a 1912 report on Maria Montessori, "stifle originality and initiative" and "[train] . . . children . . . to abject dependence." Instead, Fauset suggested, authentic, student-chosen tasks and activities could "liberate the personality of the child." For Fauset, progressive education, with its attentiveness to the individuality and autonomy of the student, constituted an antiracist pedagogy.[15]

Still, educating African American children required inoculating them against a brutalizing environment as much as fostering their capacity for meaning-making within it. Whereas white invocations of fluidity risked masking enduring structures of inequality, navigating the contradiction between modernist dreams and oppressive social structures was *the* topic of Black modernism in education. At the beginning of *The Autobiography of an Ex-Colored Man*, the novelist and former school principal James Weldon Johnson describes a row of half-buried bottles forming the edge of a garden. "Once," the novel's protagonist recounts, "while playing in the sand, I became curious to know whether or not the bottles grew as the flowers did, and I proceeded to find out; the investigation brought me a terrific spanking." Rather than encouraging the exploration of one's environment, the experience of Black racial caste, Johnson argued, was "so narrowing that the inner problem of a Negro in America becomes that of not allowing it to choke and suffocate him."[16]

The intersection of modernism, race, and progressive education shaped two celebrated novels that both Harlem intellectuals and later critics have considered landmarks in the emergence of the New Negro ethos. Jean Toomer's *Cane* and Nella Larsen's *Quicksand* both portray a northern, racially mixed Black teacher who travels south to bring modernity to the Black masses and is crushed in the failure to do so.

A transgressive text that mixes novelistic passages with poems and drama and thus assaults the boundaries and identities of segregated literary genres, *Cane* reaches a climax in "Kabnis," the story of a Black teacher's initiation into the gothic Jim Crow South. Oblivious to lurking white violence, Toomer's protagonist imagines that "they wouldn't touch a gentleman." "Nigger's a nigger down this away, Professor," Kabnis's southern Black companions counter. Racial caste trumps cultural capital.[17]

Kabnis's antagonist and perhaps the least sympathetic character in *Cane* is not a white man but rather a Black vindicationist school principal committed to Tuskegee-style training. The purpose of his school, Hanby proclaims, "is to teach our youth to live better, cleaner, more noble lives. To prove to the world that the Negro race can be just like any other race." The essence of Black teachers' pedagogy, in Hanby's eyes, is demonstrating the virtue of hard work while adhering so well to the etiquette of Jim Crow that students internalize it as well.[18]

In Kabnis's eyes, the Black masses offer no more resistance to the South's dehumanizing regime than their Black overseers. "Negroes . . . are content," he laments. "They farm. They sing. They love. They sleep." And in the South's soporific atmosphere, Kabnis also longs to sleep. "No use to read," he muses. Unable to awaken Blacks from the stupor to which Jim Crow has consigned them, Kabnis is himself subdued and silenced.[19]

"Kabnis," Jean Toomer wrote to his white friend and mentor Waldo Frank, "is *Me*." Like his character, the author sought a humanity that transcended the confines of the U.S. racial order. Noting that he had as many white ancestors as Black, Toomer passed sometimes as Black, sometimes as white. If, as he told Frank, his family "lived between the two worlds, now dipping into the Negro, now into the white," racial identities were arbitrary and fluid social constructs. Alignment with any racial identity inevitably betrayed other aspects of one's self. Individual meaning-making trumped the claims of inherited caste, culture, or community.[20]

Toomer found little value in his formal education. The Washington, D.C., schooling of his childhood was an "irksome, tedious, and unrewarding . . . mill of classroom recitations." Whereas Du Bois attributed the shortcomings of Washington's Black schools to segregation, Toomer argued that they reflected the wider failure of U.S. education. "The system of instruction" assumed that "a child is naturally recalcitrant and hostile to learning" and that schools needed to "constrain and enforce his education by cramming stuff into him and punishing him if he failed or rebelled against swallowing his allotted portion."[21]

Toomer's critique of existing schools and vision of active, individualized learning were indistinguishable from those of many white progressive educators, but he was also conscious of how oppression undermined self-directed meaning-making through explorations of one's environment. Working in New Jersey's shipyards, he encountered "doomed men" whose "faculties of speech and feeling and understanding had been paralyzed." He compared the dockworkers to slaves. "Poverty and privation," Toomer lamented to the poet and teacher Georgia Douglas Johnson, "dwarf the soul, weaken the body, dull the mind, and prohibit fruitful activity."[22]

As Toomer struggled to reconcile his ideas about education, a friend of his grandfather reported an opening at Sparta Agricultural and Industrial Institute (Sparta A&I), in Georgia. No less than New Jersey dockworkers, Toomer's students were crushed by oppression. A few months before his arrival in Sparta, one of the most infamous crimes of the Jim Crow era had occurred nearby. Black peons on John Williams's plantation were beaten daily and locked into bunkhouses at night. On Sundays, Williams ordered them to run through the woods so his hounds could practice hunting down any who tried to escape. Then, in February 1921, concerned about a possible investigation of debt peonage on his plantation, Williams began systematically killing Black workers who could offer testimony against him. And yet, Sparta A&I seemed to condone the murderous system, advertising during Toomer's time as acting principal that it offered "a thorough training in Vocational Agriculture. . . . The training creates in the boy a love for the farm, therefore it helps to keep the boy on the farm."[23]

Toomer tried without success to enable his Sparta students to see beyond the oppressive circumstances that doomed them. In his ancient history lessons on "polytheism and deity evolution," he wrote his mentor

Alain Locke, "I leap, and then look back to see the bewildered expression on my pupils' faces." Like his protagonist, Toomer sought to affirm his own identity in bringing modern ideas to the ignorant masses even though he saw no evidence that the masses had the capacity to absorb those ideas.[24]

Toomer's quest for self-realization and self-awareness pushed at the limits of race. He insisted that racial identities, whether Black or white, were traps, and he resisted anything that smacked of racial pigeonholing. His poems were "not Negro poems, nor are they Anglo-Saxon or white or English poems," he explained to James Weldon Johnson. "They are, first, mine. And second, in so far as general race or stock is concerned, they spring from the result of racial blendings here in America which have produced a new race or stock." This new race, he envisioned, was "neither white nor black nor in-between."[25]

Toomer sought in *Cane* to reconcile the slave past and Jim Crow present with a human future, but, he conceded, "I did not have a means of doing this." As he explained to the white theater producer Kenneth Macgowan, his protagonist confronted "the beauty and ugliness of Southern life. His energy, dispersed and unchanneled, cannot push him through its crude mass. Hence the mass, with friction and heat and sparks, crushes him."[26]

Kabnis's failure is not due to a particular pedagogical approach but rather to what Toomer saw as the irreconcilability of existing as both Black and human in Jim Crow America. Still, if *Cane*'s plot centers on Kabnis's defeat, its form, constructing art out of the raw material of southern Black folk culture and wildly experimental and idiosyncratic in its assault on literary genres, constitutes a testament to individual agency and thus the antithesis of that defeat. In this contradiction, *Cane* epitomizes a central theme of New Negro art and suggests the utopian, paradoxical project of New Negro education.

Toomer brought his impulse to teach and his thirst for a wholeness that transcended racial categorization to the emerging Harlem Renaissance. Shortly before publication of *Cane*, Waldo Frank introduced Toomer to his wife, the progressive educator Margaret Naumburg. She in turn introduced him to the Russian mystic George Ivanovich Gurdjieff's vision of transcending the "waking sleep" in which we live and realizing our full consciousness and potential. "The very deepest centre of my being," he would recall, "awoke to consciousness." Toomer offered lessons on Gurdjieff to Renaissance writers such as Wallace Thurman, Zora Neale Hurston, Dorothy Peterson, and Nella Larsen. Like many Harlem literati,

Larsen soon tired of Toomer's teachings, which she considered an abstruse "pseudo-religion," but, as the historian George Hutchinson argues, Toomer's Gurdjieff-inspired exercises in "self-observation with nonidentification" fostered Renaissance dreams of artistic self-expression, stimulating Larsen's ambition to write and shaping her texts.[27]

Like *Cane*, Larsen's celebrated 1928 novel *Quicksand* centers on a teacher. Helga Crane teaches at Naxos, a southern school modeled on Tuskegee. *Quicksand* opens with Helga in her room. Committed to the sensual "sweet pleasure[s]" of modern life, she exults in a cool bath, private leisure time, beautiful things, and a good book. However, the beautiful fabrics in Helga's room lie beside "her school-teacher paraphernalia of drab books and papers." Students are forced to wear dull uniforms and learn dull lessons. Whereas her room offers the kind of materials imagined by progressive educators to foster students' self-actualizing engagement with their environment, Naxos does not. The goal of its "so-called education" is the "suppression of individuality and beauty." Students and teachers are herded into the chapel to absorb the "insulting remarks" of a bigoted white preacher who commends them for knowing "enough to stay in their places." For all its talk of race pride, Naxos, Helga concludes, is not "a school" but rather "a sharpened knife, ruthlessly cutting all to a pattern, the white man's pattern."[28]

The child of a white mother and Black father, Helga had suffered an "unloved, unloving, unhappy childhood" among whites. Only when she enrolled in "a school for Negroes" did Helga discover "that because one was dark, one was not necessarily loathsome, and could, therefore, consider oneself without repulsion." Helga "ardently desired to share in, to be part of" both the community she imagined Naxos to offer and its promise of uplifting the less fortunate. Instead, her individuality, sensual existence, and "zest" for "doing good to [her] fellow men" were "blotted out."[29]

To escape the "shame, lies, hypocrisy, cruelty, servility, and snobbishness" of Naxos, Helga flees to Renaissance Harlem. But no less than Naxos schoolmen, Harlem intellectuals "slavish[ly]" imitate whites while simultaneously enforcing the color line. Either a Black or white identity would require Helga to forswear half of her roots. Defeated, she returns south with a hardscrabble preacher and is consumed by an aesthetically, psychologically, and intellectually impoverished existence.[30]

As with *Cane*, Helga's end does not constitute Larsen's vision. Like Helga, Larsen suggests, life in the United States is fundamentally interracial, challenging any notion of purity and authenticity, whether Black or white. As literary historian George Hutchinson argues, Larsen's "defiant stance toward the institution of race is not a form of 'color blindness' but precisely the opposite; it derives from and enables her genuine appreciation of human differences that reductive 'race' thinking brutalizes."[31]

As with Toomer, Larsen's writing drew on experience. Like Helga, Larsen was the child of a white immigrant mother and Black father. She attended a Chicago public high school at which the English curriculum promoted creative writing, individuality, and the dignity of the learner. Still, Larsen and her white half sister were forced to attend separate schools, a rupture no racial uplift could heal. For Larsen, as for Helga (and Jean Toomer), passing, whether as Black or white, constituted self-denial.[32]

After high school, Larsen attended Fisk. She reveled in the community of Black students, but Larsen had grown up in a milieu that embraced immigrants and organized labor, and Fisk was hostile to both. Promoting the vindicationist politics of respectability, the school left little room for expressions of individuality. When new rules required women students to wear their uniforms and no more than one ring and to be chaperoned on after-dinner walks, Larsen protested, leading to her expulsion. She then completed the nurse-training program at Harlem's Lincoln Hospital and was hired to head nursing and nurse training at Tuskegee. Tuskegee, however, showed little interest in utilizing Larsen's skill and training and, like Fisk, great interest in policing her appearance, behavior, and morality.[33]

Leaving Tuskegee after a year, Larsen returned to New York, became a librarian, began to write and entered Harlem's literary circles. Among her first publications were pieces for *The Brownies' Book*, a National Association for the Advancement of Colored People (NAACP) *Crisis* children's supplement. In presuming that Black children, no less than whites, possessed curiosity about the world, capacity for self-direction, and desire for aesthetically pleasing experience, *The Brownies' Book* drew on wider U.S. notions of childhood and progressive pedagogy. Still, as Du Bois argued, the dominant culture in the United States led "the Negro child" to associate "the good, the great, and the beautiful . . . almost entirely with white people. . . . He unconsciously gets the impression that the Negro has little chance to be good, great, heroic or beautiful." *The Brownies' Book* balanced progressive pedagogy's vision of self-directed activity with the need to transmit an alternative to the identities that a racist world had assigned Black children.[34]

Renaissance Teachers, Progressive Education, and Harlem Schools

The preoccupations of New Negro intellectual life echoed across African America, but they resounded most vibrantly in Harlem. New Negroes typically represented Harlem's racial common ground from the commanding heights of Sugar Hill, where, as Langston Hughes put it, upper-crust "colored families" lived in "nice high-rent-houses with elevators and doormen," and sent "their babies to private kindergartens and their youngsters to Ethical Culture School." (The school was known for both its willingness to enroll Blacks and its progressive pedagogy.) It was only when he entered school, James Baldwin would recollect, that he "began to be aware of Sugar Hill, where well-to-do Negroes lived. I began to be aware of it because many of my teachers lived there." For teachers and others, Sugar Hill crystallized the contradiction between possibilities that seemed to be emerging and the continuing reality of racial caste.[35]

On Sugar Hill and elsewhere, hundreds of educators made Harlem home; they were at the center of New Negro intellectual life. Harlem Renaissance impresario Alain Locke was an adult-education leader. The son of schoolteachers, he edited the Progressive Education Association's *When Peoples Meet*. The novelist and *Crisis* literary editor Jessie Fauset taught high school in Baltimore, Washington, and New York. The poet Countee Cullen taught junior high school in Harlem. His good friend, the actor, director, and bon vivant Harold Jackman was also a New York City schoolteacher. The award-winning playwright Eulalie Spence taught English and drama at Brooklyn's Eastern District High School. When not teaching Spanish at Brooklyn's Bushwick High School, Dorothy Peterson wrote a novel, promoted the Harlem literary journal *Fire*, and cofounded the Negro Experimental Theatre. Peterson's Bushwick colleague Willis Huggins headed the Harlem History Club, which trained a number of Black historians.[36]

Schoolteachers created much of Renaissance Harlem's intellectual infrastructure. When Jessie Fauset left the *Crisis* and returned to teaching in 1927, she lived with her sister Helen Lanning, also a teacher, and together they launched one of Harlem's most celebrated salons. The teacher Alta Douglass played a leading role in a number of civic and artistic groups and, according to the *Atlanta Daily World*, was "one of Harlem's most charming hostesses." W. E. B. Du Bois was the most visible presence when the 1927

Pan-African Congress met in Harlem, but behind the scenes, Layle Lane and other teachers did much of the organizing.[37]

In part, the number of New Negro luminaries working in schools reflected a job market in which relatively few occupations were open to educated Blacks. "French classes," Jessie Fauset sighed, "pay better" than writing. But it was not only economic necessity that placed educators at the center of New Negro intellectual life. Harlem was as much an ideal as a neighborhood and, in the words of the sociologist Ira De A. Reid, "not so much the Mecca of the New Negro" as "the maker of the New Negro." Teaching constituted a way of articulating and fostering new consciousness as befit a new age.[38]

Gertrude Ayer embodied many facets of this new consciousness. She was a leading light in refined Harlem society, volunteered at the Henry Street Settlement, and organized Black workers. Ayer joined with Alain Locke, James Weldon Johnson, and W. E. B. Du Bois as a featured speaker at the 1925 celebration that announced the Harlem Renaissance. And as principal of PS 24, Ayer was among Harlem's best-known educators. Adam Clayton Powell Jr.'s *People's Voice* deemed her "one of the great oaks in New York City's pedagogical forest," her school "a model of modernity" designed "to meet present day needs." Commending Ayer's commitment to progressive education, the *Amsterdam News* marveled that "they learn by doing at Harlem's only experimental school."[39]

Ayer brought a varied background to her work. Her father was an Atlanta University- and Harvard University-educated African American doctor, her mother a white English immigrant. Ayer excelled in New York's public schools, graduating from high school in 1903. She had studied bookkeeping and stenography, but her mother insisted she not work in an office, warning her daughter, "Never trust a white man." She turned to teaching.[40]

Her family history convinced Ayer that the injuries of race, and rebellion against them, were bound together with those of class and gender. Just as Ayer's mother and father had crossed the color line in a transgressive marriage, her mother's mother, Ayer maintained, "was a lady. She had fallen in love with a carpenter and paid dearly for marrying 'beneath her class.'" And just as Blacks and whites conspired to maintain the color line, "the 'lower' classes in England frown upon such social 'mistakes' as do the 'upper.'"[41]

Ayer taught until 1911, when she married the prominent Black lawyer Cornelius McDougald (Marcus Garvey was among his clients), and New

York's ban on married women teachers forced her to leave the classroom. She turned her attention from Black children to their mothers, organizing Black women laundry workers with the Women's Trade Union League. As the New York Urban League's assistant labor secretary, Ayer documented that although Black women were often far better educated than white women workers, they held the dirtiest, lowest-paying jobs. Women who had trained to be teachers and office workers were left with "their spirits broken and hopes blasted." Worse, racial discrimination at work intersected with patriarchal relations at home, creating a double bind for working-class Black women. Ayer reiterated the double oppression Black women faced on the job and at home in her landmark 1925 essay, "The Double Task: The Struggle of Negro Women for Sex and Race Emancipation," but she also claimed that "in Harlem, more than anywhere else, the Negro woman is free from . . . the grosser forms of sex and race subjugation."[42]

When New York City ended its ban on married teachers, Ayer rejoined the school system as an administrator. Building on her social welfare work and exemplifying progressive commitments to educating the whole child and connecting school to life, she focused on vocational guidance and school-based social services. "A child cannot learn if he is not physically fit," she noted. "If he needs glasses, he cannot see and therefore he cannot learn. If he is undernourished, his mind is not alert."[43]

For four years, racist school officials blocked Ayer's ascent to a principalship, despite her high score on the principal's exam. When she was finally appointed principal of Harlem's PS 24 in 1935, A. Philip Randolph excoriated a school official who had portrayed Ayer's achievement as evidence that the American Dream was within the reach of all. "The thing you call 'Americanism,'" Randolph countered, "is specious, is unsound, and doesn't warrant the fealty of black America." Still, the Urban League and the *Chicago Defender* cited Ayer's appointment as evidence of the exceptional opportunities New York afforded Black educators. Ayer's very career epitomized the contradictory mix of possibility and caste that shaped Black modernity and Black progressive education.[44]

In the 1930s, as Thomas Harbison argues in chapter 2 of this volume, Harlem increasingly condemned vocational schooling as a means of enforcing Black subordination. Although PS 24 offered vocational guidance and mental hygiene, Ayer rejected Tuskegee-style manual training. "The trades do not welcome [Black youth]," she reasoned, "so we cannot concentrate on trade specialization." Instead, Black children needed an education that countered society's image of them. "Colored people lack inspiration because they don't know what their historical background has been," Ayer argued. "The Negro woman teacher" had "the task of knowing well her race's history and of finding time to impart it." Ayer insisted that PS 24 teach the Black student to "realize: 1. That, in fundamentals he is essentially the same as other humans. 2. That, being different in some ways does not mean that he is inferior. 3. That, he has a contribution to make to his group. 4. That, his group has a contribution to make to his nation, and 5. That, he has a part in his nation's work in the world."[45]

Even as Ayer urged direct instruction to counteract society's image of Blacks, she embraced progressive approaches that affirmed Black children's full share of humanity. Teachers, she claimed, were "being trained not to want to make children do things they hate to do just because a grown person thinks it is good for them." She urged Black parents to stop "whipping, slapping and knocking children about" if they did not want them "to be slaves—humble, fearful people."[46]

The job of school, Ayer professed, was to "fill the needs the children feel." PS 24's Unit Activity Program relied on experiential learning, self-directed projects, democratic classroom living, and field trips into the neighborhood. The curriculum was intended to shift the focus of elementary school teaching from subject matter to the child. Individual abilities, especially in singing and music, were developed. "Habits and skills," Ayer insisted should be "practiced in situations created and planned by pupils and teachers together to approximate those in real life." The teacher's role, Ayer argued, was "guiding pupils in learning" with kindness rather than directing them with force.[47]

Ayer's commitment to progressive education reflected not only the particular situation of Black children but also her belief that "there is more in common than in differences between the races. . . . Harlem parents [are] native Americans for the most part, who perhaps more than others cherish the value of dignity for their personality, the value of opportunity for advancement for themselves and their children, and the values inherent in equal protection under the law."[48]

If Gertrude Ayer embodied a progressivism aimed at serving impoverished Black workers and children, Mildred Johnson represented progressivism for the Black elite. Born in 1914, Johnson was the daughter of the famed musician J. Rosamond Johnson and the niece of the poet, novelist, and civil rights leader James Weldon Johnson. Mildred was raised amid the

Harlem Renaissance elite. Paul Robeson was a family friend; the white Renaissance kingpin Carl Van Vechten and his wife were Uncle Carl and Aunt Fania.[49]

As a girl, Mildred attended the Ethical Culture School and its affiliated high school, Fieldston. The schools reflected the educational vision of the white progressive religious and political reformer Felix Adler. He sought to ground religion's ethical precepts in rational thought and actualize them in social action. In 1877, Adler founded the Society of Ethical Culture, and within a year it had established a kindergarten for poor children. The school's emphasis on rational thought, learning by doing, manual activity, problem solving, and the testing of ideas and values in social action mirrored John Dewey's educational ideals. As its reputation grew, upper-class Jewish children banned by other private schools enrolled, transforming the school from an institution serving New York's poor to one serving its elite. Unlike other New York private schools, the Ethical Culture School welcomed (a few) Black students, and many Black intellectuals and activists, Mildred's parents among them, were attracted to its progressive pedagogy and politics. In 1928, Ethical's high school division was split from the elementary school, and Fieldston was opened in the posh Riverdale neighborhood of the Bronx. Mildred was among its first students.[50]

Upon graduating from Fieldston, Johnson entered the Ethical Culture School's Teacher Training Program. After a dozen years as an Ethical/Fieldston student, Mildred was well-versed in and committed to the Teacher Training Program's progressive approach. For a nursery school course assignment, she imagined a classroom that included a doll corner, blocks, musical instruments, a nature table, paint, clay, and books for individual reading—all the elements needed for children's self-directed learning of matters interesting to them. In her first student-teaching placement, Mildred wrote a play about the planets and produced it with her third-grade class, combining her own interest in theater with students' sustained, active, multidisciplinary study of science.[51]

After her first student-teaching placement at the Ethical Culture School, Johnson needed a second placement at a different school to complete her training. She had demonstrated her teaching ability and shown excellence in subjects ranging from theater, music, and dance to science. Only one thing disqualified her from a second placement. In 1934, no New York progressive private school employed Black teachers and none other than Ethical was willing to allow a Black student teacher to apprentice in its classrooms.[52]

The twenty-year-old Johnson responded by opening her own school at the church she attended. St. Philips Episcopal was located near the 135th Street library in the heart of Harlem. In creating her curriculum, Johnson drew on her teacher training program, her own schooling, and a home life in which music, theater, and dance were ever present. With the help of one of her Ethical teachers, she adapted the classroom she had imagined for her nursery school course to her church space. With a $100 donation from an Ethical Culture board member, she bought tables, chairs, and playground equipment. "The plan," she argued, "was not only artistic but it was educationally correct."[53]

In September 1934, Johnson's school opened with eight students, young children of her Harlem society friends. Her goal, Johnson maintained, was to "provide for continuous activity, with stress on pupil self-direction." "Since it was to be a modern school," Johnson explained, "we named the school The Modern School of Harlem. The 'of Harlem' was soon dropped." The school's very name served to announce an orientation recognized by the *Amsterdam News* as "progressive." Over the years, enrollment expanded to more than two hundred nursery and elementary school students, and the school moved to a bigger space funded by Mildred's father. Even when the grades taught at The Modern School fluctuated, however Johnson's progressive curricular vision remained constant.[54]

The Modern School's initial announcement promised "a program which offers to the child opportunities to become identified with life, and so to develop to the fullest extent in body and mind, thereby becoming a healthy, effective and happy member of society." "There is no clearly drawn line between the subjects in the school program," Johnson explained. "Our program . . . is flexible and adaptable to the special needs of individual pupils, groups, and to situations as they may arise. For the most part, the classroom teacher builds her curriculum and adapts it to her particular group of children." Teachers directed science experiments, social studies projects, and conversations about news events or children's experiences. Boys learned to dance the polka, waltz, and mazurka; girls did ballet. During the period for free play, the children made use of clay, crayons, paper, scissors, paste, and paint. Blocks and "dress up" costumes served as equipment for dramatic play.[55]

Modern School students, leading Harlem journalist Sara Slack observed, were "educationally pampered" but "carefully trained." Children worked at their own pace, but academics were intense. Two–year-olds learned to listen to serious poetry and music. Students did research and wrote their own books about subjects of their choosing, encouraging them "to learn to use many sources of information, to gather many opinions, and use varied sources to find and develop a topic." By age five children were expected to read and write. "If any one of our children have a reading or language difficulty," Johnson explained, "he's given private, concentrated training. You can believe me, we have no foolishness here in reading."[56]

On weekly field trips, students explored their neighborhood. Much like the acclaimed white progressive educator Lucy Sprague Mitchell, Johnson had students visit stores and streets to observe commerce, trains, and traffic. Trips to the nearby Hudson River offered the George Washington Bridge, tugboats, barges, and a lighthouse. Rather than constituting a break from academics, Modern School field trips allowed students to observe their environment and figure out what they want to learn more about.[57]

Each year, The Modern School staged one or two original theatrical "festivals"—adaptations from children's literature or European dance and theater classics that offered "models of beauty" and a dose of happily-ever-after. Johnson prepared detailed outlines, composed songs, often adapted from the original scores, oversaw the creation of costumes and painted sets, and considered which students would be best fitted for which roles. "Children who have a certain potential," she explained, are "used in that area of the production where they excel. By following this plan no student is forced into an activity that is beyond his ability to perform. And by the same token, those students who have certain abilities are able to express them. . . . Everyone is a participant." The festivals, Johnson argued, were "the termination for many of the school's activities such as music, dance, drama, art, social studies and public speaking. . . . The children not only 'live' their part in the festival but learn thru research, stories and oral information about the reason for their contribution."[58]

Even as Johnson implemented a pedagogy of self-directed student learning similar to that of Ethical Culture and other white progressive schools, she also "indoctrinated" students with a vision of themselves that challenged the dominant ideology of Black inferiority. Johnson took great pride in the fact that her students "educated [white people] who had never seen a group of well-spoken, well-behaved colored children." In order to ensure that her charges did not resemble poorly behaved (and, implicitly, just plain poor) Black children, she reminded teachers that "children must be taught that quiet is observed in the halls of the school, on the stairway and to a large degree in the streets." Black history was a regular part of the curriculum; weekly assemblies and annual festivals ended with all singing "Lift Ev'ry Voice and Sing," the "Negro National Anthem" (Johnson's father and uncle wrote it). W. E. B. Du Bois admired The Modern School; the civil rights leader Reverend Thomas Kilgore deemed it "way ahead of its time in its approach to education."[59]

Active in organizations such as the NAACP, Jack and Jill, the Urban League, the YWCA, and Girl Friends, Johnson balanced racial solidarity and class privilege. Her students, the *New York Age* reported, were "children of the professional or white collar class." The *Amsterdam News* described the school as "exclusive." At the annual Christmas productions, the paper reported, "women dressed in minks, over chic afternoon dresses." Students collected Christmas gifts for underprivileged children who lived near the school but did not attend it.[60]

Many students loved The Modern School, but others, particularly the 10 percent on scholarships, were put off by the vindicationist enforcement of strict behavior and sense of class privilege. The future writer Toni Cade Bambara received encouragement from her fourth-grade teacher who found that the girl "evidences talent in creative writing." Still, Bambara, who attended The Modern School in the 1940s, described Johnson as "very mean, very yellow, very strict, and very snooty. She would look down at me coming in there with hand-me-down clothes. I didn't come in a cab like most of the other student[s] . . . [or] talk about going up to Martha's Vineyard for the weekend."[61]

After attending The Modern School in its early years, James C. Hall Jr. went to the Ethical Culture School and Fieldston and had a distinguished career as a university administrator. But his time at The Modern School left Hall more bitter than grateful. "Out of the group of eight" in his class, Hall claimed, "two committed suicide, one is incurably insane, one who was the brightest ended up at Oxford, and one of the loveliest ones became a drug addict and a prostitute. This mortality rate indicates the tremendous pressure that this group of youngsters was under to perform and transcend their culture and circumstances."[62]

Still, the relatively privileged status of Johnson and most of her students fostered a commitment to Black excellence that affected even poor students. Leora King was the daughter of a divorced single mother who had not graduated from high school but who insisted that Leora receive an education that made manifest and enhanced the capacity of Black people to excel. Leora transferred to The Modern School for fourth grade. "A lot of the girls were light-skinned and had long, straight hair," King recalls. "Everybody seemed so rich, and the students were very class conscious. I didn't know I was poor until I went there." Still, "there was lot of Black pride. All our teachers were intelligent, educated." The school and its accomplished teachers and families "gave me confidence in myself, that I could be well-educated, that I could be successful." The Modern School, she concluded, "was a turning point in my education. [It] made me believe I could fly."[63]

The Educational Legacy of the Harlem Renaissance

What the sociologist E. Franklin Frazier called "the high hopes that were kindled" by the Harlem Renaissance gave way to material concerns and radical organizing during the Great Depression. But the Renaissance also ran up against the contractions of its own project. As Harlem's intellectuals struggled "to uphold the American virtues of progressivism, individualism, and self-reliance," Nathan Huggins observes, they "were obliged by circumstances to be group-conscious and collective. The American Dream of open-ended possibility for the individual was for them another paradox."[64]

Still, just as progressivism in schools long outlasted the Progressive Era in U.S. politics, the Harlem Renaissance in education continued long after it had dissipated in literature and popular culture. New Negro educators' and intellectuals' hopes of thinking, writing, speaking, and living as full participants in the modern world echoed in what one might call the Long Harlem Renaissance. Although the author Richard Wright embraced the radical 1930s campaign for the material reorganization of society, he also called for "a tremendous struggle *among* the Negro people for self-expression, self-possession, self-consciousness, individuality, new values, [and] new loyalties." The militant educational activists Layle Lane, Williana Burroughs, and Ella Baker traced their politics to a capacity to imagine a different world kindled by the Renaissance. Echoing Du Bois and Locke as well as his schoolteachers Countee Cullen and Jessie Fauset, James Baldwin decried the reduction of Black people to group identities or social problems. The "insistence that it is [a human being's] categorization alone which is real and which cannot be transcended" was, he argued a "rejection of life."[65]

As Alain Locke urged a group of Philadelphia student writers, Black poets needed to create "less a chant for the dead and more a song for the living. Especially for the Negro, I believe in the 'life to come.'" In conceptualizing African American culture and identity not as inheritances that define the individual but as raw materials to interpret and transform, and in situating that identity and culture with the broadest currents of intellectual and political life, Harlem's New Negroes envisioned a society in which African Americans could both maintain group pride and be full participants in U.S. life. Even if Renaissance thinkers underestimated racism's defining power in U.S. society and thus exaggerated the possibilities within it, their ideals fostered an expansive pedagogy. Black progressive educators simultaneously built upon the capacity of Black children to construct their own understanding of the world and instilled a humanity that enduring structures of oppression sought to deny. In their attentiveness to the particularities of Black experience and its universal resonance, Black Renaissance artists, intellectuals, and educators were the authentic pioneers of the educational frontier.[66]

Notes

1. Kenneth Clark, "A Conversation with James Baldwin," in *Harlem: A Community in Transition*, ed. John Henrik Clarke (New York: Citadel, 1964), 124.
2. "Rare Library Brought to Harlem," *Amsterdam News*, January 19, 1927, 8; "Woman Principal Runs School like 'Big City,'" *Pittsburgh Courier*, February 27, 1937; and Elise McDougald, "The Task of Negro Womanhood," in *The New Negro: An Interpretation*, ed. Alain Locke (New York: Simon and Schuster, 1925), 374–76. Baldwin's teacher initially gained fame using the name of her first husband (McDougald). When she was a principal, she went by that of her second husband (Ayer). Sometimes she used Elise as a first name, and sometimes Gertrude. For the sake of clarity, she is called Gertrude Ayer throughout this chapter.
3. [Mildred Johnson], "A Few Incidents from The Modern School," n.d., 1, Modern School Papers, Schomburg Center for Research in Black Culture, New York Public Library (hereafter Schomburg); (hereafter MSP).
4. "A Few Incidents," 6; [Mildred Johnson], "Our History and Our Aims," *Silver Anniversary of the Modern School*, 1959, MSP; "Schools Plan Fall Openings: Three Progressive Groups Are Ready," *Amsterdam Star-News*, September 13, 1941, 10; and Daniel Perlstein, "Community and Democracy in American Schools: Arthurdale and the Fate of Progressive Education," *Teachers College Record* 97 (1996): 625–50.
5. Ralph Ellison, "An American Dilemma: A Review," in *The Collected Essays of Ralph Ellison* (New York: Random House, 2011), 339.
6. Gilbert Osofsky, *Harlem: The Making of a Ghetto: Negro New York, 1890–1930* (New York: Harper and Row, 1966); Nathan Huggins, *Harlem Renaissance* (New York: Oxford University Press, 1971); and David Levering Lewis, *When Harlem Was in Vogue* (New York: Knopf, 1981).

7. Houston Baker Jr., *Modernism and the Harlem Renaissance* (Chicago: University of Chicago Press, 1987); and James de Jongh, *Vicious Modernism: Black Harlem and the Literary Imagination* (Cambridge: Cambridge University Press, 1990).

8. George Hutchinson, *The Harlem Renaissance in Black and White* (Cambridge, Mass.: Harvard University Press, 1995); and Ann Douglas, *Terrible Honesty: Mongrel Manhattan in the 1920s* (New York: Farrar, Straus and Giroux, 1995).

9. de Jongh, *Vicious Modernism*, 24; see also Andrew Fearnley and Daniel Matlin, eds., *Race Capital? Harlem as Setting and Symbol* (New York: Columbia University Press, 2019).

10. Evelyn Brooks Higginbotham, *Righteous Discontent: The Women's Movement in the Black Baptist Church, 1880–1920* (Cambridge, Mass.: Harvard University Press, 1994), 185–229.

11. Daphne Lamothe, *Inventing the New Negro: Narrative, Culture, and Ethnography* (Philadelphia: University of Pennsylvania Press, 2008), 80.

12. Louis Menand, *The Metaphysical Club: A Story of Ideas in America* (New York: Farrar, Straus and Giroux, 2001), 389–90.

13. Alain Locke, "Negro Youth Speaks," in Locke, *New Negro*, 48; and James Weldon Johnson, *Negro Americans, What Now?* (New York: Viking, 1934), 102.

14. Hutchinson, *Harlem Renaissance in Black and White*; and Lamothe, *Inventing the New Negro*, 1–3. Locke and Bontemps quoted in Daniel Matlin, "Harlem: The Making of a Ghetto Discourse," in Fearnley and Matlin, *Race Capital*, 72–73.

15. Jessie Fauset, "The Montessori Method: Its Possibilities," *Crisis*, July 1912, 136–38.

16. James Weldon Johnson, *The Autobiography of an Ex-Colored Man* (Boston: Sherman, French, 1912), 4; and Johnson, *Along This Way: The Autobiography of James Weldon Johnson* (New York: Viking, 1933), 89.

17. Jean Toomer, *Cane* (New York: Boni and Liveright, 1923), 171.

18. Toomer, *Cane*, 186.

19. Toomer, 81, 159, 164.

20. Jean Toomer to Waldo Frank, January 1923, in *The Letters of Jean Toomer, 1919–1924*, ed. Mark Whalan (Knoxville: University of Tennessee Press, 2006), 116; Nellie McKay, "Jean Toomer in His Time: An Introduction," in *Jean Toomer: A Critical Evaluation*, ed. Therman O'Daniel (Washington, D.C.: Howard University Press, 1988), 3; Jean Toomer to Georgia Douglas Johnson, June 7, 1920, in *Letters*, 13; Jean Toomer to Waldo Frank, March 24, 1922, in *Letters*, 31; and W. E. B. Du Bois, *Reconstruction in America* (New York: Russell and Russell, 1935), 473.

21. Darwin Turner, ed., *The Wayward and the Seeking: A Collection of Writings by Jean Toomer* (Washington, D.C.: Howard University Press, 1980), 45–46; and W. E. B. Du Bois, "A Portrait of Carter G. Woodson," *Masses and Mainstream* 3 (June 1950): 20.

22. Charles Scruggs and Lee VanDemarr, *Jean Toomer and the Terrors of American History* (Philadelphia: University of Pennsylvania Press, 1998), 5, 60; Barbara Foley, "Jean Toomer's Sparta," *American Literature* 67 (1995): 771n17; Turner, *Wayward*, 123; and McKay, *Jean Toomer*, 44–45.

23. Cynthia Kerman and Richard Eldridge, *The Lives of Jean Toomer: A Hunger for Wholeness* (Baton Rouge: Louisiana State University Press, 1987), 81; Foley, "Jean Toomer's Sparta," 758; Barbara Foley, "'In the Land of Cotton': Economics and Violence in Jean Toomer's *Cane*," *African American Review* 32 (1998): 188–89; Gregory Freeman, *Lay This Body Down: The 1921 Murders of Eleven Plantation Slaves* (Chicago: Lawrence Hill, 1999); and Sparta Agricultural and Industrial Institute, "Give Your Boy a Chance" [Fall 1921], in John Griffin, *Biography of American Author Jean Toomer, 1894–1967* (Lewiston, Maine: Mellen, 2002), poster following 198.

24. Jean Toomer to Alain Locke, November 8, 1921, in *Letters*, 27.

25. Jean Toomer to James Weldon Johnson, July 11, 1930, in Jean Toomer, *A Jean Toomer Reader: Selected Unpublished Writings* (New York: Oxford University Press, 1993), 106.

26. Charles Larson, *Invisible Darkness: Jean Toomer and Nella Larsen* (Iowa City: University of Iowa Press, 1993), 34; and Jean Toomer to Kenneth Macgowan, March 15, 1923, in *Letters*, 141.

27. Turner, *Wayward*, 3, 126; Jon Woodson, *To Make a New Race: Gurdjieff, Toomer, and the Harlem Renaissance* (Jackson: University Press of Mississippi, 1999); and George Hutchinson, *In Search of Nella Larsen: A Biography of the Color Line* (Cambridge, Mass.: Harvard University Press, 2006), 184.

28. Nella Larsen, *Quicksand* (New York: Knopf, 1928), 4–6, 8–9, 29, 31, 44; and Hutchinson, *In Search*, 228.

29. Larsen, *Quicksand*, 7, 11, 52, 63.

30. Larsen, 18, 184; and Hutchinson, *In Search*, 28.

31. Hutchinson, *In Search*, 228.

32. Hutchinson, 19, 46–49.

33. Hutchinson, 56, 62–63, 78–79, 92–93, 101–2.

34. Nella Larsen, "Three Scandinavian Games," *Brownies' Book* (June 1920): 191; Nella Larsen, "Danish Fun," *Brownies' Book* (July 1920): 219; Katharine Capshaw Smith, *Children's Literature of the Harlem Renaissance* (Bloomington: Indiana University Press, 2004); and Christina Schaeffer, *The Brownies' Book: Inspiring Racial Pride in African-American Children* (Frankfurt: Peter Lang, 2016), 28.

35. Langston Hughes, "Down Under in Harlem," *New Republic*, March 27, 1944, 404–5; and James Baldwin, *Evidence of Things Not Seen* (New York: Henry Holt, 1995), 68.

36. Alain Locke, *When Peoples Meet: A Study in Race and Culture Contacts* (New York: Progressive Education Association, 1942); Carolyn Sylvander, *Jessie Redmon Fauset: Black American Writer* (Troy, N.Y.: Whitston, 1981), 27–31, 36, 62; Charles Molesworth, *And Bid Him Sing: A Biography of Countée Cullen* (Chicago: University of Chicago Press, 2012), 20, 49; Helen Epstein, *Joe Papp: An American Life* (New York: Da Capo Press, 1996), 43–44; "Peterson, Dorothy, Randolph," in *Encyclopedia of the Harlem Renaissance*, ed. Cary Wintz and Paul Finkelman, vol. 2 (New York: Routledge, 2004), 965–66; and John Henrik Clarke, "The Influence of Arthur A. Schomburg on My Concept of Africana Studies," *Phylon* 49 (1992): 7–8.

37. Elise McDougald, "The Schools and the Vocational Life of Negroes," *Opportunity* 1 (June 1923): 10; McDougald, "Task of Negro Womanhood," 374–76; John Howard Johnson, *Harlem, the War and Other Addresses* (New York: Wendell Malliet, 1942), 150; Thadious Davis, Foreword, in Jessie Fauset, *There Is Confusion* (Boston: Northeastern University Press, 1989), xvi; Cheryl Ragar, "The Douglas Legacy," *American Studies* 49 (2008): 137–38; "Nine Participate in Panel Discussion," *Amsterdam News*, May 18, 1935, 7; "Mrs. Alta S. Douglass, Teacher and Civic Figure," *Afro-American*, January 10, 1959, 7; and "Pan-African Congress Holds Fourth Annual Meet in N.Y.," *Chicago Defender*, August 27, 1927, 2.

38. Marion Starkey, "Jessie Fauset," *Southern Workman*, May 1932, 218; and Ira De A. Reid, "Mirrors of Harlem-Investigations and Problems of America's Largest Colored Community," *Social Forces* 5 (1927): 628.

39. "With the Sororities," *Amsterdam News*, May 16, 1928, 5; Augustus Dill, "Gertrude Ayer Is Guest at Banquet," *Pittsburgh Courier*, June 13, 1936, 9; Obituary, Mary Elizabeth Johnson, April 22, 1929, Ayer Scrapbook, Gertrude Ayer Papers, Schomburg (hereafter GAP); "Commencement Address Delivered by New York Educator," Lincoln University 1947, Scrapbook, GAP; Lauri Johnson, "Making Her Community a Better Place to Live," in *Keeping the Promise: Essays on Leadership, Democracy and Education*, ed. Dennis

Carlson and C. P. Gause (New York: Peter Lang, 2007), 271; "Negro Woman Gets Top Post in School," *New York Times*, February 5, 1935; "N. Y. Civic Club Hears Speeches on Negro Gifts," *Afro-American*, March 14, 1925, A2; "At Experimental School," *Amsterdam News*, May 21, 1938, 19; and *People's Voice*, February 19, 1944, 1.

40. Elise McDougald, "The Women of the White Strain," in *Harlem's Glory: Black Women Writing, 1900–1950*, ed. Lorraine Roses and Ruth Randolph (Cambridge, Mass.: Harvard University Press, 1996), 419.

41. McDougald, "Women of the White Strain," 411–19.

42. E. David Cronon, *Black Moses: The Story of Marcus Garvey and the Universal Negro Improvement Association* (Madison: University of Wisconsin Press, 1955), 112; Frank Crosswaith to W. E. B. Du Bois, August 28, 1925, W. E. B. Du Bois Papers (MS 312), Special Collections and University Archives, University of Massachusetts Amherst Libraries; Gertrude Ayer, *A New Day for the Colored Woman Worker* (New York: Young, 1919), 9–11, 17, 20, 23; and Elise McDougald, "The Double Task: The Struggle of Negro Women for Sex and Race Emancipation," *Survey Graphic* 6 (1925): 689.

43. McDougald, "Women of the White Strain," 419; and "Health Ass'n Hold Annual Meeting," *Amsterdam News*, February 23, 1927, 3.

44. "Mrs. Gertrude Ayer Appointed Principal," *Chicago Defender*, February 2, 1935; Nell Occomy, "Mrs. Ayer Pioneers Social Work," *New York News*, August 29, 1931; and "Mrs. Gertrude E. Ayer Tendered Testimonial Dinner," Scrapbook, GAP.

45. "Negro Woman Gets Top New York City [Job]," February 5, 1935, Scrapbook; "Rare Library Brought to Harlem," *Amsterdam News*, January 19, 1927, 8; Gertrude Ayer, "Notes on My Native Sons," in Clarke, *Harlem*, 144; Elise McDougald, "The Negro Woman Teacher and the Negro Student," *Messenger* 7 (1923): 770; and Johnson, "Making Her Community a Better Place," 272.

46. Elise Ayer, "Child Training," February 8, 1930, Ayer Scrapbook, GAP.

47. Carol Taylor, "Retiring Harlem Principal Paves Way for Race Mixing," *New York World Telegram*, June 11, 1954; Johnson, "Making Her Community a Better Place," 272; "Pupils Govern Selves," *Amsterdam News*, May 9, 1936; Ayer, "Notes on My Native Sons," 139; *New York World Telegram*, February 6, 1935; and *People's Voice*, 1.

48. Ayer, "Notes on My Native Sons," 139.

49. Jennifer Wood, "Johnson, J. Rosamond," in *Harlem Renaissance Lives from the African American National Biography*, ed. Henry Louis Gates and Evelyn Higginbotham (New York: Oxford University Press, 2009), 296–300; and Mildred Johnson Edwards, "A Few Incidents from . . . Mildred Grows Up During the Negro Renaissance," n.d., 1–2, MSP.

50. Robert Beck, "Progressive Education and American Progressivism: Felix Adler," *Teachers College Record* 60 (1958): 78–88; Ellen Tarry, *Young Jim: The Early Years of James Weldon Johnson* (New York: Dodd, Mead, 1967), 223; and Mildred Johnson, "Footnotes on the Modern School," ca. 1979, MSP.

51. Mildred Johnson, "The Plan of a Nursery School," March 13, 1933, MSP; and Johnson, "Lots of Children, or A Story of Mildred," 9, MSP.

52. Johnson, "Lots of Children," 6; and Mildred Johnson, "About: The Modern School, 1998 Edition," MSP.

53. [Mildred Johnson], "The Modern School Curriculum," n.d., 10–11, MSP; Johnson, "Lots of Children," 10; and Johnson, "About: The Modern School."

54. Johnson, "Lots of Children," 10–11; "[Faculty] Handbook for the Modern School," n.d., 10, MSP; "Schools Plan Fall Openings: Three Progressive Groups Are Ready," *Amsterdam Star-News*, September 13, 1941, 10; [Mildred Johnson], "A Few Incidents," 3; untitled 1941 report, MSP; and Charles Wolk to National Bank of Pine Bush, August 17, 1954, MSP.

55. Untitled 1941 report; Johnson, "Modern School Curriculum," 1–11; and Class of 1954, "Class History," MSP.

56. Johnson, "About: The Modern School"; and Sara Slack, "The Modern School: A Story of Progress," *Amsterdam News*, November 23, 1963, 35.

57. Mildred Johnson, "Statement Regarding Out-of-Door Program," n.d., ca. 1960, 1–2, MSP; Johnson, "Modern School Curriculum," 2; and Lucy Sprague Mitchell, "Making Young Geographers," *Progressive Education* 5 (1928): 217–23.

58. Mildred Johnson to Parent, 1955, MSP; Vernon Sinclair, "Modern School Holds Coronation," *Amsterdam News*, May 16, 1953, 34, "How T. M. S. Uses the Festival," n.d.; Mildred Johnson, "Festival: A Play for Children," March 11, 1935, MSP; and Nora Holt, "'Modern School' Children in Opera," *Amsterdam News*, July 1, 1944, 9A.

59. Mildred Johnson, "Mildred Goes to Camp," 13, MSP; "Handbook for the Modern School," 9; Mildred Johnson, "A Bit of Magic Mirror" (festival program), June 27, 1942, MSP; Sinclair, "Modern School Holds Coronation;" Johnson, "About: The Modern School"; Thomas Kilgore and Jini Kilgore Ross, *A Servants Journey: The Life and Work of Thomas Kilgore* (Valley Forge, Penn.: Judson, 1998), 55; and "Chatter and Chimes," *Amsterdam News*, October 14, 1939, 1.

60. Victoria Horsford, "Mildred Johnson Edwards, Modern School Founder, Passes," *Amsterdam News*, September 6, 2007, 41; Bessie Bell, "Women of Merit," *New York Age*, March 1, 1947; "Modern School Marks 35 Years," *Amsterdam News*, May 23, 1970, 5; "Modern School Play Notes Yule Customs," *Amsterdam News*, December 23, 1967, 11; and Mildred Johnson, "Mildred Opens Dunroven," 13, MSP.

61. Toni Cade Bambara, *Deep Sightings and Rescue Missions: Fiction, Essays, and Conversations* (New York: Knopf, 2009), 213; and Linda Holmes, *A Joyous Revolt: Toni Cade Bambara, Writer and Activist* (Santa Barbara, Calif.: ABC-CLIO, 2014), 12–13.

62. John Hall Jr., Oral History interview, 1986–87, in Anne Key Simpson, *Hard Trials: The Life and Music of Harry T. Burleigh* (Metuchen, N.J.: Scarecrow, 1990), 187; and Betty Granger Reid, "Conversation Piece," *Amsterdam News*, May 23, 1970, 5.

63. Leora King email to author, August 6, 2016.

64. E. Franklin Frazier, "Some Effects of the Depression on the Negro in Northern Cities," *Science and Society* 2 (1938): 496, 498; and Nathan Huggins, *Harlem Renaissance* (New York: Oxford University Press, 1971), 41, 59.

65. Richard Wright, in J. Saunders Redding, *No Day of Triumph* (New York: Harper, 1942), introduction; Andrew Kersten and Clarence Lang, *Reframing Randolph: Labor, Black Freedom, and the Legacies of A. Philip Randolph* (New York: New York University Press, 2015), 204; Joanne Grant, *Ella Baker: Freedom Bound* (New York: John Wiley, 1998), 26, 28; and James Baldwin, "Everybody's Protest Novel," in *Notes of a Native Son* (Boston: Beacon, 1984), 23.

66. Abby Arthur Johnson, *Propaganda and Aesthetics: The Literary Politics of African-American Magazines in the Twentieth Century* (Amherst: University of Massachusetts Press, 1991), 91.

CHAPTER 2

"A Serious Pedagogical Situation"

Diverging School Reform Priorities in Depression-Era Harlem

THOMAS HARBISON

> Whenever the public school system embarks on a program or uses proce-
> dures which provide different levels of education for different social, eco-
> nomic or racial groups, it then becomes a force in solidifying undemocratic
> class cleavages, obstructs mobility, and blocks the use of human intellectual
> resources.
>
> —KENNETH CLARK, APRIL 1954

By 1954, many parents and local leaders had reached the same conclusion as Kenneth Clark, who presented the argument quoted
above to an audience at his Northside Center for Child Development in Harlem. No matter what the intentions of educators and others
who advocated for them, differentiated educational services and the curriculum for Harlem's predominantly Black student population had become
yet another form of discrimination and injustice. Most school administrators vehemently disagreed with Clark's accusation, arguing that these programs were necessary to level the playing field for students. Harlem schools
continued to divert resources to "specialized" remedial social, vocational,
and academic training programs; the more robust and humane educational
program at Gertrude Ayer's Public School (PS) 24, as discussed in chapter 1, was the exception rather than the rule.

The school curriculum had divided Harlem parents, local leaders, and
school administrators since the Great Migration. The priorities and reform
strategies favored by many parents, community leaders, and a faction of
teachers diverged drastically from those valued by school administrators.
The divergence was sharpest during the Depression Era, when parents and
other community representatives such as civic leaders and activist teachers
questioned the fairness and equity of their schools and found new outlets
to express their discontent with educational practices that sanctioned lower
expectations for Harlem students. They rejected customized, so-called

individualized curriculum, making a strong case that when crudely applied this approach amounted to discriminatory group categorization. In response, administrators dug in their heels and intensified a long-standing remedial curricular focus that they said best served students by compensating for what they perceived to be a lack of educational experiences in their students' homes and communities. This major divide between parents and administrators in the 1930s and later differed from the pattern of the 1910s and early 1920s, when discussion of school goals and priorities was dominated by elites who generally supported school policy and agreed with school officials that specialized forms of schooling best served African American students, especially the large number who had arrived from the South.[1]

Many Black southerners and Afro-Caribbean immigrants came to Harlem aspiring to more and better schooling for themselves or their children. Yet they were met by educational practices and ideas that stymied these aspirations. At least by the time of the Great Depression, if not before, parents and community leaders pushed to make Harlem schools places that held high expectations for all students and helped them be met. These struggles reveal the dualities of the Black families' experiences in the Great Migration and pre–World War II northern cities. They achieved more unfettered access to schooling than in the Jim Crow South, but battled deeply rooted racist ideas about Black children and their futures and the educational practices they spawned. They manifest an early version of an ongoing struggle in African American experiences of schooling.

The Great Migration

Between World War I and 1930, thousands of African American families from the U.S. South and Afro-Caribbean families from the West Indies arrived in Central Harlem and dramatically changed the student population.[2] Between 1910 and 1930, New York City's Black population more than tripled, rising from 91,000 to 327,000.[3] From 1920 to 1930, over 115,000 white Harlemites left the area and nearly 90,000 African Americans and Afro-Caribbean immigrants arrived.[4]

PS 89, an elementary school located at 135th Street and Lenox Avenue, sat at the heart of Harlem's earliest Black settlement and felt the effects of early twentieth-century demographic change before any other. Even before the Great Migration accelerated the formation of a Black "city within a city" in Harlem during and after World War I, the movement uptown of Black New Yorkers from the Tenderloin district and the flight of white residents to outer boroughs transformed the blocks immediately surrounding PS 89.[5] By 1916, 84 percent of the school's students were Black and this number increased to 93 percent by 1921. Principal Jacob Ross and his administrative staff placed overage children—most of them students whose families had recently arrived from the U.S. South and the West Indies—in smaller classes (twenty-five or fewer, compared to the district average of more than forty) and opened "adjustment classes" for students whom educators judged to be farthest behind.[6]

New York City superintendents and principals in place during the late 1910s and 1920s, responding to the arrival to their schools of migrants from the South and immigrants from the West Indies, built upon a long-standing tradition of promoting specialized forms of education for migrant and immigrant groups in New York City. Since the late 1890s, administrators had pioneered the use of character education, vocational training, and the delivery of social services in the school. They sought to customize the curriculum to meet the perceived needs of their students, most of them European immigrants. As they determined that the classical school curriculum of the nineteenth century, designed to meet the academic needs of a select group of students, would not suffice for their diverse, large group of students, they offered one variation of the ongoing struggle in education over whether schools would replicate class and racial hierarchies in their curricula or seek to challenge them.[7]

One of the earliest administrators to apply this philosophy of customized curriculum to school policy targeting African American students in New York City was William L. Bulkley. Bulkley began his career in New York City public schools as a teacher in 1899 after migrating from South Carolina where he had been born into slavery. Soon after, he took over as principal of the predominantly Black school in the Tenderloin district.[8] As a close follower of Booker T. Washington, Bulkley emphasized manual training to prepare Black students for the relatively lower-status vocations open to them at the time in a segregated labor market. At the same time, he asserted that students from Black families living in poor conditions needed extra health services and recreational spaces and that his school was in the best position to provide these. In collaboration with local churches and other welfare organizations, Bulkley converted his school into a community center that offered vocational classes, basic health care, recreational facilities, and child care to neighborhood residents of all ages.[9]

Other principals in Harlem, such as Jacob Ross, began to track students into tiered levels of classes based on intelligence testing during the late 1910s and early 1920s. This fit a national trend that favored the application to schools of supposed scientific techniques developed by psychologists.[10] Using a few different types of tests derived from the Stanford-Binet (popularized during World War I as a tool for sorting army recruits), New York City school administrators teamed up with psychologists from the Education Clinic at the City College of New York and other New York universities to develop a series of cutoffs that determined minimum scores necessary for the placement of students in various academic and vocational courses, and classified students as "accelerated," "normal," or "retarded."[11]

Although they continued many educational practices that limited options for Harlem students, the public schools of Harlem during the late 1910s and 1920s offered a relative improvement in terms of material resources as compared to the vast inequalities in education spending for Black and white students in the formally segregated systems of the Jim Crow South.[12] Public leaders in the African American community of Harlem, disproportionately male and middle- to upper-class, expressed a great deal of optimism in the schools. In addition to generally validating the motives and efficacy of the administration, they gave specific support to various forms of remedial education, including character education, industrial training, and the expansion of social services. Black newspaper editors and National Association for the Advancement of Colored People (NAACP) leaders, among the strongest public voices in the Harlem Black community at the time, tended to support these approaches as they fit them into a larger strategy of racial uplift. They shared with school administrators an understanding that schools should focus on teaching middle-class cultural and social values to working-class African Americans.

The Black press generally came out in favor of character education in Harlem schools. In the mid-1920s, the *New York Age* (founded in the 1880s) backed administrators' claims that "the building of character is one of the essential aims of education" and reinforced their plea for parent cooperation to buttress in-school moral training.[13] The *Amsterdam News*, founded in 1909 as a rival to the *Age*, joined the *Age* in regularly urging parents to support the goals of the public school, including character education.[14] They also gave support to administrators' implementation of vocational curricula, even with an emphasis on lower-skilled work. As were the ideas of Booker T. Washington, or the pioneers of industrial education before him, ideas about character and labor were often intertwined. The experience of work was believed to refine students' character, and students' character would help prepare them to accept the confined work opportunities available to them due to racism.[15] The *New York Age* promoted vocational curricula in Harlem the most consistently, maintaining this position long after T. Thomas Fortune—a follower of Washington—sold the paper in 1907. During the 1920s, the paper's editorials applauded vocational guidance's effectiveness in matching the "mental capacity and adaptability of the pupil" with "channels that will qualify him for a gainful occupation."[16] For Washington and the many advocates of "uplift suasion" who followed him, vocational education and respectability-minded character education worked to reinforce one another.[17]

Both the *Amsterdam News* and *New York Age* regularly published editorials complimenting the general fairness and wisdom of prevailing school policies. Often, they explicitly noted the leadership's lack of racial discrimination or favoritism.[18] They spoke highly of Superintendent William O'Shea (who served from 1924 to 1934) and his predecessors, characterizing them as "men of executive ability and courage" who avoided racial or ethnic bias in their work.[19]

In taking this approach, they aligned closely with the racial uplift philosophy championed by the National Urban League (NUL), an organization established in 1910 to address the needs of African American migrants to northern cities and guided by sociological theories favoring assimilation and self-help strategies. NUL leaders encouraged migration, breaking with Washington's position, but perceived migrants as maladjusted to their new environment and identified vocational and moral training as the path to respectability for them.[20] In their support of an industrial education model, the NUL and leaders such as Bulkley (who played an essential role in founding the organization), were taking sides in a national debate about the goals of education for improving the position of African Americans. That debate grew out of the disagreement between Booker T. Washington and W. E. B. Du Bois, who approached the education of Black students through different strategies. Their disagreement escalated with Du Bois's public criticism of Washington's emphasis on manual labor in favor of a continued classical curriculum to educate transformational leaders in the African American community.[21]

Other Harlem residents who interacted with schools as parents or children may well have had different stories to tell, which—unless gathered into organized protest movements—were less likely to be captured by newspapers or archives. As Shannon King's study of early Harlem activism shows, working-class residents organized to contest injustice in housing, policing, and work; education may have been an area that, at that moment, drew less activism.[22] Though elites predominate in the historical record of the 1910s and 1920s, many more voices soon made themselves heard.

The Great Depression

Harlem's elite spoke less supportively of their schools during the late 1920s and 1930s as the economic situation and physical school conditions worsened and new protest movements emerged.[23] The Great Depression hit Harlem extremely hard and relatively early. The New York Urban League noted unusual increases in unemployment as early as the fall of 1927.[24] A steep economic downturn was already under way by 1928 and federal and state relief did not bring major benefits until 1936.[25] Median family income in Harlem dropped steadily after 1929, falling 44 percent by 1932, and by 1933 more than 40 percent of Black families there relied on government relief.[26] The unemployment rate in Harlem quadrupled during 1930 alone, with Black New Yorkers losing their jobs at three to four times the rate of white citizens.[27] Most Black residents of Harlem who remained employed at this time worked in low-skilled service jobs in the domestic and service sectors.[28]

School conditions, already problematic during the 1920s due to overcrowding and overdue maintenance, continued to deteriorate during the 1930s. During the Depression, many Harlem families relied on public schools as a source of benefits such as free lunches, basic health care, and job training.[29] Educational levels among Black students in Harlem rose throughout the 1930s, as did attendance rates, which equaled those among white children by the end of the decade.[30] Yet, during this time of increasing dependence on the schools, massive budget cuts led to a freeze on all new building and hiring. This disproportionately affected Harlem, by then one of the most densely populated areas of the city and an area where expansion of school facilities had already fallen behind the rapid population growth during the 1920s.[31]

By the 1930s, due to the combination of racial discrimination in the housing market that restricted Black residents to Harlem, white departures from the neighborhood, and school zoning policies that either respected residential segregation or amplified it, Harlem schools had few white students in attendance.[32] In 1920, two elementary schools were over 90 percent Black.[33] By the early 1930s, thirteen of the fourteen public schools in Central Harlem (between St. Nicholas Avenue on the west and Fifth Avenue on the east) had almost no white students. One of these schools contained 92 percent Black students, and the remaining twelve schools had Black enrollment of 97 percent or higher. This pattern paralleled the trend in other large northern urban school systems such as Chicago, Boston, and Cleveland.[34]

During the early years of the Great Depression, groups of publishers and journalists in the Black press reported on these shortcomings, which helped raise doubts about the fairness of the system. Together with groups of teachers, parents, and church leaders from Harlem, they began to question school officials' approach. They began to combine efforts to advocate more equitable education for their children. These women and men, most of whom lived in Harlem as well as some who taught there, closely connected what they identified as limited educational opportunities in schools with restricted opportunities in housing and labor markets. Education became an area that came under fire from radical political movements taking shape in Harlem, as activists turned away from the gradualist strategies favored by the "old guard" at the head of the NUL and the NAACP.[35]

The fact that both of those organizations, the two largest civil rights organizations in both New York City and the nation, often overlooked educational inequality in Harlem schools during the early 1930s created a vacuum into which teacher, parent, and citizen groups moved to air major grievances about the schools and to propose reforms that would more fairly serve the children of Harlem. They moved into the public sphere, which had been expanded in Harlem during the 1920s with the founding of weekly publications far left of the previously dominant *New York Age*, and growing Black trade unionism led by men such as A. Philip Randolph and Frank Crosswaith.[36]

Reports conducted during the 1930s, some government sponsored, some initiated by citizen groups, teachers, and other activists, revealed the extent of subpar conditions and unfair curricular tracking in Harlem schools. These studies fueled protests and further dampened community confidence in the schools. In 1930 alone, investigative reports on poor conditions in Harlem schools were released by the Better Schools Club, started by a group of six Harlem mothers; the New York City Teachers Union, the largest teachers union in the city at the time; and the Joint Committee on Education, an umbrella of civic groups such as the Junior League and the League of Women Voters. Between 1932 and 1934, parents, teachers, church leaders, and various social welfare agencies serving the community, collaborated in a Harlem Parent-Teachers' Committee to gather data on unequal conditions and to protest publicly.[37]

In the following two years, protest coalesced and intensified around two prominent government reports that put the situation in Harlem public schools under the microscope for wide audiences to see and led community activists and school administrators to stake out very different positions. The first came from a Harlem assistant superintendent, Oswald Schlockow. Schlockow was born in Germany in 1874, came to New York City at the age of eight, and attended New York City public schools through his undergraduate degree at City College of New York. As a graduate student at New York University, he took a special interest in techniques of school management and discipline, including methods for maintaining order by instilling "morality" among "incorrigible truants in the schools." He put his theories into practice as a teacher at PS 22 in Manhattan, as the principal of PS 50 and PS 109 in Brooklyn and, most productively, as the assistant superintendent in Harlem beginning in 1928.[38] Schlockow concluded that Harlem's "special educational, social, ethical, academic and vocational needs" must be met with customized school programming. Between 1932 and 1934, Schlockow made character education and vocational programming his top goal in his districts (10 and 12), which covered much of Central Harlem.[39] He described his agenda as favoring "character first," a phrase that he argued should "be inscribed over the portals of every school in these districts" since he deemed it a "pole star of vision" for Harlem students.[40]

Alongside character education, Schlockow increased vocational training programs in his Harlem districts. Schlockow teamed up with assistant superintendent Robert Frost, his counterpart responsible for Districts 13 and 14 (covering the remainder of Central Harlem), to increase the number of vocational courses in their schools. They also adjusted the academic curriculum by dropping some of the advanced classes and adding "visual instruction," which incorporated slides and other visual aides in lieu of complex texts.[41] Schlockow and Frost justified such changes as steps to accommodate "children with borderline mentalities," more likely in their districts because of "the unique make-up of the population." Yet, Schlockow and Frost failed to maintain even the illusion that the sorting into diverse curricular tracks would take place on an individualized basis, assigning vast groups of students to lower tracks based on their racial and socioeconomic characteristics and keeping students in these tracks for years on end, without opportunities to move as their achievement improved.[42]

Although he was not alone in promoting these approaches, Schlockow was extremely outspoken in his call for major curricular adjustments based on the socioeconomic, racial, and ethnic characteristics of students at any given school. In his 1933–1934 report, subsequently called "the Schlockow report" in the New York media, he called on the schools to formulate individualized plans of "academic studies, manual training, and socialized techniques of work" to best suit the specific ethnic, racial, and socioeconomic makeup of their districts.[43] In his report, he detailed the poverty and limited prior schooling prevalent among Black students in his districts, particularly those whose families had migrated to New York City from the South. He correlated these factors with poor school performance and claimed the "maelstrom of economic and social distress," presented a "serious pedagogical situation."[44]

Schlockow attempted to lay the groundwork for his programs and ward off opposition from Harlem families, who he anticipated would become offended by his program's implicit blame on their communities for school failure. Before the report's release, he contacted Harlem church and civic organization leaders and asked for their support.[45] Nevertheless, his reforms were met with major opposition, much of it quite hostile.

The *Amsterdam News* voiced the sharpest criticism. By the late 1920s, its editors had already begun to raise doubts about customized programming for Harlem schools. Immediately after Schlockow's press release, the newspaper aired its concerns about the report. The Schlockow report "augur[ed] an official move to shunt Negro pupils into certain avenues of employment deemed 'best' for them because of racial restrictions and prejudices," the editors wrote.[46]

Criticisms of the Schlockow report resonated in Black communities beyond Harlem, primarily because of the work of the African American journalist and author George Schuyler. A nationally recognized social commentator, Schuyler decided to make an example of the Schlockow report in his regular newspaper column for the *Pittsburgh Courier*, which by this time was circulated to nearly 200,000 readers and reprinted in a dozen cities.[47] The *Amsterdam News* republished Schuyler's columns as well as letters that he composed to the editor. Schuyler focused closely on Harlem schools because in his judgment, "New York City is the spearhead of the Negro's fight for full American citizenship with all of the rights, duties and privileges that go with it," and he used his attacks on Schlockow to open up a broader attack on school segregation in the urban North.[48]

Schuyler argued that Schlockow's plan represented "a quiet conspiracy . . . to segregate the Negro educationally."[49] The report, he argued, signaled the "opening gun in the threatening campaign for a lower industrial curriculum for Negro children."[50] The special curriculum for Black children could trap them permanently in the "laborer-domestic stratum."[51] Schuyler criticized school authorities in Harlem for concentrating Black students in a single district with gerrymandered boundaries and then overdosing them with industrial education. Schuyler was accusing New York school administration of more than just benign neglect. He argued that Schlockow's approach to reform was deeply racist, noting, "Now [Schlockow] is the man (and one of the exploited Jews!) who presides over the destinies of most of Harlem's school children. The education given the white children of New York is, according to this man, unsuited to colored children." Schuyler referred to Schlockow, along with Jacob Ross, by this time the principal of Junior High School 136 and a collaborator with Schlockow on his proposed curricular reforms, as "a menace to the colored people."[52]

Schuyler was by no means the first to argue against racial segregation in New York City schools. Yet his accusation of malicious intent on the part of the administration broke new ground. Schuyler's powerful response and that of the African American community in Harlem gave added impetus to the debate and represented a more confrontational tone than that of earlier discussions of Harlem schools.

Six months later, a very different type of event led to investigative journalism that triggered further cycles of protest and disagreement over school reform priorities. On March 19, 1935, a floorwalker at E. H. Kress and Company five- and ten-cent store on 125th Street spotted a teenage boy shoplifting a penknife. The guard hailed a manager, and together they apprehended the youth, Lino Rivera, and summoned the police. In an effort to defuse the situation and disperse the growing crowd of bystanders in front of the store, the manager and the patrolman who arrived on the scene took the Puerto Rican Harlem resident through the basement and released him through a rear exit.[53]

Word spread among shoppers that a young Black boy had been badly beaten by the police. An ambulance arrived to treat minor injuries suffered by the store workers during the initial scuffle while apprehending the suspect, but the crowd assumed that it had come for the boy. When the ambulance left empty and a hearse coincidentally pulled up to a building close to the store, some accused the police of murder and the gathering sidewalk crowd grew angrier.[54] A heavy object was hurled through the front window of the store and chaos escalated.[55]

When night fell, crowds broke into other stores along 125th Street, mostly white-owned and many such as Kress having reputations for refusing to hire Black employees. Disorder spread outward to Seventh and Lenox Avenues, where participants smashed over three hundred storefront windows and looted merchandise.[56] The Harlem Merchants Association wired Governor Herbert Lehman requesting military assistance. The following day, patrols by over five hundred police armed with riot guns brought the situation to a close. Ultimately, five deaths and over $500,000 of property damage were reported.[57]

As the author Alain Locke vividly recalled a year later, likening the riot to "a revealing flash of lightning," the event suddenly drew public attention across the city to the social and economic problems wracking Harlem.[58] When Mayor Fiorello LaGuardia appointed an investigative team to document the underlying problems that caused the riot, he set in motion a series of studies aimed to ensure that this moment would not soon be forgotten.

Mayor LaGuardia created the commission three days after the riot by appointing a biracial, predominantly liberal group to determine the social and economic problems underlying the outbreak and recommend government solutions.[59] He did so in consultation with leaders of church, labor, and racial uplift organizations. He appointed a Subcommittee on Education alongside seven other committees focusing on areas including employment, relief, housing, law enforcement, and hospitals.[60] He chose Oswald Garrison Villard, former editor of the *Nation*, to chair the education subcommittee. The rest of the group consisted of Countée Cullen, a poet and teacher, whose views on education are explored in chapter 1 of this volume; John W. Robinson, a Black minister; and William R. McCann, a white Catholic priest.[61]

Villard's group held weeks of formal hearings, questioning administrators, teachers, and parents about the state of the public schools serving

Harlem's children.[62] These sessions revealed a significant rift between administrators' understandings of Harlem schools and those of parents and teachers. Dozens of parent and teacher interviewees spoke—often in private for fear of retaliation by the school system—of the dilapidated state of school buildings and crowding of forty or fifty students per class, even after the scheduling of multiple shifts that disguised deeper overcrowding problems and shortened students' time in class.[63] Mrs. Eddie Aspinall, the executive secretary of the Central Committee of the Harlem Parents Associations, stated: "In this critical period . . . the Board of Education, instead of expanding the school facilities to meet the situation, has instituted a false 'economy' program in education" in which "more children are jammed into the classroom."[64] Parents questioned the implementation of vocational education and the commitment of principals and teachers to high-quality education for their children.[65] Mrs. W. J. Burroughs, speaking on behalf of the Harlem Teachers Association, the Students Association, and the League of Struggle for Negro Rights, criticized not only "scandalous conditions" in the physical plant but also a "frequent lack of sympathy" from teachers and principals as well as a "lifeless curriculum," highlighting how some teachers' perspectives differed sharply from those of school administrators.[66]

As valuable as they were for revealing contradicting views on the goals and realities of Harlem's schools, the hearings were only a part of the overall investigation into the school situation. Under Villard's chairmanship, the education subcommittee worked with the Howard University sociologist E. Franklin Frazier's research team to pull together more data and draw more sweeping conclusions than any prior study of Harlem's schools. They combed through data on the budget, age of facilities, safety ratings, staff-hiring patterns, racial demographics, and curriculum design. Frazier's team studied individual schools as well as out-of-school factors such as unhealthy living conditions that worsened student health and created obstacles to learning. The team drew information from interviews with principals, site visits, and various school records.[67]

In late August, the Subcommittee on Education submitted a highly detailed report to LaGuardia's full commission.[68] The group concluded that Harlem schools were a significant part of the problems plaguing the community and it especially criticized the physical condition of Harlem schools. "One can almost trace the limits of the Negro community through the character of the school buildings," the subcommittee wrote. The report documented segregation of students into low-skilled vocational classes and a watering down of academic courses, and it accused the school system of inequitable resource allocation, teacher hiring, and racially biased treatment of Black teachers, students, and parents by administrators.[69] A full chapter of the final report from LaGuardia's commission was devoted to education and recreation.

Upon receipt of the final version of the report, controversial enough that it was left unsigned by three commission members, Mayor LaGuardia withheld his official endorsement and decided to hold it for internal use only.[70] The overall conclusion that the incident at Kress department store was a "spark that set aflame the smoldering resentments of the people of Harlem against racial discrimination and poverty in the midst of plenty" was in line with the mayor's statements during the creation of the commission.[71] Yet, the specific accusations of discrimination by various city departments, including the school system, represented a potential political liability.

In the winter and spring of 1936, NAACP officials, groups of publishers and journalists in the Black press, and other leaders in the Harlem community urged the mayor to release the report, but he declined. Only if certain "objectionable" passages were omitted or rewritten would LaGuardia consider sharing the report more widely. However, although the mayor resisted, a copy of the report was leaked to the *Amsterdam News*, and on July 18, 1936, the paper published the entire 35,000-word report, and newspapers across the city immediately picked up the story.[72]

Release of the report fueled several Harlem-based movements to study and change the state of schools. The work of LaGuardia's riot commission and its research team put into the public record hard evidence that validated the dissent from various groups in the early 1930s and exposed the problem to a much larger audience. The riot report, combined with follow-up studies conducted by teachers, social scientists, Harlem-based civic groups, and state agencies, provided a large body of data to support arguments about discriminatory practices in the schools that had previously just been suspicions. The more evidence of inequities in Harlem schools became available, the more closely researchers and activists examined the schools and found new venues to call for change.

A group of teachers from the Teachers Union took the lead in building a protest movement based on the report findings. Since its founding in 1916 as the first teachers union in New York City, a number of members within the Teachers Union pushed an agenda reaching far beyond bread-and-butter issues.[73] In the closing months of 1935, a cadre of those teachers established a

Harlem Committee to coordinate a community-wide effort to confront the problems identified by the report of LaGuardia's riot commission.[74] As one of its first actions this group drafted a petition to the Board of Education directing its attention to a list of problems overlapping closely with those discussed in the LaGuardia report.[75] To bolster its cause, the Harlem Committee circulated reprinted copies of the commission report.

The goals outlined in the petition were quickly and emphatically endorsed by the union's leadership, as well as religious and political leaders such as the Reverend Adam Clayton Powell Jr. of Abyssinian Baptist Church and community leaders who had served on LaGuardia's commission, such as Countee Cullen.[76] The teachers on the Harlem Committee reached out to other local organizations to create a broad coalition for addressing school problems. In the spring of 1936, they pulled together a wide range of parent, religious, and civic organizations to form the Provisional Committee for Better Schools in Harlem, soon after renamed the Permanent Committee for Better Schools in Harlem. They called for new and improved school facilities in Harlem.[77]

School administrators, on the other hand, retrenched in response to the riot and criticism that emerged in its aftermath. During LaGuardia's riot commission investigation, administrators consistently focused their testimony before the Subcommittee on Education on inadequacies in the homes of Harlem children. They claimed this necessitated the widespread application of specialized curricula. Jacob Ross blamed single-parent homes for "deterioration in morals" among his 2,200 students.[78] James Marshall, the president of the Board of Education, readily admitted the inadequacy of Harlem's school facilities while adamantly denying discriminatory practices, pinning the underperformance of Black students on "deficiencies in training which result from broken homes, poverty, a vicious environment, retardation, and ill health."[79] Gertrude Ayer, New York's first African American woman elementary school principal who was pioneering community-based education at PS 24, as described in chapter 1 of this volume, argued that Harlem students' problems originated outside of the school and should thus be addressed there.

During the riot commission hearings, principals spent a great deal of time trying to justify vocational training for Harlem students. Julius Gluck, the principal of PS 89, highlighted the demand for proper equipment and teaching staff to give students failing the academic curriculum greater opportunity. "Manual training work must be extended to a great degree," he argued, "if we are to fit the children of this neighborhood for a good, profitable life after their education is completed." In his argument in favor of a broadened vocational curriculum, Gluck blamed a historical overemphasis on intellectual training for students' inability to advance through the grades at a proper pace, resulting in overage students that caused social problems in classrooms.[80] Principals of vocational high schools, such as Charles J. Pickett, the head of the New York Industrial High School, advocated for the special importance of manual training during the Depression Era when a higher number of students than normal were in school against their wishes and had no desire for an academic curriculum.[81] (Even advocates for vocational education felt the effects of underinvestment in Harlem schools, with programs lacking mere basic supplies for vocational training, as discussed in chapter 3 of this volume.)

In the same interviews, administrators continued to call for more social services in their schools, justifying the addition of mental health and social work professionals to their staffs with the goal of achieving proper psychological "adjustment" of their students. This represented a turn that was to sharpen during the upcoming war years, when principals and superintendents would be joined by teachers in an effort to infuse the curriculum with mental health services. Notably, these social services would operate alongside curricula dominated by vocational and character education, rather than the academic curriculum many Harlem residents sought.

In the heart of the Great Depression, Harlem parents, community members, and some teachers fought their version of what was then a decades-old struggle, which would prove to be enduring. They sought not only decent resources and facilities for their children, but a curriculum that reflected their aspirations rather than the constrained and oppressive employment environment they faced.

School policy makers persisted during and beyond World War II in their focus on adjusting children in an effort to counteract adverse environmental factors. During the 1940s, with a second wave of migration from the South that exceeded the first, superintendents and principals implemented a wide array of curricular initiatives that they billed as anti-juvenile-delinquency measures, continuing their strategy of expanding the school curriculum to compensate for perceived student deficits with remedial academic courses and social services. The Board of Superintendents and Board of Education began to target Harlem for special programming more aggressively than they had in the past and launched experimental programs designed to infuse "difficult schools" with social services and remedial academic programming.

The radical dissent from the Harlem community during the mid-1930s was not maintained in force during the 1940s, although this does not mean that the administration had won back support. As in most of the country, the war diverted energy and momentum from activist efforts of only a few years previously. Community spokespersons did continue to contest compensatory curricular approaches in the 1940s, expanding on public expressions of frustration first aired during the 1930s.[82]

The women and men who questioned and opposed practices in Harlem schools during the 1930s had framed the schools' mission in terms of absolute equality. They presented evidence undermining the legitimacy of so-called individualized education that in turn propelled subsequent protest. They demanded that students in their Harlem schools receive the very same paths of study, in the same quality facilities, and by the same quality teachers as the best public schools in the city. Their forceful articulation of frustrations with substandard schooling had set off a cycle by which expressions of distrust put the fairness and eventually the motivations behind school policies under close public scrutiny. Educational policies may have appeared superficially race-neutral to some, but Harlem parents and their allies in the community clearly showed that these policies were leading to a rigidly stratified system that cheated African American students of opportunity.

Meanwhile, many administrators continued to define the schools' mission as meeting what they perceived to be students' special needs, foreshadowing the use of "culturally deprived" and "disadvantaged" as terms to describe students during the 1950s and 1960s.[83] In the absence of a truly individualized custom curriculum, which was made less likely given limited resources, educators opted for a school program tailored to meet the needs of the groups as they identified them. This fraught approach risked creating a self-fulfilling cycle of low expectations built on racial and cultural stereotyping.[84]

By the end of the 1930s, these two understandings of educational approaches and priorities had grown irreconcilably far apart and trust between administrators and community members had greatly diminished, leaving little room for collaborative reform efforts at a time when such cooperation was essential to meet the needs of students. The tacit support from elite community spokespeople of the 1910s and early 1920s had dwindled and been surpassed by a wider cross-section of community members who both found and created public outlets for protest. Those voices of protest threw into question everything from school policies to the philosophies of racial uplift that undergirded them, foreshadowing debates that endured for years to come.

Notes

Epigraph quote is taken from a reprinted version of the speech in Kenneth B. Clark, "Segregated Schools in New York City," *Journal of Educational Sociology* 36, no. 6 (February 1963): 250. Clark delivered the speech to conference attendees at the "Children Apart" conference, hosted at the Northside Center for Child Development in April 1954.

1. This chapter builds on a body of historical literature that details social protest movements targeting inequality in New York City schools. Clarence Taylor, in *Knocking at Our Own Door: Milton A. Galamison and the Struggle for School Integration in New York City* (New York: Columbia University Press, 1997), illuminates the process by which Galamison and other civil rights activists organized during the 1950s and 1960s and exerted major pressure on the Board of Education in favor of school integration. Adina Back's dissertation, "Up South in New York: The 1950s School Desegregation Struggles" (PhD diss., New York University, 1997), examines roots of this 1960s protest in the preceding decade. Daniel Perlstein's *Justice, Justice: School Politics and the Eclipse of Liberalism* (New York: Peter Lang, 2004) and Jerald Podair's *The Strike That Changed New York: Blacks, Whites, and the Ocean Hill-Brownsville Crisis* (New Haven, Conn.: Yale University Press, 2002) analyze the events and politics of the Ocean Hill-Brownsville teacher strike of 1968, and more broadly show how the community steered social protest away from desegregation efforts and toward community control in the face of the school administration's resistance to desegregation. These important works answer critical historical questions about the civil rights struggles for improved schools in New York City. Yet they focus on the political complexities of desegregation efforts *after* Brown. This chapter examines some of the longer roots of community frustrations with the school administration.

2. This section draws on general studies of the Great Migration, such as Isabel Wilkerson, *The Warmth of Other Suns: The Epic Story of America's Great Migration* (New York: Random House, 2010); and Ira Katznelson, *Black Men, White Cities: Race, Politics, and Migration in the United States, 1900–1930, and Britain, 1948–68* (New York: Oxford University Press, 1973). It is also informed by publications detailing and analyzing demographic, social, political, and cultural changes in New York City during the 1910s and 1920s, including Shannon King, *Whose Harlem Is This, Anyway? Community Politics and Grassroots Activism During the New Negro Era* (New York: New York University Press, 2015); Gilbert Osofsky, *Harlem: The Making of a Ghetto: Negro New York, 1890–1930*, 2nd ed. (Chicago: Ivan R. Dee, 1996); Kevin McGruder, *Race and Real Estate: Conflict and Cooperation in Harlem, 1890–1920* (New York: Columbia University Press, 2017); and Irma Watkins-Owens, *Blood Relations: Caribbean Immigrants and the Harlem Community, 1900–1930* (Bloomington: Indiana University Press, 1996).

3. Touré F. Reed, *Not Alms but Opportunity: The Urban League and the Politics of Racial Uplift, 1910–1950* (Chapel Hill: University of North Carolina Press, 2008), 27.

4. Osofsky, *Harlem*, 130.

5. The Tenderloin ran mainly along Sixth Avenue, bounded by Fifth Avenue to the east and Eighth Avenue to the west, and by the period discussed here stretched from Twenty-Third Street up to Fifty-Seventh Street. Timothy J. Gilfoyle, *City of Eros: New York City, Prostitution, and the Commercialization of Sex, 1790–1920* (New York: W. W. Norton, 1992), 203.

6. George Edmund Haynes, "Report: Impressions from a Preliminary Study of Negroes of Harlem," 1921, George Edmund Haynes Papers, box 1, folder 1, Schomburg Center for Research in Black Culture, New York Public Library (hereafter Schomburg); and Meyer Weinberg, *A Chance to Learn: The History of Race and Education in the United States* (New York: Cambridge University Press, 1977), 72.

7. Lawrence Cremin, *The Transformation of the School: Progressivism in American Education, 1876–1957* (New York: Alfred A. Knopf, 1961), viii–ix; and "Chronological Review of Some of the Measures Taken to Effect Better Adjustment of School and Child," n.d., series 164, box 1, folder 1, Board of Education of the City of New York Collection (hereafter BOE). For other iterations of these debates, see W. E. B. Du Bois, *Souls of Black Folk: Essays and Sketches* (Chicago: A. C. McClurg, 1903), chap. 3, "Of Mr. Booker T. Washington and Others," 41–59; and Jean Anyon, "Social Class and School Knowledge," *Curriculum Inquiry* 11, no. 2 (1911): 3–42.

8. Claude Mangum, "Afro-American Thought on the New York City Public School System, 1905–1954: An Analysis of New York City Afro-American Newspaper Editorials" (PhD diss., Columbia University, 1976), 71; "Rebellion of Teachers," *New York Age*, July 8, 1909; Osofsky, *Harlem*, 20, 64; and Nancy J. Weiss, *The National Urban League, 1910–1940* (New York: Oxford University Press, 1974), 21–22.

9. Mangum, "Afro-American Thought," 71; Carleton Mabee, *Black Education in New York State: From Colonial to Modern Times* (Syracuse, N.Y.: Syracuse University Press, 1979), 116; and Seth M. Scheiner, *Negro Mecca: A History of the Negro in New York City, 1865–1920* (New York: New York University Press, 1965), 164.

10. Cremin, *Transformation of the School*, viii.

11. Haynes, "Report"; Michael W. Homel, *Down from Equality: Black Chicagoans and the Public Schools, 1920–41* (Urbana: University of Illinois Press, 1984), 116; Josephine Chase, *New York at School: A Description of the Activities and Administration of the Public Schools of the City of New York* (New York: Public Education Association of the City of New York, 1927), 14; "Vocational Guidance," *New York Age*, October 23, 1920; and Weinberg, *Chance to Learn*, 72.

12. James Anderson, *The Education of Blacks in the South, 1865–1930* (Chapel Hill: University of North Carolina Press, 1988).

13. "Lessons of School Week," *New York Age*, November 28, 1925; and "Aims of Education," *New York Age*, July 3, 1926.

14. "Getting the Children of Harlem Back to Public and High Schools," *New York Age*, September 5, 1923; "Keep Children in School," *New York Age*, June 14, 1924; "School a Necessity," *New York Age*, December 27, 1924; "Getting an Education," *New York Age*, August 30, 1924; "School Children's Needs," *New York Age*, December 25, 1920; and "When Schools Reopen," *New York Age*, September 8, 1928.

15. Anderson, *Education of Blacks*, chap. 2.

16. Editorial, *New York Age*, January 11, 1917.

17. Ibram Kendi, *Stamped from the Beginning: The Definitive History of Racist Ideas in America* (New York: Nation Books, 2016), 125, 505.

18. "School Administration," *New York Age*, October 9, 1926; "Making Schools Attractive," *New York Age*, June 1, 1929; "Important School Questions," *New York Age*, March 12, 1924; "Popular School Appointment," *New York Age*, November 27, 1926;

"A Progressive School Head," *New York Age*, April 18, 1925; "More School Accommodations"; "Two Public Appointees," *Crisis*, March 1917, 231; and Editorial, *New York Age*, January 11, 1917.

19. "School Supervision," *New York Age*, May 26, 1928; "New York's School Head," *New York Age*, April 19, 1930; "Public School System," *New York Age*, May 24, 1930; and "Dr. Maxwell's Retirement," *New York Age*, March 15, 1917.

20. Reed, *Not Alms*, 5–8.

21. Anderson, *Education of Blacks*, chaps. 2 and 3; and Michael Rudolph West, *The Education of Booker T. Washington: American Democracy and the Idea of Race Relations* (New York: Columbia University Press, 2006).

22. King, *Whose Harlem Is This?*, 16.

23. A body of historical work has explored Depression-era change in Harlem, including that related to teacher union politics: Clarence Taylor, *Reds at the Blackboard: Communism, Civil Rights, and the New York City Teachers Union* (New York: Columbia University Press, 2011); parent activism: Sara Asrat, "Harlem Is Not Dixie: The Permanent Committee for Better Schools in Harlem and the Fight for Social Justice in Depression-Era New York" (BA thesis, Princeton University, 2006); teacher activism: Lauri Johnson, "A Generation of Women Activists: African American Female Educators in Harlem, 1930–1950," *Journal of African American History* 89, no. 3 (2004): 223–40; and community-wide political change: Cheryl Lynn Greenberg, *Or Does It Explode? Black Harlem in the Great Depression* (New York: Oxford University Press, 1997); and Mark Naison, *Communists in Harlem During the Depression* (Urbana: University of Illinois Press, 1983).

24. Greenberg, *Or Does It Explode?*, 39.

25. Larry A. Greene, "Harlem in the Great Depression: 1928–1936" (PhD diss., Columbia University, 1979), i–viii, 60.

26. Eve Thurston, "Ethiopia Unshackled: A Brief History of the Education of Negro Children in New York City," *Bulletin of the New York Public Library* 69, no. 4 (April 1965): 65, 227.

27. Greenberg, *Or Does It Explode?*, 39, 42.

28. Naison, *Communists in Harlem*, 32; and Edwin R. Lewinson, *Black Politics in New York City* (New York: Twayne, 1974), 70.

29. Asrat, "Harlem Is Not Dixie," 72.

30. This was part of a nationwide phenomenon in which school attendance boomed during the Great Depression as youth faced poor labor opportunities. This was especially true at the high school level in industrial regions. Claudia Golden, "America's Graduation from High School: The Evolution and Spread of Secondary Schooling in the Twentieth Century," *Journal of Economic History* 58, no. 2 (June 1998): 345–74, 347; and Greenberg, *Or Does It Explode?*, 190.

31. Mabee, *Black Education*, 249; Asrat, "Harlem Is Not Dixie," 71; NYC Board of Education, *Annual Report*, 1933–1934, 62–63; and Thurston, "Ethiopia Unshackled," 227.

32. Historian David Ment documents the early rise of segregation in New York schools in his comparative study, "Racial Segregation in the Public Schools of New England and New York, 1840–1940" (PhD diss., Columbia University, 1975). His work does not closely examine the opposition to segregation, but rather the formation of the problem of segregation.

33. "More School Accommodations," *New York Age*, March 12, 1921; and Weinberg, *Chance to Learn*, 72.

34. Ment, "Racial Segregation," 80, 247; and Asrat, "Harlem Is Not Dixie," 24.

35. Greene, "Harlem in the Great Depression," v; and King, *Whose Harlem Is This?*, 16.

36. King, *Whose Harlem Is This?*, 9, 17.

37. Director of Publicity to Mrs. Rogers H. Bacon, June 3, 1931, part 3, series A, reel 20, NAACP Papers; "Defects Reported in Harlem Schools," *New York Times*, June 3, 1931; "Social Clubs and Fraternal News," *New York Age*, May 25, 1929; and Thurston, "Ethiopia Unshackled," 226.

38. Oswald Schlockow, "Geography," *School Work* 7, no. 1 (April 1908): 255; "Notes and News," *Journal of Educational Psychology* 9, no. 10 (December 1918): 591; Oswald Schlockow, "Discipline: Its Sociological and Pedagogical Implications" (PhD diss., New York University, 1904); and "Dr. Oswald Schlockow," *New York Times*, July 7, 1954.

39. NYC Board of Education (NYCBOE), *Annual Report*, 1933–1934, 47, 51.

40. NYCBOE, 48–49.

41. NYCBOE, *Annual Report*, 1932–1933, 364.

42. NYCBOE, *Annual Report*, 1933–1934, 45, 60.

43. NYCBOE, 46; and "Would Change Schools Here," *New York Amsterdam News*, September 15, 1934.

44. NYCBOE, *Annual Report*, 1933–1934, 47, 51, 351, 354.

45. "Would Change Schools Here," *New York Amsterdam News*, September 15, 1934.

46. "The Schlockow Report," *New York Amsterdam News*, September 22, 1934.

47. George S. Schuyler, "Segregated Schools?" *New York Amsterdam News*, September 29, 1934; "Harlem School Superintendent Charges of Prejudice," *Pittsburgh Courier*, November 10, 1934; and Aberjhani West and Sandra L. West, eds., *Encyclopedia of the Harlem Renaissance* (New York: Facts on File, 2003), 265.

48. George S. Schuyler, "N.Y. School Jim Crow Menace Arouses Parents," *Pittsburgh Courier*, December 22, 1934.

49. George S. Schuyler, "Special School Needs," *New York Amsterdam News*, October 13, 1934; and Schuyler, "Segregated Schools?," *New York Amsterdam News*, September 29, 1934.

50. "Harlem School Superintendent Charges of Prejudice," *Pittsburgh Courier*, November 10, 1934.

51. Schuyler, "N.Y. School Jim Crow Menace"; Schuyler, "Segregated Schools?"; Schuyler, "Special School Needs."

52. Schuyler, "Segregated Schools?"

53. Robert Fogelson and Richard E. Rubenstein, eds., *The Complete Report of Mayor La-Guardia's Commission on the Harlem Riot of March 19, 1935* (New York: Arno Press, 1969), 7–8; Greenberg, *Or Does It Explode?*; Lauri Johnson, "We Cannot Avoid Taking Sides," in *Teacher Education with an Attitude: Preparing Teachers to Educate Working-Class Students in Their Collective Self-Interest*, ed. Patrick J. Finn and Mary E. Finn (Albany: State University of New York Press, 2007), 221; "Says Economic Conditions in Harlem Are Bad," *Atlanta Daily World*, March 27, 1935; and Nat Brandt, *Harlem at War: The Black Experience in WWII* (Syracuse, N.Y.: Syracuse University Press, 1996), 44–45.

54. "Says Economic Conditions in Harlem Are Bad," *Atlanta Daily World*, March 27, 1935.

55. Brandt, *Harlem at War*, 44–45; and Fogelson and Rubenstein, *Complete Report*, 7–8.

56. "Harlem Riot Was Very Tough on Window Glass," *Pittsburgh Courier*, April 6, 1935.

57. "Police End Harlem Riot; Mayor Starts Inquiry; Dodge Sees a Red Plot," *New York Times*, March 21, 1935; Fogelson and Rubenstein, *Complete Report*, 9; Greene, "Harlem in the Great Depression," 487–500; Johnson, "We Cannot Avoid Taking Sides," 221; and "One Year Ago," *New York Amsterdam News*, March 14, 1936.

58. Alain Locke, "Harlem: Dark Weather-Vane," *Survey Graphic* 25, no. 8 (August 1936): 457.

59. "New York Mayor Adopts N.A.A.C.P. Riot Probe Plan," March 22, 1935, box 131-33, folder 16, E. Franklin Frazier Papers, Moorland-Spingarn Research Center, Howard University, Washington, D.C. (hereafter Frazier Papers); "Police End Harlem Riot; Mayor Starts Inquiry; Dodge Sees a Red Plot," *New York Times*, March 21, 1935; "The Harlem Riots," *Washington Post*, March 23, 1935; and Greene, "Harlem in the Great Depression," 483.

60. Fogelson and Rubenstein, *Complete Report*, 3; and "Harlem Riot Probe May Last Over 2 Months," *Pittsburgh Courier*, April 13, 1935.

61. Ment, "Racial Segregation," 244; and The Mayor's Commission on Conditions in Harlem, "The Negro in Harlem: A Report on Social and Economic Conditions Responsible for the Outbreak of March 19, 1935," 1936, box 131-117, folder 2, Frazier Papers.

62. Ment, "Racial Segregation," 244.

63. Alice Citron ["Teacher #1"], testimony, "1935 Public Hearings: Education"; President of Parents' Association, P.S. 105, testimony, "1935 Public Hearings: Education," box 3770, Fiorello LaGuardia Papers, Municipal Archives of the City of New York (hereafter LaGuardia Papers); Alice Citron, "An Answer to John F. Hatchett," *Jewish Currents*, September 1968, 12–13; Asrat, "Harlem Is Not Dixie," 9; and David Ment, "Patterns of Public School Segregation, 1900–1940: A Comparative Study of New York City, New Rochelle, and New Haven," in *Schools in Cities: Consensus and Conflict in American Educational History*, ed. Ronald K. Goodenow and Diane Ravitch (New York: Holmes and Meier, 1983), 85.

64. Mrs. Eddie Aspinall, testimony, "1935 Public Hearings: Education," box 3770, LaGuardia Papers.

65. Betty Hawley, "Public Hearing, New York State Temporary Commission on the Condition of the Urban Colored Population," typescript, December 13, 1937, Schomburg, 1118–25.

66. W. J. Burroughs, testimony, "1935 Public Hearings: Education," box 3770, LaGuardia Papers.

67. "Research Project Notebooks, Harlem Survey, Hearings, Vol. II," box 131-124, folders 1–5, Frazier Papers.

68. "New York School Conditions Attacked," *Atlanta Daily World*, August 28, 1935.

69. Ment, "Racial Segregation," 246, 255; and George Lindsey, testimony, "1935 Public Hearings: Education," box 3770, LaGuardia Papers.

70. Anthony M. Platt, *The Politics of Riot Commissions, 1917–1970: A Collection of Official Reports and Critical Essays* (New York: Macmillan, 1971), 1, 161.

71. Fogelson and Rubenstein, *Complete Report*, 77.

72. Charles Houston to Fiorello LaGuardia, April 6, 1936, microfilm reel 86, LaGuardia Papers; "Report on Harlem Survey Censored," *Chicago Defender*, August 3, 1935; Fogelson and Rubenstein, *Complete Report*, 7; and "Complete Riot Report Bared," *New York Amsterdam News*, July 18, 1936.

73. Taylor, *Reds at the Blackboard*.

74. Johnson, "We Cannot Avoid Taking Sides," 219–21.

75. "Probe Harlem School Discrimination Charge," *Pittsburgh Courier*, May 25, 1935; and Asrat, "Harlem Is Not Dixie," 68.

76. Asrat, "Harlem Is Not Dixie," 68.

77. "Harlem Pushes Campaign for Better Schools," *Pittsburgh Courier*, May 16, 1936, 7; and "Local Group Demands Schools Be Improved," *New York Amsterdam News*, July 4, 1936, 5.

78. "Education Hearing," April 4, 1935, box 131-124, folder 4, Frazier Papers.

79. "In Reply to Chapter Six," BOE; and James Marshall to Fiorello LaGuardia, May 5, 1935, LaGuardia Papers.
80. NYCBOE, *Annual Report*, 1935–1936.
81. Charles J. Pickett, testimony, "1935 Public Hearings: Education," box 3770, LaGuardia Papers.
82. "The Story of the City-Wide Citizens' Committee on Harlem," typescript, May 23, 1943, Schomburg.
83. Sylvia L. M. Martinez and John L. Rury, "From 'Culturally Deprived' to 'At Risk': The Politics of Popular Expression and Educational Inequality in the United States, 1960–1985," *Teachers College Record* 114 (June 2012): 2.
84. For recent work on compensatory education, including this dynamic, see the articles in the special issue of *Teachers College Record* 114 (June 2012).

CHAPTER 3

Wadleigh High School

The Price of Segregation

KIMBERLEY JOHNSON

[The] price of segregation that we pay . . . is already too great without adding the humiliation of "all-Negro" schools. . . . New York City is cosmopolitan in character, despite Harlem, the Lower East Side, and Yorkville.
Here there should exist the intermingling of the races aspect of democracy
at its best.

In 1954, the New York City Board of Education (BOE) closed Wadleigh High School due to its deteriorated physical condition, declining
enrollment, and poor academic performance. But the route to closure
spanned decades. Although originally an elite all-white girls' high school
when it opened in 1897, by 1940 Wadleigh appeared to many to be a failing school. White student enrollment had fallen gradually and, by the start
of World War II, the student body reflected the Harlem of the first Great
Migration: native Black New Yorkers, migrants from the U.S. South and
Puerto Rico, and West Indian immigrants. As Wadleigh's student population came to align with the demographics of its surrounding Harlem streets,
the New York City Board of Education proved unwilling to support a well-
resourced majority-Black school, or to desegregate the school. With
Wadleigh's closure, Central Harlem lost the first and only high school
located within its boundaries.

By tracing Wadleigh's transformation over time, we can better understand the educational history of Harlem in the Great Migration era. Wadleigh High School revealed the multiple forms of segregation at work in
Harlem and the high price of that segregation. Debates over what Harlem
students should learn in school, such as those outlined by Thomas Harbison in chapter 2 of this volume, were visible in both constructing and con-
testing segregation at Wadleigh.

The struggle over Wadleigh also illuminates the unfolding of the "long Civil Rights movement" in the urban North, particularly during the less-explored decades of the pre–*Brown v. Board of Education* era: the 1920s through the 1940s.[1] The Harlem riots of 1935 and 1943 revealed the growing anger and frustration that resulted when the promise of the Great Migration had stalled and economic and educational inequality had become institutionalized. Then, as now, Harlem parents, educators, and community members imagined different pathways to address this inequality. Two choices dominated the debate: whether Wadleigh should become a flagship high school for the new Black Harlem; or Wadleigh should be an integrated school that just happened to be located in Harlem? Were either possible in the context of unequal staffing and curricular policies and segregating zoning decisions by the Board of Education?

The growing reluctance of white parents to send their daughters to Harlem would eventually negate the possibility of Wadleigh developing a stably integrated student body. At the same time, the possibility of embracing an identity for Wadleigh as an all-Black high school ran aground over sharp debates about whether acknowledging the segregation of Harlem's housing and education meant acceding to "Jim Crow in the North" with its many inequalities. These two polarities created a long-standing stalemate, which New York City Board of Education policies exacerbated.

This chapter focuses on key moments in Wadleigh's transformation as a way to explore broader struggles over education in Harlem during the pre–*Brown* era.[2] One struggle was caused by tensions arising out of class, race, and ethnicity as Harlem's diverse residents all struggled to shape education in Harlem. Parents, educators, and community leaders struggled over the school curriculum and expectations, most notably in the debates over differentiated curricula and vocational training. By the late 1930s these tensions were overlaid by debates about integration versus strengthening Wadleigh as an all-Black school. By the 1940s, issues of curricular equity and integration shaped debates in Harlem over the future of Wadleigh. As Black New Yorkers gained real political power; and, as the first stirrings of the civil rights movement began to emerge, they struggled over how to conceptualize Wadleigh's identity and place in the segregated and unequal city.

Gender was also an important historical force at Wadleigh. The school was a site for the construction and expression of the troubled category of Black urban girlhood. Girls there navigated racialized ideas of age, maturity, obligation, and sexuality that, as Marcia Chatelain has shown, closed off spaces and modes of protection that white girls enjoyed.[3] An inquiry that centered gender in Wadleigh's history could draw on the nascent field of Black girlhood studies in history as well as the established examinations of gendered experiences in Harlem's pre–World War II landscape.[4] Rather than an incomplete investigation in this direction, given the constraints on space here, this important topic remains to be explored in future work.

Wadleigh Before African American Harlem

Wadleigh High School's Harlem building, which followed the original 1897 location downtown on East Twelfth Street, was one of the first schools constructed after New York City's consolidation in 1898. In a report on its opening, the *New York Times* declared the Wadleigh building the "finest high school building in the world." Now a New York City landmark, the school was the epitome of Collegiate Gothic architecture, a "massive five story building [that] housed eighty classrooms, over a dozen laboratories, executive offices, two elevators, three gymnasia, and auditorium (with 1500 seats) a library, a large boiler and engine room, two study halls, and numerous lavatories and ventilated cloakrooms."[5] Architectural ambition matched the aspirations of its neighborhood. In 1902, as Gilbert Osofsky recounts, Harlem was a "fashionable middle- and upper-middle class, mostly white neighborhood."[6]

In keeping with its architectural form, the Wadleigh High School that opened in 1902 on West 114th Street in Harlem was an academically rigorous all-girl school primarily for the white daughters of Harlem and the Upper West Side. The school's self-portrayal emphasized gentility, even as students from various class backgrounds attended. As Irving Louis Horowitz recounts in his reminiscences, although his sister's time at Wadleigh retained its "well-mannered Victorian atmosphere," the school had mostly become a "relief from immigrant drudgery rather than inflated expectations."[7] In 1925, the bulk of the advertisements in *The Owl* (the school yearbook) were for secretarial and business training institutes, suggesting that the curriculum was no longer strictly focused on academics. Many students who completed their studies in the school's academic program continued on to the City University's Hunter College, to train to be teachers.

The student body at least as pictured in the yearbook in the 1920s appeared almost exclusively white, and community members spoke of ways the school made entry difficult for Black students.[8] Among the small but growing population of Black students in the late 1920s was the future Dr. Margaret Morgan Lawrence, who graduated in 1931. The scholar Sara Lawrence Lightfoot traces the childhood and adolescence of her mother and describes a supportive academic environment at Wadleigh. When Margaret Morgan was a teenager, she fled the constant fear of violence in intensely segregated Vicksburg, Mississippi, to live in Harlem with family and continue her education. She later told her daughter that at Wadleigh she felt encouraged and challenged academically. With extensive coaching from her mentors on the Wadleigh faculty, she obtained a scholarship from the National Council of the Episcopal Church that enabled her to pursue higher education at Cornell University and later to launch a career in psychology.[9]

Colored Schools to "Mixed Schools" to Jim Crow Schools

For Black New Yorkers in the late 1800s and the first decade of the 1900s, before the Great Migration swelled their number dramatically, city schools brought an awkward mix of inclusion and segregation, as was the case in other northern cities during that era.[10] Due to their small numbers, African Americans had some access to integrated—or in the nomenclature of the time "mixed"—public schools. Even with limited integration, segregation still structured city life. African American leaders and educators struggled for inclusion of students into existing schools as well as for the hiring of African American teachers for both segregated Black schools and white schools.[11] Throughout the late nineteenth century, the condition of the city's segregated or "colored" schools such as Colored School No. 1 was dire. Charles B. Ray, a leading figure in the city's African American community, complained that the city's Black school facilities were essentially "caste schools," which were "'painfully neglected . . . old and dilapidated.'"[12]

New York City's outlawing of legal segregation in 1883 led to the start of a nominally integrated public school system that stood in contrast to other northern cities that had quickly instituted segregated school systems when faced with the beginning of the Great Migration. Nonetheless, despite the city's formal integration of its school system, the residential segregation of Manhattan's Black population into two enclaves (San Juan Hill in the West Fifties and Harlem around 135th Street at the time) meant that the schools in these areas were effectively segregated. The segregation of public schools had little effect on many of the city's Black elites during the late nineteenth century, as they often sent their children to private "colored" institutions.[13] Thus by the start of the first Great Migration, Black New Yorkers were both celebrating their inclusion into the city's "mixed" schools and facing the realities of segregation.

As the Great Migration began and as a greater Black Harlem took shape, critics began to challenge this romanticized history of New York's "mixed schools." Harlem parents noted that "mixed" schooling could impose psychological harm on Black children who were faced with teachers and fellow students who treated them with indifference, neglect, or outright racist abuse.[14] Entering previously all-white schools was no panacea either, with critics noting that the schools' all-white staffs and inappropriate curricula could push students out of school rather than keep them in. Critics of both "mixed schools" and segregated schools argued that segregated school enrollment without explicit segregation produced fewer employment opportunities for Black teachers, administrators, and staff than a formally segregated system would have created (as it did in the South).[15] Compared to other northern districts, New York also employed fewer Black teachers.[16] White control of majority Black schools also created schools with an atmosphere and a curriculum that did not lead to the educational success of Black children. Given the pervasiveness of racial discrimination, these critiques resonated with Black New Yorkers who faced enormous difficulties in securing teaching jobs in the city's school system and with parents who saw a system in which Black children found varied and often lower levels of success compared to their European immigrant peers.

Prominent figures such as the African American journalist George S. Schuyler vocally opposed practices by administrators and teachers who contributed to perpetuating social stratification in Harlem. He pressed Black Harlemites to contest the unequal conditions of education for their children and to "be prepared to roll up their sleeves and get down in the valley to fight to [the] end for full, absolute equality in everything."[17]

In contrast, editors at Harlem's main newspaper, the *Amsterdam News*, largely dismissed attacks on mixed schooling as well as calls for strong all-Black schools; suggesting that these introduced a negative southern viewpoint into a more tolerant atmosphere.[18] Indeed, Dr. Willis N. Huggins, invited by the *Amsterdam News* to write about the status of Black teachers in New York, lauded Black teachers who "refused to spinelessly ask for separate schools" and "refused to fawningly ask that discrimination be made 'for' him." Huggins added: "His methods are slow and patient, but they will attain for him full equality in appointments, in the long run, without regard to creed or color."[19] The support for New York's "mixed" or integrated schools also fit with a strong belief that these schools bestowed upon all students the benefits of a "cosmopolitan" education. For integrationists such as Lucile Spence, a Black Wadleigh teacher, the answer was simple: "If the races are to live together after maturity, they should as children go to school together."[20]

Integrationists varied in the degree to which they believed that integration could or should happen outside of or within Harlem's boundaries. Was integration meaningful if it occurred only outside of Harlem? Or was integration meaningful if it occurred only within Harlem's boundaries? Although integration within spaces like Wadleigh was preferable, integrationists did not want Harlem's children's to be solely confined within Harlem's boundaries and thus miss out on the benefits of New York's "cosmopolitan" character.[21]

When Wadleigh's Harlem building opened in 1902, the school sat about a mile south of the Black residential center developing around 135th Street and Lenox Avenue. By the Great Depression, Wadleigh was now within an area with a significant and growing Black presence. Residents faced heightened overcrowding and absentee landlord exploitation, products of continued migration into segregated spaces. The school's demographics changed more slowly than, but in parallel with, the neighborhood's. From its opening in Harlem in 1902 to the 1930s, Wadleigh saw increasing enrollment from African American and West Indian students. Given the growing resistance of white parents to sending their daughters to Harlem, the question was whether Harlem residents would have to send their children out of the neighborhood to access integrated schooling. From about one-quarter Black in 1931, the school's student body was 98 percent African American by the end of World War II.[22]

Harlem's increasing educational and spatial marginalization also reflected the limits of Black Harlem's political power. Since African Americans were still largely faithful to the Republican Party, as voters they had no influence or power within Tammany Hall. Although this loyalty to the Republican Party would fade by the 1920s, Harlem's political power was weak due to the area's gerrymandering into different city council and state assembly districts. Thus although the switch to the Democratic Party created some patronage opportunities, for the community as a whole Harlem's division meant that actual political representation did not occur until 1929 when the first Black official was elected. Unlike Chicago's Bronzeville, which elected Oscar DePriest to Congress in 1928, Harlem did not get the chance to elect its own congressional representative until 1944 when the district lines were redrawn.[23] Limited political representation and economic crisis sharpened the debates over the nature of schooling for African American children as the promise of the first Great Migration seemed to be unfulfilled.

Within this context of marginalization, support grew for the strengthening of Harlem's schools as Black institutions. For newly emerging advocates of this idea, given Wadleigh's past reputation for excellence, a possible future for Wadleigh could be as a flagship Black high school for the community, similar to Chicago's DuSable High School or Washington, D.C.'s Dunbar High School. The existence of a high school within Central Harlem was an asset, whether integrated or all-Black. The institution had played an important role for some of the few Black students that had attended during the 1920s and early 1930s, such as Ruth Dorothea Ellington, the sister of Duke Ellington, who graduated from Wadleigh in the 1930s and pursued higher education at Columbia University, or Margaret Morgan who was described above.[24]

Wadleigh's segregation was not only a product of white families' resistance to sending their daughters to Harlem or to a majority-Black school. The Board of Education zoning rules as of the early 1930s limited Harlem girls to three high schools: Haaren (Tenth Avenue and Fifty-Eighth Street), Morris (East 166th Street in the Bronx) and Wadleigh, the only high school located in the heart of Black Harlem. Two other schools, Julia Richman (East Sixty-Seventh Street and Second Avenue) and George Washington (on Audubon Avenue), were closer to most of Harlem, but in the years around World War II had much smaller numbers of Black students.[25] In the late 1930s, school officials drew attendance zones for these two high schools to include students living in white neighborhoods and ensured an all-Black student population at Wadleigh.[26] Wadleigh's resulting attendance zone was enclosed between Edgecombe Avenue to the west, Fifth Avenue to the east, Central Park to the south, and 155th Street to the north.[27] Wadleigh's zone nearly matched the boundaries of Black Harlem, defined by processes of residential segregation, by World War II. In this same time, boys living within that zone had no local high school available to them.

Debates roiled within Harlem about whether or not to accept the increasingly rigid lines of segregation that were transforming Harlem from a Black mecca to segregated ghetto with shrinking opportunities. For some migrants, accepting segregation meant accepting what they believed they had left in the South. Establishing Wadleigh as an all-Black high school (regardless of its academic status) would be a "humiliation" and a concession to "Jim Crow."[28] The potential closing of Wadleigh High School, threatened by the board as of 1937, was better than formally accepting its status as a segregated school—no matter how academically excellent.

As in earlier phases of debates over schooling in Harlem, questions of curriculum soon became central. The fall of 1934 brought into the open the simmering frustrations and debates over the integration of schools. One particularly sharp debate, described in detail in chapter 2 of this volume, pitted Harlem activists against the BOE over a proposal for "differentiated curriculum" for Harlem students.[29] The proposal submitted by assistant superintendent Oswald Schlockow argued that "upper Harlem," designating areas of African American settlement, had "special educational, social, ethical, academic and vocational needs, and these must receive special attention in terms of those needs. Fond hopes, speculation, theorizing must yield to the light of reason and the dictates of common sense."[30]

Schlockow's report met broad condemnation among Harlem leaders and journalists. They rejected his curricular prescriptions on their face, but saw also that this was the "entering wedge of segregation," a "quiet conspiracy to segregate."[31] The journalist George Schuyler called for a "standard curriculum, standard faculties, and standard administration."[32] Anything else was a tool to keep Harlem children locked into a prison of lowered expectations.

Schlockow's plan was not formally adopted. Yet several aspects, including its extreme focus on vocational training for Black students and its belief that many were mentally deficient in some way were increasingly and openly supported by many white educators in Harlem including Wadleigh's principals. Since the Board of Education's structure placed almost all of Harlem into four districts overseen by one administrator, the adoption of a differentiated curriculum there would affect the majority of the city's

Black children. Black Harlem faced the realization that despite the hopes of the Great Migration, Black migrant parents were essentially sending their children to Jim Crow schools.

Segregation could figure even within the school. The Great Depression—which limited options for youth employment—brought dramatically expanded enrollment at Wadleigh. Wadleigh and the BOE partially solved the overcrowding issue while trying to maintain the school's white racial identity with the opening of annexes. In 1933, under pressure to add more seats but faced with drastic budget cuts, the BOE opened up the second of Wadleigh's two annexes (with the first established in 1915 at Public School 179 on 102nd Street). The new annex located on 135th Street and Convent Avenue was the former site of the New York Training School for Teachers. The annexes had higher rates of white enrollment than did the main building and housed the school's academic curriculum.[33]

The First Harlem Riot and the Decline of Wadleigh

In the 1930s, Wadleigh's constituents struggled not only over the curriculum, but over whether the school would persist. They faced contradictory realities: a desire to maintain the school's reputation of academic excellence, administrators' desires to maintain a predominately white student body, and growing demand from students within Harlem as Black Harlem expanded south to 114th Street and beyond. The class composition of the white students also began to change: white students were more like Horowitz's sister, members of families in the lower-middle class, or upper-working class. For these students and their families, Wadleigh was becoming an "isolated institution in the heart of Negro Harlem."[34]

The Harlem riot of 1935 was a pivotal moment for Wadleigh and for education in Harlem. In addition to bringing long-simmering tensions into the open, the riot catalyzed investigations and official engagement with Harlem much beyond the previous decade. In addition to systematically neglected school facilities, Harlem activists cited the low expectations and sometimes hostile attitudes of Wadleigh's almost all-white teaching and administrative staff toward their African American students. This perception of hostility was revealed in government testimony. For example, as Osofsky recounts in his history of Harlem, "In 1937 an educator bluntly told an investigating commission of the state legislature: 'Let's not mince words;

let's be practical about this matter—the Negro is not employed in certain trades, so why permit him to waste his time taking such courses.'"[35] This remark echoed the early controversy over the differentiated curriculum proposed in 1934.

A number of groups such as the Permanent Committee for Better Schools in Harlem and the Harlem Parents Association sprang up in the aftermath of the riot to press for changes in Harlem's schools. Representatives of the Communist Party, Black churches, and the New York Urban League could agree to condemn the conditions of the schools and the hostility of white educators toward Harlem's schoolchildren, expressing their concerns at a mock trial of the Board of Education described in chapter 6 in this volume.[36] Many Black Harlemites had come to believe that the "unhealthful and inadequate school buildings in Harlem had much to do with the unrest which led to the disorders of March 19."[37] Nearly forty years of hard use at Wadleigh, as well as changing educational standards, made the current building obsolete and dangerous. Some described the school as a "firetrap and in such a dilapidated condition that it is unfit for the safety of human lives."[38]

White Wadleigh community members emphasized the surrounding neighborhood. In their view it had experienced a rapid decline with "pool halls and jook joints" visible.[39] Dr. John L. Tildsley, a retired associate superintendent, complained that students going to Wadleigh had "to pass through a neighborhood where gentlewomen do not like to pass."[40] He lamented the fact that Wadleigh had "adhered to cultural influences" in its surrounding area.

Coming two years after the Harlem riot, the celebration of Wadleigh's fortieth anniversary in 1937 was the beginning of a short-lived battle, this time led by white people, to preserve Wadleigh's status as what they called "a gentlewomen's school."[41] As of 1938 (the nearest year for which data are available), Wadleigh's combined population of students was about one-third African American and West Indian students. If previous patterns held, the proportion of Black students was larger in the main building than in the school's two annexes.[42] Although students, teachers, and families likely were responding to the school's increasing Black enrollment, much of the discussion emphasized the school's location in a racialized Black space. Tildsley spoke to gathered alumna and others at a celebratory luncheon at the Hotel Astor, declaring that there was an "urgent need" for a gentlewomen's school as none now existed on the West Side west of Wadleigh and up to 160th street." One proposed site for the school was located on 168th Street and Broadway, a transitional area between white Harlem and Washington Heights. However, a medical center (now part of Columbia University) took the site instead. He recognized that his desire to relocate Wadleigh was that of a "small voice in our high school education" suggesting that this perception was not in the majority. Parents, Tilsdey argued, needed to "bring pressure to bear" on the BOE for a new site for Wadleigh or its re-placements, "a new site . . . where they can send their girls in confidence and security."[43]

Tilsdey's characterization of Wadleigh's neighborhood as an unsafe one and his call for a new location were contested by some. The speech was criticized in the Women's section of *Amsterdam News* for exaggerating the dangers of Wadleigh's surrounding area and for the way the new location would be segregated. The columnist of the "feminist viewpoint" called for renovations of the existing building instead of relocation.[44]

Yet administrators largely echoed Tilsdey's depiction of the school. Wadleigh's acting principal argued that the campaign to relocate the school was not based on "prejudices," but rather, it was based simply on the issue of safety.[45] Relocating the school would protect girls "from annoyance by hoodlums who lurk in the subways, or who boldly pull on them, throw stones, or otherwise insult them." The principal noted that near the school, "police raids of disorderly houses are almost a daily occurrence."[46]

The school's anniversary coupled with upcoming BOE budget talks spurred an organized letter-writing campaign among white Wadleigh parents.[47] Although many were similar in form and content, the letters provide some insight into how some Wadleigh parents viewed the changing environment and identity of Wadleigh. In making the case for a relocated or modernized school, some parents directed their criticism at the aging building declaring it "drafty," with "overcrowded classrooms and lunch-room," overall an "unsafe" building. For many parent letter writers, however, the building's location in an "unsafe" and "immoral" neighborhood was the most important reason for the school to be relocated.[48] One parent wrote that the "neighborhood surrounding the school is most unsafe not only for young girls but also adults."[49] Still another wrote that "many days when my daughter has returned at a later hour than usual because of a play rehearsal or a club meeting, I have been terrified knowing how unsafe the neighborhood is for an adolescent girl."[50] Another was even more direct about how she equated Black residents with danger: As the "only girls school on the West Side from 59th to 192nd St., it was unfortunate and now dangerous that it was located in such a dangerous area."[51] "Many times, while going to school, [her daughter] has had fearful experiences with the negroes in the neighborhood."[52]

For some parents, one key element of their campaign for a new Wadleigh was that they no longer saw the school as one belonging to the "upper West Side." Some parents called for a new "modern high school for girls to serve the needs of the West Side of Manhattan."[53] White parents who participated in this campaign felt that they had, inexplicably, lost Wadleigh. One parent wrote, "I can find no justification for this long-standing un-just discrimination against the children of our neighborhood."[54] White parents deployed language that referred to paying high taxes to claim their rights to the school they imagined. As one parent wrote, "We who pay high rents and taxes, feel we are entitled to one of the most essential features of a residential section, an adequate high school."[55] In their view, Wadleigh's location and student population made it less than adequate.

Anxiety of decline enveloped the school, and Black students pointed to tensions regarding racial discrimination within the school itself. Black students' experiences at Wadleigh provide complex, varied accounts that point at times to a supportive environment, one in which discrimination still held sway in both open and subtle ways.[56] Although students like Margaret Morgan had found Wadleigh encouraging, a group of Black students at Wadleigh High School testified regarding racial discrimination at the school in a mass trial of the Board of Education at the Abyssinian Baptist Church. According to these Wadleigh students, although the school was over 40 percent Black in 1937, no Black girl had ever had a part in the senior play until "a militant Parent's Association won this concession."[57] Despite the school's claims to vaunted academic status, reports of dubious student behavior continued to circulate and tarnished the school's reputation. In one newspaper account, the principal denied charges that "whiskey bottles were removed from the basement . . . and that students smoked reefer."[58]

White flight (or rather the very end of the process) lay at the heart of the final shifts in Wadleigh's student population. One newspaper article charged that "white families abetted by agitation by an organization of realtors and community leaders are sending their children to schools as far away as George Washington and Julia Richman to escape association with colored children at Wadleigh."[59] Harlem's *Amsterdam News* and community leaders roundly condemned Tilsdey's anniversary speech as a "Black eye" given to Harlem, but Tilsdey's speech also touched a nerve.[60] What should happen to Wadleigh now that many both in and outside of Harlem now believed it to be a "Negro school?"

Superintendent Tilsdey, like many educators before him, approached the idea of a "Negro" Wadleigh by turning to the curriculum. Tilsdey stated what was commonly believed by some white educators about the educational as well as social prospects of African Americans: that "Negroes would be happier" especially in certain occupations—domestic, industrial and cafeteria. Tilsdey's belief in what made for African American happiness was also buttressed by a clear belief in social inequality: "You don't expect a Negro doctor to practice among whites?" According to this racial logic, the market for Black professionals was small, thus Black New Yorkers (and by extension Harlem) did not need Wadleigh as an academic school.[61] Given its location and rapidly changing student body, nothing could maintain Wadleigh as a "gentlewomen's" school, as it stood "on the edge of Harlem." The proposed solution for the school would be for it to become a "vocational school for Negroes, although colored and white would be allowed to attend the new building."[62]

Losing a School, Winning the War? "The Humiliation of All-Negro Schools"

Although white parents agitated for a new Wadleigh located farther north in Manhattan, other parents continued the fight for a better Wadleigh in its current location. In 1938, a new parent's group emerged. This group was a coalition of parents representing the school's three main racial or ethnic groups: African Americans, Puerto Ricans, and Italians.[63] The parent's group presented a petition to the BOE demanding a new school to replace the aging school building. Unlike the white parents who pressed for a location farther north, this new group began pushing for a new building that would be located "between 100th and 110th Street west of Central Park West."[64] Another group led by notable alums such as Ruth D. Ellington, pushed for keeping Wadleigh in its 114th Street location, albeit accompanied by extensive modernization.[65] Zoning restrictions meant that girls who desired an academic curriculum (and were unable to falsify their address) were restricted to attending Wadleigh. If the school closed, how would Harlem girls access an academic curriculum?[66]

With so many contending voices and with no clear political consequences to face, the BOE did nothing. In the late 1930s and 1940s a period of drift occurred. Wadleigh's growing identification as a "Negro school" held implications for its reputation in a racist context. By the early 1940s, the student body had grown smaller and had become almost exclusively African American and Puerto Rican. The total register was 70 percent black in 1943, and 98 percent by 1945. In that year, the school's total enrollment was less than half what it had been only five years earlier.[67] Part of the enrollment decline was due to the Depression-era baby bust; most of the city's schools faced declining enrollments during the 1940s.[68] White withdrawal from the school was almost complete, and so was the withdrawal of Black students whose parents feared the consequence of sending their daughters to a school with a reputation for weak academics and lack of safety. Thus, civic and religious leaders such as Reverend Robeson, pastor at Mother Zion in Harlem, as well as Margaret Byrne, the principal of the school, fretted that Harlem parents "either knowingly or unknowingly" were creating the conditions for a Jim Crow school to emerge because of their unwillingness to send their daughters to Wadleigh.[69] Margaret Byrne charged that underenrollment would lead the BOE to discontinue the school as an academic institution. Dr. Rankin, a teacher at the Wadleigh evening school, argued that "the people of the community owe it to themselves to rescue their heritage and restore Wadleigh to its former glory."[70]

Nonetheless, in the midst of this change and declining enrollment and reputation, Wadleigh presented two faces. For some Black students, the few Black teachers at Wadleigh such as Lucile Spence were invaluable. Margaret Morgan Lawrence, a former student at Wadleigh recalled that teachers such as Spence "were learned, with a concern for you as a person. . . . Being a dedicated teacher in Harlem was a life, not a job. . . . These women were mothering Harlem."[71] Other educators increasingly viewed Wadleigh's students through a lens of deprivation and hopelessness. Virginia Snitow, a white liberal teacher at Wadleigh, described her experience teaching Negro girls as teaching "minds and personalities warped and distorted like trees exposed to the wind."[72] Faced with the extreme deprivations of poverty, hunger, and homelessness, she found students were resentful of and unengaged in a curriculum based on Shakespeare, Wordsworth, Milton, and

Burns that was "not only distant in time and place but fantastically unreal and even meaningless." Schlockow believed that a special Negro history curriculum compensated for a reduced academic curriculum as the relevant solution, but Snitow argued that a relevant curriculum engaged with current events and writers such as Richard Wright energized and motivated these students toward engaging in academic work.[73]

This call to rescue Wadleigh as an academic institution points to the complexity of Harlemites' understanding of Wadleigh's history. Some parents and administrators attached the school's previous reputation to white enrollment.[74] Some, such as Mrs. William Lloyd Imes, the mother of a Wadleigh graduate, lamented underenrollment and changes in the curriculum as the remediable sources of decline.[75] The students of color who did attend present varied accounts of a supportive environment as well as experiences with discrimination, thus reflecting the ambiguous history of Wadleigh as an elite institution for Black students. This was especially true in the school's annex locations, which the BOE and school administrators treated as academic dumping grounds for students of color; and, which offered students no academic preparation at all.[76] Those who wanted a stronger Wadleigh in Harlem had to negotiate this complex history.

The call to reembrace and improve Wadleigh was complicated by the growing fear that it was essentially a Jim Crow school. Although white students were free to attend, very few did. Meanwhile, most Harlem students had no other option but Wadleigh.[77] By the winter of 1945, Wadleigh's school leadership came to publicly acknowledge the school's transformation. Margaret C. Byrne, the school's principal, convened a community meeting "to settle the matter for the good of the community" as to what the future of the school should be.[78] In convening the meeting, Byrne stated her "inference . . . that the school approaches the condition of segregation and does not have a curriculum commensurate with other schools."[79] For the Mayor's Committee on Unity, formed by Mayor Fiorello LaGuardia after the riot of 1943, the combination of segregation of Black students and low academic expectations meant that the school needed to be closed.[80] At a 1946 community meeting held by the committee, parents and education activists admitted that it was "difficult to now change the situation" of underenrollment and increased segregation that they attributed to Wadleigh's labeling as a "Negro school."[81]

Several interrelated problems faced Wadleigh: (1) declining overall enrollment; (2) an identity as "Negro school," produced both by changing neighborhood demographics in the context of residential segregation and BOE zoning policies that reinforced segregation; and (3) an inadequate and unappealing curriculum. One solution was the adoption of a new curriculum that would attract a more diverse student body and thus reverse Wadleigh's "Negro school" status. The associate superintendent relayed that although he had been in favor of closing Wadleigh "for the past five years," the board hesitated to close the school because they were not sure of [the] community reaction."[82] The BOE was correct in being unsure of the community reaction because the community had in fact been split for years. A 1945 editorial in the *Amsterdam News* reported on a meeting at Wadleigh that had attracted more than 250 parents, teachers, and community members, and remarked on this split regarding the future of the school: Cecelia Violenes, an alumna of Wadleigh called for the maintenance of the school as a "fort or frontier" of excellence within Harlem, regardless of white enrollment, whereas Mrs. Johns, a consultant for the Child Guidance Bureau, advised Black parents in Harlem to send their children to schools where they could have "interracial contacts for their girls."[83] For the author of the editorial, opposing attitudes toward the school were difficult to reconcile: "Either Harlem is asleep to the fate of their oldest institution of culture or they want it to die. If the latter, it is a cowardly procedure."[84]

The Permanent Committee for Better Schools in Harlem set forth the two alternatives to Wadleigh for Harlem residents to consider. The first recommendation was to rebuild Wadleigh and "bring into being a new building . . . so situated that the cosmopolitan character of the school may be maintained."[85] In short, a school that would be accessible to Harlem, but not necessarily located in Harlem so that it would not become a "Negro school" via the resistance of white people to schooling in Black spaces. The second alternative was a qualified one. The Permanent Committee endorsed the continuation of Wadleigh under the following conditions: (1) that the school would be thoroughly modernized and (2) that changes in zoning take place so that not all the students from Harlem would be zoned for the school. Unless those conditions were met, the committee argued that it would be "better that the school be closed than to become a 'Negro' high school."[86]

In the minds of many, *where* Wadleigh would be located was inextricably tied to *who* would attend the school, and thus linked to the racial identity of the school. Segregation had left Black people to "live in old neighborhoods" and forced them to "use old school buildings."[87] To escape these conditions, there had to be a "general rule that would allow any high school student to go to any high school in New York City and not just to a neighborhood or zoned school."[88] This meant that escaping segregation meant letting go of neighborhood schools. As one parent argued, "If the whites can't come to us, we can go to them."[89] Others felt that integration ought to be a two-way street. With the exception of Wadleigh, Black high schoolers, especially boys, had always had to leave Harlem for high school. As Cecelia Violenes, stated, "There is no reason why we should go to anyone. Let them come to us."[90]

The Price of Segregation: Closing Wadleigh

In the Harlem Riot of 1943, Black Harlemites again rebelled against the harsh conditions of northern urban Jim Crow. The issues of substandard housing, lack of employment opportunities, and the neighborhood's overcrowded and abysmal segregated educational system, remained unaddressed by the New York City government. Although for white New Yorkers the riot may have confirmed resistance to sending students to a Harlem-located school, the uprising may also have facilitated the school's continuation despite previous calls for closure.

The tense community environment in the aftermath of the Harlem riot of 1943 may have played a role in the announcement in December 1946 that the BOE would keep Wadleigh open.[91] This decision was connected to a broader issue over the development of two other "Black" high schools in New York City: Girls' High School in Brooklyn and Morris High School in the Bronx (the latter was one of the three zoned high schools for Harlem). Both of these schools, like Wadleigh, were "undergoing a rapid increase in the percentage of Negro students and an attendant drop in the enrollment of pupils."[92] Local activists rejoiced in the move, but qualified their applause by calling again for the BOE to ensure that "Wadleigh becomes what it now is not, a school which represents a fair cross-section of the school population of the city."[93]

This commitment to resuscitate Wadleigh was followed by the retirement of Principal Margaret Byrne and the appointment of a new principal, Mary C. Graham, in August 1947.[94] Graham set about trying to raise Wadleigh's enrollment numbers by developing curricula in areas such as education, nursing, and home economics that would entice not only more students but also hopefully a broader "cross-section" of students back to Wadleigh.[95] In 1950, the school established a Demonstration Nursery for students interested in future careers in nursing or child development, or for their future as homemakers. Graham emphasized that this course of study was not vocational. It was for "girls working for a general Regents diploma."[96] In 1952, Wadleigh was one of five schools and several city hospitals that established an "Earning while Learning" prenursing program as a part of a citywide effort to address a nursing shortage.[97] The effort to fill Wadleigh's seats came at a time when every other school in the city was overcrowded.

These efforts to create Wadleigh as a school of choice rather than a school of last resort proved to be too little too late. By 1953, high school enrollment in older and poorer areas of the city had dropped and elementary and junior high school enrollment had increased.[98] In areas such as Harlem and Bedford Stuyvesant, overcrowding at the elementary and junior high school level rapidly increased due to the continued migration of African Americans and Puerto Ricans to the city. Meanwhile old housing stock and old school facilities were pushing white families and Black families with means to newer areas of the city such as Queens, or to the suburbs. The newly developing areas of the city such as northern and eastern Queens faced severe overcrowding. The city confronted two issues: the growing concentration of students in poor areas with inadequate and aging facilities that faced a $75 million repair backlog as well as population shifts within the city. These new areas also needed new schools. The BOE put forward an ambitious capital campaign of half a billion dollars for the building of 312 schools over six years.[99]

Wadleigh closed at the end of the 1954 school year, part of a long-range, five-year plan for "more and better school facilities" in Harlem; and, also as result of the now two-decade-old resistance to a "Negro" high school to be located in the community.[100] Taking Wadleigh's space would be Julia Ward Howe Junior High School, a coed school. (Although this was the school's formal name, internally and sometimes externally the school continued to go by Wadleigh.) The closure of Wadleigh High School made the *New York Times* because it was the "first time in [the] history of the school system" that a city high school was "dropped from the rolls." According to the *Times*, with "two-thirds of its space unoccupied," which the newspaper attributed to "population shifts and the changing times, coupled with the lowered birth rate of the depression years," Wadleigh was regarded as "an unprofitable operation."[101]

The last Wadleigh High School graduating class was only eighty-five students, produced from a total enrollment of six hundred students. The closure brought to light conflicted feelings. Some Wadleigh students were saddened by the closure. Alumnae reactions to the school's closing reveal the profound ambivalence of the community's vision of what Wadleigh had represented. Some testified about how hard it had been to gain entry into the school. For example, the women's editor of the *Amsterdam News* recalled that she was "one of three Negro girls 'allowed' to attend."[102] With this historical struggle for access in mind, critics remarked it was "ironic that the people who had such a hard time to get into the school [Negroes], should be the ones who years later, by refusing to use it, caused its closing."[103] As had been the case at many points across the school's history, the mention of academically strong students in the last cohort sat alongside references to the school's negative reputation cited by many as a reason for its closure. Dorothy Michael, the honor graduate of the class of 1954, had been awarded scholarships to attend Hunter College, Barnard College, and Howard University.

In 1956, after a $1.4 million renovation, Wadleigh reopened as a coed neighborhood junior high school. Although still housed in the Collegiate Gothic grandeur of its early twentieth-century building, Wadleigh's academic identity as a rigorous all-girl high school was stripped away. That identity, however, had always been intertwined with New York City's segregated school system.

The closure of Wadleigh occurred just as the struggle against New York's City's school segregation accelerated after the *Brown v. Board of Education* decision. Many of the issues raised by Harlem education activists, including in and around Wadleigh over the preceding fifty years, would be taken up again by citywide civil rights and school integration activists.[104] In Harlem, as in Black communities around the country, parents, community members, and their allies would continue to struggle to choose the most favorable of a limited set of options in their efforts to secure quality schooling for their children. In the school building, over the next five decades, educators and the Harlem community continued to strive to realize the promise embodied in Wadleigh's grand collegiate halls.[105]

Notes

Epigraph source: "The Situation at Wadleigh High," *New York Amsterdam News*, February 10, 1945.

1. See Martha Biondi, *To Stand and Fight: The Struggle for Civil Rights in Postwar New York City* (Cambridge, Mass.: Harvard University Press, 2003); Jeanne F. Theoharis and Komozi Woodard, *Freedom North: Black Freedom Struggles Outside the South, 1940–1980* (New York: Palgrave Macmillan, 2003); and Thomas J. Sugrue, *Sweet Land of Liberty: The Forgotten Struggle for Civil Rights in the North* (New York: Random House, 2009).

2. On urban high schooling in the pre–World War II decades, see Kathryn Neckerman, *Schools Betrayed: The Roots of Failure in Inner City Education* (Chicago: University of Chicago Press, 2008); David Angus and Jeffrey Mirel, *The Failed Promise of the American High School, 1890–1995* (New York: Teachers College Press, 1999); and David Labaree, *The Making of an American High School: The Credentials Market at Central High School of Philadelphia, 1838–1939* (New Haven, Conn.: Yale University Press, 1992). On urban school systems more generally, the classic work is David Tyack, *The One Best System* (Cambridge, Mass.: Harvard University Press, 1974). On New York City's schools, see Diane Ravitch, *The Great School Wars: A History of the New York City Public Schools* (New York: Basic Books, 1974).

3. Marcia Chatelain, *South Side Girls: Growing Up in the Great Migration* (Durham, N.C.: Duke University Press, 2015).

4. See, for example, LaKisha Michelle Simmons, *Crescent City Girls: The Lives of Young Black Women in Segregated New Orleans* (Chapel Hill: University of North Carolina, 2015). On women in the Harlem landscape, recent works include Farah Jasmine Griffin, *Harlem Nocturne: Women Artists and Progressive Politics During World War II* (New York: Civitas, 2013); LaShawn Harris, *Sex Workers, Psychics, and Numbers Runners: Black Women in New York City's Underground Economy* (Urbana: University of Illinois Press, 2016); and Ashley Farmer, *Remaking Black Power: How Black Women Transformed an Era* (Chapel Hill: University of North Carolina Press, 2017).

5. *Wadleigh High School for Girls (Now) Wadleigh School, 215 West 114th Street, Aka 203–249 West 114th Street and 226–250 West 115th Street, Manhattan: Built 1901–02: C. B. J. Snyder, Supt. of School Buildings, New York City Board of Education, Architect* [Report] (New York: The Commission, 1994).

6. Gilbert Osofsky, *Harlem: The Making of a Ghetto: Negro New York, 1890–1930*, 1st ed. (New York: Harper and Row, 1966), 5

7. Irving Louis Horowitz, "The Yearbook: Harlem School Days in the Depression," *Antioch Review* 68, no. 4 (Fall 2010): 629–35.

8. Lauri Johnson, "A Generation of Women Activists: African American Female Educators in Harlem, 1930–1950," *Journal of African American History* 89 (2004): 223–40; and "85 Girls Graduate, Other Students Are Transferred," *New York Amsterdam News*, June 26, 1954.

9. Sara Lawrence, *Balm in Gilead: The Journey of a Healer* (Reading, Mass.: Addison-Wesley, 1988).

10. See Mary White Ovington, *Half a Man: The Status of the Negro in New York* (New York: Longmans, Green, 1911); James Weldon Johnson, *Black Manhattan* (New York: Atheneum, 1969 [1930]); Davison M. Douglas, *Jim Crow Moves North: The Battle Over Northern School Segregation, 1865–1954* (New York: Cambridge University Press, 2005); and Vincent P. Franklin, *The Education of Black Philadelphia: The Social and Educational History of a Minority Community, 1900–1950* (Philadelphia: University of Pennsylvania Press, 1979).

11. See Gilbert Osofsky, *Harlem: The Making of a Ghetto: Negro New York, 1890–1930* (New York: Ivan R. Dee, 1966); Franklin, *Education of Black Philadelphia*; and Douglas, *Jim Crow Moves North.*

12. See Osofsky, *Harlem*, 199.

13. George S. Schuyler, "N.Y. School Jim Crow Menace Arouses Parents: Resent Hint of Educators for Low Standards," *Pittsburgh Courier*, December 22, 1934.

14. For discussion of costs of "mixed" schooling, see "School Children's Needs," *New York Age*, December 25, 1920. Cited in Claude Julien Mangum, "Afro-American Thought on the New York City Public School System, 1905–1954: An Analysis of New York City Afro-American Newspaper Editorials (Volumes I and II)" (PhD diss., Columbia University, 1976).

15. Christina Collins, *"Ethnically Qualified": Race, Merit, and the Selection of Urban Teachers, 1920–1980* (New York: Teachers College Press, 2011), 37.

16. Collins, *"Ethnically Qualified."*

17. Schuyler, "N.Y. School Jim Crow Menace."

18. Mangum, "Afro-American Thought," 86, citing "Prejudice in New York Schools," *New York Age*, April 5, 1905.

19. Dr. Willis N. Huggins, "The Negro Teacher and Student Go to School," *New York Amsterdam News*, December 22, 1934. Cited in Mangum, "Afro-American Thought," 203–8.

20. "Wadleigh Still 'Melting Pot,'" *New York Amsterdam News*, December 12, 1937.

21. "The Situation at Wadleigh High," *New York Amsterdam News*, February 10, 1945.

22. Data drawn from Nationalities Statistics Surveys, 1931–1947, Series 763, Box 1 and Box 3, Board of Education of the City of New York Collection (hereafter National Statistics Surveys).

23. Charles Green and Basil Wilson, *The Struggle for Black Empowerment in New York City: Beyond the Politics of Pigmentation* (New York: McGraw-Hill, 1992).

24. On creation of a "flagship" Black high school, see Julia E. R. Clark, "Race Should Demand First-Class Separate Schools to Gain Best Education for Youth," *Pittsburgh Courier*, April 7, 1934; "Remembering a Giant," *Ebony*, April 1999, 92; and Mark Tucker, *The Duke Ellington Reader* (New York: Oxford University Press, 1995), 56.

25. "New School in Harlem to Halt Overcrowding," *Pittsburgh Courier*, May 9, 1936; and "Jim Crow Move Laid to School Official: Dr. Tildsley Opposes Any Zone Change," *New York Amsterdam News*, June 20, 1936.

26. "By 1933, geographical zones for Wadleigh and Julia Richman had been set, with Fifth Avenue serving as the boundary between the two zones. . . . As of 1938, the state survey found a pattern of zoning that effectively restricted access to the newer high schools, Julia Richman, George Washington, and Benjamin Franklin, to students living in white neighborhoods, while Black students from Harlem could generally attend only the unzoned, older buildings of Wadleigh and Haaren (as well as the various vocational annexes)." David M. Ment, "Racial Segregation in the Public Schools of New England and New York, 1840–1940" (PhD diss., Columbia University, 1975), 255.

27. Ment, "Racial Segregation," 256.

28. See William Pickens, "The Central Aim of Jim Crow Is Humiliation," *Cleveland Call and Post*, January 13, 1938.

29. The report submitted by Oswald Schlockow in the fall 1934 brought back an old, discredited idea from the 1910s, the "Gary Plan." According to Schlockow, much as he and others had advocated for Jewish and other Eastern European immigrants a generation earlier, these new migrants to New York City also needed a new differentiated curriculum. See Melissa F. Weiner, *Power, Protest, and the Public Schools: Jewish and African*

American Struggles in New York City (New Brunswick, N.J.: Rutgers University Press, 2010).

30. "The Schlockow Report," *New York Amsterdam News*, September 22, 1934; and for Schuyler, see Schuyler, "N.Y. School Jim Crow Menace."

31. "Letter Box: Segregated Schools?," *New York Amsterdam News*, September 29, 1934; and "Special School Needs," *New York Amsterdam News*, October 13, 1934.

32. See Schuyler, "N.Y. School Jim Crow Menace."

33. "Nationality of Pupils, P.S. 102 St. Annex, Wadleigh H.S.," March 1933; and, "Nationality of Pupils, P.S. 102 St. Annex, Wadleigh H.S.," January 1, 1937, Nationalities Statistics Surveys, BOE.

34. "Wadleigh Hi May Lose by Zoning Laws," *New York Amsterdam News*, June 26, 1937.

35. Osofsky, *Harlem*, 200.

36. On Harlem during the Great Depression, see Cheryl L. Greenberg, *"Or Does It Explode?" Black Harlem in the Great Depression* (New York: Oxford University Press, 1991), 222; and "People of Harlem 'Indict' School Board: Charge Overcrowding Segregation in High Schools at Big Mass Trial Next Wednesday," *Pittsburgh Courier*, January 23, 1937.

37. Osofsky, *Harlem*, 200.

38. "Wadleigh Hi May Lose by Zoning Laws," *New York Amsterdam News*, June 26, 1937. Many accounts refer to schools in Harlem as fire hazards; see, for example, "5 Harlem Public Schools Firetraps," *New York Amsterdam News*, April 14, 1934; and "Among the Worst," *New York Amsterdam News*, April 14, 1934.

39. "The Feminist Viewpoint: This Time It Is Wadleigh," *New York Amsterdam News*, December 18, 1937.

40. "Wadleigh Presses New School Plea," *New York Times*, December 12, 1937.

41. "Wadleigh Hi May Lose by Zoning Laws," *New York Amsterdam News*, June 26, 1937.

42. "Nationality of Pupils, Wadleigh H.S.," March 31, 1938, Nationalities Statistics Surveys, BOE.

43. "Wadleigh Presses New School Plea."

44. "The Feminist Viewpoint: This Time It Is Wadleigh," *New York Amsterdam News*, December 18, 1937.

45. "Wadleigh Still 'Melting Pot,'" *New York Amsterdam News*, December 18, 1937.

46. "Wadleigh Still 'Melting Pot.'"

47. Letters quoted in this section are from "Board of Education—Wadleigh High School," box 3187, folder #05, LaGuardia and Wagner Archives, LaGuardia Community College, City University of New York (hereafter LaGuardia).

48. Kyroska to LaGuardia, April 4, 1927, LaGuardia.

49. Lyon to LaGuardia, March 23, 1937, LaGuardia.

50. Milton to LaGuardia, March 25, 1937, LaGuardia.

51. Lyon to LaGuardia, March 23, 1937, LaGuardia.

52. Frisina to LaGuardia, March 25, 1937, LaGuardia.

53. Henry to LaGuardia, March 25, 1937, LaGuardia.

54. Letter to LaGuardia (NA), April 10, 1937, LaGuardia.

55. Letter to LaGuardia (NA). See also Camille Walsh, "White Backlash, the 'Taxpaying' Public, and Educational Citizenship," *Critical Sociology* 43, no. 2 (2017): 237–47.

56. Sara Lawrence, *Balm in Gilead: The Journey of a Healer* (Reading, Mass.: Addison-Wesley, 1988).

57. This 40 percent figure likely describes the main building, exclusive of the annexes at the time. "People of Harlem 'Indict' School Board: Charge Overcrowding Segregation in High Schools at Big Mass Trial Next Wednesday," *Pittsburgh Courier*, January 23, 1937.

58. "Jim Crow Move Laid to School Official: Dr. Tildsley Opposes Any Zone Change," *New York Amsterdam News*, June 20, 1937.

59. "Wadleigh Still 'Melting Pot.'"

60. "Wadleigh Still 'Melting Pot.'"

61. "Wadleigh Hi May Lose by Zoning Laws," *New York Amsterdam News*, June 26, 1937.

62. "Wadleigh Still 'Melting Pot.'"

63. "Ask New School for Wadleigh: Three Racial Groups Unite in Demands," *New York Amsterdam News*, February 26, 1938.

64. "Ask New School for Wadleigh."

65. "Place Wadleigh Building Drive Before Harlem: Circulate Petitions in Community," *New York Amsterdam News*, April 23, 1938.

66. "Both Races Need New Wadleigh High School, Audience Is Told," *New York Amsterdam News*, April 15, 1939.

67. "Nationality of Pupils, P.S. Wadleigh High School," May 1943, Nationalities Statistics Surveys, BOE.

68. "What Lies Ahead—Wadleigh? High School Faces End of Academic Career," *New York Amsterdam News*, February 1, 1941.

69. See Carrie G. Miller, "Former Wadleighite Feels That Plight of School Is Harlem's Responsibility," *New York Amsterdam Star-News*, February 22, 1941.

70. Miller, "Former Wadleighite."

71. Johnson, "Generation of Women Activists," 235–36.

72. Virginia L. Snitow, "I Teach Negro Girls," *New Republic*, November 9, 1942, 603–5.

73. Snitow, "I Teach," 604.

74. "Wadleigh Presses New School Plea."

75. "What Lies Ahead."

77. "Harlem's Schools," *New York Amsterdam News*, November 23, 1946.

77. "Race Segregation in Schools Scored: Citizens' Group Issues Report on Distribution of Pupils," *New York Times*, May 31, 1944. See also "Want Wadleigh Built Outside Harlem Locale: Committee Demands Probe on Turning School Into All Negro Institution," *New York Amsterdam News*, January 20, 1945; and "Wadleigh High Future Viewed as a Problem," *New York Amsterdam News*, January 20, 1945.

78. "To Discuss the Future of Wadleigh: Famous High School in Harlem Losing Attendance; and Important Meet Is Planned," *New York Amsterdam News*, January 6, 1945.

79. "To Discuss the Future of Wadleigh."

80. "Air Wadleigh Problem," *New York Amsterdam News*, November 23, 1946. The Mayor's Committee on Unity of New York City was created following the riots of 1943. Mayor LaGuardia named Charles Evans Hughes Jr. as chairman. The committee included "four Catholics, four Negroes, four Jews, representative each of the A.F. of L. and C.I.O., and four other members." Dan W. Dodson, "The Mayor's Committee on Unity of New York City," *Journal of Educational Sociology* 19, no. 5 (January 1946): 289–98.

81. "Air Wadleigh Problem," *New York Amsterdam News*, November 23, 1946.

82. "Air Wadleigh Problem."

83. "Wadleigh High Future Viewed as a Problem."

84. "Wadleigh High Future Viewed as a Problem."

85. "The Situation at Wadleigh High," *New York Amsterdam News*, February 10, 1945.

86. "The Situation at Wadleigh High."

87. "Place Wadleigh Building Drive Before Harlem: Circulate Petitions in Community," *New York Amsterdam News*, April 23, 1938.

88. "May Build New Wadleigh High," *Chicago Defender*, March 25, 1939; and "Both Races Need New Wadleigh High School, Audience Is Told," *New York Amsterdam News*, April 15, 1939.

89. "Wadleigh High Future Viewed as a Problem."

90. "Wadleigh High Future Viewed as a Problem."

91. "Wishing Wadleigh Well," *New York Amsterdam News*, December 21, 1946.

92. "NY Vocational High Attendance in Drop: Has Problems Like Wadleigh," *New York Amsterdam News*, November 2, 1946.

93. "Wishing Wadleigh Well"; and "School Bd. May Close Wadleigh," *New York Amsterdam News*, November 9, 1946.

94. "Board Approves School Building: $500,771 for 3 Structures at Meeting. Planned-Wade Retiring," *New York Times*, August 29, 1947.

95. "New Principal and Wadleigh," *New York Amsterdam News*, September 20, 1947.

96. "New Child Agency Aided by Students," *New York Times*, April 5, 1950; see also "Wadleigh High School Provides Parents Opportunity to See Activities at School," *New York Amsterdam News*, April 29, 1950.

97. "New Plans for Wadleigh Hi: Program for Girls Shows School's Ills; Nursing, Homemaking Seen as Inadequate," *New York Amsterdam News*, May 13, 1950; "City Plan to Recruit Nurses: Hospital Work-Study Scheme for Girl Seniors of High Schools Is the Basis," *New York Times*, June 24, 1952; and "Wadleigh Girls Earn at Nursing While Learning," *New York Amsterdam News*, February 14, 1953.

98. "Exodus from City Linked to Schools," *New York Times*, August 10, 1953.

99. "Old and New in the City's Schools: Century-Old Classroom and a Modern Counterpart," *New York Times*, August 10, 1953.

100. "Wadleigh School Faces New Status: Institution in Harlem to Be the First Secondary Center to Be Discontinued by City," *New York Times*, June 16, 1953.

101. "Wadleigh Faces New Status: Institution in Harlem to Be the First Secondary Center to Be Discontinued by City," *New York Times*, June 16, 1953," and; "Tells Why Wadleigh Hi Went Down," *New York Amsterdam News*, July 11, 1953.

102. "85 Girls Graduate, Other Students Are Transferred," *New York Amsterdam News*, June 26, 1954.

103. "85 Girls Graduate."

104. On the quickening of the northern civil rights movements and northern school desegregation see Biondi, *To Stand and Fight*; and Brian Purnell, *Fighting Jim Crow in the County of Kings: The Congress of Racial Equality in Brooklyn* (Lexington: University Press of Kentucky, 2013).

105. See Mary Anne Raywid, "The *Wadleigh Complex*: A Dream That Soured," *Journal of Education Policy* 10, no. 5 (1995): 101–14.

PART TWO

Organizing, Writing, and Teaching for Reform in the 1930s Through the 1950s

CHAPTER 4

Cinema for Social Change

The Human Relations Film Series of the Harlem Committee
of the Teachers Union, 1936–1950

LISA RABIN AND CRAIG KRIDEL

In the spring term of 1946, boys in the Youthbuilders student leadership club at James Fenimore Cooper Junior High School (JHS) 120 on
120th Street near Fifth Avenue sat down to watch and discuss *Dead End*
(1937), a film directed by William Wyler.[1] *Dead End*, starring Humphrey
Bogart as a gangster returned to the poverty-stricken neighborhood of his
childhood on Sutton Place and the East River, was based on the epony-
mous 1935 Broadway play written by Sidney Kingsley. It features a gang of
boys on the verge of embracing or resisting the fate of the Bogart character.[2]
Dramatizing the contemporary sociological discourse on the negative social
effects of poverty and deprivation, the film argued for the welfare state's
responsibility to its children, particularly via public housing and recreation.[3] Yet watching *Dead End* nearly ten years after its production, the
Youthbuilders in Harlem drew on their own knowledge and experience
to critique the film. In their lifetimes, public housing had resulted in more
neighborhood segregation—a structural form of racism that, as the African
American students at Cooper JHS 120 noted, was a root cause of delinquency. Ten years on, Cooper students judged *Dead End*'s solution to have
become part of the problem.[4]

Over the 1940s the Cooper Youthbuilders program created a space
where Harlem students used their own understanding of the world to critically reflect on media. In 1943, for example, the boys (as Cooper was an
all-boy school) staged a schoolwide forum on rectifying history textbooks

that neglected Black people's contributions to United States history, broadcast programs about race prejudice on the local radio station WNYC; and, in a major civil rights victory, successfully lobbied for the removal of the racist stereotype "Steamboat" character from a nationally popular comic book.[5] Writing about the students' work in the education journal *American Unity*, the Youthbuilders' mentor, Sidney Rosenberg, emphasized that the boys' work had moved beyond mere discussion: "After all this (talk about prejudice and discrimination), the question . . . remained: 'What can a group of pupils from Cooper Junior High School do about it?'"[6]

Cooper Youthbuilders' work in resisting and overturning racial stereotypes in the public sphere shared ideas and approaches with the critical use of media endorsed by the Harlem Committee of the New York City Teachers Union. The Teachers Union was the city's most activist teacher organization of the time and the Harlem Committee was its most politically assertive cadre, created in 1935 to mobilize Harlem civic and religious groups, parents, students, and community members as well as teachers in the struggle against pervasive school inequality. Although the specifics of the relationship between the union and Youthbuilders is not documented, Cooper students' critical discussion of the movie *Dead End* recalls the activist form of film education advocated by the Harlem Committee as part of their larger civil rights platform from the 1930s through the 1950s. One of the major strands of the Harlem Committee's work in this period was a radical multiculturalism that sought to combat damaging discourses and stereotypes of race, class, and gender in textbooks and the media (led in part by teachers at JHS 120, as discussed in chapter 5 of this volume).[7] The Harlem Committee compiled bibliographies of "films of an intercultural nature" and "human relations films," and sponsored a "human relations" film series in 1948 and 1949 at the Teachers Union Institute on West Fifteenth Street.[8] The Harlem Committee of the Teachers Union used cutting-edge documentary and animated film to teach about African American history and experience as well to explore the damaging effects of institutionalized racism.[9]

The Harlem Committee's approach to film education in city schools took inspiration, but also diverged somewhat, from earlier film-based curricular efforts. One important influence was the experimental film curriculum launched in 1936 by Alice Keliher of the Progressive Education Association's Commission on Human Relations. Known as the Human Relations Film Series (HRFS), Keliher's project consisted of edited shorts from Hollywood feature films that were shown in classrooms across the country as a way of encouraging students to address current social problems, explore their beliefs, and engage with and take action in the social world. One of the HRFS's first experimental sites was Benjamin Franklin High School in East Harlem, where English teachers Abraham Poneman and Louis Relin used the series in 1937 to prompt discussion among their Italian American, Puerto Rican, and African American students.[10] In the 1940s, Louis Relin took the HRFS to multiple educational venues across the city, including the Communist Jefferson School of Social Science in Lower Manhattan. The Harlem Committee then became acquainted with the project and adopted it for its civil rights platform in Harlem.[11]

In the 1930s and 1940s in Harlem classrooms, students and teachers came together around contemporary media in a variety of ways. Teachers often saw film as a way to recognize and interrogate oppression and racism, topics on which the traditional curriculum was silent or even racist itself. In some select but evocative cases, teachers and students together went beyond discussing film to drawing on student knowledge of racism to critique and seek to improve media representations of African American individuals and communities. This chapter contextualizes this use of film in Harlem classrooms of this period within national and local mandates on film education, paying particular attention to the activist nuances that the Harlem Committee encouraged for the classroom use of educational film.

Human Relations Film in the Classroom: Origins

The Human Relations Film Series (1936–1941) was the signature project of the Progressive Education Association's (PEA) Commission on Human Relations, directed by Alice Keliher of the Yale University Clinic of Child Development. The Commission on Human Relations, also known as the Keliher Commission, was one of three working groups that composed the PEA's Eight-Year Study (1930–1942), which collected and circulated progressive pedagogical approaches in curriculum, assessment, and teacher learning.[12] Human relations as historically conceived and developed by Keliher and her commission members represented a distinctive yet now overlooked aspect of progressive education that has become overshadowed (as well as confused with) loosely conceived notions of mid-twentieth-century intercultural, intergroup, and multicultural education. In contrast to "intercultural" education (such as Rachel DuBois's "fairs and festivals" multicultural curriculum or Hilda Taba's "intergroup education," grounded in psychological and developmental theory and addressing topics of neighborhood configurations and the nature of social relationships), human relations education as originally developed by the Keliher Commission arose from a more psychoanalytical and sociological view of adolescence.[13] Rather than focusing on the interests of the students, now viewed as a mainstay of progressive education practices, human relations programs sought to ascertain personal-social needs so that students and teachers would better understand themselves within the context of their culture and society.[14]

The Keliher Commission distributed curricular materials, including film productions, that introduced personal and social dilemmas as a stimulus for teenagers to engage critically with pressing issues of their time and to develop activist projects outside the schools as an extension of classroom discussions.[15] The materials encouraged teachers to examine social problems in relation to their effect on the individual psyche in what became known as a "psychocultural" perspective. Thus, unlike an intercultural education festival that introduced some previously unknown or unappreciated nationality (DuBois's approach) or an intergroup program that addressed classroom topics and issues related to changing community demographics (Taba's approach), Keliher's programs sought to generate students' understanding of themselves as a way to initiate social agency and community action.[16] All these approaches occupied a moderate left-liberal position in a time when the broader political continuum in the country, particularly in Harlem, included vibrant radical, communist, and nationalist perspectives.[17] Nonetheless, there were consequential variations within these approaches to thinking about racism and working with students and media in classrooms.

The Human Relations Film Series was the Keliher Commission's primary curriculum development program.[18] From 1936 to 1940, the commission produced sixty film shorts excerpted from Hollywood feature films, which they promoted as prompts for teachers to generate "instructive discussion" on personal and social problems in the secondary classroom. Selections were accompanied by a study guide containing source material, bibliographies, and suggestions for class discussion. The HRFS productions were conceived not to present content and/or an interpretive perspective, common elements for documentary film.[19] Rather, these film clips were edited to encourage the classroom audience to discuss the film's narrative as a way to address social and personal issues. In keeping with the Eight-Year Study's commitment to field testing, research, and curricular experimentation, schools submitted transcripts to Keliher's staff, who then examined classroom discourse for evidence of the film's effect on students. Benjamin Franklin High School in East Harlem served as a test site. By 1941, the Human Relations films had been distributed to over 3,000 public and private schools throughout the United States.[20]

The ambition of the HRFS was not mere discussion. Keliher and the Eight-Year Study staff hoped to encourage action among students. Keliher maintained that "young people need to sense their responsibility for assuming action as a part of their citizenship in a democracy." A distinct sense of involvement—"activity with meaning"—became the intent of the series. Keliher described students forming a welcoming committee at their school after seeing *The Devil Is a Sissy* (directed by W. S. Van Dyke, 1936), a film describing the difficulties of an adolescent entering a new school in a low-income community and planning a community recreation center after seeing *Alice Adams* (directed by George Stevens, 1935).[21] One of the most striking examples of students inspired to take action occurred at Tower Hill School in Wilmington, Delaware.[22] After watching the March of Time short film *Juvenile Delinquency* (1936) students pursued research projects on asocial behavior of youth in Wilmington, investigating the role of poor housing, low income, lack of recreational spaces, and compromised health on delinquency and reporting on governmental neglect of these problems. In words that epitomized Keliher's goals for her film series, the instructor of this class pointed out that "*Juvenile Delinquency* had the capacity to arouse student awareness to the point of motivating a study of actual conditions in the community. It seemed also to sensitize the students toward social action so that what they *did* after seeing the film seemed more important than what they *said*."[23]

Turning discussion into action depended on many factors, including school administration and community support that could enable teacher or student organizing. After its test use of the Human Relations Film Series in 1937, Benjamin Franklin High School in East Harlem adopted the HRFS across the curriculum in the late 1930s and throughout the 1940s and also screened film excerpts at schoolwide assemblies. Yet even at this high school where students had structured opportunities to pursue community outreach and activism, there is only one instance in which the HRFS was paired with social action: when Franklin students participated in Vito Marcantonio's East Harlem campaign for fair housing in the late 1930s.[24] Otherwise, despite the stated ambitions of Keliher and the HRFS, classroom discussion remained the chief outcome, at least as perceived by the HRFS and visible in the historical record.[25]

In one transcript from the experimental use of the HRFS at Franklin in 1937, for example, Abraham Poneman's English class discussed racialized violence in relation to a twenty-two-minute film clip from director Fritz Lang's *Fury* (United States, 1936). *Fury* starred Spencer Tracy as a newcomer to a small U.S. town who is wrongly accused of a crime, hunted down by an angry mob, and nearly lynched. One boy in the class complained that *Fury* featured a white man, rather than the Black men most likely to face lynch mobs in the 1930s United States: "The picture doesn't teach anything about a racial background." Another student retorted: "There's no need to tell how many negroes are lynched down South by whites . . . just because they're negroes. All the world knows it, and it is a disgrace to the United States."[26] Notably, this narrative account of East Harlem youth watching Keliher's series contrasts with the story of film education at Cooper Junior High School with which we began this essay. In 1937, the HRFS transcript suggests that at least the Franklin students who discussed *Fury* seemed to approach racism from a distant position: racialized violence was happening in the South, not East Harlem. When Cooper's Youthbuilders saw *Dead End* in 1946, their personal experience with segregation and racism informed their viewing.[27] Franklin's teachers appeared to see *Fury* and class discussion as a conduit to awakening students' understanding of social problems, but Cooper's Youthbuilders approached film as a representation of social realities that they themselves knew well.

Yet even as Franklin students' engagement with the HRFS might have been limited to abstract discussions of racism, it is important to recognize that Keliher's model of human relations film education had given students a vehicle through which they could reflect on the root causes of state-sponsored race violence, racial discrimination, and class inequality. Crucially, when human relations became conflated in the 1940s and 1950s with intergroup and intercultural education, film education became primarily focused on teaching students to develop new psychological attitudes toward diverse others. Many teachers in New York City used this more limited approach to the HRFS. As we will show in this next section, however, critical approaches to teaching film developed into the 1940s when the HRFS was repurposed by radical educators in different contexts, including via the Harlem Committee of the Teachers Union's activist approach to intercultural education.

Film and the Harlem Committee

After Alice Keliher's commission concluded its work in 1942, the Human Relations Film Series was made available to teachers through New York University's Educational Film Library (which Keliher directed until 1948) and from other university and commercial distributors.[28] In New York City, the efforts of Louis Relin, another English teacher at Benjamin Franklin High School, helped disseminate the HRFS across the city. By the early 1940s, Relin began routinely using the selections for addressing racism in multiple settings, in various schools and in citywide events. The Harlem Committee of the Teachers Union itself adopted the Human Relations Film Series for antiracist education in the late 1940s.

In the 1940s, a dominant approach to a multicultural curriculum merely exposed students to or encouraged their understanding of diverse others.[29] This approach is captured in the words of Esther Berg, a teacher who served on the Audio-Visual Committee of the New York City Board of Education and wrote often on multicultural film education in the New York City teachers' journal *High Points* in the mid-1940s.[30] As a measure of her psychological approach to teaching human relations through film, we can observe Berg describing Keliher's series as "excerpts from full-length feature films designed to provoke discussion of problems of behavior in everyday relationships."[31] The Harlem Committee practiced a type of radical intercultural education in the 1940s, one strongly differentiated from this multiculturalism focused on the matter of individual encounters.

Far from reducing social struggle to "problems of behavior in everyday relationships," the Harlem Committee instead devoted itself to a full overhaul of hegemonic approaches to the teaching of U.S. history and culture. As discussed in chapter 5 and chapter 6 in this volume, the committee lobbied against racist textbooks, taught Black history for in-service courses at the Teachers Union Institute, and developed extensive curricula on Black history and children's multicultural literature throughout the 1940s. Their curricular products included substantive descriptions of thirty-six documentaries and animated and theatrical films introducing economic and racial inequality, portraying desegregation efforts, championing the contributions of African Americans and Latinxs to U.S. culture, and debunking racial ideologies, in alignment with the committee's view of intercultural education. The committee shaped its own "Human Relations Film Series" in the fall of 1948 and 1949 and organized monthly screenings.[32]

The Harlem Committee's interest in film in the classroom also aligned with national patterns in classroom media. As film historians have noted, film education as a form of citizenship building both inside and outside the traditional U.S. classroom gained considerable momentum after World War II, capitalizing on U.S. enthusiasm for film's utility in military training and in building patriotism during the war.[33] In particular, film was judged highly useful for promoting postwar values of internationalism and tolerance for diverse others in the school and the workplace.[34]

The Harlem Committee's work with film reflects transitions in the organization's work during the World War II and postwar years. Founded in part in response to the Harlem riots of 1935, amid high levels of unemployment and insufficient public services in the area, the initial activities of the Harlem Committee were firmly oriented toward structural change: the desegregation of Harlem schools, the improvement of infrastructure, the provision of equal material resources and qualified teachers, the parity of employment of Black teachers with white ones in the city school system.[35] As World War II and rising anticommunism in the postwar years constrained the space for radical activism, the committee's turn to more inclusive curricula and school materials represented a less controversial field of work (although one that was not without controversy and consequences, as detailed by Jonna Perrillo in chapter 5 of this volume).

Like the radical writers and artists, as Julia Mickenberg describes, who used juvenile genres as a method to sidestep censorship and to keep the politics of the Popular Front alive into the 1950s and 1960s, the Harlem Committee continued in the spirit of earlier efforts via their film program.[36]

The Harlem Committee's film series and corresponding bibliographies represent one way in which the Teachers Union's dedication to civil rights survived in an extremely constricted era. The committee's film project made prodigious use of documentary film, in contrast to Keliher's original series of film excerpts from current-run theatrical film. Indeed, twenty-seven of the thirty-six films on the Harlem Committee's list—nearly 80 percent—were documentary, and four of the remaining films were animated. A number of films on the Harlem Committee's lists focused on racism and segregation: *For Us the Living* (Freedom Films, n.d.) argued for desegregated housing, *An Equal Chance* (New York State Commission Against Discrimination, 1949) called attention to employment discrimination, *Color of a Man* (International Film Foundation, 1946) exposed Jim Crow policies in the South, *Sydenham Plan* (World Today, n.d.) showcased the work of the first interracial hospital in the United States, located in Harlem, and *That All May Learn* (Mexico, EMA Mexico and the United Nations, 1949) documented the exploitation of a Mexican family that had not received formal schooling.

Several films sought to portray the dangers of racism to a democracy, as in the U.S. Army's *Don't Be a Sucker* (1946) and Freedom Films's *Hidden Wall* (1951). A number of other films demonstrated the contributions of people of color and of immigrant communities, like the films on Black servicemen in World War II, *The Negro Soldier* (directed by Stuart Heisler, 1944) and *Teamwork* (U.S. Army Signal Corps, 1946); a film on World War II refugees and their work in the United States, *New Americans* (directed by Slavko Vorkapich, 1944); and a film on the labor of world peoples in contributing natural resources to manufacturing, *Made in the U.S.A.* (Association Films, n.d.). Another grouping of films aimed to debunk ideologies of racial superiority, not only *The Races of Mankind* (United Film Productions, 1946), based on the work of Columbia University anthropologists Ruth Benedict and Gene Weltfish, but also *One Man-One Family* (B.I.S., n.d.). Relatedly, some films pictured antiprejudice and intercultural activities across the country and the world, such as *Americans All* (*March of Time*, 1944), *It Happened in Springfield* (directed by Crane Wilbur, 1948), *Make Way for Youth* (directed by Robert Disraeli, 1948), the *Cummington Story* (directed by Mervyn LeRoy, 1947), *For All the World's Children* (directed by William K. McClure, 1949), and *Picture in Your Mind* (directed by Philip Stapp, 1948).

Even as the Harlem Committee sought to leverage these films for pedagogy against racism, the films themselves contained problematic elements or silences. *The Negro Soldier* addressed segregation in the military abroad and proposed integration as crucial to the war effort but wholly elided segregation at home; although the animated film *The Brotherhood of Man* debunked the biological rationale for racism, it also included troubling caricatures of ethnic minorities. The extent to which these limitations became grounds for student critique and reflection depended on teachers' use of the films.[37]

In the Harlem Committee's creation of their own film series with documentaries on social and economic justice, desegregation, history, and antiracism, they updated intercultural education through contemporary and in some cases pioneering media. As the documentary film scholar Jonathan Kahana has argued, subtending all documentary work since its inception in the early 1920s—whether avant-garde in the 1920s, state-sponsored in the 1930s and 1940s (which characterized most of those on the committee's list), observational in the 1960s and 1970s, or performative in the contemporary period—is the filmmaker's intention to make a social intervention, a contribution to discourses obtaining in the public sphere.[38] Accordingly, along with their teaching of Black history and their resistance to racist textbooks, the Harlem Committee's use of documentary was part of its long and concerted effort to provide accurate knowledge on the historical and contemporary world.

The committee saw documentary film as a vehicle for human relations teaching in both its subject matter and its form. The group sought to resist stereotypes not only in the media, but also in textbooks, including through efforts based at Cooper JHS 120 and discussed in chapter 6 of this volume. At the 1951 annual conference of the Teachers Union, Harlem teacher and committee member Alice Citron asked: "Radio, T.V., films, the theatre, publications—what are they doing to the minds of our children?" "How are the schools meeting this threat?"[39] By turning to documentary films, the Harlem Committee's version of midcentury film education sought a corrective to the products of white-dominated commercial media.

Both Keliher's Human Relations Film Series and the Harlem Committee's film project hoped to encourage viewers to craft a critical stance on social problems and to take action to address them. Far more common in the city and the country in the 1940s was the use of film for a decidedly less expansive intercultural or human relations education model than that of the Teachers Union's Harlem Committee—one that teachers such as Esther Berg recommended for changing attitudes and developing new psychological stances toward diverse others. This mainstream model of film education was visible even at Cooper JHS 120. In addition to the Youthbuilders' program described above, Cooper had a schoolwide "human relations film" program under way in 1946. Writing in *High Points*, the Cooper teacher Dina Bleich described the program as a series of assemblies in which students across the school watched documentary films on U.S. internationalism and better race relations "emphasiz[ing] the development of *worthwhile attitudes* in the field of human relations."[40] Bleich reported that the assembly screenings were structured toward guiding students to "analyze their attitudes" and to "grow emotionally as well as intellectually."[41] Consistent with the rise in post–World War II discourses promoting film education for multiculturalism and internationalism, Bleich and many educators asserted that film was the best means by which to "provide our children with information and cultivate in them attitudes that will enable them to act intelligently as citizens of a world community."[42]

The Cooper Youthbuilders club approached film very differently compared to the approach of the school assemblies. Rather than teachers and administrators managing students' speech and behavior to conform to pre-established directives on film discussion, the Youthbuilders' mentor, "Mr. Rosenberg," asked the boys to use *Dead End*'s story as a prompt to consider the problem of youth delinquency in their neighborhood and how it might be solved. Notably, film viewing and discussion here were presented as means by which students could think critically about the roots of social problems in their local world—and what they themselves knew about these problems and could do about them. Bleich wrote that the discussion included the boys' reflections on "lack of parental control, segregation, and the large number of 'crime movies' marketed to their neighborhood." Although "lack of parental control" and the danger of "crime movies" as causes of delinquency might suggest that the students' thinking mirrored dominant and often racist social discourses of the day, some elements suggest otherwise. They discussed "segregation" as delinquency's root cause, interpreting the film via their lived social experience with institutionalized racism. In 1946, this allowed them to actualize *Dead End*'s original social message: by worsening the segregation of African Americans and Latinxs in the city, "fair housing" (the film's term for public housing) had in fact contributed to (instead of resolving) inequality.

"Mr. Rosenberg" identified himself in connection with the Harlem Committee of the Teachers Union in an article he wrote in 1943 about the Youthbuilders for the teachers' journal *American Unity*. Viewing films such as *Dead End* provided a springboard to several club actions to combat racist stereotypes in textbooks and the media: lobbying publishers to remove racist stereotypes in national comic books; directing a schoolwide assembly at Cooper on the representation of African Americans in history textbooks and planning the writing of a supplement to textbooks on the contributions of diverse racial and ethnic groups to U.S. history; and broadcasting three radio programs over WNYC radio—"How Do Comic Books Affect Our Education?" "What Is Our Responsibility to Improving Pan-American Relations?" and "And How Can Pupils Combat Race Prejudice?"[43] These critical engagements with media represented the most assertive form of the radical multicultural education advocated by the

Harlem Committee in the 1940s. Cooper JHS's 120 students merged film viewing with knowledge of their communities in dealing with their larger struggles against racism and inequality.

The multiple uses of film in Harlem schools in the late 1930s and 1940s revealed the intersection of two fundamental forces in U.S. education: the rise of public secondary schooling in socializing U.S. children on a mass level and the rise of institutions of educational film (and later television) to deliver on technology's promise in instructing these mass numbers of students. As media historians have pointed out, in spite of the utopian strands in the long history of educational technology over the twentieth and twenty-first centuries, instructional media have been primarily characterized by instrumentalism, or use in the education of citizens to adapt and compete under advanced capitalism.[44] So too, as Brian Goldfarb relates in his history of media education in the United States, technological approaches to education have typically been associated with compensatory education and curricular approaches targeting low-income children of color in schools.[45]

Even when progressive modules of educational media have been developed—notably, Keliher's HRFS for the PEA's Commission on Human Relations—they have been almost invariably adapted and turned into something far less expansive by educational institutions in latter years.[46] Despite striking examples such as the Youthbuilders' program at Cooper JHS 120 and despite Alice Keliher's stated ambition to facilitate not only enlarged student consciousness but also action, most film education work lost its potential for larger social critique in the 1940s and 1950s. As exemplified by the work of Esther Berg in the New York City school system, the hegemonic understanding of human relations came to be understood as an educational process through which peaceful and tolerant interactions among individuals from different backgrounds could be facilitated in the classroom, playground, and eventually the workplace.[47]

As educational film became institutionalized as a vehicle for differentiating and racializing students, or at best for sugarcoating social inequalities, Harlem's educational uses of film stood in relief. At Benjamin Franklin High School, film helped provoke student discussion of state-sponsored violence and unemployment discrimination; at James Fenimore Cooper Junior High School 120, students and teachers built on film and student knowledge to resist racism in schools and the media. For the Harlem Committee of the Teachers Union, the Human Relations Film Series became a mode in which civil rights work could continue even as larger forces inhibited structural change in the Harlem schools. Film education in 1930s and 1940s Harlem appears not as new technology fad or a panacea for solving social conflict but as another space in which Harlem students and educators sought to perceive and act upon their social realities.

Notes

1. Dina Bleich, "A Film Program for Social Living," *High Points* 28, no. 7 (1946): 37.

2. See also Mr. DuLac, "Review: Dead End," *Letterbox*, accessed January 4, 2017, https://letterboxd.com/mr_dulac/film/dead-end/. The young actors in the play *Dead End* re-created their roles in the movie and went on to play members of the same neighborhood gang in a series of spinoffs, becoming successively the Dead End Kids, the Little Tough Guys, the East Side Kids, and the Bowery Boys all the way into the 1950s. Pamela Robertson Wojcik, *Fantasies of Neglect: Imagining the Urban Child in American Film and Fiction* (New Brunswick, N.J.: Rutgers University Press, 2016), 41–42.

3. Amanda Ann Klein, "Realism, Censorship, and the Social Promise of *Dead End*," in *Modern American Drama on Screen*, ed. William Robert Bray and R. Barton Palmer (Cambridge: Cambridge University Press, 2013), 9–28; and Wojcik, *Fantasies of Neglect*, 55–61. The 1935 play *Dead End* was considered influential in the passage of the Wagner-Steagall Housing Act of 1937 and the expansion of Boys' Club facilities in the late 1930s. Klein, "Realism, Censorship," 12.

4. Bleich, "Film Program," 37.

5. Sidney Rosenberg, "They Go After the Comics," *American Unity: A Monthly Manual of Education* 2–3 (1943): 10–11; see also Sidney Rosenberg, interview, cited in New York Board of Education Advisory Committee on Human Relations, *Administration of Human Relations Program in New York City Schools: Report to Honorable F. H. LaGuardia Mayor of the City of New York* (New York: New York Department of Investigation, 1946), 77.

6. Rosenberg, "They Go After the Comics," 10.

7. Jonna Perrillo, *Uncivil Rights: Teachers, Unions, and Race in the Battle for School Equity* (Chicago: University of Chicago Press, 2012), 47–82. See also Clarence Taylor, *Reds at the Blackboard: Communism, Civil Rights, and the New York City Teachers Union* (New York: Columbia University Press, 2010), 75–100, 237–71; and Celia Lewis Zitron, *The New York City Teachers Union, 1916–1964: A Story of Educational and Social Commitment* (New York: Humanities Press, 1968), 94–97.

8. The Teachers Union Institute, "Human Relations Film Discussion Series," October 18, 1949, in "Audio-Visual Material" and "Reference List," box 44, folder 7, Teachers Union of the City of New York Records, 1920–1942, Collection no. 5445, Kheel Center for Labor-Management and Documentation, Cornell University (hereafter TUCNYR).

9. Perrillo, *Uncivil Rights*, 60–61; and Anna McCarthy, "Screen Culture and Group Discussion in Postwar Race Relations," in *Learning with the Lights Off: Educational Film in the United States*, ed. Devin Orgeron, Marsha Orgeron, and Dan Streible (Oxford: Oxford University Press, 2012), 397–423.

10. "Project Progress," December 24, 1937, in General Education Board Collection, Record Group 632.1, PEA—Commission on Human Relations—Motion Picture, 1939–1941,

Rockefeller Archive Center, Sleepy Hollow, New York (hereafter GEB), series 1.2, box 284, folder 2965. "Appraisal, Motion Picture Project," January 1940, 4, in GEB, series 1.2, box 284, folder 2962.

11. The Teachers Union Institute, "Human Relations Film Discussion"; Esther L. Berg and George E. Levinbrow, "The Use of Motion Pictures to Develop Better Human Relations," *Educational Screen* 23, no. 3 (1944): 112–14. "The Road to Life," *New York Teacher News* 6, no. 13, December 8, 1945, 2; "School Reminders: For High School Students," *New York Teacher News* 6, no. 31, April 20, 1946, 2; and "In Short: "Film[s] That Fight Prejudice," *New York Teacher News* 7, no. 19, January 25, 1947, 2.

12. Craig Kridel and Robert V. Bullough Jr., *Stories of the Eight-Year Study* (Albany: State University of New York Press, 2007).

13. DuBois launched the PEA–sponsored "Commission on Intercultural Education" in 1936 and quickly developed a major profile in pluralist circles, frequently carrying out workshops for educators and interfaith organizations, for example, in New York City and across the nation. Diana Selig, *Americans All: The Cultural Gifts Movement* (Cambridge, Mass.: Harvard University Press, 2008), 197–202, 240; and Ethel J. Alpenfels, "Principles Underlying Education for Better Group Relations," in *The Study of Intergroup Relations: Papers from the 1945 Meeting of the Council on Cooperation in Teacher Education* (New York: American Council on Education, 1945), 11.

14. Alice Keliher, *Life and Growth* (New York: D. Appleton-Century, 1938).

15. "Commission on Human Relations: Motion Picture Project, Appraisal," January 1940, in GEB, series 1.2, box 284, folder 2962, 1.

16. The HRFS must be viewed as a component of the Eight-Year Study where both the Keliher and Thayer Commissions were articulating a conception of personal-social needs. When placed within this context and when the series is recognized not as a form of documentary film or aligned directly with the Rockefeller Foundation film efforts (rather, the project was guided by the General Education Board staff), the HRFS's "personality and psychological self" theme is not as pronounced as some have interpreted. Rob Aitken, "'An Instrument for Reaching Into Experience': Progressive Film at the Rockefeller Boards, 1934–1945," *Journal of Historical Sociology*, accessed January 16, 2015, doi:10.1111/johs.12094, http://dx.doi.org/10.1111/johs.12094.

17. Nikhil Pal Singh, *Black Is a Country* (Cambridge, Mass.: Harvard University Press, 2005).

18. Craig Kridel, "Educational Film Projects of the 1930s," in Orgeron, Orgeron, and Streible, *Learning with the Lights Off*, 215–29.

19. We thank Dan Streible for pointing out the HRFS's relation to trigger films. Edward F. Newren, "The Trigger Film: Its History, Production, and Utilization," Association for Educational Communications and Technology Annual Convention, Atlantic City, New Jersey, 1974.

20. "Project Progress," December 24, 1937, in GEB, series 1–2, box 284, file 2965; and "Appraisal, Motion Picture Project," January 1940, in GEB, series 1–2, box 284, file 2962, 4.

21. Alice Keliher, "Human Relations Series of Films," *New England Educational Film Association* (n.d.), xii, in Alice Virginia Keliher Papers, Bobst Library, New York University, manuscript collection 139, box 17, folder 7.

22. Tower Hill School served as one of the twenty school sites for both the PEA's Eight-Year Study and one of the seven sites for the American Council on Education Motion Picture Project that measured the effect of film curricula on students' learning outcomes. For a report on all seven projects, see Charles Hoban Jr., *Focus on Learning: Motion Pictures in the School* (Washington, D.C.: American Council on Education, 1942).

23. "A School Uses Motion Pictures," 48–49, cited in Hoban, *Focus on Learning*, 87, 172; emphasis added.

24. Lisa Rabin, "The Social Uses of Classroom Cinema: A Reception History of the 'Human Relations Film Series' at Benjamin Franklin High School, East Harlem, 1936–1955," *Velvet Light Trap* 72 (2013): 58–70. In addition to showing films in classrooms and to students involved in citywide debates, Franklin also used the HRFS series for at least one community discussion in East Harlem itself. The student newspaper in the East Harlem community, *East Harlem News*, announced in its October 1941 issue "*Captains Courageous* and an Excerpt from an Andy Hardy Film" (most likely, *A Family Affair*) were to be shown at the Franklin auditorium on November 6, 1941, with Franklin students along with their principal Leonard Covello, English teacher Louis Relin, and the chairperson of the New York City Schools Motion Picture Committee to lead discussions. "Franklin Stages Film Program," *East Harlem News*, October 1931, 3, col. 2, Covello Papers, Historical Society of Pennsylvania, box 131, folder "*East Harlem News*."

25. Michael C. Johanek and John L. Puckett identify a historical struggle between Franklin's original "community-centered" ethos and its need to conform to a more traditional curriculum, which won out in the 1940s. Michael C. Johanek and John L. Puckett, *Benjamin Franklin High School: Education as If Citizenship Mattered* (Philadelphia: Temple University Press, 2006).

26. Alice Keliher, stenographic notes of "Student Discussion Following Showing of Excerpts from 'Fury,'" Benjamin Franklin High School, New York, New York, August 10, 1937, in GEB, series 1.2, box 284, folder 2966, 44–73, 66.

27. We are grateful to Ansley Erickson for helping us develop this argument.

28. "PEA—Commission on Human Relations—Motion Picture Project—Draft," in GEB, series 1.2, box 284, folder 2962, 2.

29. Perrillo, *Uncivil Rights*, 47–82; Taylor, *Reds at the Blackboard*, 75–100, 237–71; and Zitron, *New York City Teachers Union*, 94–97.

30. Esther Berg et al., "The Use of Motion Pictures to Teach Better Human Relations," *High Points* 26, no. 2 (1944): 39–49, adapted by Berg and George E. Levinrow, the director of Child Guidance for New York City Schools as "The Use of Motion Pictures to Develop Better Human Relations," in the national publication *Educational Screen* 33, no. 3 (March 1944): 112–14; Esther Berg, "A List of Films for 'Human Relations,'" *High Points* 27, no. 6 (1945): 74–51; Berg, "Films to Better Human Relations," *High Points* 27, no. 5 (1945): 17–22; Berg, "Recent Visual Aids for Intercultural Education," *High Points* 28, no. 10 (1946): 65–72; and Charles G. Spiegler and Esther Berg, "Films Can Fight for Democracy," *High Points* 28, no. 5 (1946): 44–47. A 1946 report by the Board of Education's Advisory Committee on Human Relations to Mayor LaGuardia referenced the use of film in human relations teaching across the city school system. New York Board of Education Advisory Committee on Human Relations, *Administration of Human Relations Program in New York City Schools*, 76, 78, 86, and 91.

31. Berg, "List of Films," 74.

32. The TU Institute, "Human Relations Film Discussion Series"; "Audio-Visual Material"; and "Reference List," TUCNYR.

33. Charles Acland, "Curtains, Carts and the Mobile Screen," *Screen* 50, no. 1 (2009): 148–66; and Acland, "Classrooms, Clubs, and Community Circuits: Cultural Authority and the Film Council Movement, 1946–1957," in *Inventing Film Studies*, ed. Lee Grieveson and Haidee Wasson (Durham, N.C.: Duke University Press, 2008), 145–81; and McCarthy, "Screen Culture."

34. Zoë Druick, "Reaching the Multimillions: Liberal Internationalism and the Establishment of Documentary Film," in Grieveson and Wasson, *Inventing Film Studies*, 66–92;

Acland, "Classrooms"; McCarthy, "Screen Culture"; and Lisa Rabin, "A Social History of US Educational Documentary: The Travels of Three Shorts, 1945–1958," *Film History: An International Journal* 29, no. 3 (2017): 1–24.

35. See Thomas Harbison, chapter 2 in this volume; Taylor, *Reds at the Blackboard*, 237–71; Perrillo, *Uncivil Rights*, 47–82; Lauri Johnson, "A Generation of Women Activists: African American Female Educators in Harlem, 1930–1950," *Journal of African American History* 89, no. 3 (2004): 223–40; and Johnson, "Making Democracy Real": Teacher Union and Community Activism to Promote Diversity in the New York City Public Schools, 1935–1950," *Urban Education* 37, no. 5 (2002): 566–87.

36. Julia Mickenberg, *Learning from the Left: Children's Literature, the Cold War, and Radical Politics in the United States* (Oxford: Oxford University Press, 2005).

37. Thanks to Clarence Taylor for this helpful interpretation.

38. Jonathan Kahana, *Intelligence Work: The Politics of American Documentary Film* (Berkeley: University of California Press, 2008).

39. "Forum II: Bigotry and Thought Control—Threats to American Culture," Schools and the Fight for Peace and Freedom, Fifteenth Annual Educational Conference of the Teachers Union, Local 555, UPW, Saturday, April 7, 1951, in box 46, file 9, 1, TUCNYR.

40. Bleich, "Film Program," 32, emphasis added. Bleich wrote two other essays on the use of films for citizenship building in the late 1940s. Dina Bleich, "Films and Attitudes," *High Points* 29, no. 8 (1948): 18–31; and Bleich, "Strengthening Democracy Through Films," *High Points* 32, no. 8 (1950): 5–16. Cooper School's human relations film program appears in Advisory Committee of Human Relations, *Administration of Human Relations Program in New York City Schools*, 76, 91.

41. Bleich, "Film Program," 36.

42. Bleich, 38; see also note 43 below. On the institutionalization of film education in the United States midcentury, see Zoë Druick, "The Myth of Media Literacy," *International Journal of Communication* 10 (2016): 1125–44; Acland, "Classrooms," 145–81; and Gregory A. Waller, "Projecting the Promise of 16mm, 1935–45," in *Useful Cinema*, ed. Charles Acland and Haidee Wasson (Durham, N.C.: Duke University Press, 2011), 125–48.

43. Sidney Rosenberg, interview, cited in Advisory Committee on Human Relations, *Administration of Human Relations Program in New York City Schools*, 77. Rosenberg himself wrote about the program in the education journal *American Unity*. Rosenberg, "They Go After the Comics," 20.

44. Druick, "Myth"; Acland, "Classrooms"; and Waller, "Projecting the Promise."

45. Brian Goldfarb, *Visual Pedagogy: Media Cultures in and Beyond the Classroom* (Durham, N.C.: Duke University Press, 2002), as cited in Druick, "Myth," 1131.

46. Druick's recounting of the co-optation of critical media studies by educators and technocrats as "media literacy" has been helpful to us here. Druick, "Myth." See also Kridel's treatment of the HRFS's "transition" to Film Custodians. Craig Kridel, "Examining the Educational Film Work of Alice Keliher and the Human Relations Series of Films," Rockefeller Archive Center Research Reports, 2010, accessed August 14, 2016, http://www.rockarch.org/publications/resrep/kridel.php.

47. Perrillo, *Uncivil Rights*; McCarthy, "Screen Culture"; and Rabin, "Social History."

CHAPTER 5

Bringing Harlem to the Schools

Langston Hughes's The First Book of Negroes
and Crafting a Juvenile Readership

JONNA PERRILLO

L angston Hughes's *The First Book of Negroes* (1952) opens with a vibrantly painted scene. A Black man, dressed in a red velvet hat, wearing a loose tunic and pantaloons, sword tucked into his belt, gazes off into the horizon of seemingly endless desert. It is the Moroccan-born Estevanico, the explorer of what would become Florida and the U.S. Southwest, American Indian translator, treasure-seeker, and, eventually, murder victim of the Zuni. It is a unique, relatively obscure choice of beginning figures, but the enthralling story of Estevanico captures many of the major themes of the book and Hughes's larger corpus, including Black achievement, intercultural contact and tension, and the import of language and the African diaspora to understanding Black identity. In *The First Book of Negroes*, young readers are introduced to Black people who were widely recognized and celebrated (Booker T. Washington, Harriet Tubman, Louis Armstrong), the lesser known (the Peruvian priest Martin de Porres, W. C. Handy) and the anonymous (African slaves, the thirty Black men who accompanied Balboa on an expedition). Interspersed with biographical and historical accounts of these figures are stories of Terry Lane, a fictional walnut-hued child whose phenotype tells the story of Black Americans; hundreds of years ago, Hughes writes, Africans, Indians, and Europeans met in the New World and "their children's children are the American Negroes of today."[1] A resident of Harlem, Terry stands in as a Black everychild, connecting ordinary children of all races to the often larger-than-life figures they meet in the book. The son of a United Nations translator and the great-grandson of a slave, Terry makes the histories of Black accomplishment and Black servitude relevant and accessible at once to a wide range of juvenile readers. In addition, he ties the history of Black people in Africa and the Americas to Harlem of the 1950s and, through his southern grandmother and cousin, to Jim Crow (a "holdover from slavery") and the Black folktale tradition that Hughes often drew on and celebrated in his own writing.[2]

This chapter examines Hughes's production of the often-overlooked *The First Book of Negroes* because it offers a particularly compelling vantage point for examining how the author transformed ideas, images, and business practices that he developed as a young Harlem Renaissance writer to educate the nation's youth. Moreover, thinking about the book's readership provides a view into the politics of the books Harlem and New York City children otherwise were reading in 1950s classrooms. Over his career, Hughes authored a wide collection of works for children, including pieces he published in *The Brownie's Book* in the 1920s; children's poetry in the 1930s; his five-volume *First Book* textbook series that he published from 1952 to 1960; and his three-volume set of *Famous Negroes* (1954–1958), published by Dodd, Mead.[3] *The First Book of Negroes* was not his first children's publication, therefore, but it represented a unique and important response to Hughes's long commitment to critiquing and reenvisioning the books children encountered in school.

Hughes's political critique in *The First Books of Negroes* dated to some of his most seminal works as a writer in the Harlem Renaissance. Throughout his life and career, Hughes remained committed to the same questions that thrived at the heart of the Renaissance, including: What constitutes Black culture and art? What are the responsibilities of the Black artist to himself and his or her community? Can cultivating a Black readership serve as a pathway to community advancement? And what is the role of a Black aesthetic—and the Black diaspora—within a larger U.S. culture?[4] Hughes, like the Renaissance figures discussed by Daniel Perlstein in chapter 1 of this volume, saw many threads linking education, broadly conceived, and these questions.

Hughes did not work formally as a teacher, other than a brief stint in Toluca, Mexico, in 1920, and a three-month guest appointment at the University of Chicago in 1949. This burdened him to make writing a constant source of income, but it also compelled him to engage with a wider range of schools and teachers. Throughout the 1930s, 1940s, and 1950s, he visited hundreds of schools in Harlem and across the country and he developed significant relationships with collectives of teachers, many of whom taught his work and helped him to promote his books. All these aspects of his career—from Renaissance philosophies to the importance of promoting his works in schools—came together in the course of *The First Book of Negroes*, making it an embodiment of Hughes's long-standing ambition to provide Black children with "books that will give them back their souls."[5] Hughes thus shared with the educators and writers Perlstein describes a common pedagogical ambition rooted in New Negro thought that endured well beyond the New Negro era: building Black personhood through teaching practices and materials.

The First Book of Negroes came at an important time in Hughes's career; in 1953, the year after its publication and in a time of widespread fear about the Cold War, he was summoned before the Senate to testify about his ties to communism. In his trial, Hughes deftly explained that although he had "never read theoretical books of socialism or communism," he had developed "non-theoretical, non-sectarian" ideas "born out of my own need to find some kind of way of thinking about this whole problem of myself, segregated, poor, colored and how I can adjust to this whole problem of helping to build America when sometimes I cannot even get into a school or a lecture or a concert or . . . library."[6] Hughes's testimony captured many of the enduring preoccupations found in his poetry and prose, including his belief that racial oppression was legitimized and entrenched in educational and aesthetic institutions as much as in political ones. Despite the book's purposeful omission of figures such as Walter White, Paul Robeson, and W. E. B. Du Bois, who served as easy targets for Cold War censorship, *The First Book of Negroes* embraces the same ideas Hughes professed in his trial.[7] The book's treatment of "the profitable business" of slavery—a topic that had long challenged Black writers when writing for children—offers a powerful critique of the collusion between race and capitalism, as well as a celebration of the aesthetic traditions slavery helped to birth. "Not only did slaves work the fields," Hughes writes, "but some became fine builders, brick masons, carpenters, and iron smiths," creators of the distinctive ironwork of New Orleans and Charleston and of slave songs alike. The Ethiopians and Egyptians of whom Terry's grandmother tells him stories were great artisans and craftspeople. According to her, because Europeans were "more interested in conquering people than teaching them," Africans still had not learned "to build factories or make gunpowder," and instead called on the great traditions of "civilization" that were integral to the African past.[8] Throughout the book, Hughes offers a compelling narrative of Black people who served as aesthetic, cultural, and scientific contributors of a wide range, despite or because of racial oppression.

In *The First Book*, Hughes's Terry Lane embodies African diasporic history, and Harlem appears as the prime ground from which to narrate African and African American history.[9] Terry Lane's Harlem is a place that many children in the United States would have found appealing. From early in the book, readers learn that it is the home of famous Black Americans such as Joe Louis and Duke Ellington. It is multicultural and multilingual; in stark contrast to the school his cousin Charlene attends in Alabama, Terry's classmates, like his teachers, are both white and "brown as Terry." Some of his classmates are Puerto Rican and "just learning English," but "all of these children are good friends, learning and playing together."[10] In this sometimes idealized description of Harlem, Hughes corrects absences and silences in historical understanding and counters one-sided or pathologizing depictions of contemporary urban Black life.

Critical response to the book was divided ideologically, which was typical for Hughes's work in this period. *The Crisis* deemed that Hughes's "presentation of his materials elicits pride and admiration. He is successful in his attempts to subtly but carefully counteract the usual stereotypes about Negroes and to integrate their lives with those of Americans of other races and nationalities." Referring both to the book's treatment of the past and its criticisms of Jim Crow, the *Journal of Negro Education* proclaimed that "one reads between the lines of this new book that not all is sweetness and light and that the need for a new earth and new heaven grows increasingly insistent." Yet still, the reviewer continued, the book served to balance Hughes's "obviously overdrawn pictures of the goings on in the Negro ghetto" in some of his other recent works, including *Simple Speaks His Mind* and *Montage of a Dream Deferred*. In contrast, the *New York Times* found the biographical descriptions too brief and the "space given to the regional treatment of the Negro a little out of proportion."[11] These reviews offer some perspective into what critics recognized (or failed to recognize) as the project of *The First Book of Negroes*, including Hughes's adoption of the juvenile biography genre to tell a history of accomplishment as well as racial oppression for children. This was no simple feat within a Cold War culture that frequently limited young readers' access to authentic stories about Black life. To understand one's own time, Hughes argued, is to understand the past. To be a boy like Terry, living happily and comfortably in Harlem, is to be the son of a multilingualist, the great-grandson of a slave, and a descendant of a regal heritage at once. In his highlighting of Harlem as both an actual place and an ideal to be sought, Hughes used *The First Book of Negroes* to provide readers with a new vision of Black identity and social politics. It was a vision grounded in political beliefs he had developed since his early days as a Renaissance writer and now translated into a genre for the people he saw as the most vulnerable in the face of racial oppression, and thus most in need of nuanced and humane accounts of Black experience and accomplishment: children.

Black Identity, Black Art, and Books

In his 1926 seminal essay, "The Negro Artist and the Racial Mountain," Hughes lodged what amounted to a thinly veiled critique of some of his Harlem Renaissance colleagues. Writing about Countee Cullen, whom he identifies only as a "young Negro poet," Hughes set out what he saw as the responsibilities of the Black artist. Paraphrasing Cullen in the *Brooklyn Eagle* two years before, Hughes criticized Cullen's claim that he "want[ed] to be a poet—not a Negro poet," and chastised his friend for fueling "an urge within the race toward whiteness."[12] Cullen was symbolic to Hughes of the Black middle class more broadly, which he described as "people who are by no means rich yet never uncomfortable nor hungry—smug, contented, respectable folk, members of the Baptist church." The children of Harlem's elite, he wrote, "go to a mixed school. In the home they read white papers and magazines. . . . The whisper of 'I want to be white' runs silently through their minds." The essay, published in the *Nation*, constitutes one of the Renaissance's most powerfully rendered arguments for the idea that there must be something authentically "Black" about Black literature. For Hughes, the source of this art was found in the aesthetics of the Black working class: jazz, the blues, dance, and the call and response traditions of the Black church. Overlooked by many in the larger mission of his essay, however, is another important claim: that the cultural curriculum of the middle-class home and the cultural curriculum of the school reinforced each other. By 1926, as historians including Thomas Harbison have shown, "mixed" public schools were becoming increasingly rare in Harlem.[13]

Most Harlem students attended schools that were exclusively Black. Nonetheless they, like their wealthier peers who may have attended school alongside white students, often encountered powerful lessons in whiteness as "a symbol of all virtues" through the texts they were assigned to read.[14]

Throughout his life Hughes contemplated the role that schools played in cultural transmission and in how they shaped—or failed to shape—a sense of cultural identity and pride. A year before he published *The First Book of Negroes*, he wrote his famous 1951 poem "Theme for English B." The narrator of the poem is a twenty two-year-old Black southerner who boards at the Harlem YMCA and attends "college on the hill above Harlem," the only Black student in his class. He is asked by his white instructor to "go home and write / a page tonight / And let that page come out of you—/ Then, it will be true." Hughes wonders "if it's that simple" and the poem becomes a meditation on race and authenticity. The poem's first stanza tells us that as a child the narrator attended Jim Crow schools first in Winston-Salem and then Durham; now a student at City College of New York, he believes "I'm what / I feel and see and hear, Harlem, I hear you." In contrast to the poet of "The Negro Artist and the Racial Mountain," the narrator here creates a theme that "[is] not white" and does not try to be. One implication, particularly when compared with Hughes's earlier essay, is that the student is successful because he has been taught to "work, read, learn, and understand life" in segregated southern schools and in the streets of Harlem. But could students receive such an education in northern schools, where the great majority of Black children's teachers were white and racist?[15] The question of how to teach self-possession to Black youth appears across a wide span of Hughes's work, from his turgid and didactic 1933 poem "Letter to the Academy" (in which he challenged "all you gentlemen who . . . are now old . . . come forward and speak upon / The subject of Revolution . . . I mean the gentlemen who wrote lovely books . . . that sold in the hundreds of thousands and are studied in the high school"); to his regular column in the *Chicago Defender*, where he exposed the lack of diversity in textbooks; to essays like "Books and the Negro Child," in which he argued that to make Black children "feel that they will be men and women, not 'just niggers,' is a none too easy problem when textbooks are all written from a white standpoint."[16]

In his interest in textbooks, Hughes echoed a major undercurrent in Harlem education politics and, more specifically, the political activism of Black parents and radical educators. Wartime patriotism and the popularity of interculturalism, coupled with ongoing school inequities, focused both groups' attention on what students read in school. Beginning in the 1940s, Harlem parents worked with and independently of teachers to survey the content of textbooks. Mother Enid Tyler struck much the same chord as Hughes when she testified before the Board of Education (BOE) in 1950, "When I look into textbooks, the manner in which the Negro has been portrayed is that of an inferior personality."[17] Working at the famed Schomburg library on 135th Street, Augusta Baker supported parents and pressed for better inclusion of Black authors' work in the curriculum, calling on many of the arguments about Black representation from the Harlem Renaissance and imbuing them with a wartime flavor. In her 1945 article, "The Negro in Literature," she explained that "books play an important part in combatting or fostering racial prejudice, and no one working with books and children will deny the powerful influence of the printed word on them. . . . The time has come to . . . show the Negro in his true light—giving freely of his gifts and asking for nothing in return except a chance to live harmoniously and decently with others."[18] From books, Baker argued, children, Black and white alike, stood to learn courage and the skills of citizenship.

Although Black parents pressed on the BOE to address racist texts, teachers were often in a better position to enact change, both through the selections they made for their students and through political action. Few white teachers seemed concerned about the issue, but the Teachers Union of New York City, the more radical and leftist of the city's two teachers unions in the period (as discussed in chapter 6 of this volume), represented an exception. The Teachers Union began publishing Negro History Week supplements to their union's newspaper during the 1930s. These nationally recognized supplements contained Black history quizzes, literary excerpts by notable Black writers, including Hughes, and bibliographies. The Teachers Union's Harlem Committee had served as the political backbone of the entire union since its inception in 1936, and its unique commitment to Black achievement and Black representation in the curriculum was important but hardly mainstream. Hughes corresponded with the Teachers Union and spoke at their conferences through the 1950s, and he was likely aware of the Teachers Union's 1950 booklet *Bias and Prejudice in the Textbooks of the Schools of New York*, a publication that was the cornerstone of their work on textbooks and was written under the direction of Norman London, a teacher at James Fenimore Cooper Junior High School (JHS)

120 in Central Harlem, where Hughes had visited more than once. The booklet, reported on in the local Black press and disseminated by the Teachers Union to every teacher in the city, identified "approved poison" in Board of Education–sanctioned textbooks such as *Our America*, a book adopted for the fourth through six grades that claimed, "It is true that most slaves were happy. They did not want to be free," and *The Treasure Chest of Literature*, an anthology edited by two New York City school principals that included passages such as this: "The degradation and suffering of the old leaders of the South was pitiful. Deprived of their homes, bankrupt, and terrorized by the Negroes and 'carpet-baggers,' they finally organized the Ku Klux Klan which, although wrong in principle, gave them some relief from their sufferings."[19] Across grade levels and academic subject areas, the Harlem Committee's research persuasively showed, New York City children were presented with racist portrayals of Black Americans and minimized accounts of white racism. Perhaps students at JHS 120 also protested these texts, like they did racist advertising and media, as discussed in chapter 4 of this volume.

The committee reserved particular criticism, however, for the New York City school superintendent William Jansen, author of the widely-adopted geography textbook, *Distant Lands*. The Teachers Union exposed Jansen's racist beliefs about Black Africans and white colonialism, echoing critiques that Hughes had made earlier of geography textbooks' depiction of "African natives as bushy headed savages with no culture of their own."[20] And without offering any specific figures, they also exposed the ways in which Jansen profited financially from these beliefs by requiring or encouraging the book's use in schools. The sophisticated attention the Unionists afforded to Jansen's work highlighted the ways in which racism and racial inequities in New York City schools were not, as school administrators often contended, produced by political factors that were out of their control but rather were a product of their own failings and their willingness to profit, financially and otherwise, from the marginalization of students of color. In retribution for the Teachers Union's work on this one publication, the Board of Education effectively dismantled it by targeting involved teachers. In 1950, the year *Bias and Prejudice* was published, eight Teachers Union members were suspended by the Board of Education for reasons that they saw as directly connected to their work on race and equity in the city's schools. "Our children's minds are poisoned by race hate in school books," a Teachers Union flyer announced in prominent lettering. It named as one

of the eight Alice Citron, a veteran teacher with nineteen years of experience, who taught the subject of "Negro History and Achievement" to her
students.[21] Because of the risk Teachers Unionists posed in empowering
the activism and claims of Harlem parents through *Race and Bias* and other
means, approximately four hundred Teachers Union members were suspended or forced to resign by the end of the decade. The BOE's censure of
the Teachers Union, as well as additional waves of teacher firings as Cold
War anticommunism grew in power, weakened an antiracist vision of
unionism, as Clarence Taylor explores in chapter 6 of this volume, and left
parents and community members to protest racism without teachers as
strong allies.

The production of *Race and Bias* itself had a far greater effect on the
union—and Harlem schools—than it did on the curriculum. Text adoption
in New York City in the 1950s, despite a highly bureaucratized system, was
a politically inconsistent process of contestation between multiple, competing ideologies. Hughes's novel *Not Without Laughter* appeared on a 1958
list of recommended readings by and about "American Negros" for a
district-mandated eleventh-grade unit on "The Individual and the American Heritage," but there is little evidence that teachers were encouraged
to teach Black literature outside of units focusing on multiculturalism or
in other grades.[22] In fact, a great deal of racist literature remained in the
curriculum and in the schools. In 1960, for example, a BOE committee
unanimously approved the inclusion of the ten-volume set of children's
literature *Through Golden Windows* in school libraries, including the volume that contained "Little Black Sambo," which was praised for its "historical as well as aesthetic value." By contrast, committee members protested Astrid Lindgren's *Sia Lives on Kilimanjaro* on the grounds that "while
the photographs are beautiful . . . there seems to be no justification for the
children's disobedience to their parents."[23] As these examples show, race
representation competed with a Cold War reverence for authority and suppression of dissent—as well as a host of other factors—as city administrators made decisions about texts.

When New York education officials did assign texts that included Black
Americans, the images students encountered were often deeply problematic, particularly in the history and social studies curriculum. Importantly,
students read virtually no original writing by Black authors and instead
were assigned white authors' representations and stereotypes. A survey
of social studies texts in use in the New York City schools from 1950 to

1960 revealed that of the books' combined 183 depictions of Black men, 164 portrayed them as farmers or laborers, as opposed to professionals or sports, arts, or entertainment figures. Of the 45 portrayals of Black women, 36 were as laborers or domestics.[24]

The First Book of Negroes offered a portrait of Black Americans that radically differed from depictions in the books that New York City and other northern children encountered in their social studies readings; southern children, due to the region's politics and textbook adoption policies, most often encountered none at all. Importantly, Helen Hoke Watts, who oversaw the production of *The First Book of Negroes* for Franklin Watts publishers, instructed Hughes not to worry about the southern book market. "We have no hopes of it anyhow, except for the enlightened," she wrote, and left Hughes to appease northern antileftists.[25] In addition to his publisher's political support, the genre of the Black biography offered Hughes an advantage in creating a book that would "effect social change" by documenting Black achievement and contribution, as he hoped *The First Book* would.[26] Its elementary grade-level intended audience reflected his longstanding commitment to and concern for young children, who may yet have received fewer damaging messages about the desire to be white. Moreover, as Julia Mickenberg has illustrated, the genre of the Black juvenile biography allowed writers to teach "children African American history in a way that implicitly challenged postwar racial hierarchies, communicated radical ideas about citizenship, and made a direct connection between past struggles against slavery and present struggles for civil rights" all in the guise of biographical stories.[27] Hughes's representations of Africa in the book, a striking contrast to the arguments made by Jansen and others, offer one clear example of how this worked.

In his early work, Hughes had often conceived of Africa, as did other Renaissance writers, as a symbolic motherland and a metaphor for the "otherness" of Black Americans (see the poems "Negro" and "The Negro Speaks of Rivers"). In *The First Book of Negroes*, by contrast, Hughes is more interested in African resistance to European colonialism, symbolized in the African rejection of technologies of conquest, including factories and guns. His stories of the University of Sankore in Timbuktu and of Ethiopian society pre-Christ offer more than simple historic lineages for African Americans (in fact they appear halfway through the book); they offer an argument about the importance of African independence and the flourishing of African civilization before European colonization. These arguments, made explicit in other of Hughes's work of the period, as well as his travel to and relationship with Africa and African artists, are embedded throughout *The First Book of Negroes*.[28] They demonstrate how Hughes shared interests with Harlem-based intellectuals who had long looked to Africa for a historical and aesthetic foundation beyond the confines of U.S. racism and with U.S.-based activists attuned to growing anticolonial movements on the continent.

Since the *First Book* was a trade book that read like a social studies text, rather than a textbook by one of the larger publishing houses that produced many of the books taught in the city schools, its best chance stood in its being adopted by school librarians, who were often more progressive and took a greater leadership role than teachers in pushing for text diversity (in this light, it is of little surprise that Hughes thanked the influential Chicago librarian Charlemae Rollins and included a brief sketch of her in *The First Book of Negroes*).[29] Then, teachers could read or assign the book to their classes. In the decade following the book's publication, letters that Hughes received from students prove that this happened with frequency. Fourth-grader Emily Elefant wrote to Hughes to tell him that her teacher assigned her to read *The First Book* after she gave a report on Harriet Tubman for her class; Elefant confided, "I am glad she did because this way I learned about great American Negroes in our time."[30] At Public School (PS) 29 in Queens, a fourth-grade class wrote to Hughes to let him know that they used the *First Book* as their source text for a play they wrote for Negro History Week.[31] After Hughes spoke about the *First Book* at PS 184 in Harlem in January 1953, many fifth-grade students wrote to him to tell him that they and their class were saving their money to buy the book for their school library and for themselves.[32]

Simultaneously, Hughes's other works were taught across grade levels and to older students in Harlem and elsewhere in the city. One Harlem junior high school teacher sent Hughes her students' writing in response to a column he wrote in the *New York Post*, "Fray or Pray?" Most of the students argued for fighting. Seventh-grader Joyce Rembert wrote, "I would go with flay [*sic*] because if they, the white people fight us, we can fight them back too. . . . We could picket stores and get dogs of our own. Build our own stores, schools."[33] "I say violence because I do not believe in a person or persons who believe in no non-violence," classmate Mary Smallwood concurred, "because in someway [*sic*] or other you have to take up for yourself."[34] "The world doesn't belong to the white man," wrote yet another student. "If we had colored executives maybe some people would have more faith in them and they will have more faith in themselves."[35] According to Harlem students, their self-image was vastly different and more civil rights–focused than it was when Hughes wrote "The Negro Artist and the Racial Mountain" nearly forty years earlier. And Hughes's own writing, he was delighted to see, played no small part in bringing about the change. "I found the resulting student essays most intriguing . . . and I must admit that I sometime feel that a little fraying might make the speed of desegregation less deliberate," Hughes wrote to teacher Nancy Bowe.[36] By the 1960s, Hughes was frequently included in Negro History Week performances and was treated, like Dr. Martin Luther King, as a symbol of brotherhood and tolerance.[37]

Time and again, teachers and students who thought of themselves as "brotherhood conscious" saw Hughes, despite his alleged communist affiliations, as one of their best role models. Often this impulse, as was also the case for King, required teachers to sanitize and depoliticize Hughes's ideas to a certain extent and reify some works while ignoring his more provocative and critical essays, poems, and other writings. But correspondence between Hughes and students shows that teachers asked their classes to read a broader range of his works than those often canonized in the elementary and secondary curriculum today. Teachers' desire—if not that of the textbook adoption committees—to make Hughes a part of their literary education certainly stemmed from his deep and residing confidence in the capacity of Black Americans and in his larger sense of concern for children, a group to whom many writers of Hughes's stature gave little attention.

Harlem and Its Publics

From his Harlem apartment window, Terry can see City College and the Empire State Building. The A-train takes him to Broadway or Radio City, or ice skating at Rockefeller Center. What might have appeared to be a seemingly simple detail to many readers was, in fact, an important point for Hughes to highlight. As a young man, he explained in a 1963 essay, he believed that Harlem was "a world unto itself." But he soon learned that "it was seemingly impossible for Black Harlem to live without a white downtown. My youthful illusion . . . did not last very long. [Harlem] was not even an area that ran itself."[38] Hughes's seemingly rosy version of Harlem in

The First Book of Negroes inverted many people's assumptions about it; it is not just white people who patronize Harlem but Harlemites who were at home in the rest of the city. Terry's father translates at the United Nations or Terry and his cousin visit the Statue of Liberty. Implicitly, *The First Book of Negroes* points to the ways in which Harlem and Harlem residents were intrinsically linked to the rest of Manhattan, often through their labor or art. Terry's neighborhood is a place where "different people get along all right," an ideal that Hughes never abandoned.[39] It is no small coincidence that Terry lives on Convent Avenue, a "nice tree-lined street" that Hughes once disparaged as a place where "even though you're colored, it would never occur to you to riot and break windows."[40] In contrast to the children of "The Negro Artist and the Racial Mountain," Terry belongs to the Black middle class, but without compromising a sense of self-identity and respect.

Hughes's decision to figure Harlem as a place of thriving cosmopolitanism stands as both his statement on an ideal race politics and a response to his own role in making Harlem a place both symbolic and real for Americans Black and otherwise. That children across the nation, including many who had never traveled to New York, would have recognized Harlem as an epicenter of Black life was due largely to the aesthetic corpus and accomplishments of Renaissance-Era artists of all types, including Hughes. Yet by the 1950s, the incipient suburbanization of New York's Black cultural, intellectual, and financial elite was under way. Harlem no longer served as the physical home for most Black artists, even as it continued to serve as a setting for some of the decade's most important Black-authored texts, including James Baldwin's *Go Tell It on the Mountain* (1953) and Ralph Ellison's *Invisible Man* (1952).[41] Hughes's lifelong commitment to residing in Harlem, like his faith in racial diversity and multiculturalism, was seen by some Black artists whom he had once mentored, including Baldwin, as out of vogue. But for Hughes, to leave Harlem for somewhere more avantgarde, in New York or abroad, would also have meant abandoning the decades of work and relationships he had established there, including his own personal history. Like Hughes, Terry Lane could also have lived elsewhere. Hughes's decision to present a happy child from Harlem against the history of Black America captured his very argument that Black achievement was compatible with a deep sense of history, identity, and place. Owning and telling this history, in literature and in lore, was key to the process.

At the same time, Hughes feared the Harlem Renaissance had failed to cultivate what he would describe in 1930 to Walter White, executive secretary of the National Association for the Advancement of Colored People, as "an interest in racial expression through books" for many Americans. He believed that much of its literature (if not his own) had neglected the concerns of working-class Black people who faced more imminent problems and held more pragmatic concerns than questions of art and representation. In response, backed by the Rosenwald Fund, Hughes toured the South in the 1930s to introduce, promote, and ultimately sell his work and to build what he called "a black public."[42] For Hughes, these tours were important not only for bringing literature to the masses, but for doing so on his own terms, unmediated by white publishers or philanthropists who might "giv[e] a million dollars to a Jim Crow school, but not one job to a graduate of that school."[43] Hughes would speak out about the publication of literature that addressed the "race problem" for the rest of his life, precisely because he saw its importance to societal enlightenment and true Black advancement. At times, he feared that his efforts to create a Black reading public had failed. In 1954, he wrote to his Renaissance colleague and ongoing friend and collaborator Arna Bontemps: "Negro professional folks are building 80 and 100 thousand dollar homes in suburbs, with landscape lawns and swimming pools. We're rising!" he contended. "And they have practically NO books to go with the rest of the furnishings."[44] And yet Hughes never gave up on his convictions, nor his experimentation with "book caravans" as a means to sell his work, including in schools.

Schools and teacher networks played an especially important role in Hughes's conception of how to promote and disseminate his work. When developing a plan for promoting *The First Book of Negroes*, Hughes sent to the publisher Helen Hoke Watts a list of Black librarians and teachers whom he considered "especially active in racial and intercultural fields." He encouraged Watts to send promotional materials to them; many of the teachers worked in Harlem schools where the Teachers Union's Harlem Committee had been particularly active.[45] In his letters to Arna Bontemps, Hughes charted his success in selling *The First Book of Negroes* through his relationship with teacher groups and PTAs.[46] He maintained contact with some Teachers Unionists and other progressive teachers and visited their schools when he could. Listening to Hughes read his work, reported a ninth-grade student from Harlem's J.H.S. 136, was "as if he were talking and telling his listeners all about his troubles and personal affairs . . . his experiences seem very familiar and interesting to us."[47] Both teachers and students praised Hughes for the readings and talks he gave, lauding particularly his accessibility, approachability, and interest in students. More than seeing this work as a simple financial necessity, Hughes appears to have enjoyed developing a relationship with his audience and was particularly kind and attentive to his juvenile readers. With great regularity, he responded to letters children wrote to him, particularly when they did so of their own accord rather than as part of a class assignment. Repeatedly, young people wrote to him with vague or repetitive questions about his life or about how to become a writer, yet he responded to them at length, personally and individually. Often he included a book with his letters, in an act of what seems to be both simple generosity and another means by which to build a reading public.

At the heart of the Harlem Renaissance a belief had existed among its members that images mattered and that changing the cultural images of Black Americans and creating what Hughes termed in "The Negro Artist and the Racial Mountain" as "racial art" could lead to society's changed treatment of them. For children, he argued, these images took on particular import. When students only saw in their civics textbooks "Negro neighborhoods as the worst quarters in our cities" and in their history texts "the backwardness of the South but none of its amazing progress in only three score years of freedom," both white and Black people believed that the images represented blanket fact.[48] What Hughes sold in his books written for young writers was an image of Black Americans—young and old, renowned and ordinary—as talented, high achieving, and vital contributors to American culture. Predominant sociological and cultural arguments of the 1950s held that Black children possessed "damaged psyches" from economic and social isolation; these arguments were employed more than they were challenged by civil rights campaigns, most especially in the 1954 *Brown v. Board of Education* case. By contrast, in characters such as Terry Lane, whose life was far from typical for most children growing up in Harlem, readers met a boy who is happy, successful, and aspiring, despite living in a city where "colored people find it difficult to rent a house except in streets where Negroes live." His cousin Charlene, who grew up in Jim Crow southern schools, is valued for "know[ing] a great many things that [Terry] did not know," including many of the most important skills required in rural living.[49] Children in *The First Book of Negroes* are both shaped by and come to terms with race politics at once, much as Hughes wanted for the readers of the book. It can be easy to dismiss the political importance of these messages over sixty years later, or to see the book as simply an idealistic portrait Hughes created because of the age of his audience. To do so, however, is to misread the importance of the *The First Book of Negroes* as well as its continually adaptive writer, who sought to bring central, long-developing principles of political rights and aesthetic representation to some of the nation's youngest and most impressionable citizens.

Notes

1. Langston Hughes, *The First Book of Negroes* (New York: Franklin Watts, 1952), 18.
2. Hughes, *First Book of Negroes*, 40.
3. Hughes's ideas for *Famous American Negroes* series came under much greater revision and censoring from Dodd, Mead than did his work for *The First Book of Negroes*, which is the reason that it is not a subject of this essay. See Arnold Rampersad, *The Life of Langston Hughes*, vol. 2 (New York: Oxford University Press, 1988), 229–30.
4. For a broader look at Hughes's literature for children, see Katherine Capshaw Smith, *Children's Literature of the Harlem Renaissance* (Bloomington: University of Indiana Press, 2004); Gizelle Liza Anatol, "Langston Hughes and the Children's Literary Tradition," in *Montage of a Dream: The Art and Life of Langston Hughes*, ed. John Edgar Tidwell and Cheryl R. Ragar (Columbia: University of Missouri Press, 2007), 237–58; Dianne Johnson, *Telling Tales: The Pedagogy and Promise of African American Literature for Youth* (New York: Greenwood Press, 1990); and Langston Hughes, *Collected Works for Children and Young Adults (The Collected Works of Langston Hughes, v. 12)*, ed. Steven C. Tracy (Columbia: University of Missouri Press, 2001).
5. Langston Hughes, "Books and the Negro Child," *Children's Library Yearbook*, vol. 4 (Chicago: American Library Association), 108–10.
6. Testimony of Langston Hughes, before the Senate Permanent Subcommittee on Investigations of the Committee on Government Operations, Tuesday, March 24, 1953. For more on the effect of red baiting on intellectuals and artists, see, for example, Ellen Schrecker, *Many Are the Crimes* (Princeton, N.J.: Princeton University Press, 1999); Martha Biondi, *To Stand and Fight: The Struggle for Civil Rights in Postwar New York City* (Cambridge, Mass.: Harvard University Press, 2006); and Gerald Horne, *Black Liberation/Red Scare: Ben Davis and the Communist Party* (Newark: University of Delaware Press, 1994).
7. Although no known records exist proving that Hughes was specifically pressured to omit these figures, he later regretted that "it was impossible at that time to get anything into children's books about either Dr. DuBois or Paul Robeson." See Langston Hughes to William G. Horne, October 25, 1965, folder 1225, box 213, Langston Hughes Papers, James Weldon Johnson Collection in the Yale Collection of American Literature, Beinecke Rare Book and Manuscript Library, Yale University (hereafter LHP).
8. Hughes, *First Book of Negroes*, 12–13, 25. In contrast to the support Franklin Watts showed to Hughes, Henry Holt publishers fired every editor who worked with Hughes on his *Montage of a Dream Deferred* (1952) and *Laughing to Keep from Crying* (1952) in response to the trial. Rampersad chronicles this and the financial pressures Hughes was under when he signed on to write *The First Book of Negroes*; see Rampersad, *Life of Langston Hughes*, 189–230.

9. In contrast to many of Hughes's other writings, *The First Book of Negroes* marked an important contribution to the social studies (rather than literature or reading) curriculum. The scholarship on the teaching of Black history and African American contributions to social studies education is extensive, but for an understanding of developments predating *The First Book of Negroes*, see Clare Corbould, *Becoming African Americans: Black Public Life in Harlem, 1919–1939* (Cambridge, Mass.: Harvard University Press, 2009); Pero G. Dagbovie, *African American History Reconsidered* (Urbana: University of Illinois Press, 2010); Jonathan Zimmerman, *Whose America? Culture Wars in the Public Schools* (Cambridge, Mass.: Harvard University Press, 2002); LaGarrett J. King, "When Lions Write History: Black History Textbooks, African American Educators and the Alternative Black Curriculum, 1890–1940," *Multicultural Education* 22, no. 4 (Fall 2014): 2–11; Jarvis Ray Givens, "'He was, undoubtedly, a wonderful character,' Black Teachers' Representations of Nat Turner During Jim Crow," *Souls* 18, no. 2 (October 2016): 215–34; James A. Banks, "African American Scholarship and the Evolution of Multicultural Education," *Journal of Negro Education* 61, no. 3 (Summer 1992): 273–86; and Jacqueline Goggin, *Carter G. Woodson: A Life in Black History* (Baton Rouge: Louisiana State University Press, 1993).

10. Hughes, *First Book of Negroes*, 18.

11. June Shagaloff, "Book Reviews," *Crisis*, January 1953, 61–63; John W. Parker, "A Book of Positive Faith in America," *Journal of Negro Education* 22 (Autumn 1953): 496–97; and "Terry's People," *New York Times Book Review*, November 16, 1952, 32.

12. Margaret Sperry, "Countee P. Cullen, Negro Boy Poet, Tells His Story," *Brooklyn Eagle*, February 10, 1924.

13. Davison M. Douglas, *Jim Crow Moves North: The Battle Over Northern School Segregation, 1865–1954* (New York: Cambridge University Press, 2005); David Ment, "Patterns of School Segregation, 1900–1930: A Comparative Study of New York City, New Rochelle, and New Haven," in *Schools in Cities: Consensus and Conflict in American Educational History*, ed. Ronald K. Goodenow and Diane Ravitch (New York: Holmes and Meier, 1983), 67–110, 72; Jonna Perrillo, *Uncivil Rights: Teachers, Unions, and Race in the Battle for School Equity* (Chicago: University of Chicago Press, 2012); and Mark Naison, *Communists in Harlem During the Depression* (Urbana: University of Illinois Press, 1983).

14. "The Negro Artist and the Racial Mountain," *The Nation*, June 23, 1926, 692–94.

15. On city teachers' racial attitudes, see Perrillo, *Uncivil Rights*; Zoe Burkholder, *Color in the Classroom: How American Schools Taught Race, 1900–1954* (New York: Oxford University Press, 2014); Clarence Taylor, *Reds at the Blackboard: Communism, Civil Rights, and the New York City Teachers Union* (New York: Columbia University Press, 2011); and Jennifer deForest, "Tilting at Windmills? Judge Justine Wise Polier and a History of Justice and Education in New York City," *History of Education Quarterly* 49, no. 1 (February 2009): 68–88.

16. "Books and the Negro Child," *Children's Library Yearbook*, vol. 4 (Chicago: American Library Association), 108–10.

17. "Address Made at the Meeting of the Board of Education on April 6, 1950, in Re Item #26, Banning Teachers Union," folder 13, box 2, Charles J. Bensley Papers, 1947–1954, Board of Education of the City of New York Collection (hereafter BOE).

18. Augusta Baker, "The Negro in Literature," *Child Study* 22 (Winter 1944–45): 58–63.

19. Quoted in Celia Zitron, *The New York City Teachers Union, 1916–1964* (New York: Humanities Press, 1968), 102–3.

20. See Hughes, "Books and the Negro Child."

21. "Our Children's Minds Are Poisoned by Race Hate in School Books" (flyer), May 19, 1950, folder 3, box 44, Papers of the Teachers Union of the City of New York,

1916–1964, Kheel Center for Labor-Management Documentation and Archives, Cornell University Library. On Citron, see also chapter 3 in this volume.

22. Teachers were instructed to teach with a focus on "American heritage" throughout the year, but they were not required to do so in a way that addressed or included race. Board of Education of the City of New York Bureau of Curriculum Research, *Reading List for the Theme Center on "The Individual and the American Heritage"* (New York: Board of Education, 1958), 49, folder 30, box 3, series 661, BOE.

23. Bureau of Libraries, Board of Education, "Sixth Supplement to Library Books for Elementary and JHS, 1960," January 1960, folder January 20, 1960, series 617, BOE.

24. Fred Turetsky, "The Treatment of Black Americans in Primary Grade Textbooks Used in New York City Elementary Schools," *Theory and Research in Social Education* 2 (December 1974): 25–50, 33–34.

25. Helen Hoke Watts to Langston Hughes, March 3, 1952, folder 1225, box 63, LHP. For a more extended analysis of Franklin Watts's decision to commission and publish *The First Book of Negroes*, and the publisher's relationship with Hughes and other leftist writers, see Julia L. Mickenberg, *Learning from the Left: Children's Literature, the Cold War, and Radical Politics in the United States* (New York: Oxford University Press, 2006), 151–58.

26. Quoted in Mickenberg, *Learning from the Left*, 157.

27. Julia Mickenberg, "Civil Rights, History, and the Left: Inventing the Juvenile Black Biography," *MELUS* 27 (Summer 2002): 65–93, 65.

28. For more on images of Africa in the work of Hughes and other Renaissance writers in the 1920s, see Corbould, *Becoming African American*; Jeff Westover, "Africa/America: Fragmentation and Diaspora in the Work of Langston Hughes," *Callaloo* 25, no. 4 (Autumn 2002): 1206–23; and David R. Jarraway, "Montage of Otherness Deferred: Dreaming Subjectivity in Langston Hughes," *American Literature* 68, no. 4 (December 1996): 819–47. For more on Hughes and anticolonialism in the 1950s and 1960s, see Daniel Won-gu Kim, "'We, Too, Rise with You': Recovering Langston Hughes's African (Re)Turn 1954–1960 in 'An African Treasury,' the 'Chicago Defender,' and 'Black Orpheus,'" *African American Review* 41, no. 3 (Fall 2007): 419–41.

29. For more on librarians and liberalism, see Louise S. Robbins, *Censorship and the American Library: The American Library Association's Response to Threats to Intellectual Freedom, 1939–69* (Westport, Conn.: Greenwood Press, 1996); Christine Jenkins, "International Harmony: Threat or Menace? U.S. Youth Services Librarians and Cold War Censorship, 1946–1955," *Librarians and Culture* 36, no. 1 (Winter 2001): 116–30; E. J. Josey, ed., *The Black Librarian in America* (Metuchen, N.J.: Scarecrow Press, 1970); and Sara L. Schwebel, *Child-Sized History: Fictions of the Past in U.S. Classrooms* (Nashville, Tenn.: Vanderbilt University Press, 2011).

30. Emily F. Elefant to Langston Hughes, January 22, 1964, folder 3586, box 212, LHP.

31. Michael Graham to Langston Hughes, February 17, 1965, folder 3672, box 219, LHP.

32. Shirley Givens to Langston Hughes, January 13, 1953; Irvins Maleare to Langston Hughes, January 13, 1953; and Mildred Clark to Langston Hughes, January 13, 1953, all in folder 3676, box 220, LHP.

33. Joyce Rembert, "Flay or Pray?" JHS 136, Class 7–4, November 16, 1962, folder 3671, box 219, LHP. The terminology in these letters is confusing because the teacher, students, and Hughes himself go back and forth between using "fray" and "flay." I have recorded all terms as they are found in the original documents.

34. Mary Smallwood, "Violence," JHS 136, Class 7–4, November 15, 1962, folder 3671, box 219, LHP.

35. Mildred D., "Flaying or Praying," JHS 136, Class 7–4, November 16, 1962, folder 3671, box 219, LHP.

36. Langston Hughes to Nanny Bowe, January 17, 1963, folder 3671, box 219, LHP.

37. See, for example, PS 53, "Brotherhood Is Everyday," February 1959, folder 3671, box 219, LHP; and PS 9, Brooklyn, "Negro History Week and Brotherhood Program," February 26, 1953, folder 3672, box 219, LHP.

38. Langston Hughes, "My Early Days in Harlem," *Freedomways* 3 (1963): 312–14.

39. Hughes, *First Book of Negroes*, 16, 18, 38.

40. Langston Hughes, "Down Under in Harlem," *New Republic*, March 27, 1944, 404–5.

41. For more on this, see James Smethurst, "'Don't Say Goodbye to the Porkpie Hat': Langston Hughes, the Left, and the Black Arts Movement," *Callaloo* 25, no. 4 (Autumn 2002): 1224, 1237, 1228.

42. Quoted in Arnold Rampersad, *I, Too, Sing America* (New York: Oxford University Press, 1986), 214. See also Rampersad's account of Mary McLeod Bethune's influence in convincing Hughes to conduct a reading tour, 211–14; and Langston Hughes, *I Wander as I Wander* (New York: Hill and Wang, 1993), 56–57.

43. Langston Hughes, "To Negro Writers," *American Writers' Congress*, ed. Henry Holt (New York: International Publishers, 1935), 139–41. For more on the relationship between Harlem Renaissance writers and publishers, see John K. Young, *Black Writers, White Publishers: Marketplace Politics in Twentieth-Century African American Literature* (Jackson: University Press of Mississippi, 2006); George Hutchinson, *The Harlem Renaissance in Black and White* (Cambridge, Mass.: Belknap Press of Harvard University Press, 1996); and Elizabeth Davey, "Building a Black Audience in the 1930s: Langston Hughes, Poetry Readings, and the Golden Stair Press," in *Print Culture in a Diverse America*, ed. James P. Danky and Wayne A. Wiegand (Chicago: University of Chicago Press, 1998), 223–43, 227.

44. Langston Hughes to Arna Bontemps, February 10, 1954, in *Arna Bontemps-Langston Hughes Letters, 1925–1967*, ed. Charles H. Nichols (New York: Dodd, Mead, 1980), 320.

45. Langston Hughes to Helen Hoke Watts, September 28, 1952, folder 1225, box 63, LHP.

46. Langston Hughes to Arna Bontemps, December 19, 1952; and Langston Hughes to Arna Bontemps, February 18, 1953, in Nichols, *Arna Bontemps-Langston Hughes Letters*, 299, 302–3.

47. Ivetty Santana, "With the Poets," *Views, Reviews, Interviews*, January 1956, folder 3676, box 220, LHP.

48. Hughes, "Books and the Negro Child."

49. Hughes, *First Book of Negroes*, 57, 53.

CHAPTER 6

Harlem Schools and the New York City Teachers Union

CLARENCE TAYLOR

M any parents in Harlem schools complained that teachers were indifferent to the children they taught. In 1949, a report examining a project to provide counseling to children in four schools in Harlem with high delinquency rates described teachers in those schools as punitive and unsympathetic to students. Forty percent of the teachers were labeled inexperienced and close to 50 percent were seen as indifferent to students.[1] Speaking before the Urban League in 1954, Kenneth Clark, a professor of psychology at City College, declared that the "average reading and math levels were two years behind grade level for those schools studied. In some classes there was no improvement in scores from the beginning to the end of the school year. Most teachers in Harlem schools were inexperienced and poorly supervised; there were 103 local classes for children with "retarded mental ability," in the lexicon of the time. However, only three schools had classes for "intellectually gifted children."

Clark believed that institutional racism was responsible for poor education in Harlem. "It is no longer necessary to have specific techniques for gerrymandering schools and excluding Negro children from academic and other specialized high schools. These children are not prepared to pass the tests for these academic and specialized high schools. This is a most effective form of racial exclusion" for Harlem's Black children, who had been born in the city, migrated from the South or immigrated from the West

Indies.[2] In the 1950s and 1960s, segregated Black schools "stood in marked contrast to those in white areas" of the city and the suburbs, as the historian Jerald Podair noted. They were "overcrowded, poorly maintained, and often staffed by teachers who had 'washed out' elsewhere in the system." Diminished material and human resources accompanied diminished expectations from many white teachers for their Black students. Many Black teachers were "angered by what they perceived as [white teachers'] matter-of-fact acceptance" of the then-ascendant culture-of-poverty thesis. Its adherents, following the anthropologist Oscar Lewis and later the sociologist Daniel Patrick Moynihan, conceived of poverty not as momentary or changeable material privation but as a cause of enduring changes that defined personality and ability across generations.[3] In schools, teachers could follow the culture-of-poverty logic to suggest that the fact of students' impoverishment indicated their current and future intellectual promise. Teachers "responded to this self-fulfilling prophecy with indifference and benign neglect."[4] Although Harlem had more Black teachers than did many parts of New York City, racist hiring practices limited their number sharply.[5] Recounting his experience as a child growing up in Harlem, the author James Baldwin wrote: "We hated many of our teachers at school because they so clearly despised us and treated us like dirty, ignorant savages."[6]

Some New York City teachers organized behind a different view of Harlem and other Black and Latinx communities. Before the Cold War and before the founding of today's United Federation of Teachers (UFT) and the recognition of its collective bargaining rights, the New York City Teachers Union (TU) was the largest teachers union in the city with six thousand members. The TU was founded in 1916 by social democrats who maintained that teachers should receive decent salaries and respect from administrators. It opposed loyalty oaths and called for academic freedom. After a few decades of internal debate about the focus and scope of its organizing, the TU identified with industrial unionism and called for organizing workers at all levels, including part-time and unemployed teachers, toward building a strong working class. This meant eliminating walls, such as racism, that divided the class. Thus, the TU led a major campaign to end institutional racism in the educational system, similar to what is known today as social-justice unionism. The union fought for higher wages and improved working conditions for its members, and also made social and racial justice for people of color in the city a central mission. Members of the

TU contended that structural factors robbed Black children of a decent education.

What distinguished the multiracial TU from other teachers unions and organizations was that it promoted a form of unionism that cultivated strong ties with parents, civil and religious organizations in Black and Latinx communities. The TU, parents, and community groups in Harlem fought together for better services to schools and students, new school buildings in communities where the oldest school buildings existed, and an elimination of racist and biased textbooks from schools. However, anticommunist repression during the Cold War helped marginalize the TU.

Over the 1950s, the rival Teachers Guild (the Guild) became the dominant teachers union in the city, and its approach to unionism differed from that of the TU. The Guild was founded in 1935 when seven hundred teachers left the TU because of the growing number of communists in its ranks. The Guild members asserted that the TU was pushing the agenda of the Communist Party of the United States of America, and it was not concerned with the interest of teachers. The Guild's major objective was to provide better pay, improved working conditions for teachers, and other benefits for its members. The Guild, unlike the TU, did not build strong alliances with parents of color and civic organizations in Harlem and other Black communities in New York.

Before a targeted anticommunist campaign by the New York City Board of Education helped dismantle the TU, the union forged a working alliance with parents in Harlem in search of a decent education for the children of that community. At a time when many Harlem teachers harbored racist ideas about their children, the TU had been an unusual activist presence. When it was dismantled, Harlem and New York City lost an important alliance between parents and teachers.

This chapter documents three episodes in the history of the TU, noting the way its type of unionism enabled it to forge a cooperative relationship between Black parents and teachers. The first incident, in the mid-1930s, involved a principal in Harlem who was accused of brutalizing a Black child. Although the TU joined with many in the Harlem community calling for the removal of the principal, the Guild came to his defense, thus opposing the community's effort to have a voice in determining who was appropriate to educate and supervise children of Harlem.

The second issue, emerging in the late 1930s and early 1940s, was juvenile delinquency and its roots in racial segregation and inequality. Several

Harlem-based advocacy groups were operating in the post–World War II landscape, targeting multiple forms of segregation in housing and employment.[7] In a similar vein, the TU accused the Board of Education of racial discrimination because it segregated Black and white children and discriminated when allocating resources and personnel. Meanwhile, the Guild downplayed racial discrimination and inequality as a major factor in student conduct. It blamed a deficient Black culture that needed rehabilitation. The TU sought to work with the Harlem and other predominantly African American and Latinx communities of the city to develop solutions that would tackle structural inequality, and the Guild called for tough punitive action against juveniles, more often restricting than supporting their access to schooling.

In the 1950s, after the TU's influence had waned, but as parent and community advocacy against segregation peaked, the integration of the teaching force became a third issue that often divided many in the Black community and teachers. After the Supreme Court handed down its *Brown v. Board of Education* decision, New York City activists placed greater pressure on the New York City Board of Education to integrate its student body and to provide equal resources and services to all children regardless of race. Parent activists understood unequal teacher qualifications along with substitute rather than permanently assigned teachers as manifestations of segregation in Harlem schools. When the Board of Education Commission on Integration recommended an involuntary transfer plan to bring more experienced teachers into communities of color, the Guild alienated Black and Latinx activists and parents by vigorously opposing the recommendation.

These three cases illustrate the nature of the TU's advocacy, the limits of the Guild's vision of teacher activism, and the displacement of the former by the latter by the 1960s. This transition helped form and nurture a feeling of resentment and distrust among African American and Latinx parents and activists against teachers long before the Black Power era or the headline-grabbing Ocean Hill-Brownsville conflict and teachers' strike of 1968.[8]

The Schoenchen Case

On October 21, 1936, fourteen-year-old Robert Shelton escorted his sister to her first grade class at Public School (PS) 5 on Edgecombe Avenue between 140th and 141st Streets. The historical record is not clear about the sequence of events but Shelton claimed that principal Gustav Schoenchen took him to his office and beat him across the head and arms with a stick. The Permanent Committee on Harlem Schools, made up of parents, activists, and members of the New York Teachers Union, called for the removal of the principal. Two physicians examined the fourteen-year-old and wrote in an affidavit that "there were contusions of the left forearm about the wrist and postero-laterally about three inches below the left elbow." Shelton also had contusions on his left shoulder and "traumatic injury to the muscles involving the area between the sixth and eighth ribs. . . ." There were injuries on his scalp, "one and a quarter inches long in [the] left frontal region."[9]

Schoenchen had a reputation for being hostile and insulting to parents who attempted to talk with him about problems with their children. The PS 5 Parent-Teacher Association also accused him of interfering in its activity. As a result of Shelton's injuries and complaints from parents, the TU passed a resolution calling on the Board of Education to "investigate thoroughly the charges against Mr. Schoenchen" and to discharge him as principal.[10]

The New York Teachers Guild was critical of both the TU and Harlem activists. The Schoenchen case, the Guild contended, demonstrated how communists manipulated racial tension for their own benefit. It accused the TU of "promoting a highly prejudiced handling" of the case. It blamed the so-called Committee for Better Schools in Harlem (which counted powerful figures like Ella Baker among its leaders) for circulating an "alleged" statement of facts that accused the principal of brutally beating Shelton. The committee "caused an 'emotional outburst' and a prejudging of the principal." In condescending and insulting language, the Guild claimed a crowd of "overwrought persons" at the trial helped to create the "impression that Principal Schoenchen was guilty."[11] The Guild ridiculed the committee for passing out leaflets calling for mass action and asserting that "Schoenchen Must Go." One handout even labeled Schoenchen a "savage child beater." The Guild questioned the severity of Shelton's injuries, noting that although photos showed him covered in bandages, "the boy was in bed only during the normal sleeping hours." Echoing the tactics of southern racists who blamed Jews and communists for Black protest and thus denied Black agency, the Guild declared that "demonstrations were conducted by white leaders with a following of Negro children from the school."[12]

Claiming that it held "no brief in support of a principal or teacher who used corporal punishment," the Guild did "hold a brief for the maintenance of the process of orderly inquiry into all charges before the courts as well as before the Board of Education." Accusing the Teachers Union of creating hostility between principals and teachers and promoting racial tension, the Guild called on its members to "guard against race riots, and against class war."[13] On the question of a New York City principals' treatment of a Black student, the Guild appeared to side with the school system.

The Guild's statements revealed its attitude toward Black communities, brushing off the grievances that Harlem addressed to school officials. That the Guild was silent about PS 5's Parent-Teacher Association's claim that the principal interfered with its functions indicated how far divorced the new union was from the Harlem community. Rather than explore complaints by parents, the Guild accused the TU of exploiting Black anger. The Guild's criticism of Black activists and their white allies demonstrated it had no interest in building strong ties with parents, working with them, and taking part in a movement that would empower them when confronting school officials.

The Teachers Union, unlike the Guild, connected the Schoenchen case to the socioeconomic conditions in Harlem. According to the TU, the case represented another, if dramatic, example of the systemic discriminatory treatment of Black people. Black children in Harlem were provided the poorest school facilities, their parents were relegated to the lowest-paying jobs and experienced the highest unemployment in the city. Prefiguring arguments that other New York City activists would make through the 1960s, the TU claimed that the "educational policies of New York City did not differ fundamentally from the Jim Crow practices in other parts of the country." The Teachers Union declared that the schools in Harlem were overcrowded and segregated, having a 90–100 percent Black and Latinx student body. Children were malnourished and came to school "in revolt against their unhappy lot and resentful to discipline." The curricula ignored the contribution African Americans made to the nation. In the view of the TU, these were the conditions that underlay protest against Schoenchen.[14]

Activists lodged their complaints in dramatic fashion, via a mock trial of the Board of Education staged at Harlem's Abyssinian Baptist Church in January 1937. Some of the nation's most prominent Black leaders played a major role; Abyssinian was one of the largest Black churches in New York City and one of the most important Black institutions in Harlem. The Reverend Adam Clayton Powell Jr., then the assistant pastor of Abyssinian before becoming its pastor in 1937, played the role of the judge. The jury featured an esteemed group of leaders: Charles Hamilton Houston, the dean of Howard University Law School; Frank Crosswaith, the onetime organizer of the Brotherhood of Sleeping Car Porters, the chair of the Negro Labor Committee, and a close ally of A. Philip Randolph; Lester Granger, the organizer of the Los Angeles branch of the National Urban League (and later the executive director of the organization nationally); and East Harlem's United States Congressman Vito Marcantonio. Two thousand people who attended the trial listened to condemnation of the Board of Education (BOE). The board was found guilty of not addressing the deteriorating conditions in Harlem schools.[15] The trial's location, its illustrious participants, as well as its large audience revealed the depth and breadth of frustration over education in Harlem, a frustration the TU sought to help address.

The Schoenchen incident and the responses it provoked highlight the differences between the Guild and the TU. The Guild's more cautious response demonstrated a concern for due process. But the union was also concerned about the role that parents and community leaders played in education. As its criticism of parents and civic leaders of Harlem hinted, the Guild opposed what it saw as the intrusion of parents into the professional realm of the education of their children, including monitoring the performance of teachers and administrators. When the TU and parents demanded that their children not be physically abused by school officials or denied a decent education, the Guild accused them of attacking a principal without evidence. For the Guild, protecting the principal was part of protecting the tenure of teachers against community action. If the Harlem community could have a principal fired, it could take the same action against teachers. The Teachers Union formed an alliance with parents and Harlem leaders in an effort to empower the community in addressing their concerns with the Board of Education, but the Guild and its successor the UFT did not foster such a relationship. The Guild repeatedly responded to Black community efforts to shape and improve the education of their children with concern for due process for teachers. This tension appeared in the mid-1930s, but recurred frequently through the late 1960s—when the tension between Black parents and predominantly white professional authority and union power boiled over in the Ocean Hill-Brownsville controversy and citywide teacher strike.

Rehabilitation of Black Children

One of the major problems plaguing Harlem was juvenile crime or misbehavior. After a fifteen-year-old white male was killed in Harlem by three Black teens in 1941, the white-owned press published a number of articles claiming that there was a crime wave in the predominantly Black Manhattan neighborhood.[16] Despite the sensationalism of the coverage and complaints from the Black press that its white counterparts were conducting a "crime smear" campaign, juvenile crime in Harlem was a reality. Although crime among juveniles throughout the city was increasing, in Harlem it was 50 percent higher in the post–World War II years.[17]

The Guild represented the problem as a matter of cultural deficiencies of African Americans and Latinxs. Calling the situation in Harlem an "abnormal one," the Guild claimed that it was "futile to expect the schools in those problem areas to function adequately by normal standards." The TU and the Guild diverged on their understanding of the origins of juvenile crime, particularly in relationship to segregation and the inequalities it accompanied and compounded.

Before 1954, the Guild did not focus on school segregation as a problem. Instead the union portrayed the children of Harlem, Bedford-Stuyvesant, and other communities of color as below par, in desperate need of social and psychological healing. The Guild did not point out that these students were denied essential services, given the least experienced teachers and denied a full day of instruction. Instead of stressing the lack of educational services the Guild argued that pathological conditions in the ghetto hindered children's learning. Hence, the answer, as the Guild saw it, was the need for special services and the modification of behavior on the part of children and adults of color.[18]

The Guild, like the TU, blamed juvenile crime on inadequate school financing, oversized classes, the war and its emphasis on brutality, and bad housing. The Guild did offer solutions to juvenile crime—often referred to as "juvenile delinquency" in Harlem. It called for reducing class sizes to twenty-five students, building new schools in ghetto areas, creating adult education classes, extending "child guidance and social services as an integral part of the schools," and offering industrial training in an effort to address job insecurity. It also urged the BOE to hire more teachers. The Guild's program emphasized a social contract that demanded state responsibility to fight against juvenile crime and called on the government to provide vital funding for education and job training.[19]

A report prepared in 1945 by the Guild's Committee on Delinquency was far reaching, but revealed a commitment to ideas of racial uplift, with education leading to mobility and individual opportunity. Broader structural or institutional change of the sort supported by the TU and particularly its leftist and communist members was not necessary. The Guild called for physical and dental inspections, adequate nutrition, and vocational training. Vocational training respected the bounds of a segregated labor market, focusing on the demands of "specialized groups" via classes for "Negro beauty culture," for example. The elimination of discrimination in the schools would lead to a "more cooperative attitude on the part of minority groups toward government, school, and society. Equality of opportunity in public education," the report maintained, "will encourage minority groups toward increased efficiency and will raise the compensation in unskilled trades by somewhat reducing the number of those seeking employment in these fields, thus raising the standard of living." The Committee on Delinquency argued that "well-adjusted family relations" were essential for preventing delinquency, but "only in a small proportion of our homes do these relations exist." Proposed solutions included a school curriculum dealing with family relations, vocational guidance, "physiology, personal hygiene, boy and girl relationships and community responsibility."[20] Elizabeth L. Danin, who was the chair of the Guild's Educational Policies in Wartime Committee, blamed juvenile crime on the negligence of city authorities, poor funding, crowded classrooms, and the war but she also claimed that "parental neglect" was a major cause.[21]

With its focus on what the Guild identified as the social pathology of the ghetto,[22] the union supported policies that would further segregation. The Committee on Delinquency called for immediate steps, including the segregation of troublesome students in special schools. It also sought to institutionalize teacher resistance to working in "underprivileged areas" and called for teachers so assigned to have "preferred status in obtaining transfers to vacancies in schools in other areas."

Some of the Guild's specific policy suggestions aligned with ideas furthered by the TU as well. But the two organizations were miles apart in their understandings of impoverished Black communities and their schools. The TU argued that the major problem was racial bigotry on the part of school officials; the solution included hiring additional African American and Latinx staff and integrating the student body as well as providing adequate services. The *New York Times* asserted in November 1941 that a "wave of terror" had hit Harlem, consisting of boys between the ages of twelve and sixteen."[23] In response to the problem, the police commissioner proposed more police be assigned to Harlem to reduce juvenile crime.[24] Citron declared that she had witnessed increasing rates of unemployment, the "most wretched of housing conditions," and thousands of mothers who were forced to work for low wages to supplement the family income. Refuting the Guild's implicit claim that Harlem parents were responsible for juvenile crime, Citron wrote that her "intimate contact with the people of Harlem," showed her "how deep and strong are the aspirations of Negro mothers and fathers for their children."[25] Rather than more police, Harlem needed a slum-clearing project, thousands of jobs for young people, and the enforcement of Roosevelt's executive order 8802 outlawing discrimination in industry.[26]

Citron also called on the school system to change its curriculum by adding a "full program of Negro history and culture." Like Citron, the TU contended that teaching Black history and culture was beneficial to Blacks and children of other races and ethnicities because it would make them aware of the role Black people played in building America. Such knowledge would challenge the racist notions that Black people were inferior to other groups.[27] Lucile Spence, one of the few African American teachers in the public school system and also a leading member of the TU, helped form the union's Harlem Teachers Committee. The Harlem Committee led a campaign to include "Negro History" as part of the schools' curricula. As described in chapters 4 and 5 of this volume, the Harlem Committee created and distributed to school teachers literature on the accomplishments of African Americans. Black history was seen as a way of uplifting Black students because it would challenge the racist distortions in textbooks that depicted Black people as inferior. The TU member Virginia L. Snitow, who taught in Harlem, claimed in an article she wrote for *The Nation* magazine, that her students came from maladjusted homes and extreme poverty. Despite their difficulties, Snitow maintained that "it is not money we lack, but honest understanding, courage and the will to wipe out an old evil." According to Snitow, "So simple a thing as introducing discussions of Richard Wright's *Native Son*, of important figures in Negro history and culture, of the Negro newspaper" and the *"People's Voice* [a Harlem Black weekly], produced a changed class."[28]

The TU did not want the teaching of Black history and culture to be limited to students. The Harlem Committee attempted to help teachers gain greater knowledge of the children they taught by providing educators an opportunity to study Black history and culture. Under Spence's leadership, the Harlem Committee created a number of in-service courses for teachers, including, The Contribution of the Negro People to American Civilization, the Negro in Early American History, the Negro in the Reconstruction Period, and the Negro in Literature, Art and Music. The goal of these and other in-service courses on Black history and culture was to furnish teachers with a better understanding of the social, economic, and political conditions of African Americans.[29]

Both the Guild and the TU called for changes in Harlem schools in response to popular concern over "juvenile delinquency." The TU took a more expansive and systematic understanding of the problem, however, but the Guild resorted to blaming Harlem families, echoing the developing "culture of poverty" view of Black children and urban communities.

Blackboard Jungle

After the 1954 *Brown v. Board of Education* decision finding school segregation unconstitutional, New York City activists highlighted segregation in many areas of the city's schools. One type of segregation emerged in teacher assignment. Unlike many other urban school systems that typically assigned larger populations of Black teachers to Black-majority schools, New York City continued to have a radically smaller proportion of Black teachers than Black students. Yet segregation appeared in a different form—with far fewer experienced and fully certified teachers assigned to Harlem schools than in other whiter neighborhoods in the city.

On this issue as in earlier cases, TU aligned itself with Harlem parent and community activists whereas the Guild alienated itself from those groups. The Guild had been outspoken on the issue of desegregation. In September 1954, the Guild president, Charles Cogen, pointed out that Richard Parrish, who was an African American and an executive board member of the Teachers Guild, helped bring forth the amicus curiae brief submitted by the American Federation of Teachers in support of the *Brown* desegregation case. Cogen contended that in "every area of living we need to overrule in practice every vestige of discrimination." He attempted to put the Guild's position on desegregation in a trade-union context claiming that the Guild proudly followed the leadership of its international, the American Federation of Labor (AFL). The AFL, immediately following the *Brown* decision, urged Congress to establish a billion-dollar fund to build new schools and hire teachers. For Cogen and the Guild, the Supreme Court's ruling in *Brown* meant that race was becoming less significant as a factor in hindering advancement. Reading *Brown* as a statement to the Cold War world was a "fitting reply to our totalitarian and fellow traveling critics."[30] Cogen drew on remarks by Buell G. Gallagher of City College in claiming that Blacks had advanced from bondage to first-class citizenship faster than any group in human history. Despite the Guild's rhetorical celebration of *Brown*, desegregation, and the growing civil rights campaigns in the South, the union became locked in a heated battle with community and civil rights organizations in New York City over its position on desegregating the city's teacher resources.

A few months after the *Brown* decision and after the City College professor Kenneth Clark's charge that the school system was racially segregated, the New York City Board of Education created a Commission on Integration and tasked it with deriving methods of promoting desegregation. The commission was divided into five subcommissions, including one examining the assignment of school personnel. On December 7, 1956, the Sub-Commission on Personnel and Assignments issued a report with sixteen recommendations, including providing schools with large proportions of Black and/or Puerto Rican students more supervisory personnel, relieving teachers of clerical and nonteaching duties, establishing smaller classes, modernizing school facilities, and improving the physical plant. These were largely uncontroversial, but one recommendation set off a firestorm as it sought to address the comparatively low levels of experienced and certified teachers in schools that served New York's African American students. Although the BOE's practice was to allow teachers to transfer to their choice of schools once they had achieved sufficient (usually only a few) years of seniority, the Sub-Commission called for more active and equity-minded teacher assignment. The BOE had the power to transfer teachers "when they are needed," and this power should be used to aid "improvement of teaching conditions in the difficult schools." "It may be difficult to get teachers' acceptance at first," the Sub-Commission recognized, but "it can and must be done."[31] To ensure that skilled teachers were present in schools that needed them, the Sub-Commission recommended that transfers begin in the fall of 1957 and be completed by September 1959. Although it suggested that a voluntary transfer list be created first, vacancies in the predominantly Black and/or Puerto Rican schools that the BOE referred to as "subject schools" should be filled with regular appointed teachers by "declaring in excess the number of teachers necessary to bring the school to the ratio established."[32]

The TU joined with parents in their support for the transfer plan, arguing that it was needed to overcome racial disparity in access to qualified teachers. The TU maintained that the major reason that children in Harlem and other Black and Latinx communities performed so poorly in the classroom is that they had so few experienced teachers.

The Guild, usually a vocal supporter of civil rights causes, opposed the plan as "forced transfers" that violated teachers' rights as professionals. It also opposed such a scheme because the involuntary transfers were based on the racial composition of the schools involved. Guild leaders contended that such race-conscious policy would undermine a merit-based system, a system it thought had been assured with the end of legal segregation after *Brown*. The scholar Daniel Perlstein notes that the Guild had an "ideological commitment to social democracy" and wanted to "extend America's political democracy to economic life." It believed that the trade union movement was the best means of gradually moving the United States to socialism without changing the political order. Once economic conditions improved, race would no longer be a factor in a more perfect meritocracy. Eventually, the logic suggested, "America might achieve a universally held culture, with universal standards of judgment, in which all would assimilate."[33]

The Guild had condemned and continued to condemn racial bigotry and celebrated the contributions of African Americans. By the early 1940s, the Guild was presenting strategies for addressing the needs of poor Black and Latinx children, strategies consistent with its social democratic ideals. However, it never condemned racism as an overarching reason for African American and Latinx inequality. It also did not contend that bad schools were the result of a flawed political system, or a problem of structural barriers. Instead, the union concerned itself with people unable to take advantage of meritocracy.[34] Thus, the solution, the Guild emphasized, was to help provide opportunities to the "disadvantaged" so they could take advantage of a political and economic system that had provided opportunities to others. Race-conscious teacher assignment seemed to threaten the Guild's hope for a race-blind meritocratic future.

The Guild campaigned against the teacher transfer plan, declaring, "Integration Yes! Forced Rotation No!" Cogen justified the Guild's opposition to involuntary transfers by claiming that such a plan would lead to a "transient teaching staff," lowering the quality of education and antagonizing the professional staff whose goodwill was essential for implementing integration. Cogen argued that "difficult schools" were not a "racial problem," but he quickly turned to blaming families and communities, as the Guild had done before. The children required more remedial and guidance services, not because of inadequate resources to African American, Afro-Caribbean, and Latinx neighborhoods, but because of "complex socio-economic causes."[35]

Cogen also shifted to criticizing schools in Harlem and other Black communities of the city as far too dangerous (presumably for his constituent teachers, rather than for children). Student behavior, "varying from child to child, run[s] the gamut from annoyances to serious crimes." In classrooms, children of color refuse to "stay in their seats, using obscene language toward the teacher and fellow pupils, ringing false fire alarms and in general refusing to obey the necessary rules and regulations of a school situation. Criminal behavior includes assaults, robbery, extortion, destruction of property, starting fires and other types of action which bear some similarity to the Blackboard Jungle."[36] Cogen was referring to a contemporary motion picture that portrayed the daily hardships in the classroom of a new teacher with his students from the inner city.

Civil rights and civic groups attacked the Guild's position. Edward Lewis, the executive director of the Urban League of Greater New York expressed "shock" at the Guild's opposition to placing more seasoned teachers to teach in Harlem and other predominantly African American and Latinx communities.[37] Speaking to four hundred people attending a conference of the United Neighborhood Houses, Lewis claimed that New York City teachers were involved in an organized campaign to avoid serving children of color. In what the *New York Times* reporter Murray Illson described as a "bitterly worded keynote speech," Lester Granger said, "One of the most disturbing symptoms that have recently appeared," among teachers, is their "organized and sanctioned effort" to avoid serving in predominantly African American and Latinx schools. The Intergroup Committee on New York City Public Schools, which represented twenty-six organizations, publicly denounced the Guild's and the High School Teachers Association's opposition to the transfer plan. One member of the Commission on Integration said that the teachers lacked courage. In a letter to the Board of Education president Charles Silver, the Intergroup Committee urged the board to implement the teacher transfer plan without delay. The Guild, which was part of the group, refused to sign the letter to Silver.[38] The president of the National Urban League, Granger, argued that it was more than a coincidence "that these difficult schools are almost invariably those with heavy concentrations of mainland and territorial children of dark complexion. Call them Negroes, or call them Puerto Rican, the schools that these children attend are those which too many school teachers seek to avoid—and their avoidance in far too many cases is viewed by their superintendents and principals with a tolerant eye."[39]

Cogen accused Granger of confusing dark-skinned children with difficult children, claiming that the problems of integration and difficult schools were two separate issues. Despite this defense, the Guild could not eradicate the perception that it cared more for its teachers than for the children of color they served. By focusing on children's "deficiencies," the Guild had failed to address the clearly discriminatory policy that had resulted in unequal teacher assignment. To make matters worse, years of stressing professionalism had left little or no room for parents to become partners with teachers in their children's education, and the union's unwillingness to work with community networks had only alienated it from those communities.[40]

Taking a view much more in line with the views of many Black parents in Harlem and elsewhere, Rose Russell, the legislative representative for the TU, criticized the Board of Education for not taking steps to prepare, educate, and encourage teachers to volunteer to transfer. In a letter to the editor of the *New York Times* on February 7, 1957, she argued that the board did not mention the improvements it planned to make in the schools or offer an incentive to teachers. She wrote, perhaps naively, that if the "Board discharges its responsibilities teachers will respond, for besides the fear of change there is also a feeling of unpreparedness for the problems to be faced." As had the Sub-Commission on Assignments and Personnel, Russell urged that transfers had to go hand in hand with a commitment to smaller classes, additional remedial and clerical assistance, and adequate supplies in the subject schools. Incentives for teachers should include "liberalized sabbatical leaves, credit towards salary increments and similar fringe benefits along with a program of reorientation and inter-group education." By listing all the corequisites for the transfer, Russell was attempting to placate teachers. Accusing them of being racist would only alienate them from the union. Russell hoped that with incentives enough teachers would volunteer so there would be no need for forced transfers.[41]

Teachers Union leaders knew that if there were any chance of getting teachers to support the plan, they could not afford to alienate them. On the other hand, the union wanted to maintain its commitment to the Black community. Union leaders claimed that principals had organized their faculties and PTAs to conduct a letter-writing campaign against the Sub-Commission's report. According to Lederman and Russell, it was not too late to undo the damage and they called on the Board of Education to explain the facts of its plan, stop principals from using scare tactics, create school and district conferences, and create a program of improvement and incentives to persuade teachers to transfer to "subject schools." At its February 20, 1957, meeting, the Executive Board of the TU voted to urge the Board of Education to institute reforms in the schools in African American and Latinx communities and call for volunteers to solve the staffing problem.[42]

Despite its optimistic statements about voluntary transfers, the TU knew that forced transfers would be necessary, a fact signaled when it publicly backed the Sub-Commission's recommendations.[43] On February 28, the Board of Education officially approved the Sub-Commission's plan and agreed to submit an estimation of implementation costs to the Board of Estimate. In a letter to the board president Charles Silver, the union asked that the school agency "lay the groundwork for a successful call for volunteers" by creating improvements in the schools, offering incentives for teachers, distributing material, and holding discussions. The call for volunteers, the union argued, was the key ingredient to successful implementation.[44]

Teacher transfers were not the only issue the TU took on in the 1950s, joining other activists in concern about the "obsolete" condition of many New York City school buildings in Black and Latinx areas. The Urban League invoked the Cold War struggle to make its case for equality in education, quoting Valerie Hawkins, the education director of the Interracial

Agency, who argued that the successful Soviet launches of Sputniks 1 and 2 should challenge the system to educate all children "to the best of our ability, without discrimination." Schools "must develop all our manpower to its utmost potential if we are to retain our self-respect and our security in the world today."[45]

In the 1950s, both the Guild and the TU spoke in support of civil rights for New York City school children. Faced with the question of whether they would help redistribute the unequally divided resources—human as well as material—in New York City schools, however, the TU and the Guild took divergent routes. The Guild pointed again to community and family failure as a source of educational inequality, and lodged complaints against race-conscious policy making, which they thought competed with their race-blind meritocratic ideal. The TU, aware also of potential teacher opposition to transfers, nonetheless spoke of the need to equalize teacher resources as well as strengthen Harlem schools.

Ann Matlin taught at PS 184 in Harlem from the early 1940s until she was forced to leave because of her membership in the Communist Party. She recalled that her students would arrive at school hungry because their families could not afford to provide them breakfast. To make matters worse for learning, the school building was dilapidated and classes were overcrowded. Matlin joined the Harlem Committee for Better Schools, a group of parents, teachers from the TU, and community leaders, who conducted rallies, lobbied administrators, and demanded improved conditions for the children of Harlem. Matlin worked with the Harlem Committee to assure that new school buildings be constructed in Harlem. Even though the Board of Education declared that it would not build any new schools during the war, the committee managed to get four new schools built. Matlin joined the TU activists Alice Citron, Norman London, and Morris Seltzer, all members of the Harlem Teachers Committee who worked steadfastly to improve conditions for the children of Harlem.[46]

Citron, Matlin, London, Seltzer, and other TU members had a broad view of unionism that went beyond providing benefits and higher wages for its members. The Teachers Union's objective—building a radical movement for social change—connected its concerns to the working-class African American and Latinx communities. TU members established a teacher and community relationship unparalleled in the city's history. But due to the anticommunist ethos and, at times, hysteria of the Cold War, the TU became a target of the BOE. More than 1,100 members were called before the superintendent of the Board of Education or his representatives and viciously grilled on their political beliefs and associations. Close to 500 TU members were fired, forced to resign, or forced to retire. By 1950, the BOE had passed the draconian Timone Resolution, which denied recognition of the union. Despite its efforts to function, by 1964, the Teachers Union had folded.

With the TU's demise, a model of teacher-parent cooperation in Harlem and elsewhere was over. In Harlem and other African American and Latinx communities of New York City, members of the New York City Teachers Union forged an alliance with parents and community leaders to help build a coalition to challenge Board of Education policies that denied the children of that community an adequate education. This included eliminating overcrowded classes and dilapidated school buildings, securing experienced teachers and administrators who did not physically abuse students, and using textbooks that did not denigrate people of African origins.

Harlem parent and community organizing alongside the TU managed to persuade the Board of Education to build new school buildings in Harlem, eliminate racist and biased textbooks, and take other steps to improve education in that community. Because of the TU's isolation and eventual collapse, its rival, the Teachers Guild prospered. Eventually, its brand of unionism became the only game in town. The Guild and later the UFT worked to improve wages and working conditions for teachers but did not cultivate strong alliances with the parents of Harlem and other communities of color in the city. Instead of working with parents, community activists, and civil rights organizations to challenge Board of Education policies that were harmful to students, the Guild's emphasis on social pathology as the cause of African American and Latinx failure in schools rather than structural inequality only alienated Harlem and other communities of color.

The contrast between the TU and the Guild illustrates that teacher-parent conflict is not inherent in teacher unionism, and that New York City's teaching force was never a homogeneous entity. By the late 1960s, with the UFT as the dominant voice of teacher unionism, New York City became home to multiple potent confrontation between a predominantly white teachers union and predominantly Black and Latinx communities. From Intermediate School 201 in East Harlem (discussed in chapter 8 of this volume) to Ocean-Hill Brownsville, and across teacher strikes from 1967 through the early 1970s, conflict often characterized teacher-parent relationships. The roots of these confrontations lay in the demise of the TU's vision of strong teacher and community relations.

Notes

1. Rachel Ellen Lissy, "From Rehabilitation to Punishment: The Institutionalization of Suspension Policies in Post–World War II New York City Schools" (PhD diss., University of California, Berkeley, 2015) 23. See also "Harlem Project: The Role of the School in Preventing Maladjustment and Delinquency (1947–1949)," series 240, Board of Education of the City of New York Collection, Municipal Archives (hereafter, BOE, MA), 150.
2. Clarence Taylor, *Knocking at Our Own Door: Milton A. Galamison and the Struggle to Integrate New York City Schools* (New York: Columbia University Press, 1997), 52–53.
3. On the origins of the "culture of poverty," see Alice O'Connor, *Poverty Knowledge: Social Science, Social Policy, and the Poor in Twentieth-Century U.S. History* (Princeton, N.J.: Princeton University Press, 2001), chap. 4. For its consequences in education, see, among others, Jack Dougherty, *More than One Struggle: The Evolution of Black School Reform in Milwaukee* (Chapel Hill: University of North Carolina Press, 2004), chap. 3; and John Spencer, "From 'Cultural Deprivation' to Cultural Capital: The Roots and Continued Relevance of Compensatory Education," *Teachers College Record* 114, no. 6 (2012), 1–41.
4. Jerald Podair, *The Strike That Changed New York: Blacks, Whites and the Ocean Hill-Brownsville Crisis* (Princeton, N.J.: Princeton University Press, 2002), 154.
5. Christina Collins, *"Ethnically Qualified": Race, Merit, and the Selection of Urban Teachers, 1920–1980* (New York: Teachers College Press, 2011).
6. James Baldwin, "Negroes Are Anti-Semitic Because They're Anti-White," *New York Times*, April 9, 1967.
7. Martha Biondi, *To Stand and Fight: The Struggle for Civil Rights in Postwar New York City* (Cambridge, Mass.: Harvard University Press, 2003).
8. A growing number of scholars have blamed 1960s Black Power proponents for the tension between Black communities and public-school teachers. For example, see Richard Kahlenberg, *Tough Liberal, Al Shanker and the Battle Over Schools, Unions, Race and Democracy* (New York: Columbia University Press, 2009); Jonathan Kaufman, *Broken Alliance: The Turbulent Times Between Blacks and Jews in America* (New York: Scribner, 1988); and Joshua Zeitz, *White Ethnic New York: Jews, Catholics and the Shaping of Postwar Politics* (Chapel Hill: University of North Carolina Press, 2007).
9. "Step-Children of New York," *New York Teacher*, February 1937, 9.
10. "Step-Children of New York."
11. "The Schoenchen Case," *Bulletin*, December 15, 1936, United Federation of Teachers Collection (hereafter UFT), box 1, folder 2, Tamiment Library and Robert F. Wagner Labor Archives, New York University Bobst Library.
12. "The Schoenchen Case," *Bulletin*, December 15, 1936, UFT, box 1, folder 2.

13. "The Schoenchen Case."

14. "Step-Children of New York," 9–10.

15. Robert Michael Harris, "'Teachers and Blacks': The New York City Teachers Union and the Negro, 1916–1964" (MA thesis, Brooklyn College, 1971), 40–41; and *New York Age*, January 16, 1937.

16. Eric Schneider, *Vampires, Dragons, and Egyptian Kings: Youth Gangs in Postwar New York* (Princeton, N.J.: Princeton University Press, 1999), 57.

17. "Harlem, South Central or Cabrini Greens," City-Data.com, September, 22, 2007, www.city-data.com, accessed March 10, 2017,

18. *Guild Bulletin*, November 24, 1941, January 16, 1942, UFT, box 1, folder 9.

19. *Guild Bulletin*, November 24, 1941.

20. *Guild Bulletin*, October 22, 1943, UFT, box 1, folder 10.

21. *Guild Bulletin*, October 22, 1943.

22. *Guild Bulletin*, October 22, 1943.

23. "Crime Outbreak in Harlem Sours Drive by Police," *New York Times*, November 7, 1941, 1.

24. "250 More Police in Harlem to Stamp Out Crime Wave," *New York Times*, November 8, 1941, 1.

25. Alice Citron, Letter to the Editor of the *New York Times*, November 12, 1941, 22.

26. Alice Citron, Letter to the Editor of the *New York Times*.

27. Clarence Taylor, *Reds at the Blackboard: Communism, Civil Rights, and the New York City Teachers Union* (New York: Columbia University Press, 2011), 289–90.

28. Taylor, *Reds at the Blackboard*, 252.

29. Taylor, 287–88.

30. Charles Cogen, "De-Segregation: A Historic Decision, The President's Column," *Guild Bulletin*, September 1954, 2, UFT, box 2, folder 46.

31. Report to the Commission on Integration, Board of Education, City of New York by Sub-Commission on Teachers Assignments and Personnel, December 7, 1956, BOE, MA.

32. Report to the Commission on Integration, December 7, 1956,

33. Daniel Hiram Perlstein, "The 1968 New York City School Crisis: Teacher Politics, Racial Politics and the Decline of Liberalism" (PhD diss., Stanford University, 1994), 39.

34. Perlstein, "1968 New York City School Crisis," 45–46.

35. Charles Cogen, "Integration YES! Forced Rotation No!" *Guild Bulletin*, February 1957, UFT, box 2, folder 46.

36. Cogen, "Integration Yes! Forced Rotation No!"

37. Benjamin Fine, "Teachers Oppose Integration Plan, *New York Times*, January 18, 1957, 13.

38. "26 School Groups Urge Integration," *New York Times*, January 1, 1957, 33.

39. Murray Illson, "Race Bias Is Laid to City Teachers," *New York Times*, November 17, 1957, 68.

40. "Teachers Reject Bias Accusation," *New York Times*, November 18, 1957.

41. Russell to Editor of the *New York Times*, February 7, 1957, TU Press Release, February 7, 1957, box 44, folder 9, Teachers Union of the City of New York Records, Kheel Center for Labor Management Documentation and Archives, Cornell University Library (hereafter TUCNYR).

42. Russell to Editor of the *New York Times*, February 7, 1957; and Minutes of Special Executive Board Meeting, February 20, 1957, box 44, folder 14, TUCNYR.

43. TU Press Release, February 26, 1957, box 44, folder 14; and Resolution (n.d.), box 44, folder 14, TUCNYR.

44. TU Press Release, March 2, 1957, box 45, folder 3, TUCNYR.

45. Urban League of Greater New York Press Release, November 20, 1957, box 45, folder 3, TUCNYR.

46. "Ann Matlin: Matlin Remembers the Classroom," Dreamers & Fighters: The NYC Teacher Purges, accessed August 2, 2016, www.dreamersandfighters.com/matlin /inter_amatlin.aspx. For the Harlem Committee, see Taylor, *Reds at the Blackboard*, 287–91.

PART THREE

Divergent Educational Visions in the Activist 1960s and 1970s

CHAPTER 7

HARYOU

An Apprenticeship for Young Leaders

ANSLEY T. ERICKSON

A conversation unfolded in November 1962, in an office in the Harlem YMCA on 135th Street. In earlier decades, the "Y" offered accommodations to scores of Black performers and intellectuals who needed lodging when downtown hotels barred them. By 1962 the Harlem Y also housed offices of community organizations—including HARYOU, or Harlem Youth Opportunities Unlimited. HARYOU's funding came first from the New York City government, then from President Kennedy's Committee on Juvenile Delinquency, and later from the War on Poverty's Community Action Program.[1] HARYOU proposed to study and to intervene in Harlem's neighborhoods to improve the lives and prospects of local youth. The organization endured in various forms for over a decade. But in the fall of 1962, it was still trying to find its way.[2]

In HARYOU's small offices, Dr. Kenneth Clark and a colleague sat in conversation with two young men—Ford Saltus and Charles Coleman. A tape recorder ran as the esteemed social psychologist and City College professor and the sixteen- and seventeen-year-old Harlem teenagers talked about their neighborhood. The boys lived about ten blocks away from the Harlem Y, near 125th Street. They had recently established the social organization they called the "Chessmen Fraternity," taking advantage of a time when there had not been "any gang battles for a while." We "try to encourage the boys to be somewhat ambitious in other activities, other than going out and fighting each other. . . . We had this idea that we wanted to help each other in the community," the young men explained.[3]

Saltus and Coleman came to HARYOU in search of guidance, but Clark wanted to learn from them instead. The two young men became the first members of the "HARYOU Associates," a group of Harlem youth involved in planning the organization's work. In keeping with social science parlance of the day, HARYOU leaders hoped to create an "action research laboratory."[4] Youth energy and ideas, from Saltus and Coleman and many peers who joined them, helped shape HARYOU.

HARYOU valued youth knowledge and skill but also recognized the need to cultivate and further develop that knowledge and skill. Prompted by its vision of youth-led community change, HARYOU created a dynamic educational space that included a mix of formal and informal approaches to youth learning and fostered opportunities for young people to share and act on what they had learned. HARYOU's history matters, then, not only because it offered an early and influential model for what became War on Poverty Community Action programs.[5] And it matters not only as a window into the thinking of Kenneth Clark.[6] It illustrates what emerged when a group of professional-class Harlem adults created an educational enterprise guided by a robust sense of respect and need for young people's capacities. Such a vision commands attention especially given the ways it cut against many elements of the social and intellectual context in which it developed. Material obstacles to Black young people's flourishing were many, and they were only worsened by social science and policy frameworks of the day that identified young African Americans only as problems to be solved, as embodiments of deficit rather than potential.[7]

Teens of Coleman and Saltus's generation were coming of age in a Harlem that showed both the long-term ravages of racist oppression and economic exploitation and their new forms in the post–World War II years. Strictures on Black residential mobility remained tight, as shiny new suburban developments and discounted mortgages lured white urbanites to the suburbs. The country's Levittowns and similar mass-produced suburban developments barred all but the most daring few Black families, through a web of segregationist home finance and real estate practices reinforced at times with neighborhood violence. But many white suburbanites moved outward from previously segregated neighborhoods in the New York City boroughs of Queens and the Bronx, or to the neighborhoods of Washington Heights and Inwood farther north in Manhattan. Their movement opened spaces for working- and middle-class Black families who sought opportunities for home or apartment ownership, or more space and light, or better schools.[8]

Around 124th Street, where Saltus and Coleman lived with their families, Black middle-class outmigration left a Harlem that was increasingly segregated not only by race but also by class. Fewer of Harlem's doctors, teachers, and white-collar government workers lived in the immediate area. More and more families navigated poverty, facing low-wage work or dependence on welfare payments or the informal economy. From beauty parlors to lunch counters to numbers-running, Harlem residents had long worked in small-scale and at times illicit economic enterprises, while also trying to make a way in the sharply racially divided labor market of the broader city.[9] The neighborhood became the geographic center of a national informal economy in the late 1950s and early 1960s: the heroin trade. Its distribution and sales network reached residents all over Manhattan, the five boroughs, and beyond, but its hub was Central Harlem.[10] With the trade and its human consequences visible on the streets, heroin was the starkest of the dangerous choices that Saltus and Coleman hoped to help their fellow teens avoid. The young men also worried about peers' decisions to disengage from school or other social networks and supports.[11]

Alongside their material struggles, many Harlem residents faced obstacles in the form of ideas—the way city and national leadership thought about them. Even those who sought to help traded in concepts that proved dangerous. The sociologist Oscar Lewis coined the term "culture of poverty" in his 1959 study of Mexican village life, but his assertions gained tremendous traction in U.S. social policy circles in the 1960s. Lewis argued that poverty marked families not only at the moment of material privation but also in enduring and generational ways. Fighting poverty meant, in Lewis's view, changing the culture of poor people. Policy makers, scholars, and welfare officials working in this tradition saw more deficits than sources of strength, knowledge, and ideas in poor communities. At times, too, HARYOU's Kenneth Clark spoke in his own terms that closely echoed Lewis's in focusing on the "pathology" of the ghetto.[12] A deficit orientation characterized a wide array of poverty-focused interventions of the era, from Title I federal funding in schools to moralistic and often racist regulations on public housing and welfare recipients' family structures and uses of funds. When Clark and his HARYOU colleagues sat down with Saltus and Coleman and they committed to including Harlem youth in research and program development, their actions diverged from this developing norm. Some scholars have interpreted Clark as a pathologist, by focusing on the ideas of damage that ran through his work from the doll studies that informed *Brown v. Board of Education* through his language in *Dark Ghetto*. But the process of Clark's work with HARYOU provides another layer of complexity.[13]

HARYOU operated with initial funds from the Kennedy administration's Committee on Juvenile Delinquency. But Clark and his colleagues forcefully rejected the "delinquency" language. HARYOU sought to call attention not to the supposed faults of Harlem youth—as much delinquency discourse did—but to the injustices of the broader world they inhabited. "The President's committee wanted us to direct ourselves to delinquency control, but we refused to do so. What HARYOU is talking about is the built-in delinquency which exists in the type of racist society which accepts ghettos as norms and which gets irritated when the people within the ghetto get mad and defiant. The type of delinquency which HARYOU is trying to deal with is that of social delinquency."[14]

The network of Harlem-based social workers, community activists, educators, and health professionals who composed HARYOU's first leaders chastised earlier New York City social programs as "social work colonialism" for failing to involve Harlem residents in the planning of programs for their benefit.[15] Clark claimed that they wanted to do more than target programs at youth. They wanted to create alongside them. When Clark sat down with Saltus and Coleman, he was following through on this idea, seeing the young men as people who knew what HARYOU should do. For Clark, these boys and their knowledge about their community and its youth should be the heart of the organization's efforts. In essence, Clark was working out an early form of "maximum feasible participation" of local residents. The concept helped shaped other efforts such as the Lower East Side's Mobilization for Youth, and even more so the War on Poverty's Community Action Programs nationally.[16]

In their conversation at HARYOU's offices, Clark tried to set Coleman and Saltus at ease, explaining that they were the experts on a subject that he cared about but was still trying to figure out. He had been inspired, as had many, by the powerful example of youth activism in the southern Black freedom struggle, from the Montgomery children's march to lunch counter sit-ins, and by the absence of "anti-social" activity accompanying these intense protests.[17] But Clark did not claim to understand fully Harlem's youth culture, nor the approaches adults could take to engage and motivate young people to protect and improve both their own lives and those of their community. He argued, in writing and in actions such as listening to Saltus and Coleman, that the most important questions about Harlem's current challenges and future possibilities for youth had to be answered not only by experts but also by local youngsters.

HARYOU staffers' appreciation for the "zeal" and "enthusiasm" of youth came alongside a desire to cultivate "real *understanding* of the issues and their implications, an *awareness* of the many operative forces within and without" Harlem, and exposure to "the various possibilities for action."[18] Guided by respect for and desire to cultivate youth knowledge, HARYOU's youth program created an intensive educational, developmental space that offered young people the training and platform to share the ideas they had and the new ones they cultivated.

After describing HARYOU's initial foray into youth research, this chapter examines three aspects of HARYOU's work that illustrate the desire and the complications of seeing young people as knowers. HARYOU ran a Leadership Training Workshop, engaging young people in a variety of internship and learning experiences. Africana studies pioneer John Henrik Clarke sought to train HARYOU teens as vessels for African and African American history too often missing from local schools. Dance students and other artists crafted their technique and then displayed their work to local and citywide audiences. It notes too that youth helped organize Harlem into multiple elected neighborhood boards, seeking to counter city disinterest with heightened political organizing at the micro scale.

None of these venues for youth research and youth contribution fully achieved the "action-research laboratory" that Clark and his colleagues envisaged. Various strains appeared, as youth voices diverged from and challenged adult perspectives, as adults failed at times to cede authority even as they sought to cultivate youth knowledge and leadership, and as HARYOU at times did not recognize or credit the networks of knowledge and action that women had created. Despite these limitations, HARYOU (and HARYOU-ACT, as the entity was called after 1965) created an educational space that developed young people as agents in the advancement of their communities. A variety of kinds of instruction, mentorship, and apprenticeship together constituted an intentional curriculum for engaged young Black life and leadership. HARYOU pursued this work even as powerful national and local discourse viewed city neighborhoods like Harlem and

Black youth like HARYOU's participants as symbols of pathology rather than possibility. HARYOU wrestled deeply but imperfectly with the question of who knew Harlem, who knew African American youth and Black urban life, and how to build and share this knowledge.

HARYOU's work shifted significantly from the early 1960s through the late 1960s and early 1970s, prompted by major transitions in leadership, scale, and focus. Yet its central commitment to identifying and cultivating local youth knowledge and leadership animated the work across the decade. This commitment helped the organization develop a dynamic set of educational experiences that provided young people expert guidance, apprenticeship, and low-stakes exposure to a variety of learning settings.[19] In today's era of national-scale educational expertise and educational interventions celebrated for their portability across communities, HARYOU offers a reminder that, previously, those committed to strengthening local communities first thought to ask what the children knew. Then they built educational spaces to support and further develop that knowledge and its power. Thus HARYOU asks educators and policy makers today to reflect on which epistemic orientations and assumptions their work reflects.

HARYOU was suffused with a social science research ethos, and staffers recorded the project's work in intricate detail, via audio recordings or extensive field notes. A HARYOU staffer recorded the conversation of Clark, Coleman, and Saltus at the offices in the Harlem Y, then transcribed it and filed it with the organization's research director, Kenneth Marshall. The social science approach symbolized by the presence of the tape recorder in many HARYOU venues may have created a barrier for some Harlem residents and made them feel less welcome and more examined than HARYOU's rhetoric promised. But it also provided a robust and detailed documentary record. This record indicates that HARYOU not only claimed to seek out, listen to, and build on the experience and ideas of local teens, but it in fact did so in at least a portion of its work.[20] Because of the project's unusually extensive documentation of conversations with and among young people, it offers a strikingly direct—if certainly not unmediated, disinterested, or comprehensive—account of teens' ideas about their neighborhood and their futures.

HARYOU operated for just over a dozen years, first with Clark as director and with a cadre of powerful African American social work professionals alongside him, a group that was heavily but not exclusively male. In 1964, Clark lost a political tussle with Harlem's congressman and the longtime pastor of the Abyssinian Baptist Church, Reverend Adam Clayton Powell Jr., and HARYOU merged with a community organization called Associated Community Teams, which was led by Powell and his allies, including many longtime Harlem activists.[21] HARYOU-ACT continued operations for the remainder of the decade, largely via funds obtained through the federal Community Action Program it had helped inspire.

The leadership transition changed HARYOU, but so did Harlem itself. The organization had been growing at a slow pace—with a year and half of research before an intensive summer program for thirty-two students in 1963, and three hundred in the summer of 1964. This scale no longer felt sufficient after the July 1964 Harlem uprisings. Prompted by the police killing of a Harlem teenager near his Upper East Side summer school, days of street violence and property destruction worried officials from New York to Washington, D.C. Seeking to bring more youth into "constructive" structures quickly, to discipline their anger and their desire for change, HARYOU-ACT moved quickly to a summer employment model to reach more than six thousand students.[22]

The transition from Clark's to Powell's leadership as well as the quick escalation in scale strained the organization's capacity and its public perception. Controversy around HARYOU seemed to fit with long-standing views of the War on Poverty. In these accounts, grand ambitions of "community action," "maximum feasible participation," and democratic engagement almost always foundered on the shoals of local political conflict. Recent scholarship, however, focuses not exclusively on leadership and politics, but on practice and grassroots action, and challenges this story of decline and failure.[23] HARYOU had more than its share of conflict and it failed to achieve its most ambitious goals. But, like many Harlem visions that were not fully realized, the story resounds with hopes and strategies that merit consideration for another era.

Youth Research as Education

Describing HARYOU in its earliest years, Kenneth Clark explained, "It is the fundamental premise of HARYOU that the youth of the community are the chief victims of the frustration, despair, apathy, and the quiet and strident conflict and dehumanization which characterize the ghetto. . . .

Too many of Harlem's youth are doomed to live lives of despair and hopelessness and have become the human casualties of pervasive social neglect and injustice." These words ring with tones of pathology and deficit—but as he did throughout his work at HARYOU, Clark pivoted from pathology to power. "The youth of Harlem can be salvaged, nurtured, and stimulated to assert and attain their rights to dignity as human beings."[24] In his work as a community psychologist at the Northside Center, Clark spoke of the necessary "maladjustment" Harlem residents needed intentionally to cultivate rather than overcome—a maladjustment to the unjust constraints they faced, rather than any "adjustment" to them.[25]

By the early 1960s, Clark and his early colleagues from organizations such as the Harlem Neighborhood Association, local churches, and social work networks began to see community research as part of the process of necessary maladjustment, a precursor to powerful action. In addition to their commitments to youth engagement in principle, they were seeking ways to bridge what they felt to be a growing gulf between themselves and Black urban-dwelling youth. Some of this distance was geographic. By the mid-1960s, many middle- and upper-class Black professionals, such as those who led HARYOU, had left Harlem for more suburban areas inside or beyond the city limits. Some of the distance felt cultural, as adults worried that they would be perceived as "placating sops" by young people enthralled with "hipsterism" or "sub-cultures" of "bobs," "cool cats," and "slicksters." Adults worried that youth would not accept their "honest efforts at social reform." HARYOU leaders (in at times exoticizing tones) desired access to "authentic" youth, to inform their work.[26]

Alongside Ford Saltus and Charles Coleman, a group of students from early high school through college age became the HARYOU Associates and made themselves frequent figures at the Harlem Y offices. HARYOU's own writers thought the young people were motivated by the altruistic, the practical (as in the acquisition of skills and opportunities for themselves), and the social benefits of participation, but that the overriding attraction was "the opportunity . . . to be involved in real and serious dialogues concerning their own future."[27] In 1963, students accompanied adult staffers or completed their own ethnographic-style observations and fieldwork in various community centers, on stoops, and on street corners.[28] One recording captures an example of the practice: a team of two teenagers and a college-aged student spent an hour or so on the corner of 133rd Street and Eighth Avenue, starting conversations with young passersby about their lives and their community. They heard from children recently returned home from reform school and others who expressed their desires to grow up to be scientists. The youth conducting the interviews commented on wanting Harlem youngsters like themselves to participate in HARYOU, not to be "under the spyglass" of other researchers as "indigenous informants," but as researchers themselves.[29]

Through their research, young people contributed to a report of more than six hundred pages that, although its format resembled an unpolished typescript, circulated in New York City and beyond in social work and urban affairs circles. The report later provided the empirical base for Clark's 1965 national bestseller, *Dark Ghetto*. Young people did not write either the 1964 HARYOU report or *Dark Ghetto*, but they were part of the knowledge-creation mechanisms that shaped HARYOU's understandings of Harlem's needs and its proposed solutions.

As they participated in research efforts and organized projects including the Harlem event aligned with the August 1963 March on Washington, some tensions emerged. The students who had presented themselves at the Harlem Y offices to become involved in the HARYOU Associates were largely middle class or from upwardly mobile families, and HARYOU staffers judged some to be "reluctant or unable to function with the other less privileged young people."[30] When pressed to expand their group to include what HARYOU adults described as the "more marginal," "damaged," or "obviously deviant young people," the participating youth resisted. When these "marginal" youth did join, they often left quickly because, as HARYOU adults perceived it, they felt unable to meet the challenges of the research tasks involved "either because of lack of training and skill or inadequate motivation or other types of character defects."[31]

Youth research participation created many tensions with HARYOU's adult professionals. The HARYOU Associates youth were "virtually a 'staff team'; yet, their youthfulness and lack of experience warranted close direction and supervision by adult staff members." Some of those adults felt the expected power dynamic shifting: "The [youth] group held the adult staff team in a 'heads I win, tails you lose' bind." A program could falter because the staff had "not . . . really shown faith in the group." Or the staff could err in allowing them "to go off half-cocked."[32] Youth could have at once too much authority, and not enough.

The presence of adolescents in typically adult-only work spaces brought quotidian challenges. The young people thought that they had been invited to fully participate in HARYOU's work and expected to be welcomed at HARYOU's offices at all times. "They often seemed to 'take over' the HARYOU offices," at the Harlem Y, testing the patience of the professional and secretarial staff. The youth group won assignment of their own space in the office. Adult staffers hoped to confine them there, but "this hope was not fulfilled."[33] When given a space where their contributions felt welcome, these Harlem youth seized it enthusiastically.

Alongside their work as junior social scientists, interviewing neighbors and tallying U.S. census data alongside research associate and sociologist Olivia Frost, HARYOU Associates did crucial leg work for multiple organizing efforts, including a mayor's youth summit and the major school boycotts in New York in 1964.[34] HARYOU youth helped conceptualize a wide range of programs, institutions, and opportunities that ultimately drew more than $4 million in federal and local support for youth-led Black history workshops, youth-run coffee shops as community centers, and a "neighborhood board" program that would elect block-level leadership for Harlem neighborhoods.[35] Although it is hard to know exactly which of these suggestions originated with youth ideas, some adult comments linked proposals to youth contributions. Early HARYOU documents proposed conventional "job training"—testing, training, and placement services for out-of-school Harlem youth.[36] A few years later, however, Kenneth Clark reported having learned from his young associates that "Negro youth in Harlem did not have the opportunity to learn how to manage even a small business or store since, unlike other lower-middle-class groups in the city, their parents did not own stores." For a few years, HARYOU shifted to creating youth-run businesses as more locally based and richer sites for on-the-job training.[37]

Both the contributions and the tensions that came from youth presence attest that youth participation in HARYOU was significant for the organization. Participation changed the young people as well—and at times, HARYOU adults complained about this. As social work professionals, they had been in search of "authentic" Harlem youth voices who could inform and translate their program ideas. Rather than celebrating the increase of skill and social capital that youth participants demonstrated, HARYOU colleagues complained that "these workers often lose the very qualities for which they were recruited from the community once they are placed on the payroll and brought into contact with professional colleagues whose style they sought to imitate."[38] As they learned from their new context,

HARYOU Associates were no longer the "authentic" youth HARYOU sought to understand and access. Another aspect of HARYOU's work, however, wanted to cultivate change in participating young people.

An Apprenticeship for Leaders

In the summer of 1963, as HARYOU was wrapping up its research phase, a selected group of thirty-two adolescents, some from HARYOU Associates and some new to the organization, participated in a six-week-long Leadership Training Workshop (LTW). The LTW was an educational space committed to listening to and furthering youth knowledge and skill. Students of high school and college age spent their mornings working on research and action teams on housing, heritage (African and African American history), group social work, and a coffee shop/cultural center. These placements put the young people in positions of authority and contribution, as they organized tenants or led groups of children of elementary school age. Like historic forms of apprenticeship, young people in the program learned through example, experience, and low-stakes engagement with informed adults. As one adult participant described it, the goal was to build not only on young people's "apparent 'knowledge' of 'what makes things wrong in Harlem,'" but also on "a real *understanding* of the issues and their implications; an *awareness* of the many operative forces within and without the Harlem community," to help develop leaders "in a systematic, honest, and rigorous fashion."[39]

Afternoon discussions and debates motivated and informed students' continued civic action. The LTW's schedule demonstrated the power of HARYOU's connections, with figures from a New York City deputy mayor to parent activists to Malcolm X all making time in their schedules for extended conversations with the young trainees. If the program had been shaped in part by the idea that Harlem youth should have the opportunities for learning that came within a family business, it was a family where local political leaders came to dinner.

Many pressing issues came up for discussion in the LTW. The question of school desegregation was one contentious example. In 1963, Kenneth Clark was only nine years past his contribution to the *Brown v. Board of Education* litigation, and was still deeply enmeshed in New York City integrationist activism. Many of the adults working with HARYOU in its early phases shared his focus on desegregation as a strategy for educational equity. Yet Clark also invested heavily in attempts to improve the lives of Harlem students and residents immediately, not waiting for desegregation's stuttering progress given the many forms of resistance on display in New York City. Before HARYOU, Clark helped initiate the Higher Horizons program that brought additional human and material resources into select Harlem schools.[40] For HARYOU's adults like Clark, desegregation remained an important strategy for equity, but not the only one.

When the Leadership Training Workshop scheduled an afternoon of student discussion about schools and segregation, the young participants likely sensed that HARYOU's leadership favored an integrationist perspective. In conversation, though, students were clear on their ideas and their concerns, even when they diverged from those of HARYOU's head staffers. Laura Pires, a recent graduate of Columbia University's School of Social Work and a key staff leader (and documenter) of the Leadership Training Workshop, described school "integration" as the students' "favorite topic." They relished the opportunity to argue against integrationist currents and in favor of "improvement" instead. The local activist Mildred Bond visited the workshop for an afternoon discussion, and students opined that "it was not necessary to have Susie Cohen sit next to the little black boy to have better schools." For Sherron Jackson, a Harlem native home for the summer from college and participation in the Black freedom struggle in the South, "The biggest problem in Harlem schools is that to learn to read and write is impossible." Jackson resisted the idea of integration as facilitating school improvement, saying it was a "white yardstick" applied to a "black community."[41]

At times HARYOU adults bristled at the ideas youth expressed in the organization's educational spaces. Pires captured students' resistance to Bond's arguments in favor of integration, and criticized them for it. Students, including Sherron Jackson, had "pulled out all of their 'black' arguments—emotional and moral as they may be." HARYOU staffer Larry Houston pressed against this: did the students want "separate but equal"? Houston took an extreme view of the students' ideas, equating them with those of a Mississippi segregationist: "You sound like Senator Eastland."[42] Despite these sharp comments, HARYOU youth continued to press their position. Elsewhere Pires worried that some youth were increasingly interested in Malcolm X and his leadership, or were enamored of what some at HARYOU thought of as the more separatist approaches of John Henrik

Clarke and his cultural heritage work, to be described later. Pires, like many of her HARYOU colleagues, was both professionally and personally committed to valuing youth knowledge and ideas. But she and some of her colleagues were afraid of youth frustration and anger produced by the many manifestations of racism and divestment in Harlem. Would tensions simmer, or explode?

Brenda McCoy was a high-schooler when she participated in the Leadership Training Workshop. Her team worked alongside Jesse Gray of the Community Council on Housing, to organize tenants against decrepit and dangerous conditions on a block of West 117th Street. The students' efforts helped set the groundwork for a major 1964 rent strike that Gray led.[43] But at the end of the summer, what mattered most to McCoy was not what she had contributed, but what she had learned. McCoy grew up in what she described as a "bourgeois black area"—the Riverton Houses on 135th Street, built as the segregated Black counterpart to Metropolitan Life's segregated white Stuyvesant Town farther south in Manhattan. Talking about the gap between her own relative comfort and the conditions she observed via her summer work reduced her to tears. Her Riverton neighbors "seem to have no identity with the type of people [she] worked with on 117th St." She took home a message of unity in Black identity that cut across class: "Until all of our black brothers are free, the ones down on 117th St. nodding [in a heroin trance] and the ones up in [Riverton], we can never be free."[44]

HARYOU created spaces for young people to hear various ideas and try their hands at civil discourse about these concepts. The Leadership Training Workshop provided a political and intellectual apprenticeship. It presented a striking counterpart to the often low-skill job placement and training ethos of the era's Job Corps or manpower programs that had been conceptualized with a much less powerful, or, in Clark's terms, less constructively and purposefully "maladjusted" Harlem young person in mind.

In her remarks at the end-of-summer banquet for the Leadership Training Workshop, Sherron Jackson expressed the ideas of participation and youth influence that Kenneth Clark and his adult colleagues had articulated at the project's inception. "HARYOU must be taught by the young person in Harlem. HARYOU must be molded by the young person in Harlem. HARYOU must in essence *be* the young person in Harlem."[45] The LTW engaged only a small group of Harlem youth, and at times it was clear that HARYOU adults struggled to accept the youth perspectives they said they wanted. Nonetheless, the LTW exemplified a dynamic learning space motivated by respect for and desire to cultivate youth as knowers and leaders in their community.

John Henrik Clarke and Youth History Teachers

Another distinct feature of HARYOU's work with young people—and its approach to community development more generally—was the infusion of historical learning throughout the organization. As one HARYOU leader put it, teaching Harlem residents about African and African American history helped "give them memories they can respect, and use to command the respect of other people . . . to develop an awareness and a pride in themselves, so that they can become a better instrument for living together with other people."[46] HARYOU imagined historical knowledge to be central to building self, community, and change in Harlem.

Some Leadership Training Workshop participants spent portions of their days on HARYOU's "Heritage Program." They worked as history teachers at St. Philip's Church day-care center, the Dunlevy-Milbank Center for children, and other spaces. Teenagers could benefit from learning as they taught, and the placing of youth in positions where they could make direct contributions to their community was consistent with the project's overall vision. But HARYOU and Harlem needed youth history teachers because so few schools and other state-run educational venues in the early 1960s made African and African American history central to their work. Some Harlem teachers created materials to fill this gap for their students, but they were exceptions in an educational landscape that gave people of African descent too little attention and often the wrong kind of attention in the curriculum. (This was a problem that some educators and artists sought to contest in Harlem from the 1930s onward, as discussed in chapters 4 and 5 of this volume.)

HARYOU's historical work was led by John Henrik Clarke, a pioneering scholar and a founder of the field of Africana studies. Educated in a mixture of Harlem-based study circles and periodic classes at New York area universities, Clarke served stints as a faculty member at the New School and Hunter College. He made HARYOU his base of operations in the mid-1960s. Clarke's mentee Ronald Drayton was a teenager and LTW participant in 1963, working alongside Clarke in preparing materials and teaching approaches for Harlem youngsters. Drayton continued on as Clarke's partner after that initial summer, teaching history classes in after-school settings for children and evening sessions for adults through the mid-1960s. Clarke, Drayton, and a few colleagues contributed to the rapidly growing HARYOU staff, offering introductory heritage workshops to new hires.[47]

Black educators had worked for decades to comment on the shape of the dominant U.S. curriculum and its effects in reinforcing white supremacy rather than celebrating or even including Black humanity. Clarke's work, both inside and outside the academy, sought to address this distortion in myriad ways—from producing original classroom-friendly illustrated materials and circulating them to anyone who wrote to request them, to crisscrossing metropolitan New York to deliver lectures whenever invited, to contributing to media as an expert on Black history. Either because of the particular nature of historical knowledge or Clarke's own preferences, his history pedagogy had a less distributed view of knowledge production than did other aspects of HARYOU.

Clarke had been educated in study circles and other community-generated—and in some cases less hierarchical—venues for sharing and building historical knowledge. Yet in his work at HARYOU he held to a pedagogical vision in which young people could become conveyors of scholarly knowledge more than generators or contributors to it. He taught by lecturing, and the available documentation suggests that this was the approach he encouraged among his fellow heritage teachers. His young HARYOU colleague Ronald Drayton, however, began to explore more interactive pedagogical modes in the late 1960s.[48] But neither saw youth as producers of historical knowledge.

The Heritage program may not have embodied the fullest view of the "action research laboratory" that HARYOU promised, yet Clarke made an important contribution to the educational space that was HARYOU. Largely thanks to him, HARYOU made history inseparable from the other elements of community action. He offered a rationale for historical understanding as foundational for HARYOU staff, HARYOU youth, and Harlem residents engaged in any aspect of community improvement. As he put it, "African and Afro-American" history offered them "a greater awareness of themselves and the role they must play if their community is to be revitalized," seeing history as a force in teaching "the people of Harlem to use their talents . . . and love their own memories in order to fulfill themselves more completely."[49] Clarke made Black history available by creating the materials and the venues in which he could spread historical knowledge within HARYOU and farther. Both the absence and the demand for such materials well beyond Harlem had been so profound that Clarke soon found himself responding to requests for his pamphlets and curricular guides from educators and Freedom School leaders around the country and presenting to school districts and other groups in the New York area.[50]

HARYOU Arts—Youth Ideas in Performance

HARYOU underwent a major leadership transition in late 1964 and 1965, alongside a transformation in the scale of its work. HARYOU's executive director, Livingston Wingate, characterized the growth in terms of dollars. Over six weeks, the organization went from a $96,000 per week program to a $396,000 per week program. HARYOU had planned to grow, but the July 1964 Harlem uprising created a new sense of immediacy and a new set of goals. Both local and federal leaders feared African American urban youth as "social dynamite," in James Conant Bryant's term that appeared in HARYOU discourse.[51] Officials wanted HARYOU to bring as many young people into its net as possible, in the not-at-all-veiled hope that youth engagement in summer programs could reduce the likelihood of further unrest. Now HARYOU-ACT tried to serve thousands of children—and its previous intensive engagement with a small cadre of young people took a backseat to broader-scale efforts.

Nonetheless, HARYOU's core modes of working with young people—in research, organizing, and display and performance of arts and culture—remained the center of the project's youth programs. Dance, music, and theater, offered in summer intensive as well as yearlong training programs became new spaces for student knowledge to be both fostered and shared.

HARYOU's research director and veteran social worker Kenneth Marshall had already spoken of the centrality of "art as equipment for living" in his work for HARYOU. Addressing a 1962 gathering of Harlem-based painters, musicians, playwrights, and others who were interested in shaping HARYOU's work in the arts, Marshall explained his appreciation for youth culture as a meaningful response to the conditions of young Black people's lives. Marshall hoped to recognize the artistic and cultural contributions of Harlem youth and to pair it with expert artistic guidance. Rather than add to the era's censorious discourse about culturally disconnected youth, Marshall saw "some of the so-called 'sub-cultural' stances . . . [as] a kind of collective poem or creation." Black youth saw a society "based on the comings and goings of commodities," but a society that denied them the ability to acquire these commodities. Experiencing this exclusion, they "utilized the very scraps and dregs of our rich society to form and mold a world that has some coherence and purpose to it . . . to seize upon the scraps and fuse them into a kind of mystique and make of this a kind of life."[52] Marshall's appreciation for young people as resourceful culture makers paralleled Kenneth Clark's interest in learning from young people's views of their community in HARYOU's research endeavors. And both shared a commitment not only to valuing but to developing youth skill.

HARYOU's dance program looked much like an intensive preprofessional training endeavor that linked interested (but not necessarily previously trained) young people with highly skilled instructors. The discipline of dance structured much of the day (especially in the summer), and students felt a culture of high expectations and striving for aesthetic and physical accomplishment that pushed them beyond where they had been previously. One HARYOU dancer, George Faison, recalled the intense physical and emotional effort required to reach the professional standards his instructors expected. Success in dance depended on rigorous discipline, and the lessons extended beyond the studio. Otis Sallid participated in HARYOU's dance program in 1964 and 1965. By chance he dropped in at a community center where classes were under way, a step that launched him toward a career in performing arts. He appreciated the dance training as well as the development of disciplined work that carried him to Juilliard. "HARYOU-ACT was really a big deal because in the midst of all this poverty, this mis-education, just being out there on your own in a lot of ways, they taught you really big things. They taught you how to show up on time. How to . . . make sure you cleaned your tights before you come in the next day. And put them by the door and get ready for your next class. They taught you . . . how to be in the pursuit of excellence."[53]

Although apprentice housing advocates in the Leadership Training Workshop had an experience that was different from that of apprentice dancers like Faison and Sallid, both found in HARYOU a platform for expression and growth. Dance performances became venues for expression not unlike the opportunities that other parts of HARYOU created for young people to speak out about housing conditions or lecture about Black history. HARYOU dancers performed for audiences all over the city. Faison recalled the power of expressing his frustration with the world through his body and his movement, looking directly at his audience in the final movement of a trenchant dance piece.[54]

Youth knowledge shaped other kinds of performances as well. HARYOU's theater program created and staged a play at a 1968 local conference on the problem of school suspension. In a setting focused on enrollment and graduation statistics and school construction plans, HARYOU youth brought their knowledge to bear via drama, in a work titled *The Voice of the Ghetto*.[55]

From Kenneth Marshall's early comments through community performances in the late 1960s, artistic performance and training was one of the ways in which HARYOU created spaces for the cultivation and expression of youth ideas and knowledge. At times, as in the controversy over Amiri Baraka's Black Arts Repertory Theater that led to HARYOU's withdrawing its federal funds, arts programming became the center of political conflict. But beneath the controversy, adults and youth worked together as creators of culture.[56]

HARYOU saw young African American Harlem residents as sources of knowledge, energy, and contribution. This commitment was visible in part in the organization's initial 1961–1962 conversations with the New York mayor's office, and in the proposals that led to funding via President John F. Kennedy's Committee on Juvenile Delinquency. It became clearer via the engagement of young people such as Ford Saltus and Charles Coleman, Brenda McCoy and Sherron Jackson. Despite major leadership transitions and new pressures brought to bear by the fast-shifting landscape of urban life and politics in the mid-1960s, this commitment remained in HARYOU's work into the late 1960s.

HARYOU has enjoyed attention from historians interested in its fate as an embattled War on Poverty program. And Kenneth Clark's difficult and often paradoxical language of pathology and deficit have likewise attracted attention. The educational ideas and educational spaces HARYOU generated, however, provide a different perspective.

HARYOU built a dynamic set of educational spaces—some formal, such as summer dance instruction, and some much more informal, as when young people milled about the offices on 135th Street—guided by a commitment to Black youth as powerful interpreters and actors in their communities. HARYOU thus offers an example of an educational space designed to respond to and foster the knowledge and skill of local youth. In the context of social science, educational, and social policy discourse of the early and mid-1960s, when so many attempts both to support and denigrate urban Black communities emphasized forms of pathology and deficit, HARYOU made a conscious turn in a more affirming direction. In some ways, the centrality of this idea even in HARYOU's work speaks to the power of the deficit-focused, often demeaning discourse about young Black people that was circulating at the time.

Elements of HARYOU's work can be seen in later educational efforts in Harlem, including in the continued development of autonomous (and often more radical) educational spaces (as discussed in chapter 9 of this volume) or efforts at local democratic governance of schooling (as discussed in chapters 8 and 12 of this volume) that followed HARYOU's initial foray into "Neighborhood Boards" to organize local Harlem residents.

Over its lifespan, HARYOU encountered many critics, some rightly frustrated about the organization's initial investment in programs for a few rather than broadly distributed benefits for many. Others questioned, especially given the depth of poverty in Central Harlem at the time, whether extensive federal resources could be fairly distributed if so many went to professional staff.[57] Despite these and other limitations, in its initial years of the mid-1960s HARYOU exemplifies a commitment to viewing young people not only as students but as thinkers, contributors, and leaders— people who know things, and can be supported in knowing and doing in the interest of themselves and their communities. Like other educational visions that developed in Harlem in the twentieth century, this one was only partially realized in practice historically, but nonetheless is worth the attention of educators and those who imagine a different future today.

Notes

1. HARYOU's work first started with a $330,000, eighteen-month-long study of conditions and opportunities for Harlem youth, funded by the Kennedy administration's presidential Committee on Juvenile Delinquency, and the City of New York. This study phase ran from mid-1962 to early 1964; programs for youth began in the summer of 1963. HARYOU, *Youth in the Ghetto: A Study of the Consequences of Powerlessness and a Blueprint for Change* (New York: HARYOU, 1964), 22–29.
2. I would like to thank Deidre Flowers for early research assistance on this paper.

3. Harlem Youth Opportunities Unlimited, Inc., "First Meeting of the HARYOU Associates," November 1962, Schomburg Center for Research in Black Culture, New York Public Library (hereafter Schomburg), Kenneth Marshall papers (hereafter KMP), box 5. This encounter is also memorialized in a comic book created by HARYOU: William Robinson, *Harlem Youth Report #5: Youth in the Ghetto* (New York: DC Comics, 1964), 31, reprinted in Cyril Tyson, *Power and Politics in Central Harlem, 1962–1964: The HARYOU Experience* (New York: Jay Street, 2004).

4. "HARYOU Associates: An Action-Research Laboratory," Schomburg, Northern Student Movement Papers, folder 3, box 24.

5. Noel Cazenave, *Impossible Democracy: The Unlikely Success of the War on Poverty Community Action Programs* (Albany: State University of New York Press, 2006) explores the consequences and struggles of HARYOU as a War on Poverty precursor and example. For recent work on War on Poverty programs, see Lisa Gayle Hazirjian and Annelise Orleck, eds., *The War on Poverty: A New Grassroots History* (Athens: University of Georgia Press, 2011); and on New York particularly, Tamar W. Carroll, *Mobilizing New York: AIDS, Antipoverty, and Feminist Activism* (Chapel Hill: University of North Carolina Press, 2015).

6. On Clark, see Daryl Michael Scott, *Contempt and Pity: Social Policy and the Image of the Damaged Black Psyche, 1880–1996* (Chapel Hill: University of North Carolina Press, 1997); Daniel Matlin, *On the Corner: African American Intellectuals and the Urban Crisis* (Cambridge, Mass.: Harvard University Press, 2013); Matlin, "Who Speaks for Harlem? Kenneth B. Clark, Albert Murray and the Controversies of Black Urban Life," *Journal of American Studies* 46, no. 4 (November 2012): 875–94; and Gerald Markowitz and David Rosner, *Children, Race, and Power: Kenneth and Mamie Clark's Northside Center* (Charlottesville: University of Virginia Press, 1996).

7. On the power of the "culture of poverty" idea in the era's policy and politics, including the impact of the work of Oscar Lewis and Daniel Patrick Moynihan, see Alice O'Connor, *Poverty Knowledge: Social Science, Social Policy, and the Poor in Twentieth Century US History* (Princeton, N.J.: Princeton University Press, 2002).

8. In an extensive literature on white suburbanization, leading works include Kenneth T. Jackson, *Crabgrass Frontier: The Suburbanization of the United States* (New York: Oxford University Press, 1985); and David M. P. Freund, *Colored Property: State Policy and White Racial Politics in Suburban America* (Chicago: University of Chicago Press, 2007). On Black suburbanization, see Andrew Wiese, *Places of Their Own: African American Suburbanization in the Twentieth Century* (Chicago: University of Chicago Press, 2004); and Steven Gregory, *Black Corona: Race and the Politics of Place in an Urban Community* (Princeton, N.J.: Princeton University Press, 1998).

9. On Harlem's informal economy, see LaShawn Harris, "Playing the Numbers: Madame Stephanie St. Clair and African American Policy Culture in Harlem," *Black Women, Gender and Families* 2, no. 2 (Fall 2008): 53–76.

10. Eric C. Schneider, *Smack: Heroin and the American City* (Philadelphia: University of Pennsylvania Press, 2008).

11. Harlem Youth Opportunities Unlimited, Inc., "First Meeting"; and HARYOU, *Youth in the Ghetto*.

12. The most expansive version of Clark's thinking in this regard is found in his bestselling *Dark Ghetto: Dilemmas of Social Power* (New York: Harper Torchbook, 1967 [1965]).

13. *Brown v. Board of Education of Topeka, KS*, 347 U.S. 483 (1954); and Clark, *Dark Ghetto*.

14. "Summary of the Dinner Meeting of the Arts and Cultural Affairs Committee, July 8, 1963," Schomburg, John Henrik Clarke papers (hereafter JHCP), box 21, folder 56, 4;

and "CAI Staff Meeting, Tuesday, Dec. 8, 1964, Community Action Institute 1965," JHCP, box 21, folder 13.

15. Kenneth B. Clark, "Profile of HARYOU," n.d. [1963], Schomburg, Harlem Neighborhood Association papers (hereafter HNAP), box 7, folder 5.

16. Cazenave, *Impossible Democracy*.

17. "Summary of the Dinner Meeting," JHCP, box 21, folder 56, 4.

18. "Leadership Training Workshop," JHCP, box 21, folder 56.

19. These ideas resonate with present-day calls for youth participatory action research in school improvement. See, for example, Nicole Mirra, Antero Garcia, and Ernest Morrell, *Doing Youth Participatory Action Research: Transforming Inquiry with Researchers, Educators, and Students* (London: Routledge, 2015).

20. This is a more favorable view of youth participation in the organization than that offered by Cazenave, *Impossible Democracy*. Most previous accounts of HARYOU have focused chiefly on the political conflict between Kenneth Clark and his allies and Congressman Adam Clayton Powell Jr. and his, and the media debates that followed from this. Asking less about the structure of control of HARYOU and its more quotidian practices with young people offers a different view of the organization.

21. Cazenave, *Impossible Democracy*, 105–16.

22. HARYOU-ACT, "1/2 Way Report: Is the Demonstration Experiment Working?" 1965, Library of Congress, Kenneth Clark Papers, box 133, folder 4.

23. Orleck and Hazirjian, *War on Poverty*.

24. Clark, "Profile of HARYOU," 1–2.

25. Matlin, *On the Corner*; and Markowitz and Rosner, *Children, Race, and Power*.

26. "HARYOU Associates: An Action Research Laboratory."

27. HARYOU, *Youth in the Ghetto*, 90.

28. Hundreds of pages of transcripts from this fieldwork as well as planning meetings are available in the papers of Kenneth Marshall, Cyril Tyson, Kenneth Clark, and the Harlem Neighborhood Association at the Schomburg Center.

29. Harlem Youth Opportunities Unlimited, Inc., Program Planning Department, "Street Interviews: Hilton Clark and Liz Ulla, by William Jones," n.d. (ca. 1963), KMP. Note that Hilton Clark was the teenage son of Kenneth and Mamie Clark.

30. HARYOU, *Youth in the Ghetto*, 84.

31. HARYOU, 84.

32. HARYOU, 575–76. These questions about how to balance youth autonomy and the need for guidance still engage those working in youth participatory action research today.

33. HARYOU, 91.

34. Tyson, *Power and Politics*, 42; and HARYOU, *Youth in the Ghetto*, 580–81. On Frost's work at HARYOU and later at Youth in Action in Bedford Stuyvesant, see the Olivia Pleasants Frost Papers, Schomburg.

35. HARYOU, *Youth in the Ghetto*, 585–96; and Clark, *Dark Ghetto*, xiii–xiv.

36. "A Proposal for the Planning of a Comprehensive Youth Services Program in Central Harlem Submitted by Harlem Youth Opportunities Unlimited, Inc., in Association with Harlem Neighborhoods Association, Inc. Under Public Law 087-274," May 15, 1962, HNAP, folder 7, box 7, n.p.

37. Clark, *Dark Ghetto*, 40.

38. Clark, 53.

39. "Leadership Training Workshop," n.d. (ca. 1963), JHCP, box 21, folder 56.

40. Markowitz and Rosner, *Children, Race, and Power*, 113–14.

41. Harlem Youth Opportunities Unlimited, Inc., "Leadership Training Workshop 'End of Program' Banquet, September 5, 1963," September 11, 1963, KMP, box 2, folder Haryou Leadership Training Workshop, 6–11.

42. L. [Laura] Pires, "Memo to J. Jones and K. Marshall," August 12, 1963, KMP, box 2, folder Haryou Leadership Training Workshop.

43. Roberta Gold, *When Tenants Claimed the City: The Struggle for Citizenship in New York City Housing* (Urbana: University of Illinois Press, 2014).

44. Harlem Youth Opportunities Unlimited, Inc., "Leadership Training Workshop 'End of Program' Banquet, September 5, 1963," 43–46.

45. Harlem Youth Opportunities Unlimited, Inc., 11; emphasis added.

46. John Henrik Clarke, "Workshop #1," May 16, 1985, JHCP, box 20, folder Course Outlines—NYC Board of Ed., District 17 Workshop on African-American History for Teachers, 1985, 6.

47. John Henrik Clarke to Robert MacBeth, n.d., JHCP, box 21, folder 46; "Heritage Classes," n.d., JHCP, box 21, folder 43; and Documentation on HARYOU staff workshops, JHCP box 21, folder 25.

48. "Proposal for a Community Action Institute," n.d., JHCP, box 21, folder 29.

49. Clarke to Organizing Committee, Community Action Institute, September 15, 1965, JHCP, box 21, folder 29; and Prospectus for A Summer Heritage Program, n.d., JHCP, box 21, folder 29.

50. See, for example, letters in JHCP, box 21, folder 1.

51. James Bryant Conant, *Slums and Suburbs: A Commentary on Schools in Metropolitan Areas*, 1st ed. (New York: McGraw-Hill, 1961). The term appears, for example, in "Summary of the Dinner Meeting."

52. "Summary of the Dinner Meeting."

53. Otis Sallid oral history with Ansley Erickson and Deidre Flowers, November 30, 2015. Recording in author's possession.

54. Sallid oral history and George Faison oral history with Ansley Erickson and Dina Asfaha, December 12, 2016. Recording in author's possession.

55. "HANA Confab Stars HARYOU-ACT Youth," *New York Amsterdam News*, February 10, 1968.

56. Larry Neal, "The Black Arts Movement," *Drama Review: TDR* 12, no. 4 (1968): 29–39, 32.

57. See, for example, Lee Cook, "Harlem Youth Seek Power," *Amsterdam News*, July 8, 1972.

CHAPTER 8

Intermediate School 201

Race, Space, and Modern Architecture in Harlem

MARTA GUTMAN

Faced with intransigent bureaucracy, struggling schools, deteriorating buildings, and entrenched racial segregation, parents in Harlem demanded direct control over the core functions of public education in the 1950s and 1960s. One new building became a flashpoint in the battle for community control—Intermediate School (IS) 201, the infamous windowless school that abuts the Park Avenue railroad viaduct two blocks north of East 125th Street, straddling Central Harlem and East Harlem. White architects and politicians, including the mayor, John Lindsay, rallied to defend "Harlem's besieged masterpiece," but parents in Harlem disagreed.[1] The location and the architecture, which many of them opposed, stood as a constant reminder of their unmet demands, from exclusion in policy making to broken promises of integration.

Well after the Supreme Court held racial segregation unconstitutional in the landmark *Brown v. Board of Education* decision (1954), New York City lagged in desegregating schools. Fed up with the glacial pace, pent-up anger about school facilities and ingrained racial segregation exploded in the late 1950s. Mae Mallory, Viola Waddy, and seven other women formed the Harlem Nine and organized a 162-day boycott of three junior high schools in 1958. This grassroots activism, coupled with court action, forced the Board of Education (BOE) to create an open enrollment policy—four long years after *Brown*.[2]

More protests followed. Civil rights activists, led by Reverend Milton Galamison, organized a citywide boycott in 1964. A photograph of an African American boy staring through a dirty, broken window illustrated the flyer that urged participation in "Freedom Day" (figure 8.1). The caption reads, "I Don't Have A Good Integrated School." More than 460,000 pupils—half of the students enrolled in the city's public schools—stayed home on February 3, making for the largest civil rights protest in U.S. history.[3] The generous explanation is that demands from white parents for segregated neighborhood schools and from Black parents for integrated schools were irreconcilable in the face of extraordinary demographic change: 1.5 million white residents left the city between 1950 and 1965, and the number of school-age children increased with Black and Puerto Rican boys and girls making up 75 percent of students by 1960.[4] Less generously, the BOE was, whether for reasons of racist ideology or inertia, comfortable operating a segregated school system.

Two years later, angry parents upped the ante in Harlem. They demanded that their community exercise direct control over IS 201, a stellar example of the BOE's intransigence. With the school scheduled to open on April 1, 1966, the Board of Education announced that mixing Blacks and Puerto Ricans in equal number would achieve racial integration. Black and Puerto Rican integration advocates wanted their children to share in the resources and political power that they knew accompanied white student enrollment.[5]

Pressured to do better by parents and community representatives at IS 201, the BOE tried to make its plan tolerable. It delayed the school opening and touted the building's advantages in a leaflet that it distributed to thousands of families in Queens and the Bronx who would have the option of enrolling. The response was lukewarm at best. Exactly nine white children from overcrowded junior high schools in Queens registered, and anger escalated in Harlem as it became clear that voluntary transfer had replaced compulsory zoning as the BOE's mechanism for desegregation. When the chair of the Board of Education, Lloyd Garrison, told the community that white children would come to the school once it had "proven" itself, the community answered in-kind: their children would stay out of school "until the school had proven itself" to them.[6]

To challenge segregation at IS 201 and its predicted consequences, parents turned to the time-honored tools of grassroots organizing and public

Figure 8.1 City Wide Committee for Integrated Schools, "School Boycott! Flier," 1964. Credit: Queens College Civil Rights Archives, accessed August 5, 2016, http://archives .qc.cuny.edu/civilrights/items/show/130.

protest.[7] The Harlem Parents Committee, chaired by Isaiah Robinson, and other community groups called for a boycott, determined that the school would not open until their demands were met. When the picket line formed on the opening day, September 12, 1966, fewer than 600 students (of the 1,800 who could have been enrolled) crossed it to attend classes; 80 percent were African American, 20 percent were Puerto Rican, and none were white. "A New Air-Conditioned School Means Nothing Unless the Children Attending It Are Learning," one leaflet read.[8] "I don't want segregation, but if I have it I want it on my own terms," David Spencer, a parent and community leader, told a reporter. "I feel I know what's best for me."[9] Mae Mallory, Stokely Carmichael, and other members of the Student Nonviolent Coordinating Committee, the Congress of Racial Equality, the Black Panther Party, and other community groups joined Spencer, Alice Kornegay, Helen Testamark, Suki Ports, and other parents on the picket line.[10]

The boycott, which lasted almost three weeks, succeeded. Parents forced the white principal, Stanley Lisser, to resign, and pressured the Board of Education to hire a Black administrator and integrate African and African American history and culture into the curriculum. Their victory paved the way for an experiment in local self-governance in education that the Ford Foundation funded in 1967; defined formally as a "demonstration district," at IS 201 and two other schools, this experiment was known informally as community control. And although New York's ultimate decentralization of school governance in 1970 was far from what community-control advocates had sought in the 1950s and 1960s, the IS 201 activism helped propel that change as well.[11]

This chapter directs attention to architecture—to the polarization that design caused, and the opportunities that it also afforded. IS 201, designed by Nathaniel Curtis and Arthur Q. Davis, white architects based in New Orleans, is an example of an equalization school. Southern school districts in the pre–*Brown* years sought to fend off desegregation by bringing segregated educational facilities for Black children closer to parity with those for white children. In the 1950s an equalization school in the South was materially better than one from the Jim Crow period, but it was not exactly the same in every aspect of its design as one built for white children. These modern schools benefited African Americans in that they were Black-run institutions and they employed African American teachers. However, the new schools continued to constitute Black children as social subjects with inherently unequal citizenship rights.[12]

IS 201 served the purposes of equalization in New York City even though the BOE did not adopt a formal policy of equalization or admit that it built equalization schools deliberately. However, this school, a modern school, designed and built to higher standard than any other one in Harlem, reinforced existing patterns of racial segregation, much to the dismay of parents and civil rights activists. And the process of planning and building IS 201 exposed the political disempowerment that reinforced school segregation in New York City. In keeping with its top-down, stratified management, the Board of Education reluctantly incorporated new methods of citizen participation into its planning process but did not value this input, even though public hearings and other mechanisms for expanding local democracy had been in use in the city since the early 1950s.[13]

Harlem parents wanted to harness opportunities in the built environment to make better lives for themselves and their children, and they used urban space to make their demands known to the public. Whether they articulated a vision for the future based in integration or Black autonomy, whether they embraced modern architecture or disdained it, urban places figured in their aspirations for a just society. The exceptional design of IS 201, the heated disputes about the boycott in 1966, the teachers' strikes in 1967 and 1968, and decentralization of the Board of Education have obscured the interplay between space and society that took place at the school.

Henri Lefebvre, who theorized the dynamic relationship between space and society in architecture, helps frame the discussion. IS 201 is an excellent example of Lefebvre's argument that the physical, social, and discursive constructions of space work simultaneously in buildings, and that each aspect is open to and a cause of contestation. Famously, Lefebvre insisted that space is at once a physical, social, and discursive construction, and that space is made through the way it is built, lived, and imagined. He also asserted that citizens win their rights to the city, which he defined as the right to urban life, through temporal and spatial struggles as well through public debate and electoral politics. He maintained that appropriating urban space has an emancipatory potential in liberal capitalist democracies, but he also cautioned that appropriated spaces are likely to replicate at least some of the power relations of the dominant society.[14]

Set back from Madison Avenue, supported by tapered concrete piers, and without a single window in a classroom, IS 201 was the first fully air-conditioned public school in the city. It took Curtis and Davis almost two years to design the building, prepare construction documents, and bid the job; this time frame, typical for a public project, stood out as expeditious in New York City in the early 1960s.[15] Contractors broke ground in 1964, and the $5 million price tag made IS 201 the most expensive school yet built in the city.[16] Babette Edwards, a community leader who served as chair of the East Harlem Union for Equal Achievement in Schools in the mid-1960s, expressed that it horrified parents to see first the concrete frame and then the brick enclosure rise up next to the railroad viaduct. Forty years later, her voice conveyed anger at the memory.[17]

The architectural form of IS 201, closed to the community and the world, embodied Cold War ideologies and deficit-minded views of African American and Latinx communities circulating in domestic social policy in the same years. The school doubled as an air-raid shelter (as did IS 55 in Ocean Hill-Brownsville, Brooklyn, designed by the same architects). According to the architecture historian David Monteyne, the defensive posture of both schools is racist, expressing containment, control, and fear of the other that were part and parcel of Cold War politics.[18] Harlem education activists often called on this example, Vietnam War imagery, to decry the violence done to Black and Latinx young men called to fight in a war not of their own choosing.

A perspective drawing of IS 201 helps to explain Monteyne's point. Helmut Jacoby, an architect and highly regarded renderer, delineated the view in 1963, showing the building from the southeast corner of Madison Avenue and East 127th Street. He deliberately included the Harlem context in his rendering, insisting that it was his "specific task to show a not yet existing building in its real surroundings."[19] And yet the view is idealized. The three-story building, shown as an impermeable abstract block, glistens in the sunshine and is surrounded by elegant row houses (and a tenement or two), graceful street trees, clean streets and sidewalks, and relaxed children. Idealized or not, this broader view did not persist in later reproductions of the rendering.[20] The frequently published version (figure 8.2), cropped to emphasize the defensive posture of the building, shows only a few neighborhood features—some trees, the street and sidewalk, and a train spewing smoke as it chugs along the viaduct. The inclusion is deliberate: the noise and air pollution caused by the train was one

Figure 8.2 View of IS 201, Curtis and Davis, 1963.
Credit: Office of Civil Defense, Department of Defense, "New Buildings with Fallout Protection" (Washington, D.C., 1963), 20–23. A copy of the drawing is in the National Archives.

reason for making the school windowless.[21] The drawing also suggested that this school could obviate the deleterious influences of the East Harlem environment on children and remedy the systemic, acute failure of public education in the ghetto.

African American boys left high school at an alarming rate—75 percent across New York City in the mid-1960s.[22] Crime, vandalism, delinquency, and drug addiction were also of great concern as were the battles over turf that erupted between young men in Harlem and other areas of Manhattan.[23] In this context, Jacoby made sure to depict a policeman in the architectural rendering; he is standing on the sidewalk near the main entrance to the school with one hand extended, and the other one resting near his gun. In deference to the promise of a racially integrated school, white and Black children are shown even though it was unusual for them to play or live together in the same place in this moment in East Harlem. Black boys and girls stand inside the fenced playground, while white boys and girls pass by, walking to school. White children, privileged in public space, glance at Black children, contained by a tall metal fence.[24]

Modern architecture beckoned to African Americans and Puerto Ricans who were eager to shed the strictures of the past, but this school was not what they had hoped for.[25] Even though the building was modern, up-to-date, and full of amenities that were not found in public schools in Harlem, the design valorized abstraction, monumentality, and technical virtuosity at all cost. At best, Curtis and Davis designed a school that did not square with the community's vision for its children's future; at worst the building ingrained racial inequalities (and the power of an authoritarian school board) in the present.

To Curtis and Davis and their liberal allies in the architecture community, the windowless school exemplified best practices. Angry parents called it a "prison," "a tomb on stilts," a "warehouse," or a "fortress."[26] They didn't want us to look in," Babette Edwards recalled. Her scathing comment echoed a cartoon published in the *New York Amsterdam News* and reprinted in the *New York Times*.[27] To Preston R. Wilcox, the sociologist and community organizer who advised the negotiating team during the 1966 boycott (and the governing board afterward), this school was an equalization school, "a palliative for anger" in a community that had sought desegregation for decades. It symbolized "the worst in community planning and public education." He wrote, "The die has been cast in architectural form. The architecture has soothed the guilt of the Board; it has failed to handle the legitimate anger of the ghetto."[28]

Segregated and Windowless by Design

Who selected the site? Who decided to make the school windowless? Who decided to hire white architects from New Orleans? Alas, the archival record is silent on who made these crucial decisions. The architectural model survived, thanks to Lillie Crowder, an African American architect who worked at the Board of Education for thirty years, and the working drawings are housed in the New York City Municipal Archives. However, researchers noted that in the late 1960s the BOE started refusing to share information about the school.[29] Potentially rich sources for it, the monthly meeting minutes of the BOE's Committee on Buildings and Sites, were collected only sporadically after the Board of Education reorganized in 1961, just as IS 201 entered its purview.

According to community leaders, the battle for an integrated school started in 1958. Parents learned that the Board of Education intended to build the new junior high school to relieve overcrowding in James Fennimore Cooper Junior High School (JHS) 120 and JHS 45.[30] When parents warned the superintendent of schools, John Theobald, that the proposed location near the East Harlem Triangle would obviate their goal of desegregation, he set aside the proposal to build the new school and supported instead the community's plan to bus a modest number of students from East Harlem to Yorkville schools.[31] The pledge not to build in East Harlem proved to be the first of many broken promises.

For some Harlem parents, though, a new junior high school in the Triangle was much preferable to other options. The New York City Planning Commission announced in June 1961 that it intended to rezone a substantial portion of East Harlem as an industrial park. Outraged, Alice Kornegay, already renowned as an activist, organized the East Harlem Triangle Community Association and demanded a new junior high school as part of her strategy to defeat the rezoning plan. Kornegay saw a racially integrated, up-to-date school as the surest guarantee of a high-quality education for Harlem children. She called for the BOE to make a new school "with superior standards and with unique facilities." Such a school "must attract students from all parts of New York, resulting in an exchange of ideas, ambitions, and interests between students of all racial, economic, and cultural backgrounds."[32]

By 1961 the Board of Education had selected a site for the school: the short city block from East 127th to East 128th Street, between Madison Avenue and the Park Avenue viaduct. When the proposal for what was promised to be an integrated school was released, the Harlem community raised questions about several matters, especially segregation, air-conditioning, and the lack of space for play.[33] The chairman of the City Planning Commission, James Felt, concurred about the playground, and at the public hearing held on August 14, 1962, he instructed the BOE to "initiate proceedings now for acquisition of property for a playground for this school."[34] As in earlier slum-clearance projects, a warehouse, a church, tenements, row houses, and an apartment house—worn buildings, but the places where everyday life was lived in East Harlem—would be demolished to make way for a public project that was planned with minimal citizen participation.[35]

Proximity to the Triborough Bridge, the Board of Education claimed, would make it possible for children from overcrowded schools in Harlem, the South Bronx, and Queens to attend the new school. Dumbfounded, Harlem parents pointed out that white parents would refuse to send their children to school in an impoverished community of color that had more than its fair share of social problems. They demanded that the BOE relocate the school, present a clear plan for integration, and hire a Black male principal.[36]

The Board of Education refused to budge. Eugene F. Hult, the head of the Office of School Facilities Planning, offered this explanation to a reporter in 1966: "In a big system like this, where we build 30 or 40 schools a year, we just don't have time to consult the local people," he said. Even if the consultation had taken place, Hult indicated that a change in the architectural concept would have been unlikely because "the design was a new concept which the pedagogy people wanted."[37]

Hult referred to the open-plan, windowless classrooms that the Educational Facilities Laboratories (EFL) promoted for schools. Organized in 1958 and backed by the Ford Foundation, the EFL funded experiments in all matters pertaining to schools including design and construction.[38] In 1962, the EFL invited a research unit at the architecture school at the University of Michigan to test the desirability of the windowless classroom, and published the findings in a report that hailed the design.[39] Explaining that advances in air-conditioning and artificial illumination rendered windows technologically obsolete, the EFL counseled architects to discard them altogether in schools. The long-standing symbolic association of light with education was ignored.[40] Because windows distracted children, especially boys, by drawing their attention to the world outside the school, the EFL asserted that a windowless classroom would improve the attention span of students, offer economy in construction, increase security, and engender flexibility in planning. A windowless classroom facilitated the open classroom and "interdependence among teachers," including those who were reluctant to embrace new informal methods of instruction.[41]

When news of the Michigan experiment was leaked to the press, the *Wall Street Journal* published a front-page exposé. Teachers were concerned about autonomy, noise, and claustrophobia, parents about the use of their children as human subjects, and the glass industry about the loss of business. Even Jonathan King, the chief administrator of the EFL, expressed some ambivalence.[42] Not so the New York City Board of Education: it forged ahead, and not only for purposes of pedagogical innovation.

The BOE faced a perfect storm of competing regulations pertaining to school design. School buildings in New York State needed to be located in areas relatively free from "injurious chemicals and dust"—not the case next to the railroad.[43] An experimental windowless school could resolve that problem, but regulations also required generously sized windows (but not necessarily ones that opened) in each classroom.[44] The Cuban Missile Crisis helped resolve the regulatory conundrum. In response to the prospect of nuclear war, the state's education department announced in 1963 that it would permit windowless classrooms in the basements of schools that were used as fallout shelters.[45] Although school districts in cities of over one million inhabitants were exempt from obtaining state review and approval of plans and specifications, the green light was welcome. One year later, the Board of Education informed the Office of Civil Defense that IS 201 also could double as a fallout shelter because of "many inherent features" in the design. By way of proof, it sent the perspective view and two photographs of the architectural model.[46] One photo had been published in *Time* magazine in 1963, illustrating a story that touted the benefits of air-conditioning in windowless schools and other institutional buildings.[47]

An Equalization School in East Harlem

Enter Curtis and Davis. Controversy had touched the firm again and again because of contentious buildings and charges of unethical practice, but it was well regarded in 1960 including for the innovative public schools that it designed for Black neighborhoods in New Orleans—high-quality equalization schools such as the Thomy Lafon Elementary School in "Back of Town." Winner of the National AIA First Honor Award, this public school was widely publicized (featured in *LIFE* magazine in 1954) and even exhibited in Moscow in 1959; a photograph of the school was hung at the entry to the United States Trade and Cultural Fair in Sokolinki Park (site of the famous kitchen debate between Richard Nixon and Nikita Khrushchev).[48]

With that kind of publicity (and the backing of powerful mentors such as the architect Walter Gropius, Davis's teacher at the Graduate School of Design at Harvard University), Curtis and Davis's practice flourished. A junior partner, Walter Rooney, led the New York branch office. He looked for commissions for hotels that would, along with prisons and correctional facilities, embassies, and sports arenas, provide bread-and-butter work for the firm. The hotel commissions did not pan out, and Rooney set out to find other work, including IS 201.[49]

While the architects developed the design for a new junior high school, the Board of Education and the New York Chapter of the American Institute of Architects cosponsored a seminar on urban schools in 1963 with a new advisory committee on school design and construction. The list of participants included Dr. Benjamin Willis, the superintendent of schools in Chicago, Edward Logue, the director of the Boston Redevelopment Authority, and Jonathan King from the EFL. John F. Hennessy, a board member, committee chair, and prominent engineer, explained in the press release, "Much thought has been given suburban schools, but there has been virtually no extensive consideration of the requirements for City schools. These include, among others, special designs to confirm to limited sites, restricted play areas, relocation of tenants, and problems presented by temptations to vandalism."[50]

Is it a coincidence that Hennessey highlighted the design challenges that Curtis and Davis faced in IS 201, including the small site, restricted play area, vandalism, and tenant relocation? Is it a coincidence that the EFL helped to fund the conference? Is it a coincidence that Rooney handled the arrangements? Clearly, the seminar set the stage for promoting a building that was already controversial in the community and among planning professionals.

Curtis and Davis called on lessons learned in New Orleans as they satisfied the strict requirements for a junior high school in New York City—classrooms for 1,800 students, an auditorium, a cafeteria, a gymnasium, and a playground.[51] The site proved to be an intractable problem. Hult and his supervisor, Adrian Blumenfeld, ignored Felt's mandate to provide additional playground space because it required clearing more buildings and relocating more tenants in a community weary of both (as a confidential memo had apprised BOE members in 1962).[52] As a consequence, the problem of play remained where it had landed at the start of the design process, which was squarely in the architects' laps. To address this pressing need, Curtis and Davis set the school back from Madison Avenue (to make space for the fenced playground), lifted the front end of the building fourteen feet off the ground, and supported it on concrete piers to create a covered plaza, intended as a public space and area for play. Unfortunately, to fit the building on the site, the architects had to push the school close to the railroad viaduct, with the attendant noise and air pollution.

The 1961 Zoning Resolution, which made the office tower and plaza ubiquitous in midtown Manhattan, likely influenced the decision to set the school back from Madison Avenue, as did the mentality of equalization.[53] Two blocks north of the IS 201 site, a parochial school run by All Souls Church showed that a fine school, with generous operable windows, could be built on a short block that abutted the railroad viaduct. However, the short block did not have enough space for a junior high school and a playground given the preference for a low-slung, sleek, freestanding, modern school. The mentality of equalization required a midcentury modernist building with a small playground, not a multistoried, traditionally fenestrated building like All Souls.

Enter the windowless solution, favored by the professional staff in the pedagogy and construction departments at the BOE. A windowless school allowed flexibility in classroom use, facilitated the use of audiovisual aids, and promised to reduce operating and maintenance costs.[54] Architects were starting to take note of the cost of energy (one reason the EFL promoted the windowless solution, the express concern being with the cost of heating, not air-conditioning).[55] Vandalism had also caused window replacement to skyrocket in public schools. Broken windows figure prominently in *The Diary of a Harlem Schoolteacher*, the haunting account that Jim Haskins wrote about his experience in Harlem schools.[56] And the Office of Civil Defense preferred a windowless school because it created an air-raid shelter at no cost to the federal government.

IS 201 does, in fact, have windows—to light its four entries and the administrative offices on the ground floor and the corridors upstairs. The "floor-to-ceiling and wall-to-wall expanses at the end of each corridor" are placed to "avoid a closed-in feeling," Leonard Buder, the education reporter for the *New York Times*, explained in May 1966.[57] Buder (often an apologist for the BOE) did not make clear that the cladding, perforated brick screens, rendered the hall glazing invisible from the street and masked the mechanical system of fresh air intakes. Rather, he emphasized that they protected glass from vandals.

For all the investment in the physical structure, for all the attention to detail, the emotional and psychological needs of Harlem children did not enter the discussion until it came time to promote the school to a public that was dubious about its merits. By design, children in a windowless classroom lose contact with the outside world; they have no measure by which to check the clock time that sets the pace inside the building against the rhythm of the world outside. Lillie Crowder alluded to these issues when she discussed IS 201: "This school had an interesting concept, captured by the architects, with the notion that the parents and administrators in Harlem would comprehend and like it," Crowder said. But they gave "little thought at the time of the potential psychological effect on students on the inside . . . or other drawbacks, such as . . . the stench from [the use of covered exterior spaces] as a rest room" (Preston Wilcox also criticized the open arcade, used by homeless people).[58] Crowder went on to criticize the architects for failing to grasp the specificities of the urban context or evince concern for the varieties of human experiences in buildings, especially among children.

Even so, the New York chapter of the American Institute of Architects singled out the building for its top honor in 1966.[59] Focusing on their perception of the area rather than students' experiences, the jury applauded the school as "a courageous solution of the difficult problems inherent in the school's neighborhood and in its restricted site." The "imaginative and effective solutions to the problems of 'environmental control'" also won praise.[60] In keeping with the equalization schools that the architects had designed in New Orleans, no expense was spared inside the high-end iteration in New York. The Board of Education did not explain its reasoning for making this decision, but this much seems clear—on the one hand, the professional staff hoped the high-end design would attract white students to the school, and on the other hand, it expected that the promise of architectural excellence would produce acquiescence in Harlem, stifling protest about a segregated school—serving as "a palliative for anger," as Wilcox stated. The basement was equipped with a wood shop, science lab, and other special classrooms; high-quality, durable finishes were used in the public spaces, including the auditorium and gymnasium on the second floor; and the classrooms were designed to be generous in scale. Curtis and Davis clad the building in red brick screens, and alluded to classical European, African, and Native American architecture with tapered columns and beams, a hypostyle hall, arcade, and kiva-inspired seating in the playground.

The criticism intensified so much so that the Board of Education asked Curtis and Davis to produce a brochure to explain the design rationale of the school.[61] The architects described the organization of each floor and

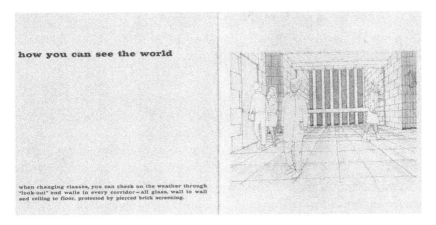

how you can see the world

when changing classes, you can check on the weather through "look-out" end walls in every corridor—all glass, wall to wall and ceiling to floor, protected by pierced brick screening.

Figure 8.3 "How You Can See the World," Curtis and Davis, 1966.
Credit: To the Pupils and Parents, Arthur A. Schomburg Junior High School, from the Architects, Curtis and Davis, 1967. A copy is in New York City Municipal Archives.

provided sketches to answer these questions: "Why is your school up in air?" "What makes rooms for thought? "What lights the scene?" "How does your classroom grow?" "How you can see the world?" "How does the air conditioning work?" In each case, the sketches emphasized protection, containment, and separation, and underscored the assumption that a child needed to be removed from the world outside the school if the child was to learn.

At this historical moment, an architectural argument predicated on enclosure and exclusion did not make sense in Harlem. Wilcox and many others argued that the world outside the school, the ghetto, ought to be embraced as a source of strength and pride. This sketch, titled "How You Can See the World," is the most troubling, for its allusion to prisons (figure 8.3). Wilcox may have had this area of the building in mind when he wrote that, "I.S. 201 stands as a monument to absentee-decision-making, colonialism." It is "a personal affront."[62]

To a thinker like Henri Lefebvre, abstract space, endemic in the mass-produced buildings of modern societies, diminishes "affective, bodily, lived experience." This diminution has grave consequences; it does not "permit a continual back-and-forth" that all members of society need to forge the "consensus" that "confers upon them the status of 'subjects.'"[63] Through Lefebvre's lens, the physical space of IS 201 cast children as objects. Yet the relations between a building and the larger world are not fixed at the time of construction, as Lefebvre also insisted. And, as bell hooks reminds us, places on the margins can incubate creative challenges to hegemonic social orders.[64]

A Space of Radical Openness for Children

"If one believes that a segregated white school can be a 'good school,'" Preston Wilcox stated, "then one must believe that a segregated Negro and Puerto Rican school, like I.S. 201 can be a 'good' school also."[65] As the controversy at IS 201 escalated, the Ford Foundation entered the stage. McGeorge Bundy became president of the foundation in 1966, soon after John Lindsay, his good friend and college roommate at Yale University, had been elected mayor of New York City. Lindsay, who inherited the explosive situation in the city's public schools, turned to Bundy for help.[66]

Under Bundy's leadership, the foundation funded three experiments in local self-governance in 1967—"demonstration districts" in Brooklyn, the Lower East Side, and East Harlem—as a means of improving education. Harlem's demonstration district centered on the IS 201 Complex, including the new intermediate school, four elementary schools, and a building where the governing board rented an office.[67] The governing board of the IS 201 Complex, a key component of the self-governance plan, reflected the interracial, interfaith, and multiethnic coalition that had coalesced in support of community control. The board elected Isaiah Robinson president (he went on to become the first African American president of the Board of Education), and hired teachers, staff, and administrators of color including the acting principal, Ronald Evans. Ann Crary Evans, his partner, taught at Public School (PS) 133, one of the affiliated elementary schools.

The short-lived experiment in self-governance at IS 201 had identifiable accomplishments amid the controversy. Evans (like Wilcox) berated the central Board of Education for locating the new building near the railroad, hiring white architects, spending a fortune on an experimental design, and refusing to countenance citizen participation in the planning process. But he appreciated that the new building was well built, fully equipped, and without any rats. "So, it didn't have any windows," he said, shrugging his shoulders.[68] The governing board issued a comprehensive manual full of information for Harlem and East Harlem residents, developed a community education center (Wilcox was the chief consultant), placed graduates in the city's specialized high schools, and ran summer tutoring programs to prepare students for college (Smith College was one partner). It also reached out to the Latinx community (Evelina Antonetty, the president of United Bronx Parents, was an ally), supported bilingual education (the IS 201 Complex's newspaper, *Kweli*, was published in Spanish and English), integrated Black and African studies into the curriculum, experimented with pedagogy, and fought for resources for students. Providing evidence that the curricular struggles that activist teachers and authors (as described in chapters 4 and 5 of this volume) had waged in earlier decades continued, Evans noted that "books by black scholars and writers like Claude McKay, James Baldwin, Zora Neale Hurston, Langston Hughes . . . were not on the approved book list," but Evans included them.[69] He found a mentor in Herbert Kohl, the radical educator and activist in East Harlem schools, and learned about other experimental pedagogies, including from the woman who would become his wife.[70] Not every parent welcomed professionals relatively new to the struggle for better schools in East Harlem. Some (Helen Testamark was one) targeted radical educators who they believed had co-opted their hard work, promoted racial hatred, excluded them from the governance experiment, and ignored their demands for a community-based education that would empower their children.[71]

For Ann Evans, the IS 201 Complex was "magical." "It was Camelot."[72] Ann taught for seven years at PS 133, where the principal, Dellora Hercules, agreed to participate in an experiment funded by the Center for Urban Education. The child-centered Gattegno approach to reading and math instruction was introduced into the first-, second-, and third-grade curricula in the fall of 1968. Like almost all the teachers in the IS 201 Complex, Ann stayed on the job during the citywide teachers' strike that fall. "We were learning to start where we found each child and to build from there," she said.[73] Barbara Wilson-Brooks, who attended PS 133 from kindergarten through the fifth grade, benefited from the child-centered pedagogy. "The school really stood out for me because . . . we learned . . . that's where we blossomed. Everybody cared for us."[74]

The experiment ended abruptly, when the principal left for another school. This happened as the demonstration districts were being dismantled and replaced with a weaker form of governance known as community control. Ann Evans set aside teaching for other work. Looking back on this time in her life, she wrote, "The experiment in community control . . . will always be remembered as one, brief shining moment when the black and Hispanic community united to take charge of their own schools, and when education flourished as students and parents and teachers worked together in an atmosphere where the humanization of education . . . was taking place. . . . I disagree with those who dismiss the P.S. 133 project as a failed project because it didn't last."[75]

Wilson-Brooks moved to IS 201 for seventh and eighth grades, attending it after the demonstration district had been shut down. Although she was wary about coming to a school that had engendered so much controversy, she came to enjoy the place. She received what she felt was a fine education, one that included discussions of Black Power, African history, and culture. The building's distinct design figured in her understanding of the school, and not only because it was a cause of the boycott. She took the high quality of the design, including the air-conditioning, to mean that IS 201 was intended for white students, too. "This is our community," she said. "Why isn't it good enough to have our children go there?"[76]

Michael Darby and Derrick Black attended IS 201 during Evans's tenure and, as Wilson-Brooks did, they valued the school and their education. They also held Evans in high esteem, because he was personable and accessible, strict and fair, and he encouraged them to achieve. Black's mother sent him to IS 201 because it was a good school with a strong academic program, and it was close to home, but not so close that it would expose him to the unwanted influences of "the crew." He took the city bus, an "upscale" way for a student from Harlem to travel to public school. IS 201 appealed to both children because of its architectural presence; it also had amenities that other schools in Harlem lacked—the gymnasium ("pretty amazing," Darby said), shops, labs, a cafeteria, and so forth. If their friends teased them about going to a windowless school, one that looked like a prison, they corrected the misapprehension, referring to the windows at the end of the hallways and in the administrative suite. "Outside in" was one way to see the school; "inside out" was another.[77]

Inside, teachers experimented with design, setting aside the front-facing layout of the traditional classroom for less authoritarian open-plan arrangements (also promoted by the EFL).[78] Each classroom had an accordion wall, making it possible for up to four rooms to be joined into one. Black explained that teachers took advantage of this feature to encourage students to collaborate on group projects. Desks were not arranged in straight rows, and teachers did not sit at the front of the classroom; rather students worked in small groups and appointed a spokesperson who would present the work at the end of the session. Black emphasized that the traditional classroom, which he had experienced in elementary school, was less useful. "In a different environment people can face each other, share different ideas, just like we're doing here," he said.[79]

Students also learned that they could turn the architectural logic of the building inside out. Blondell Cummings, who had a brief experience as a substitute teacher at IS 201, remembered that pupils would walk down the hallways, reach into the classrooms, switch off the lights and then let the door close behind them, leaving the classroom in total darkness. Her story puzzled Darby and Black who remember that teachers controlled the lights with a special key, but they do agree with Cummings that the hallways enticed experimentation (and not of the sort that Evans encouraged). They played ball at the light wells, shooting a small ball, a spaldeen, over the railing. "It was like a league," Black said, and went on to point out humorously that this game "helped us with hand and eye coordination."[80] He did not play sports after school because his mother wanted him to study, determined that he would go to college.

For Darby and Black, the boycott and strike have slipped from active memory ("we were kids"), but not the broader cause of Black Power and empowerment that shaped schooling at IS 201. Black mentioned dress and hair, and turned to other matters when asked if he recalled the assassination of Malcolm X. He nodded yes and went on to say that he also remembered that the assassination of "Dr. King had a huge impact on the country." He reflected that "it was a moment. I got to be proud of my heritage, even though I wasn't marching up and down the streets."[81]

The governing board made it a priority to promote Black empowerment and Black Power. Architecture helped because the state-of-the-art school contained a beautiful auditorium. In this room, Herman Fergusson delivered an incendiary tribute to his mentor and friend, Malcolm X; James Baldwin and Betty Shabazz attended the ceremony and heard Fergusson call the Harlem community to arms (figure 8.4).[82] Russell Rickford's discussion (in chapter 9 of this volume) of IS 201 in the context of alternative Black educational spaces further illustrates how the school engaged Black culture and politics.

IS 201 also focused on the arts. Curtis and Davis expected that a windowless school would free a child's imagination, but teachers knew better.

Figure 8.4 Program for Malcolm X Memorial Service, February 21, 1969, cover. Credit: New York Public Library, Schomburg Manuscripts, Archives, and Rare Books Division, Schomburg Center for Research in Black Culture, Babette Edwards Education Reform in Harlem collection, SC MG 809, box 6, folder 6.20, Malcolm X.

They offered classes in dance, music, and theater, took their students outside to draw and paint, and displayed artwork in parks and playgrounds.
They published catalogs (one title was "The Children Speak: Art from
I.S. 201"); they included artwork in the school's yearbook; and they engaged parents in activities that they ran for pupils in the streets alongside
the school. The artwork was of such high quality that the American Museum of Natural History exhibited it in 1971.

And finally, IS 201 spawned other experiments, including those that
centered on design. Both Isaiah Robinson and Preston Wilcox joined the
board of directors of the Architects Renewal Committee in Harlem
(ARCH) in the spring of 1968 after radical African American architects,
engineers, and planners, led by J. Max Bond Jr., took over the leadership.
ARCH developed a master plan for the East Harlem Triangle (at Kornegay's
request), created educational programs, such as Architecture in the Neighborhoods, which Mary Dowery directed, and proposed new buildings.
High on the agenda was a new high school for Harlem.[83]

IS 201, a "monument to absentee-decision-making," remains an enduring emblem of the violence that equalization schools and segregationist
policy making caused for everyday people and their communities in the
middle of the twentieth century. But, following Lefebvre's point that spaces
are constructed and appropriated, there is no single story to tell about IS 201.
At this school, parents, teachers, administrators, and children of color engaged in the back-and-forth that made them *subjects*, not merely the objects
of a technocratic, racist, architectural determinism. In the process, they also
made this school belong to them.

Their activism changed Harlem and contributed to the broader cause
of citizen participation in New York City, showing that the time-honored
tools of protest, boycott, and community organizing at the neighborhood
scale can change cities, schools, and architecture for the better. Their efforts even changed the city's position on the school's most derided feature.

The Board of Education's Advisory Committee on School Construction met each month through the 1960s. The committee discussed all sorts
of issues pertaining to design and construction. The minutes of the meeting held on June 13, 1968, noted that "the following items were reviewed."
This is the first item on the list: "The matter of windowless schools was
discussed briefly. In the opinion of the committee, windowless schools were
psychologically controversial and should not be encouraged in future work,
unless for exceptional reasons."[84] The Educational Facilities Laboratories

concurred, having executed a complete about-face as to the merits of the windowless classroom.[85]

Notes

1. James Bailey, "Harlem's Besieged Masterpiece," *Architectural Forum* 125, no. 4 (1966): 48–51. The name of this school has changed several times. In this essay I call it, "IS 201."
2. Adina Back, "Exposing the 'Whole Segregation Myth': The Harlem Nine and New York City's School Desegregation Battles," in *Freedom North: Black Freedom Struggles Outside the South, 1940–1980*, ed. Jeanne Theoharis and Komozi Woodard (New York: Palgrave Macmillan, 2003), 65–91.
3. Clarence Taylor, *Knocking at Our Own Door: Milton A. Galamison and the Struggle to Integrate New York City Schools* (New York: Columbia University Press, 1997); and City Wide Committee for Integrated Schools, "School Boycott! Flier," *Queens College Civil Rights Archives*, accessed August 5, 2016, http://archives.qc.cuny.edu/civilrights/items/show/130.
4. State Education Commissioner's Advisory Committee on Human Relations and Community Tensions, "Desegregating Public Schools in New York City" (New York: New York State Department of Education [hereafter NYSDOE] and New York City Board of Education [hereafter NYCBOE], 1964); and New York City Planning Commission [hereafter NYCPC], *Plan for New York City 1969*, vol. 1: *Critical Issues* (New York, 1969), cited in Prashant Banerjee et al., "Mid-Century Modern Schools: Preserving Post-War Modern Schools in New York," Student project (New York: Columbia University Graduate School of Architecture Planning and Preservation, Historic Preservation Program, 2013), 8n5.
5. On community control, see among others Jerold Podair, *The Strike That Changed New York: Blacks, Whites, and the Ocean Hill-Brownsville Crisis* (New Haven, Conn.: Yale University Press, 2004); and Heather Lewis, *New York City Public Schools from Brownsville to Bloomberg: Community Control and Its Legacy* (New York: Teachers College Press, 2013).
6. "I.S. 201: Symbol of the Struggle for Justice in Urban Education," *East Harlem Protestant Parish Newsletter*, October 1966, 4–5, in Municipal Archives of the City of New York Board of Education of the City of New York Collection (hereafter MA BOE), series 385, Rose Shapiro Papers 1961–1969 (hereafter RSP), subseries c, box 6, folder 18.
7. Michael R. Glass, "'A Series of Blunders and Broken Promises': I.S. 201 as a Turning Point," accessed February 19, 2019, http://www.gothamcenter.org/blog/a-series-of-blunders-and-broken-promises-is-201-as-a-turning-point.
8. The leaflet is reproduced in Thomas K. Minter, *Intermediate School 201, Manhattan: Center of Controversy* (Cambridge, Mass.: Harvard Graduate School of Education, 1967), 3.
9. Quoted in Jeremy Larner, "I.S. 201: Disaster in the Schools," *Dissent* 45, no. 1 (1967): 27–33.
10. "A 'Brick Concentration Camp,'" *Jet*, October 13, 1966, 16–17; Thomas A. Johnson, "Black Panthers Picket a School," *New York Times*, September 13, 1966, 38; and William Knapp, Commanding Officer, Bureau of Special Services, Memo to Chief Inspector, re Dispute Between the Board of Education and East Harlem Parents and Community Leaders Involving Intermediate School #201 in Harlem, September 23, 1966, B.S.S. #548-M (Supplementary #10) in Numbered Communication Files, New York Police Department Surveillance Records, 1939–1973, MA.

11. Podair, *Strike That Changed New York*.

12. Rachel Devlin, *A Girl Stands at the Door: The Generation of Young Women Who Desegregated America's Schools* (New York: Basic Books, 2018), 14–18, 58–65; James E. Ryan, *Five Miles Away: One City, Two Schools, and the Story of Educational Opportunity in America* (New York: Oxford University Press, 2010), 26–27; and Amy S. Weisser, "Marking Brown v. Board of Education: Memorializing Separate and Unequal Spaces," in *Sites of Memory: Perspectives on Architecture and Race*, ed. Craig E. Barton (New York: Princeton Architecture Press, 2001), 97–108.

13. Marci Reaven, "Neighborhood Activism in Planning for New York City, 1945–1975," *Journal of Urban History*, first published April 28, 2017, https://doi.org/10.1177/0096144217705446.

14. Henri Lefebvre, *The Production of Space*, trans. Donald Nicholson-Smith (Oxford: Blackwell, 1991); and Lefebvre, "The Right to the City," in *Writings on Cities*, ed. and trans. Eleonore Kofman and Elizabeth Lebas (Oxford: Blackwell, 1996), 147–59.

15. NYCBOE, *Journal of the Board of Education of the City of New York* (New York: City of New York, v.d.), entries dated January 4, 1962: 67, January 25, 1962: 162, February 28, 1962: 266, March 8, 1962: 399, April 16, 1962: 586, May 8, 1962: 730, July 8, 1962: 1104, August 22, 1962: 1371, 1469, October 11, 1962: 1524–25, May 12, 1964: 732, and November 18, 1964: 1723.

16. Diane Ravitch, *The Great School Wars: A History of New York City Public Schools*, 3rd ed. (Baltimore: Johns Hopkins University Press, 2000), 294–95.

17. Babette Edwards, telephone conversation with author, June 16, 2014.

18. David Monteyne, *Fallout Shelter: Designing for Civil Defense in the Cold War* (Minneapolis: University of Minnesota Press, 2011), 194–98.

19. Cited by Claudius Coulin, "Introduction," in Helmut Jacoby, *Architectural Drawings* (New York: Frederick A. Praeger, 1965), 5; and Alison Isenberg, *Designing San Francisco: Art, Land and Urban Renewal in the City by the Bay* (Princeton, N.J.: Princeton University Press, 2017), 243–46. (My thanks to Alison Isenberg for directing me to these sources.)

20. Department of Defense, Office of Civil Defense and National School Boards Association, "School Boards Plan for Civil Defense" (Washington, D.C.: Government Printing Office, 1965), 20.

21. Ronald Evans suggested as much in an interview with the author, New York City, April 21 and 22, 2014.

22. "Background: Public Education in the Ghetto," *East Harlem Protestant Parish Newsletter* (October 1966), 1, in RSP, subseries c, box 6, folder 18.

23. See, for example, Eric Schneider, *Vampires, Dragons, and Egyptian Kings: Youth Gangs in Postwar New York* (Princeton, N.J.: Princeton University Press, 1999).

24. For similar points, see Monteyne, *Fallout Shelter*, 196.

25. Margaret Ruth Little, "Getting the American Dream for Themselves: Postwar Modern Subdivisions for African Americans in Raleigh, North Carolina," *Buildings & Landscapes: Journal of the Vernacular Architecture Forum* [hereafter *B&L*] 19, no. 1 (2012): 73–88; Amber N. Wiley, "The Dunbar High School Dilemma: Architecture, Power, and African American Cultural Heritage," *B&L* 20, no. 1 (2013): 95–128; and Jennifer V. O. Baughn, "Where's the White Columns? Architectural Imagery in *The Help*," paper presented at the Southeast Chapter Society of Architectural Historians, Athens, Georgia, 2012 (unpublished paper in author's possession).

26. Bailey, "Harlem's Besieged Masterpiece," 50.

27. Fred M. Hechinger, "I.S. 201 Teaches Lessons on Race," *New York Times*, September 25, 1966, 199.

28. Preston R. Wilcox, "Architecture: A Palliative for Anger (draft)," 1, 2, 6, in Schomburg Center for Research in Black Culture, New York Public Library (hereafter Schomburg), Preston Wilcox Papers, MG 235, box 10, folder 10.6.

29. Carolyn Woods Eisenberg, "The Parents Movement at I.S. 201: From Integration to Black Power, 1958–1966: A Case Study of Developing Ideology" (PhD diss., Columbia University, 1971); and David Rogers, *110 Livingston Street: Politics and Bureaucracy in the New York City Public School System* (New York: Vintage Books, 1968).

30. "I.S. 201: Symbol of the Struggle for Justice in Urban Education," *East Harlem Protestant Parish Newsletter*, 4. The Board of Education also intended to close down JHS 172 located inside Benjamin Franklin High School. The BOE's records indicate that a new school was being considered for East Harlem in 1961, not 1958. Board of Education, School Planning and Research Division, Status of Projects, Prepared for the 1-12-1961 meeting of the Committee on Buildings and Sites, in MA BOE, series 134, box 4, folder dated January 19, 1961.

31. Dorothy Jones, Inteview, January 1968, cited in Eisenberg, "Parents Movement at I.S. 201," 41, 53; and Preston Wilcox, "Releasing Human Potential: A Study of East Harlem-Yorkville School Transfer. Prepared by The East Harlem Project and the NYC Commission on Human Rights" (1961), in MA BOE, series 321, James B. Donovan, 1961–1963, Subject Files, box 2, folder 32.

32. Alice Kornegay and Rev. George T. Fuller, "Statement of the East Harlem Triangle Community Association and Chambers Memorial Baptist Church Regarding the Construction of the Proposed Junior High School 201," 1962, in Schomburg, Babette Edwards Education Reform in Harlem Collection (hereafter BEERHC), SC MG 809, box 3, folder 3.17. A copy of this statement, sent to Board of Education members, has yet to be found in the Municipal Archives. See also Earl Caldwell, "The Harlem Parents State a Case on IS 201," *New York Post*, September 23, 1966; and Murray Kempton, "Insulted and Injured," *New York Post*, September 22, 1966, clippings in RSP, subseries c, box 6, folder 16.

33. Parents and Community Groups from Harlem on I.S. 201, "Sequence of Events Surrounding Community Involvement with Public School 201," June 20, 1966, 1, in RSP, subseries c, box 6, folder 18; and Melvin E. Schoonover, *Making All Things Human: A Church in East Harlem* (Eugene, Ore.: Wipf and Stock, 1969), 117–19. (My thanks to Brian Goldstein for directing me to this remarkable memoir.)

34. NYCPC, Meeting Minutes, January 3, 1962, 21, January 17, 1962, 81; August 14, 1962, 638–39 (quote). The Board of Education had an eye on a site for the playground across from the school on East 127th Street, one that would have required more building clearance; when it made these plans known to the community, they collapsed quickly. M. A. Farber, "I.S. 201 Play Site Stirs New Dispute," *New York Times*, December 24, 1966.

35. For historic photographs of this fabric, see OldNYC, accessed February 10, 2019, https://www.oldnyc.org.

36. Parents and Community Groups from Harlem on I.S. 201, "Sequence of Events," 4–5.

37. Quoted in Bailey, "Harlem's Besieged Masterpiece," 50.

38. For an overview, see Judy Marks, *A History of Educational Facilities Laboratories (E.F.L.)* (Washington, D.C.: National Clearinghouse for Educational Facilities at the National Institute of Building Sciences, 2000; reprint, rev., 2001, 2009).

39. Architectural Research Laboratory, Department of Architecture, University of Michigan, *The Effect of Windowless Classrooms on Elementary School Children: An Environmental Case Study by the Architectural Research Laboratory, Department of Architecture, University of Michigan* (New York: Educational Facilities Laboratories, 1965), 17.

40. Catherine Burke, "Light: Metaphor and Materiality in the History of Schooling," in *Materialities of Schooling: Design, Technology, Objects, Routines,* ed. Martin Lawn and Ian Grosvenor (Oxford: Symposium Books, 2005), 125–44.

41. Architectural Research Laboratory, *Effect of Windowless Classrooms,* 21–22.

42. Lawrence G. O'Donnell, "Windowless Buildings: Do They Hurt Morale or Boast Efficiency?" *Wall Street Journal,* March 12, 1962, 1.

43. Paul W. Seagers, "A Study to Define the New York State Statutes, Written and Implied, on Schoolhouse Ventilation," for the NYSDOE, Division of School Buildings and Grounds (Albany: University of the State of New York, 1944), 8.

44. NYSDOE, Division of Educational Facilities Planning, *Manual of Planning Standards for School Buildings* (Albany: University of the State of New York, 1965), 27, 28.

45. My thanks to David Monteyne for sharing his copies of this document and the one cited in the note directly below this one. A. D. Dotter, Acting Director Division of School Buildings and Grounds, "Fallout Shelters. Memo to City, Village and District Superintendents, Supervising Principals, and Architects and Engineers, Dated February 1, 1963, State Education Department, University of the State of New York, Albany," cited in Monteyne, *Fallout Shelter,* 321n10.

46. Office of School Buildings, NYCBOE, "Letter to James E. Roembke, Director, Architectural & Engineering Development Division, Office of Civil Defense, Dated May 8, 1964, New York, N.Y.," cited in Monteyne, *Fallout Shelter,* 321n12.

47. "The Cool Age," *Time,* August 2, 1963, 60.

48. "The No-Corridor School," *Architectural Forum,* April 1953, 132–33; Keith Weldon Medley, "A Reason for Smiles in 'Back-of-Town,'" *LIFE,* March 1954, 59–62; Arthur Q. Davis, *It Happened by Design: The Life and Work of Arthur Q. Davis* (New Orleans: Odgen Museum of Southern Art, University of New Orleans, and University Press of Mississippi, 2009), 17–18, 75–76; and Francine Stock, "Is There a Future for the Recent Past in New Orleans?" *MAS Context* 8 (2010): 1–17. AIA is the abbreviation for the American Institute of Architects.

49. Davis, *It Happened by Design,* 30–31; and Nathaniel Curtis, "Curtis and Davis: The Way to New York," in *My Life in Modern Architecture* (New Orleans: University of New Orleans, 2002), chap. 5, accessed February 23, 2019, http://www.curtis.uno.edu/curtis/html/frameset.html.

50. NYCBOE, "Press Release (April 29, 1963)," in RSP, subseries b, box 4, folder 4.

51. Davis, *It Happened by Design,* 19, 78.

52. NYCBOE, *Journal of the Board of Education of the City of New York,* entries dated January 9, 1963: 14, January 23, 1963: 84. The 1962 memo is mentioned in Rose Shapiro, Memo to Sylvia Jaffee, November 4, 1966, and Sylvia Jaffee, "I.S. 201, Manhattan [November 1966]," in RSP, subseries c, box 6, folder 19.

53. The architects did not take advantage of the extra density, "the bonus," that the new zoning resolution offered to developers who provided plazas in front of skyscrapers. The image, not the development process, was influential. (My thanks to M. Christine Boyer for helping me think through this point.)

54. For example, C. J. Arnold, "'Take Out the Windows'—1961," *Educational Screen and Audiovisual Guide,* June 1961, 280, 296; R. A. Frye, and Frank M. Standhardt, "See More—Hear More—Learn More in Windowless Rooms," *Educational Screen and Audiovisual Guide,* June 1961, 275–77; and Eva G. McDonald and Eleanor Burts, "Opinions Differ on Windowless Classrooms: The Windowless Classroom Is a Controlled Laboratory; Windows Help to Promote Better Learning," *NEA Journal* (October 1961): 12–14. (My thanks to Fr. Stephen M. Koeth for pointing me to these references.)

55. Leonard Buder, "New Schools Win Honors in Design," *New York Times*, May 29, 1966, R1.

56. Jim Haskins, *Diary of a Harlem Schoolteacher* (New York: New Press, 2007 [1979]); and Leonard Buder, "Schools Seeking to Foil Vandals by Hiding Windows from View: One New Building Will Not Have Any—Screens to Protect Another," *New York Times*, November 18, 1963, 35.

57. Buder, "New Schools Win Honors."

58. Lily Mae Brown Crowder, email message to author, February 14, 2014; and Wilcox, "Architecture: A Palliative for Anger," 3.

59. Buder, "New Schools Win Honors."

60. Buder.

61. The brochure, "to the parents . . ." is in MA BOE, series 283, Office of the Secretary, Beatrice Steinberg, Subject Files, box 4, folder labeled Demonstration project-I.S. 201 Man. 1969-68-67.

62. Wilcox, "Architecture: A Palliative for Anger," 2.

63. Lefebvre, *Production of Space,* 224; Adrian Forty, "Space," in *Words and Buildings: A Vocabulary of Modern Architecture* (New York: Thames and Hudson, 2000), 270–75.

64. bell hooks, "Choosing the Margin as a Space of Radical Openness (1989)," in *Women, Knowledge, and Reality: Explorations in Feminist Philosophy,* ed. Ann Garry and Marilyn Pearsall (New York: Routledge, 1996), 48–55.

65. Preston Wilcox, "The Controversy Over I.S. 201: One View and a Proposal," *Urban Review* 1, no. 3 (1966): 13–16. The argument continues to resonate: Eliza Shapiro, "'I Love My Skin!' Black Parents Find Alternative to Integration," *New York Times*, January 8, 2019.

66. Karen Ferguson, *Top Down: The Ford Foundation, Black Power, and the Reinvention of Racial Liberalism* (New York: Oxford University Press, 2011), 94–96.

67. Miriam Wasserman, "The I.S. 201 Story: One Observer's Version," *Urban Review* 3, no. 6 (1969): 3.

68. Evans interview, April 21 and 22, 2014.

69. Ronald Evans, email message to author, July 12, 2016. See also Haskins, *Diary of a Harlem Schoolteacher*; and Herbert R. Kohl, *36 Children* (New York: Plume, 1988 [1967]).

70. Evans interview, April 21 and 22, 2014.

71. "Testimony Regarding the Appointment of Charles E. Wilson as Consultant to Act as Admininstrator of I.S. 201 Demonstration Project (April 23, 1968)," in RSP, subseries d, box 17, folder 7.

72. Evans interview, April 21 and 22, 2014.

73. Ann Crary Evans, "An Experiment in Humanizing Education," in *The Gattegno Effect: One Hundred Voices on One of History's Greatest Educators,* ed. Educational Solutions Worldwide (http://www.calebgattegno.org/2011), 112; and "Dr. Caleb Gattengo," *Kweli, Truth, Veridad,* November 1969, cover, in BEERHC, SC MG 809, box 6, folder 6.9.

74. Barbara Wilson-Brooks, oral history interview and Neatline map exhibit, by Nina Wasserman with Viola Huang, Ansley T. Erickson, and Esther Cyna, New York City, 2014, 2016, in "Barbara Wilson-Brooks' Harlem Community," Harlem Education History Project, harlemeducationhistory.library.columbia.edu.

75. Evans, "Experiment in Humanizing Education," 114. See also Lewis, *New York City Public Schools.*

76. Wilson-Brooks, oral history interview and Neatline map exhibit.

77. Michael Darby and Derrick Black, interview with author, New York City, July 28, 2016.

78. Inés Dussel, "Digital Classrooms and the New Economies of Attention: Reflections on the End of Schooling as Confinement," in *Designing Schools: Space, Place, and Pedagogy*, ed. Kate Darian-Smith and Julie Willis (New York: Routledge, 2017), 233–34; and Amy F. Ogata, "Educational Facilities Laboratories: Debating and Designing the Postwar Schoolhouse," in Darian-Smith and Willis, *Designing Schools*, 55–67.

79. Darby and Black interview. See also Herbert R. Kohl, *The Open Classroom: A Practical Guide to a New Way of Teaching* (New York: Vintage Books, 1969).

80. Darby and Black interview; and Blondell Cummings, Personal communication with Ansley T. Erickson, New York City, October 2, 2014, summary shared with the author by email, July 13, 2016.

81. Darby and Black interview.

82. Ferguson, *Top Down*, 146–48.

83. Marta Gutman and Richard Plunz, "Anatomy of Insurrection," in *The Making of an Architect, 1881–1981*, ed. Richard Oliver (New York: Columbia University Press and Rizzoli, 1981), 206–7; and Brian Goldstein, *Roots of Urban Renaissance: Gentrification and the Struggle Over Harlem* (Cambridge, Mass.: Harvard University 2017), 86–87. See also Mary Dowery, oral history interview with author, New York City, April 14, 2014. On the protest demanding a high school, rather than a state office building, see chapter 9 of this volume; and Goldstein, *Roots of Urban Renaissance*, chap. 2.

84. New York City Board of Education Advisory Committee on Construction, "Minutes of Meeting Held in the Office of Hugh Mclaren (June 13, 1966)," in RSP, subseries a, box 3, folder 30.

85. Marks mentions EFL's interest in open-plan classrooms, but not in windowless ones. Marks, "History of Educational Facilities Laboratories."

CHAPTER 9

Black Power as Educational Renaissance

The Harlem Landscape

RUSSELL RICKFORD

arlem is a collage of conflicting images," one of the community's
adopted sons wrote in the 1960s.[1] Indeed, the contradictions of
the Upper Manhattan locale were never more pronounced than
they were during that tumultuous decade. Contemporary journalists and
social scientists tended to see Harlem as a metaphor for decay; they adopted
a weary sociological tone when discussing the blight and social disarray of
the "Dark Ghetto."[2] Beyond the tales of pathology, however, lay the mystique of the most famous Black neighborhood on the planet. Despite its
poverty and deferred dreams, Harlem remained a cultural and intellectual
mecca and a capital of Black and Puerto Rican activism.[3]

Harlem's dueling identities—as both a locus of oppression and a vibrant
"city within a city"—converged in the realm of education. A 1964 study
by the community agency Harlem Youth Opportunities Unlimited
(HARYOU) reported that by third grade, Central Harlem youths were a
full year behind the academic achievement of their New York City peers;
by eighth grade they had fallen about two and a half years behind.[4] At the
same time, Harlem was the site of some of the era's most powerful educational crusades. Although the modern age of school protest in the neighborhood began in the 1950s following the *Brown v. Board* decision, many of the
most dynamic local struggles unfolded in the 1960s and early 1970s against
the backdrop of escalating liberation movements across the country and
around the world.[5]

This essay examines several alternative and community education efforts in Harlem during the decade after the neighborhood's 1964 street uprising.[6] That rebellion, combined with the devastating 1965 assassination of Malcolm X in Upper Manhattan, deepened liberating impulses within local organizing campaigns and expanded the influence of Black nationalist initiatives. The heyday of such activities roughly coincided with the Black Power phase of the African American freedom movement. By the mid- to late 1960s, an array of grassroots ventures sought to imbue Harlem youngsters with a potent sense of racial pride and awareness. Taken collectively, such "black consciousness" projects constituted a tremendous wellspring of militant energy.[7]

Black Power in Harlem was in many respects a renaissance of educational thought and practice. Questions of pedagogy were at the heart of the community's most innovative political and cultural endeavors, from the formation of "liberation schools" to the quest for control of Intermediate School (IS) 201 to the battle against the construction of the 125th Street State Office Building. The contemporary "build where you are" ethic and spirit of experimentation led local activists to develop an array of models beyond the conventional structures of public schooling. The greatest elements of ingenuity in contemporary Harlem education sprang from below.

The institutions discussed here did not constitute a uniform movement. No single ideology shaped the terrain of alternative education in Harlem. I use the moniker *Black Power* to encompass a range of efforts—from classroom strategies to informal practices—that stressed Black and Puerto Rican self-determination and downplayed or rejected integrationist philosophies. Since the 1950s, the local drive for improved schooling had largely centered on integrationist rationales. Yet as of 1964, of the 31,000 students registered for public school in Central Harlem, 91 percent were Black and almost 8 percent were Puerto Rican.[8]

Educational activities emphasizing Black and Puerto Rican pride and awareness were undertaken by explicitly Black nationalist formations such as the Organization of Afro-American Unity and the Harlem branch of the Black Panther Party. They were pursued, as well, by a politically diverse cohort of parents, organizers, and poverty workers. Local activists such as Babette Edwards, David Spencer, Preston Wilcox, and Audley "Queen Mother" Moore played a central role in crafting and implementing Black Power visions of schooling.

Those visions did not emerge fully formed amid the ascent of the Black Power concept in 1966. Instead they materialized during ongoing quests for educational and social advancement. As early as 1964, the Harlem rent strike leader Jesse Gray had urged residents of the community to draw on "the mass reservoir of black power" to unify and develop what he called "the ghetto." That same year another local activist, the singer and educator Josephine Buck Jones, declared that, "The Negro people have been at the mercy of a self-perpetuating power structure in the schools."[9] Even as Harlem parents joined the massive 1964 boycotts against racial segregation in New York City schools, the pursuit of local democratic power in education was replacing more narrowly integrationist frameworks as the critical paradigm of struggle.[10]

The ensuing years brought further radicalization, often expressed in the language of global anticolonialism. Local activists described Harlem as an "underdeveloped" nation in need of self-government. The officials who oversaw the community's public schools were not simply negligent bureaucrats—they were "colonialists." Far from a consequence of mere prejudice, the ghettoization of Black people was "for the express purpose of educational, political, economic and social exploitation."[11] Some of these ideas had long germinated within Harlem's political circles. As faith in appeals to white conscience continued to wane and more residents embraced the principles of Black consciousness and community control, local activists helped convert a "Negro Revolution" into a larger crusade for Black and Puerto Rican liberation.

That cause required a reckoning with the possibilities and limits of the enterprise of education. Few of Harlem's community education efforts eschewed the human-capital logic of equipping poorer children with marketable skills and preparing them for life in a highly technological society. Social mobility and escape from menial employment were widespread ambitions; local parents vowed to spare the next generation the indignity of having to scrounge for jobs in an affluent land. That meant either redeeming or circumventing a bloated public school system that stigmatized so-called disadvantaged children and at the same time often played a custodial role in minority neighborhoods.

To fulfill the tenets of liberation, however, Harlem organizers had to do more than ensure that local youth were considered educable for employment. They had to end the alienation of Black and Puerto Rican students within the unwieldy regime of New York City schools. They had to equip such children with a sense of cultural dignity. They had to confront the larger political and economic subjugation of the community. And they had to deliver "a total education"—one that exposed the corruption of the existing power apparatus and evoked more humane possibilities.[12]

Though they failed to accomplish all these objectives, Harlem's grassroots educational models did a great deal. They operationalized Black Power ideals. They repudiated the term *Negro* and engaged children of color in a meaningful quest for self-definition. They combined the language of American rights with a boldly Third Worldist orientation. They critiqued Western materialism and the Cold War premise of the inherent virtue of capitalist democracy in the United States. They challenged the assumption that the transmission of middle-class values was an imperative of formal learning. Finally, they enriched the intellectual life of a community that pulsated with radical ideas.

Even a cursory survey of alternative education in Harlem during the era of Black Power reveals a spectrum of aspirations. Many of the ventures outlined below might today be derided as symbols of identity politics because they favored racial empowerment over ostensibly universalist ideals. Yet the initiatives were far from provincial. Indeed, they were often intellectually expansive and cosmopolitan. They remind us that poor, working-class, and lower middle-class Black and Puerto Rican urbanites were more than passive consumers of educational services. They were also creators of institutions and staunch defenders of their right to ensure the proper training of their children.

The Forerunners

Black nationalist activity in the early 1960s laid the groundwork for educational experiments later in the decade. Though Harlem's nationalist traditions date back to Marcus Garvey and other early twentieth-century figures, the surge of contemporary organizing generated an extraordinary cultural revival. On any given day, a colorful assortment of Afrophiles propagandized local residents, combating what they saw as the malign tendencies of Negro assimilationism. The African Jazz Art Society Studios picketed wig shops and promoted "naturalism" (unprocessed hairstyles) with its Grandassa fashion shows. Meanwhile the Nation of Islam held African Bazaars at the 142nd Street Armory; the Yoruba Temple taught West

African languages at its 116th Street headquarters; and the Afro-Caribbean militant Richard B. Moore lectured at a 125th Street gallery on behalf of the "Committee to Present the Truth about the Name 'Negro.'"[13]

The hub of nationalist engagement was the septuagenarian Lewis Michaux's National Memorial Bookstore on 125th Street and Seventh Avenue. Known affectionately as "professor," Michaux was a fount of Black folk wisdom. His shop, which he had operated since the 1930s, contributed to the edification of generations of Harlemites. The writer Larry Neal later remembered arriving in Harlem in 1961 and discovering in Michaux's place a veritable shrine to Black history and culture:

> On that Saturday, after the speeches and the book buying, Mr. Michaux took us in the back room of his store. It was a crowded room jammed with books and other artifacts. Photographs of Marcus Garvey, Harriet Tubman, Sojourner Truth stared down at us. There was a heaviness about the room, as if it were crowded with ghosts. The spirit that drew the people to Harlem Square every day was being manifested in the room; ghosts emanated out of old books, photos, and the sounds and rhythms of Mr. Michaux's voice.[14]

Michaux's store was not just a repository of books by and about Black people; it was also a nexus of political expression, a source of knowledge about the nonwestern world, and a destination for African leaders and other dignitaries who visited Harlem. The back of the shop served as a radical salon where ideologues debated each other and where Malcolm X often huddled with his notes before mounting a speaker's platform erected just outside the building. Michaux himself regularly occupied the street-corner podium, offering evening lectures in Harlem's "stepladder preacher" tradition. In a 1960s speech titled "Babylon Is Falling," the elder explained "why we the black people in America should return to thy mother land (Africa) before it's too late, because there is no room in this white man's inn, because of the color of your skin."[15]

Dubbed the "House of Common Sense and the Home of Proper Propaganda" and "Repatriation Headquarters" of the Back-to-Africa movement, the National Memorial Bookstore exemplified the belief that erudition was crucial to Black advancement. As Michaux once told the boxer Sugar Ray Leonard, "What you put on your head will rub off in your bed. It's what you put in your head that will last you 'til you're dead."[16]

A more formal vehicle for Black nationalist education lay a few blocks from Michaux's place at the 116th Street mosque of the Nation of Islam (NOI). The NOI's stern regimen of racial and moral uplift was designed to rescue "so-called Negroes" from "the grave"—the sea of ignorance and debauchery in which the unconverted were said to wallow. Under Malcolm X's leadership the Harlem mosque featured a number of educational projects designed to shield the faithful from such degradation. Among them was a youth training program that offered basic academic instruction (the "Three R's" plus Arabic and Black history) and conveyed the religious body's austere doctrines. According to the sacred teachings, "A" was for ALLAH, "B" was for "the BLACK MAN," and "C" was for CLEANLINESS.[17]

The Harlem mosque greatly expanded its educational offerings in the late 1960s. A bitter political and organizational dispute led to Malcolm X's ouster from the pulpit (and ultimately from the NOI) between late 1963 and early 1964, and a firebomb destroyed the 116th Street temple after Malcolm was slain in 1965. But the Muslims rebuilt with gusto, constructing a modern, five-story facility that included a house of worship, several NOI businesses, and a school. (This primary and secondary institution bore the name held by all NOI schools—"The University of Islam.") By the early 1970s, more than seven hundred children ages three to eighteen, Muslim and non-Muslim alike, attended full-time classes at the Mosque No. 7 complex, the brisk efficiency of which seemed to reflect the larger NOI mission of achieving total independence from white America.[18]

NOI schools cultivated a fiercely entrepreneurial ethic. "Get an education, but not an education that leaves us looking to the slavemaster for a job," Elijah Muhammad, the organization's supreme leader, commanded.[19] A more radical agenda shaped the instructional efforts of the Organization of Afro-American Unity (OAAU). The erstwhile NOI spokesman Malcolm X established the OAAU as his secular organ after splitting with Muhammad in 1964. Run by sharp, young intellectuals, including the journalists Lynne Shifflett and A. Peter Bailey, the upstart organization aimed to infuse the Black freedom struggle with the principles of Pan-Africanism and human rights. Political education was central to this mission, so the OAAU launched a Saturday morning Liberation School that held free classes for youths and adults at the storied Hotel Theresa on 125th Street.[20]

The OAAU had been patterned after the spirit of the Organization of African Unity, a new federation of (some recently) independent nations.

That international perspective strongly influenced the Liberation School curriculum, a fact that appealed to local anti-imperialists such as the Japanese American activist Yuri Kochiyama, a Malcolm X ally who attended the school. Liberation School instructors emphasized African and African American history, seeing the absence of such knowledge as "a definite handicap to Black children in their quest for identity." The OAAU also decried the shortage of material on Black life and culture in New York City schools, and dismissed as "tokenism" the Board of Education's modest attempts to diversify the curriculum.[21]

The Liberation School and the embryonic OAAU dwindled rapidly amid the fear and confusion that followed Malcolm X's assassination in February 1965. Yet both the organization and the school had lasting effects. They helped popularize the term *Afro-American* as an honorable self-designation for a rising people, and they prepared militants such as the Liberation School director James E. Campbell for future social justice work within and beyond Harlem. The phrase *liberation school*—a reformulation of the "freedom school" concept—was itself influential. If Malcolm's death marked the arrival of an era of unapologetic Black consciousness, the liberation school motif helped inaugurate a whole generation of radical ventures.[22]

A final Black nationalist project in Harlem signaled the advent of a new age of parallel institutions. Galvanized by the death of Malcolm X, the poet-playwright LeRoi Jones (later Amiri Baraka) founded the Black Arts Repertory Theatre/School (BARTS) in a once-elegant West 130th Street brownstone, opening the school's doors to "the people of the ghetto" in the spring of 1965. The outfit, which briefly secured federal antipoverty funding via HARYOU, sponsored plays, exhibits, and outdoor performances, attempting to embody a revolutionary cultural ethos and serving as "a bridge of communication between the contemporary artist and the Black community at large."[23]

BARTS offered young Harlemites classes in the arts and other subjects taught by some of the most gifted Black artist-intellectuals of the day. The jazz composer and bandleader Sun Ra directed the music class; the poet Sonia Sanchez ran the remedial skills course; and Harold Cruse, the talented and curmudgeonly writer, oversaw the "History of the Afro-American Presence as a Culture Within a Culture." Fees for an eight-week term stood at $1.40 for adults and $.75 for children. Summer sessions enrolled four hundred students; remedial reading and math courses served eighty children ages seven to thirteen.

Law enforcement agents and politicians accused the institution of fostering hatred of white people. BARTS, they insisted, was the locus of "an extreme Negro nationalist society," a cabal devoted to sponsoring "vile racist plays in the language of the gutter."[24]

Yet Cruse called the establishment "one of the most positive institutions developed in Harlem during the last twenty-five years, with the support of a very broad representation from the Harlem youth."[25]

Though BARTS folded in 1966 amid bitter internal strife, the venture proved deeply influential. It birthed the Black Arts Movement and inspired the creation of a host of independent schools nationwide. It also exemplified the contemporary theme of African-American self-discovery; celebrated Black vernacular life (in contrast to the cultural constraints imposed by the NOI's strictures of "respectability"); and projected the idea—soon to become emblematic of uptown dissidents—that Harlem needed to "gain its sovereignty" to be truly free.[26]

The Coming of Black Power

Some activists focused on creating new educational spaces. Others sought the power to govern existing Harlem schools. As the "Black Power" slogan arose in 1966, several strands of militancy coalesced under the new political creed. The nascent Black Panther Party branch in Harlem captured the spirit of resistance. The fledgling organization introduced itself to local residents as a force that would "attack the rats and roaches, that will attack racist school teachers, that will attack racist cops."[27]

The Panthers wished to convert the community's public schools into instruments of Black consciousness. They joined civil rights groups in pressing for inclusion of African and African American history in Harlem classrooms and even attempted to recruit to the cause neighborhood street gangs and other fringe elements. They also agitated for the appointment of Black principals and for the renaming of schools "to reflect the history and achievements of our people."[28]

Other Black Power outfits sought a broader restructuring of public education. In 1967 the Harlem chapter of the Congress of Racial Equality (CORE) unveiled a plan to sever Central Harlem schools from the New York City Board of Education and form a completely independent district. Spearheaded by the local CORE leader Roy Innis and his educational chair

Victor Solomon, the proposal called for the creation of an autonomous entity encompassing 40 neighborhood schools and approximately 50,000 children. The reorganization would have produced the third largest school district in New York State.[29]

CORE officials presented the plan as an ode to pragmatism. Harlem schools, they insisted, were "bulwark[s] of mediocrity" managed by a distant and cumbersome bureaucracy. Compared to the existing system, an autonomous school board chosen by Harlem residents and chartered by the state would prove far more responsive to local needs. At the heart of the proposal lay the logic of indigenous government, a precept of community control and a source of mounting opposition to the external domination of Harlem. "As in the South," CORE leaders maintained, "we have a situation where white overlords are overseeing the education of black children." An independent school district would "give Harlem a place on the map" and offer residents a taste of genuine power.[30]

This position marked a stark departure for CORE. As recently as 1965, the national civil rights group had viewed the desegregation of northern urban districts as the only effective way to end "the perniciousness of ghetto schools." Now, amid the turn to Black Power, Harlem CORE was demanding an autonomous district as a means of "improving the lives of black people where they are." What Innis and Solomon envisioned was not a Bantustan-style territory endowed with nominal authority, but a meaningful step toward self-rule.[31]

Economic liberation was a further goal. An independent school system would enable local administrators to negotiate contracts with suppliers of their choosing, channeling millions of dollars to indigenous businesses and bringing decent jobs to a community plagued by unemployment. However, the main rationale for the breakaway district was neither financial nor material. Like other Black Power advocates, Innis and Solomon were preoccupied with what they called "the psychology of the black man."[32] One odious consequence of Harlem's powerlessness, they believed, was the self-loathing that it engendered in community members. There was a certain irony in this perspective. By reducing power relations to the question of mental well-being, CORE's Black nationalists replicated a key premise of those liberal integrationists who linked racial segregation to the purported anomie of the Black child.

In any case, most New York State legislators declined to seriously consider the autonomous school board plan. Harlem CORE formed a committee of Black and Puerto Rican parents, educators, social workers, and community leaders to prepare a detailed study of the proposal. Support for the effort came from a white liberal group (Friends of Harlem CORE) that hoped to better understand "the new level at which the Black intellectual community is now operating."[33] In the end, however, proponents of the independent district failed to overcome the odor of racial separatism that clung to the plan.

Still, the campaign was hardly fruitless. Though the CORE proposal appeared to lack widespread local backing, many of its premises gained a broader hearing as Harlem's community control struggle intensified between 1967 and 1970. The view of Black urban enclaves as social entities that must be elevated and preserved; the emphasis on changing the lives of masses of people rather than working toward incremental reform; and the audacious belief that local schools could become "the central institution in the renaissance of Harlem"—all became axioms of struggle in years to come.[34]

Indeed, some of these outlooks helped shape another local battle in 1967. As Harlem CORE was promoting its school district plan that year, organizers of the West Harlem Liberation School (WHLS) were forging their own visions of educational redemption. The WHLS appeared during a boycott of Public School (PS) 125 on West 123rd Street. For months, parents of students at the 85 percent Black and Puerto Rican elementary school had attempted to gain a role in selecting a principal and establishing a curriculum. A community voice in decision making, they argued, was needed to improve conditions at the school, where the vast majority of children were reading below grade level. After their demands produced "only frustration, antagonism, and heartache," they launched the strike.[35]

The protest unfolded amid the rebellious zeitgeist of 1967, a year that witnessed massive street uprisings in Newark and Detroit. Militancy pervaded the rhetoric of PS 125 parents and activists, some of whom inhabited the "brick pill boxes" of Harlem's nearby Grant Houses, a sprawling public complex. Organizers declared that "miseducation is a form of genocide" and urged parents to "bring your children to the [picket] line," rejecting the bourgeois impulse to shield youngsters from political confrontation.[36] Hoping to demonstrate the validity of alternative educational methods, the boycott committee adopted a dual strategy: it would operate WHLS—an interim academy for PS 125 students—while negotiations with the Board of Education continued.

WHLS reflected the diversity of its creators, who included Black nationalists such as the Columbia University Social Work professor and former Malcolm X associate Preston Wilcox, white liberals from the Morningside Heights area, and leftists such as the veteran activist Maude White Katz, the chair of the boycott committee. Parents, students, and other neighborhood volunteers taught an innovative curriculum at three temporary locations, including two nearby churches and a community center. The course of study occasionally reinforced American triumphalist narratives. For example, students learned that George Washington had led his troops against the British in the Battle of Harlem Heights. But they also discovered through their studies that Northern capitalists had profited from the slave trade, and they engaged in discussion and role-play designed to celebrate and contextualize Harlem's fight for a local say in school affairs.[37]

WHLS pupils worked from a special "Liberation Notebook" designed by parents. They perused mimeographed pamphlets on Harriet Tubman and Malcolm X. They studied African and Puerto Rican history. They recited folk songs and Langston Hughes poems, including "The Ballad of the Landlord," a piece about a defiant tenant living in slum conditions. They even mounted a brief takeover of City Hall to publicize boycott demands. Though the atmosphere of WHLS was often raucous, students seemed to enjoy the school's air of exuberant improvisation. They also appreciated its borrowed facilities, which included classrooms in Riverside Church on Manhattan's Upper West Side. As one child remarked, "This school is better than 125 because 125 has roaches—but Riverside don't have roaches."[38]

By reprising the OAAU's "liberation school" theme, WHLS projected an image of uncompromising resistance. Though the school operated only nine days, more than two-thirds of PS 125 students attended its freewheeling sessions. In so doing, they gained exposure to key concepts in democratic education. The organizers of WHLS embraced the principle that no youngster is "culturally deprived." They provided free lunches for students and arranged afterschool and preschool programs for the children of working parents. Most important, by constructing an evocative alternative, they dramatized "the failure of P.S. 125 to provide our children with the kind of education that will enable them to deal with the inequalities that exist in the world."[39]

Other contemporary liberation schools appeared, including one conceived by the Young Lords, a cadre of radical Puerto Rican nationalists that briefly seized a church in East Harlem (or El Barrio) in 1969 to house the make-shift academy. Acting against the backdrop of the larger community-control movement in New York City, the group attempted to expose the coercive tactics by which both the state and religious authorities resisted radical re-form. "The Board of Education needs cops to keep the Public School prisons open," one Young Lords flyer read. "The Methodist Church needs cops to keep the Liberation school closed."[40]

The Young Lords saw the liberation school as one component of a larger program of parallel services designed to supplement the crumbling social infrastructure of El Barrio. During their occupation of the church the Puerto Rican activists operated a free breakfast program for children, a day-care center, and free health clinics.[41] The aim was a complete reordering of existing arrangements. The bourgeois church, a site of propriety and law-and-order, was to become a "people's church" (la iglesia del pueblo), a zone of replenishment and reallocation.

Of course, the Young Lords also wished to reconstruct the architecture of knowledge. Surrounded by racism, poverty, and unemployment, East Har-lem children were denied the critical skills necessary to fully comprehend the origins of their suffering. Liberation school organizers hoped to arm such youths with an anticolonial epistemology. Pupils discussed Puerto Rico as a subjugated nation, urban renewal as class warfare from above, and the story of Columbus's "discovery" of the New World as the propagation of settler mythology. Before the intervention of the Young Lords, one youngster con-fessed, "I always thought Puerto Ricans had no history or culture."[42]

Though "liberation schools" offered formidable models, by the late 1960s the struggle for community control of IS 201 had emerged as Har-lem's main educational battlefront. The IS 201 affair began with the quest for desegregation. Harlem parents had long believed that the presence of white children in local schools would compel officials to upgrade instruc-tional services in the neighborhood. But even militant resistance to segre-gation had proved futile. When IS 201, a new facility in East Harlem, was unveiled in 1966, parents refused to accept the introduction of another seg-regated school on the familiar terms of inferior "ghetto education."[43] (For more on the siting and design of IS 201, see chapter 8 of this volume.)

Adopting a fresh approach, activists demanded that IS 201 become a test case in local control. Boycotts, sit-ins, and other pressure tactics forced the city to concede. In 1968 a twenty-one-member governing board of parents, educators, and other local representatives formed to oversee the "Schomburg complex" or "I.S. 201 Complex," a four-thousand-student entity comprising IS 201 and its feeder elementary schools.[44] IS 201 had become a prototype of community control in an urban context.

Much has been written about the IS 201 struggle and the urban community-control movement it precipitated.[45] In chapter 8 of this volume, Marta Gutman examines the school's architecture to explain what prompted activism there, and to document how activists reclaimed the space of the building. The campaign at IS 201 should also be viewed in the context of the local thrust for alternative establishments. Several organizers of Harlem's past and future autonomous institutions converged in the IS 201 affair. (The former OAAU Liberation School coordinator James E. Campbell, for example, served as an IS 201 assistant principal.) And though the East Harlem "demonstration district" evolved within the framework of public education, the effort embodied many of the principles that guided experimental models. As IS 201 Governing Board member Babette Edwards later asserted, the Schomburg Complex (also called at times the IS 201 Complex) reflected a desire "to build an alternative structure of our own outside the system."[46]

From the beginning, the Governing Board and its supporters envisioned a radical departure from conventional schooling. They hoped to embody institutionally the seemingly paradoxical concept of "quality education in the ghetto," feeling that they could ill afford what Edwards called "the loss of another generation of children" while seeking desegregation.[47] An East Harlem mother had echoed a familiar integrationist refrain when she told a citywide task force on poverty in 1966 that "the [educational] system as it is now deprives Negroes, Puerto Ricans, and Whites of a chance to get to know and appreciate each other's backgrounds."[48] By 1968, however, few local activists wished to further petition a remote Board of Education for reforms that never seemed to materialize. Now they resolved to create new models themselves.

Doing so meant harnessing the creative impulses of alternative education. The Governing Board pursued standard amenities such as a modern, updated curriculum and a fully equipped library. Yet it also attempted to reimagine the entire community-school relationship. The Schomburg Complex would not function as a colonial outpost—another impenetrable agency governed from afar. Instead its campuses would become vibrant centers of culture and recreation. The schools hosted community meetings and "black awareness" events, including Harlem Repertory Theatre productions. *Kweli*, a Spanish-English community newspaper with a crusading, race-conscious spirit, was published within the complex. The cluster of campuses even officially observed Malcolm X's birthday on May 19, thereby sanctifying an occasion that had been celebrated only in informal ceremonies—if at all.[49]

Of course, the chief innovations of the Schomburg Complex were curricular. For years Harlem activists had demanded teaching materials that acknowledged the "contribution of cultural groups." This approach rested on a paradigm of "accepting difference" that implicitly accepted white subjectivity—the presumptive norm against which minority existence was to be cast. The rise of Black Power, however, had revitalized assertions of Black and Puerto Rican autonomy. The expressed goal of curricular reform shifted from mere *inclusion* to the fulfillment of more cogent and affirming theories of Afro-American history. Embracing this cultural imperative, the IS 201 Governing Board adopted an array of programs in Black and Puerto Rican studies. The administrative body developed a Community Education Center and an African-Hispanic History and Culture Institute designed to correct "prevailing images of African Americans, Puerto Ricans, and Mexican Americans."[50]

The Third World sensibilities of such initiatives also shaped the complex's bilingual education program. Parents had long complained about the neglect of Spanish-speaking students in Harlem schools. When they inquired about the academic progress of such children, however, they had been scolded for failing to speak English at home.[51] By contrast, the Schomburg Complex attempted to honor the whole linguistic and cultural identity of its students. Bilingual classes, still rare in New York City at the time, included exploration of the Taino Indian and African roots of Puerto Rican culture, as well as discussion of Spanish colonialism and American imperialism. Students sang Puerto Rico's anthem (*La Borinqueña*) in Spanish. They traced links between African and Puerto Rican dance styles and culinary habits.[52] In short, they received a cosmopolitan and culturally relevant education at a time when Cold War ideals and white supremacy still governed much of schooling and American life.

Despite these accomplishments, activists had hoped for more. The Governing Board complained that it had never been granted full control of the complex. As early as 1968, some of its members declared that they were "being used to make black and Puerto Rican people all over this city believe that society is concerned about the education of their children."[53] Endowed with limited authority, local administrators had been unable to meet fully the raised expectations of parents, teachers, and students. Bickering and recrimination among educators only exacerbated the chaos that beset the intermediate school. Amid mounting strife, Babette Edwards, David Spencer, and other key members of the Governing Board resigned.[54]

Even with these limitations, community control drew powerful opposition from the teachers union, Board of Education, and local political establishment. After only three years, the demonstration districts were effectively mothballed, absorbed into the weakened democracy of "decentralization" by 1970. Now school governance operated on a smaller geographic scale. Crucial fiscal and personnel decisions remained in the hands of the central board, with local administrators relegated to a subordinate role. The new governance structures subverted the robust vision of community control that had motivated the IS 201 experiment.

Symbolically and otherwise, however, the IS 201 struggle was quite significant. In many respects, Harlem's quest for control of its schools marked the apex of Black and Puerto Rican consciousness in the community. The Governing Board had rejected what it saw as ingrained assumptions about the antisocial nature of poor children of color. It had moved to ban the word *Negro* from local classrooms and to combat racial stigma by elevating African-descended people to the dignified status of "Afro-Americans." Most of all, it had demonstrated that indigenous experimentation could lead to the creation of new and democratic structures. As the Harlem parent and Governing Board chairman David Spencer proclaimed, "Direct community participation in the operation of the public schools is our right as Black and Puerto Rican people in this land."[55]

The Death and Life of Community Education

The demise of the IS 201 demonstration district was demoralizing enough in itself. "We are beginning to understand what it must have been like after Reconstruction, when the Jim Crow laws destroyed the few liberties Black southerners had achieved after the Civil War," Spencer wrote in 1969.[56] Yet even then, another debacle was looming. The contemporary battle against the construction of the Harlem State Office Building (SOB) further highlighted both the appeal of grassroots theories of education and the powerful resistance such outlooks encountered.

The people's campaign against the SOB escalated in 1968. It was then that many Harlemites learned that plans were being completed to erect a large office building for New York State agencies and other interests on 125th Street and Seventh Avenue. Supporters of the redevelopment project argued that the initiative would bring jobs and economic vitality to the community. But many residents saw the proposed building as an intrusion that would benefit elites and displace people of color and their cultural institutions. (Lewis Michaux and his historic bookstore had already been ousted to make way for the construction project.) Those who viewed the SOB as a harbinger of gentrification ridiculed Governor Nelson Rockefeller's suggestion that the edifice would stand as a memorial to Martin Luther King Jr., who had been assassinated in April 1968. "King had planned a Poor People's March," one observer noted. "What the Governor has given us is a Rich People's March—right through the ghetto."[57]

By early 1969 the SOB construction site had spawned a vigorous opposition movement. Meanwhile, a broad-based coalition of Harlem organizations promoted alternative plans for the plot. Though proposals for a day-care center and medical facilities emerged, the call for the creation of a public high school—possibly named in honor of Malcolm X—remained a rallying point. Because Central Harlem lacked such a public institution (the last one had closed with Wadleigh's conversion to a junior high school in 1954, as detailed in chapter 3 of this volume), thousands of local youths were forced to travel great distances every day, journeying north or south in Manhattan or the Bronx simply to get an education. Securing a new high school appeared to be the logical next step on the path to community control. As one Harlem mother proclaimed during a public hearing on the SOB issue, "The only way for us to protect our children is to arm them with the necessary education—taught and controlled by the Black community."[58]

By now the concept of regenerating Harlem's social infrastructure from below had become almost axiomatic. Those who envisioned a truly relevant local high school drew from a pool of democratic ideals established through years of struggle. The Committee for a Harlem High School, a group of local organizers, professionals, and everyday residents, pictured an institution in which students graded themselves, planned their own classes, and worked with community groups for academic credit. The U.S. schoolhouse, the organization declared, "can no longer stand as the bastard offspring of a racist society, remote and separate from the community."[59] Another vision for the structure came from Charles F. Gordon, a playwright associated with Harlem's Black Theatre Workshop. Gordon imagined a cultural center featuring a library, child-care services, and a school for ages 3 to 103, "staffed from top to bottom with conscientious Black educators."[60]

What Harlem ultimately received was not an educational marvel but a towering symbol of its own subjugation. In the months after the last protesters were driven from the excavation site, the SOB rose above the 125th Street junction where Malcolm X had once delivered his mesmerizing harangues. Not everyone had supported Harlem's campaign to "reclaim" the contested plot of land. Figures such as CORE's Roy Innis, the increasingly conservative leader who had once authored a plan to establish a separate Harlem school district, embraced the tales of capitalist development spun by SOB boosters. "You wouldn't want to build a high school on Times Square or Wall Street," he maintained, "and this [125th Street] is our Wall Street."[61] For Harlem's rank-and-file organizers, however, the state building's completion in 1973 marked a sobering defeat. The edifice, one writer predicted, would loom over Harlem "like a gun turret in a maximum security prison."[62]

Of course, some Harlemites refused to relinquish notions of emancipatory education. The local icon Audley "Queen Mother" Moore never abandoned the quest for alternative schools. A septuagenarian by the 1960s, Moore had labored for decades within a host of social movements. She had championed Pan-Africanism, socialism, tenant rights, and reparations for slavery, always maintaining a distinctly Black nationalist worldview. In the 1960s she remained a fervent supporter of Black consciousness causes. She agitated for African American principals in Harlem schools, memorialized Malcolm X, and backed both the IS 201 struggle and the campaign against the SOB.[63]

Born in 1898, in New Iberia, Louisiana, Moore had left school after the fourth grade. Yet she harbored a firm belief in the redemptive power of education. The veteran activist argued that many public schools damaged African American children academically and culturally. But in her view, the crisis ran much deeper than that. Moore felt that Black people would never be free until they repudiated the social identity imposed on them by the majority culture. The process of reconditioning was to begin with emphatic rejection of the term *Negro*. As she explained in 1968, "We were brought over here as Africans, then denatured, dehumanized and turned into Negroes."[64]

Moore imagined an independent school that could stimulate a collective transformation of consciousness. She and her sister, Loretta Langley, hoped to establish the Eloise Moore College of African Studies (the name honored yet another sibling) on twenty-five acres of their spacious farmland estate in the Catskills region of Upstate New York. Dubbed "Mount Addis Ababa," the Parksville, New York, property was to serve as a citadel of racial awareness. Moore and Langley envisaged it as the site of a crusade against "oppression psychoneurosis," the syndrome Moore believed plagued African-descended people. The college, she maintained, would provide a place "where people could come to us from all over the world to be decolonized and de-Negroized."[65]

The institution was to play a more concrete role, as well. Moore and Langley wished to equip poor and working-class Black youths with "skills that automation could not erase," thus combating the forces that were reducing many Black Americans to lives of precariousness within an army of reserve labor. The desire to impart such expertise—from soil conservation to poultry-rearing—also reflected a long-standing Pan-African goal of sending technicians to Africa to assist in the development of postcolonial states.[66]

Moore sustained the dream of a school at Mount Addis Ababa throughout the 1960s as she toiled on behalf of the Republic of New Africa and her own organization, the Universal Association of Ethiopian Women. The institution evolved in her mind's eye even as she participated in Harlem's Conference for Quality Education (she spoke on "The Danger of Miseducation Among Our Children") and joined an occupation of the New York City Board of Education's meeting hall in 1966. However, the Eloise Moore College of African Studies never materialized. New York City schoolchildren occasionally visited Mount Addis Ababa to plant crops and engage in survivalist exercises, and activists gathered there for political summits. Intelligence agents duly monitored these activities as part of the government campaign against Black militants. But no physical campus emerged to embody Moore's contention that "Negro" was simply "a state of mind" that could be exchanged for a more empowering subjectivity.[67]

Beset with financial problems, Mount Addis Ababa fell into disrepair in the 1970s. Moore, however, clung to her visions of autonomous education. Her concept of an establishment "totally embracing the cultural, educational and industrial needs" of Black people proved remarkably resilient.[68] Indeed, comparable ideals had inspired an array of educational efforts in Harlem during a period of intense mobilization.

Space prohibits a full account of the range of local establishments that strove to cultivate Black and Puerto Rican identity. Those Harlemites not served by the institutions mentioned above might have attended "master liberation workshops" at the National Black Theatre on 125th Street; learned African and African American history at the Afro Arts Cultural Center on 134th Street; or studied Yoruba, Kiswahili, and Spanish at Our School, a Pan-Africanist outfit on 117th Street.[69] Between the eruption of the Harlem street rebellion of 1964 and the completion of the State Office Building in 1973, these and other autonomous enterprises attempted to provide academic training as well as something akin to what the Nation of Islam called "knowledge of self"—the ability to comprehend one's past, to engage one's present, and to pursue a future free from exploitation.

Viewing Harlem's educational landscape as an alternative infrastructure enables us to appreciate the social geography of community resistance. Harlem was never merely the locus of an inescapable "urban crisis." It was also the site of a radical public sphere, a place where wisdom about domination and struggle flowed through multiple, intersecting channels. Similarly, the neighborhood's indigenous educational ventures were neither dens of extremism nor vehicles for the narrow pursuit of professional status. Rather, they were expressions of collective desire for true dignity and cultural citizenship. Today, when careerism and mercenary values govern the ethos of learning at practically all levels of schooling, we would do well to revive such humanist impulses.

Notes

The author wishes to thank Rachel Klepper for research assistance with portions of this essay.

1. "Visions of Harlem," manuscript, n.d., box 7, folder 24, Lawrence Neal papers (hereafter LNP), Schomburg Center for Research in Black Culture, New York Public Library (hereafter Schomburg).
2. Ray Rogers, "Harlem of Yesteryear Is No More," New York Times, June 12, 1969, B1; and Kenneth B. Clark, Dark Ghetto: Dilemmas of Social Power (New York: Harper and Row, 1965).
3. For more on grassroots activism and the quest for Black self-determination in Harlem, see Garrett Felber, "'Harlem Is the Black World': The Organization of Afro-American Unity at the Grassroots," Journal of African-American History 100 (2015): 199–225.

4. HARYOU, *Youth in the Ghetto: A Study of the Consequences of Powerlessness and a Blue-print for Change* (New York: HARYOU, 1964), 237.

5. Adina Back, "Exposing the Whole Segregation Myth: The Harlem Nine and New York City's School Desegregation Battles," in *Freedom North: Black Freedom Struggles Outside the South, 1940–1980*, ed. Jeanne Theoharis and Komozi Woodard (New York: Palgrave Macmillan, 2003), 65–92.

6. This essay complements existing works that focus on struggles in Harlem's public schools, including William H. Watkins, "A Marxian and Radical Reconstructionist Critique of American Education: Searching Out Black Voices," in *Black Protest Thought and Education*, ed. William Henry Watkins (New York: Peter Lang, 2005), 107–36; Martha Biondi, *To Stand and Fight: The Struggle for Civil Rights in Postwar New York City* (Cambridge, Mass.: Harvard University Press, 2003), 241–49; Jennifer de Forest, "The 1958 Harlem School Boycott: Parental Activism and the Struggle for Educational Equity in New York City," *Urban Review* 40 (2008): 21–41; Adina Back, "Up South in New York: The 1950s School Desegregation Struggles" (PhD diss., New York University, 1997); and Hasan Kwame Jeffries and Patrick D. Jones, "Desegregating New York: The Case of the 'Harlem Nine,'" *OAH Magazine of History* 26 (2012): 51–53.

7. For a related discussion, see Russell Rickford, *We Are an African People: Independent Education, Black Power, and the Radical Imagination* (New York: Oxford University Press, 2016).

8. HARYOU, *Youth in the Ghetto*, 165.

9. Transcript of Jesse Gray keynote address to the Federation for Independent Political Action Conference, December 1964, box 2, folder 9; and Josephine Buck Jones to Lyndon B. Johnson, April 7, 1964, box 10, folder 10, Babette Edwards Education Reform in Harlem Collection, Schomburg (hereafter BEERHC).

10. "Harlem Parents Support Boycott," *New York Times*, January 22, 1964, 28.

11. "East Harlem Project" statement, June 1964, box 18, folder 10, Preston Wilcox Papers, Schomburg (hereafter PWP); Preston Wilcox to Berlin Kelly, July 27, 1970, box 5, folder 6, BEERHC; and Isaiah Robinson, "Educational Determinism," *Liberation*, September 1968, 27.

12. Patricia Albjerg Graham, "Educating the City's Children," box 54, folder 9, Ewart Guinier Papers, Schomburg; and David X. Spencer Press Release, May 21, 1970, box 9, folder 7, BEERHC.

13. "Wig Salon Opens New Harlem Shop," *New York Amsterdam News*, August 17, 1963, 42; "African Bazaar Muslims 369th Armory," 1963 flyer, box 11, folder 5, Malcolm X Papers, Schomburg (hereafter MXP); Thomas A. Johnson, "Black Nationalists Gain More Attention in Harlem," *New York Times*, July 13, 1966, 1, 29; Earl Caldwell, "African Influence Thriving in Harlem," *New York Times*, March 12, 1968, 45; "African Courses at Yoruba Temple," *New York Amsterdam News*, November 3, 1962, 32; and Dear Co-Worker letter, n.d., ca. March 1962, box 5, folder 81, Richard B. Moore Papers, Schomburg.

14. Lawrence Neal, "Black Power/Liberation," manuscript, n.d., box 6, folder 15, LNP.

15. "Hear Dr. Lewis Henri Micheaux's Philosophy," pamphlet, n.d., box 23, folder 25, Universal Negro Improvement Association Records, Manuscript Archives and Rare Book Library, Emory University.

16. John Henrik Clarke, "The New Afro-American Nationalism," *Freedomways* (Fall 1961): 288; "Lewis Michaux: The World's Greatest Seller of Black Books," *Third World*, November 3, 1972, 13; "Lewis Michaux: I Advocated Going Back to Africa," *Third World*, November 24, 1972, 7, 11; "Lewis Michaux: The World's Greatest Seller

of Black Books," *Third World*, December 8, 1972, 13; and "Lewis Michaux: The World's Greatest Seller of Black Books," *Third World*, December 22, 1972, 12.

17. Theodore 4X and Hattie 2X to Brother Minister Malcolm X, October 12, 1962, box 11, folder 11; University of Islam materials, box 11, folder 3 "Plans for Youth Training Program"; and "ABC of Divine Knowledge," box 11, folder 11, MXP.

18. "Black Muslims in Harlem Build on Racial Pride and Prosperity," *New York Times*, January 13, 1969, 44; "The Nation of Islam: Education and Enterprise," news clipping, box 33, folder 7, BEERHC; Charlayne Hunter, "Muslim Center Blends Business, School and Mosque," *New York Times*, August 25, 1970, 38; Lesly Jones, "Muslim Teaching Makes Impact on Harlem," *New York Amsterdam News*, August 29, 1970, 1, 43; Naomi Tucker, "Muslims' Progress, a New Image," *New York Amsterdam News*, April 29, 1972, 10; and Thomas A. Johnson, "Minister and Mosque Have History of Dependability," *New York Times*, April 15, 1972, 16.

19. University of Islam materials, box 11, folder 3, MXP.

20. "Organization of Afro-American Unity Statement of Basic Aims and Objectives," July 1964, box 14, folder 1, MXP. See also William W. Sales, *From Civil Rights to Black Liberation: Malcolm X and the Organization of Afro-American Unity* (Boston: South End Press, 1994).

21. Diane C. Fujino, *Heartbeat of Struggle: The Revolutionary Life of Yuri Kochiyama* (Minneapolis: University of Minnesota Press, 2005), 148–49; and "Board of Education Tokenism," *OAAU Backlash*, November 9, 1964, box 14, folder 7, MXP.

22. The OAAU Liberation School was one of the first formations in the country to use the *liberation school* moniker. See Transcript of June 22, 1970, Robert Wright Interview with Herman Ferguson, Ralph J. Bunche Collection, Moorland-Spingarn Research Collection (hereafter MSRC).

23. Transcript of May 3, 1965, letter to "Dear Brothers and Sisters," Black Arts Repertory Theater/School FBI File, F. B. Eyes Digital Archive, accessed April 29, 2017, http://omeka.wustl.edu/omeka/exhibits/show/fbeyes/theatreschool.

24. Michael Stern, "Police Look Into Harlem Racists," *New York Times*, March 18, 1966, 18; and "The War Within the War," *Time*, May 13, 1966, 33.

25. "U.S. Cash Aids Negro Spiel of White Hatred," *Chicago Tribune*, December 1, 1965, B4; and Harold Cruse, *The Crisis of the Negro Intellectual* (New York: New York Review of Books, 2005), 440.

26. Hollie West, "Negro Poet Whips Up Hate in Harlem 'Black Arts' Body," news clipping, n.d., Black Arts Repertory Theater/School FBI File, F. B. Eyes Digital Archive, accessed April 29, 2017, http://omeka.wustl.edu/omeka/exhibits/show/fbeyes /theatreschool.

27. "Who Does What and Why in the Black Panther [Party?]," Pamphlet, n.d., box 1, folder 7, Black Panther Party Harlem Branch Papers, Schomburg (hereafter BPPHBP).

28. "Unite for Black Power!" flyer, 1966, box 1, folder 8; "Read About the Black Panther and Black Power" flyer, n.d., box 1, folder 9; and George M. Miller to "Dear Brothers and Sisters," August 20, 1966, box 1, folder 8, BPPHBP.

29. "Minutes of Document Committee Meeting, November 16, 1967," box 9, folder 14, Annie Stein Papers, Rare Book and Manuscripts, Columbia University (hereafter ASP); and "Harlem CORE Nearer to Goal of Independent Harlem School System," September 1967 Press Release, box 29, folder 17, BEERHC.

30. Harlem CORE, "A Proposal for an Independent Board of Education for Harlem," March 1967, box 162, folder 7, United Federation of Teachers; Roy Innis and Victor Solomon to "Dear Citizen of Harlem," September 16, 1967, box 29, folder 17, BEERHC.

31. Carl Rachlin, "CORE and the Schools," ca. 1965, box 32, folder 8, BEERHC; Roy Innis to "Dear Friend," July 1969, box 3, folder 8; and Civil Rights Documentation Project Vertical File, MSRC.

32. Harlem CORE, "A Proposal for an Independent Board of Education for Harlem," March 1967, box 162, folder 7, United Federation of Teachers Records (hereafter UFTR), Tamiment Library and Robert F. Wagner Labor Archives, New York University (hereafter Tamiment).

33. Doris Ullman to Annie Stein, n.d., box 9, folder 14, ASP.

34. Roy Innis and Victor Solomon, "Harlem Must Control Its Schools," *New Generation* (Fall 1967): 4–5.

35. Robert L. Allen, "Harlem Youngsters Boycott P.S. 125, Study on Own: 'Liberation Schools': Parent Power?" *National Guardian*, March 25, 1967; and "SOS: Save Our Students," PS 125–36 Parent/Community Committee flyer, 1967, box 160, folder 4, UFTR.

36. Preston Wilcox, "Teaching and Caring: One Teacher in Action," unpublished essay, box 32, folder 14, BEERHC; Leonard Buder, "Boycott Keeps 1,450 Out of School in Harlem," *New York Times*, March 14, 1967, 49; and "S.O.S." 1967 West Harlem Liberation School flyer and attached materials, box 160, folder 4, UFTR.

37. "Teacher's Guide," 1967, box 32, folder 14, BEERHC; and "Riverside Special," "Discussion Guide for Upper Grades and High School," 1967, box 31, folder 8, BEERHC.

38. Lois Prager, "PS 125 Boycott Involves 1700 Pupils," *Columbia Daily Spectator*, March 14, 1967, 1, 3; Preston Wilcox, "The 'Educated' and the 'Unlettered,'" unpublished essay, box 12, folder 1, PWP.

39. Preston Wilcox, "The 'Educated' and the 'Unlettered,'" unpublished essay, box 12, folder 1, PWP.

40. "Support the People's Church" January 1969 flyer, box 5, folder 8, Christiane C. Collins Collection, Schomburg.

41. "Support the People's Church."

42. *El pueblo se levanta*, Video (New York Third World Newsreel, 1970).

43. Babette Edwards, "A Review and Analysis of Three Educational Strategies for Positive Change in the Public School System of the City of New York," box 39, folder 2, and "Brief History of the Community Control Struggle," box 2, folder 3, BEERHC.

44. Preston Wilcox, "To Be Black and to Be Successful," February 1966, box 9, folder 5, and Proposal for I.S. 201 Complex Governing Board, 1967, box 5, folder 1, BEERHC.

45. See, for example, Daniel H. Perlstein, *Justice, Justice: School Politics and the Eclipse of Liberalism* (New York: Peter Lang, 2004); and Diane Ravitch, *The Great School Wars: A History of the New York City Public Schools* (Baltimore: Johns Hopkins University Press, 2000), 192–211.

46. Babette Edwards, "A Review and Analysis of Three Educational Strategies for Positive Change in the Public School System of the City of New York," 47, box 39, folder 2, BEERHC.

47. "Minutes of Second Negotiation Session of Parents, Community Representatives, and Board of Education Concerning Intermediate School 201," September 1966, box 2, folder 5; and E. Babette Edwards, Statement to "Equal Achievement in Schools," Conference, April 18, 1966, box 32, folder 8, BEERHC.

48. "CBS Testimony Before Lindsay Task Force on Poverty," January 1966, box 36, folder 19, BEERHC.

49. "Demands of Parents and Community to Make I.S. 201 a Model School," box 3, folder 13, BEERHC; 1970 I.S. 201 Complex Position Paper, box 9, folder 7, BEERHC; "Black Awareness: Malcolm X Memorial Service" flyer, 1969, box 6, folder 20, BEERHC; "I.S.

201 Complex Unit Administrator's Calendar," February 15–February 28, 1969, box 1, folder 20, BEERHC; and "El Hajj Malik El Shabazz," *Kweli*, June 1969, box 6, folder 9, BEERHC.

50. "Proposal for Massive Economic Neighborhood Development," October 1964, box 20, Folder 8, Preston Wilcox Papers, Schomburg; and "African-Hispanic History and Culture Institute," box 1, folder 1, BEERHC.

51. "Statement by Gilberto Gerena Valentin at Public Hearing on Proposed Grade Reorganization of New York City School System," March 1966, box 32, folder 8, BEERHC.

52. Angela Gilliam to Berlin Kelley, March 11, 1970, box 1, folder 6, BEERHC; "Folklore Festival," *Kweli*, May 1970, box 6, folder 10, BEERHC; and "The Idea of Freedom and the Puerto Rican," and "Discovery of Puerto Rico," box 9, folder 11, BEERHC.

53. I.S. 201 Governing Board, "Position Paper," *Liberation*, September 1968, 30.

54. Lesly Jones, "IS 201 Parent Dispute Rages On," *New York Amsterdam News*, May 1, 1971, 1; Babette Edwards and Hannah Brockington to Dave Spencer, February 5, 1971, box 3, folder 10, ASP; and Martin Arnold, "2 on I.S. 201 Board Resign in Protest," *New York Times*, March 9, 1971, 44.

55. Isaiah Robinson, "Educational Determinism," *Liberation*, September 1968, 27–28; David Spencer to Preston Wilcox, October 14, 1968, 10, 11, BEERHC; and Dave Spencer, "School Strike: A Parent's View," *Harlem News*, October 1967.

56. David Spencer Press Release, April 30, 1969, box 24, folder 6, Isaiah Robinson Files, series 378, Board of Education of the City of New York Collection, Municipal Archives of the City of New York (hereafter BOE, MA).

57. "The Site and the Scene," *Kweli*, July 1970, 5, box 3, folder 11, BEERHC; Daniel H. Watts, "Rockefeller's Negroes," *Liberator*, June 1967, 3; and Barbara Butler, "Gov. Rockefeller's Plan for Harlem Removal," *Liberator*, May 1968, 11.

58. Harlem Committee for Self-Defense, "Don't Let Them Destroy Harlem!" flyer, ca. 1969, box 54, folder 13, John O'Neal Papers, Amistad Research Center; Architects' Renewal Committee in Harlem, "The Case for a Harlem High School," February 1969, box 31, folder 20, BEERHC; "Raping the Children," *Kweli*, November 19, 1969, box 6, folder 9, BEERHC; "Reclamation Site! What's It All About?" *North Star*, December 1969, box 20, folder "The North Star," Paul M. Washington Papers, Blockson Collection, Temple University; and "Harlem Group for Self-Defense Seek to Achieve Unity to Save Community," *Muhammad Speaks*, December 27, 1968, 12.

59. "New Harlem High School: A Dream Moving Toward Reality," clipping, box 6, folder 26, ASP; and The Committee for a Harlem High School, "Study Design for a High School Program in Harlem," 1969, box 31, folder 20, BEERHC.

60. Charles F. Gordon, "Out of Site," *Black Theatre*, April 1970, 29–30.

61. Michael T. Kaufman, "CORE Offers Plan for Harlem Site," *New York Times*, October 11, 1969, 35.

62. Institute of Afrikan Research, "The S.O.B. in Harlem: Dig on This," box 15, folder 10, PWP.

63. Minutes of United Federation of Black Community Organizations Meeting, October 7, 1969, box 27, folder 11, BEERHC; M. A. Farber, "Brooklyn Sit-In Bars 2D Hearing by School Board," *New York Times*, December 21, 1966, 1, 32; "This is a poem written by Queen Mother Moore," December 1966, box 35, folder 5, BEERHC; and "The Brothers & Sisters for Afro-Am. Unity," flyer, ca. 1970, box 35, folder 5, BEERHC.

64. "This is a poem written by Queen Mother Moore," December 1966, box 35, folder 5, BEERHC; and C. Gerald Fraser, "Negro History Week Stirs Up Semantic Dispute," *New York Times*, February 15, 1968, 29.

65. "Activities at Mt. Addis Ababa," box 1, folder 25, Audley Moore FOIA File (hereafter AMFF), Tamiment; and Interview with Audley (Queen Mother) Moore, June 6 and 8, 1978, Black Women Oral History Project, Schlesinger Library, Radcliffe College.

66. "The Black Scholar Interviews: Queen Mother Moore," *Black Scholar*, March–April 1973, 50.

67. "Harlem Conference for Quality Education" program, December 1966, box 2, folder 9, BEERHC; Victor Reisel "Queen Mother's Mission: Veteran Communists Organize to Seize Black Power," December 1968, clipping, box 1, folder 25, AMFF; and Eric Pace, "Queen Mother Moore, 98, Harlem Rights Leader, Dies," *New York Times*, May 7, 1997, 15.

68. "The Universal Association of Ethiopian Women, Inc.: A Brief History," pamphlet, box 23, folder 30, Dabu Gizenga Collection, MSRC.

69. Simon Bly Jr. to Isaiah Robinson, April 13, 1970, box 1, folder 4, Isaiah Robinson Files, BOE, MA; National Black Theatre pamphlets, 1974, box 21, folder 26, Dabu Gizenga Collection, MSRC; and Federation of Pan African Educational Institutions Pamphlet, box 10, folder 13, Ronald W. Walters Papers, MSRC.

CHAPTER 10

"Harlem Sophistication"

Community-Based Paraprofessional Educators in Central Harlem and East Harlem

NICK JURAVICH

Winifred Tates applied to work at Public School (PS) 72 in East Harlem "to be an inspiration to her children," as she told an evaluator in 1976. This evaluator described Tates as "very community oriented," an educator who did "great things with children." She "was involved with everything" at her school, including classwork, home visits, and field trips, and she had guided a reading group of "the lowest achievers in the class" up to grade level. When observers from the Board of Education visited PS 72, they "constantly mis[took] her for the classroom teacher."[1]

In fact, Tates was a paraprofessional educator, working in a new kind of community-based position that was envisioned by parents, educators, and activists in Harlem in the 1960s. As part of their struggles for educational equity and self-determination, these Harlemites pushed the Board of Education to hire local residents—primarily the mothers of schoolchildren—to work in public schools. Local hiring, they argued, would create jobs for poor and working-class Black and Latina women, improve the quality of education for their children, and connect local schools to their communities. To transform Harlem's schools, these activists reimagined the work of education: who should do it, how they should do it, and how communities should know about it.

Plans for community-based hiring germinated in Harlem's antipoverty organizations, where staff and participants challenged psychological and cultural explanations of poverty by empowering Harlem's residents in the early 1960s.[2] Harlem Youth Opportunities Unlimited (HARYOU) played a central role, cultivating demonstration programs and petitioning the Board of Education to deploy federal funds for local hiring. Their efforts yielded fruit when the board hired its first paraprofessional educators in the spring of 1967.

By then, Harlem was in the midst of a "renaissance of educational thought and practice" inspired by the Black Power movement.[3] Community-based educators blossomed in this hothouse. The first generation of "paras" went beyond official expectations for their positions, implementing new pedagogies, curricula, and community outreach. Their labor proved so valuable to students, teachers, and parents that the board hired over ten thousand paras by 1970.

To secure their jobs during the political upheavals that rocked New York's schools in these years, paraprofessional educators organized, waging an innovative campaign in their neighborhoods and within their union, the United Federation of Teachers (UFT). The contract they won provided living wages, job security, and opportunities for advancement to thousands of working-class Black and Latina women. As a result, the ideas, practices, and organizing strategies of Harlem's community-based educators became models for a national "paraprofessional movement" that brought half a million new workers into U.S. public schools by the time Winifred Tates was interviewed in 1976.[4]

Despite the movement's success, New York City's 1975 fiscal crisis generated severe cuts in programs and positions for paraprofessional educators.[5] The politicians who emerged from this crisis in power sought to perpetuate austerity policies and to redefine the work of education as the province of elites. Community-based educators fought back and kept their jobs; 25,000 paraprofessional educators work in New York City today, out of 1.2 million nationally. However, the broad, emancipatory vision of community-based educational work that Harlem's first generation of paras practiced became a casualty of the crisis as the resources, institutions, and activism that had sustained it withered in this new, hostile educational climate.

This essay explores the evolving practice and meaning of educational work for Harlem's community-based paraprofessional educators over two decades. In their struggle for good jobs and permanent careers in public schools for local mothers, Harlem's activists channeled demands for jobs and freedom that reverberated through the Black freedom struggle, from the March on Washington to New York City.[6] By asserting that working-class Black and Latina women could work as educators and improve schooling, these Harlemites challenged the views of elite policy makers who believed poor women and their neighborhoods were in thrall to a "culture of poverty."[7] Through their labor, the first generation of community-based paraprofessional educators remade the classroom experience and relationships between schools and communities. Through their organizing, they made their jobs permanent, institutionalizing a new kind of educational work that persists to this day as a legacy of the Black freedom struggle.

The meanings of this work were always contested, even within the coalition of Harlemites who supported and worked in community-based jobs. The integrationist socialist Bayard Rustin and the radical nationalist Preston Wilcox both campaigned for local hiring. They debated the ways in which these workers should be prepared, how they should be organized, and what they should do in classrooms. The decision to unionize, in particular, cast these contests in stark relief: a contract offered stability, legitimacy, and advancement in schools, but institutionalization necessitated trade-offs and compromises that dismayed radical organizers. Across the city, the women who did this work struggled constantly to assert the value and legitimacy of their labor in the face of elite critiques and, later, tightening budgets. At one level, this is the story of a Harlem struggle that produced lasting changes in the American educational workforce. At the same time, charting the rise and fall of community-based educational work in Harlem reveals a rich, forgotten praxis that was undermined not by ineffectiveness, but by austerity politics.

Envisioning New Kinds of Educators in Harlem

Three factors generated demands for local hiring in Harlem schools in the early 1960s. First, New York City's teaching corps was very segregated by northern standards; Harlem's teachers knew little of their students' lives and often feared their neighborhoods.[8] Second, as students weathered segregated, indifferent learning environments, their parents struggled in a segregated, deindustrializing economy. As New York lost thousands of manufacturing jobs and added thousands of public-sector ones in the postwar era, access to city work took on heightened importance. Finally, the rise of federally funded antipoverty programs in New York, including HARYOU (founded in 1962), created spaces for experimentation in local employment.[9]

Parents and educators affiliated with HARYOU used demonstration programs and direct advocacy to push the Board of Education to hire locally. Richard Parrish was a Harlem teacher and union organizer who coordinated volunteers for Virginia's freedom schools in the summer of 1963. That fall, Parrish recruited two hundred teachers to work with students alongside four hundred mothers hired by HARYOU.[10] The afterschool program helped students "associate with adequate role models on a more personal level" and promoted "parent and teacher cooperation."[11] Later that year, Thelma Johnson, the chair of HARYOU's Committee on Education and the Schools, petitioned local administrators "to pay female recipients of Welfare" to walk children to and from school. The program, Johnson argued, "would serve the dual purpose of getting the children to school and providing the Welfare recipient with a sense of pride."[12] Johnson and Parrish knew that Harlem's parents would make talented educators if given the opportunity, and they understood that working-class people needed to get paid for their work.

HARYOU summarized its educational philosophy in its 1964 report, "Youth in the Ghetto." Among "ten anticipated needs" for Harlem's youth, HARYOU listed "parent aides" who would "demand for them [Harlem youth] what middle-class parents demand." The social worker Laura Pires wrote in the report that hiring "indigenous nonprofessionals" in public roles would "improve the giving of service" and create "meaningful employment for Harlem's residents."[13] Pires's colleague, the sociologist Frank Riessman, agreed. He quoted her in the frontispiece of his 1965 book with Arthur Pearl, *New Careers for the Poor*, adding, "This statement, taken from the HARYOU proposal, forms the basic thesis of this book."[14] Pearl and Riessman's book pushed the idea of local hiring into the policy mainstream and spawned a "New Careers Amendment" to the Economic Opportunity Act, introduced by Congressman James H. Scheuer of the Bronx in 1966. The core concepts, as Riessman acknowledged, were forged in Harlem.

The call for community control of Intermediate School (IS) 201 in 1966, discussed at greater length in chapters 8 and 9 of this volume, reshaped educational organizing in Harlem and amplified demands for local hiring. The scholar-activist Preston Wilcox called for a "fundamental restructuring of the relations between school and community based on a radical redistribution of power," which included "training local residents as foster teachers."[15] The Harlem Parents Committee called for local hiring in their newsletter, as did the mayor's commission in its 1967 report on decentralization.[16]

Starting in 1966, Wilcox chaired the board of the Women's Talent Corps (WTC), a job-training institute for women funded by the Office of Economic Opportunity. The WTC began training Harlem-based women for paraprofessionals jobs after Wilcox organized meetings with local community associations to forge partnerships. Seeking to place aides not just in community-run programs but the public schools themselves, the WTC and its trainees conducted letter-writing campaigns and a sit-in at the Board of Education. Their seventy-five trainees became the first paraprofessional educators hired by the board in 1967.[17]

Community-Based Educators at Work, 1967–1970

The Board of Education expanded hiring to 1,500 people in the fall of 1967 and employed more than 10,000 paraprofessionals by 1970. A study conducted in that year offers a statistical portrait of these educators. Half of New York's paras were African American and close to 40 percent had Spanish surnames (for context, only 42 percent of students were white but 91 percent of teachers were). Some 93 percent of paras were women, 80 percent of whom were mothers living within ten blocks of the schools where they worked. Their children attended these schools, and 85 percent regularly saw their students outside the classroom. Furthermore, 60 percent of paras reported formal involvement in a community institution, and nearly all cited increased engagement with neighbors through their new jobs. They worked an average of twenty-two to twenty-five hours a week and took home roughly $50, just above minimum wage. Federal regulations required that all job applicants be on welfare or eligible for it.[18]

As this study indicates, paras entered classrooms with intimate knowledge of the needs of local families and long-standing connections to community organizations. The Board of Education's hiring structure cemented these connections. Half of paras were nominated for their positions by city-recognized "Community Action Agencies," including HARYOU-ACT.[19] Principals hired the other half from among parent leaders and existing school staff. Organizations including HARYOU-ACT and the Women's Talent Corps provided training.

The talents and connections paras brought to their work completely undermined the "culture of poverty" thesis then in vogue with many poverty warriors. Anne Cronin, the training director at the WTC, rejected this framework explicitly, writing that the WTC's training program "reflects a basic philosophy about the 'teachability' of uneducated people. It assumes that the 'culture of poverty' does not affect the attitudes of most of the low-income groups in New York City."[20] As Cronin added in 1968, her students "were people who are alert and active in community affairs . . . PTA officers, den mothers, community council members, church volunteer workers . . . with a rich life-knowledge and wisdom about the ways of their world."[21] Laura Pires, who moved from HARYOU to the WTC to support trainees in the field, developed her own shorthand for this combination of local knowledge and organizing savvy. She called it "Harlem sophistication."[22]

Paraprofessionals in Central Harlem and East Harlem represented the diversity of these neighborhoods by design, and they tailored their work to the needs of their particular school communities. Across these diverse settings, they deployed three general strategies to succeed in their new roles. First, they practiced "activist mothering," the promotion of youth and community survival through the use of "indigenous knowledges."[23] Second, they built cross-class, interracial solidarity among working women that connected local mothers, paras, teachers, and union organizers. These alliances helped paras secure their jobs.[24] Third, paraprofessional educators consistently sought education and training to turn their jobs into teaching careers, espousing a philosophy of collective advancement that sought to rise with Harlem rather than from it.[25]

A detailed look at a single program reveals the many facets of community-based educational work. Parent-Teacher Teams (PTT) was developed jointly by HARYOU-ACT, Local School District 5, and Teachers College. The program employed 130 parents in 27 schools in Harlem and the Upper West Side, serving 3,900 students between 1967 and 1970.[26] At one cluster of four schools in Southern Harlem, 26 of 27 paras hailed from the same ten-block radius (one lived just outside), but only one teacher lived in the neighborhood, on Morningside Avenue. These mothers, who were in regular contact with the families they served, connected the schools to the community in ways that teachers, who were often commuting from outside Harlem, could not.

The proposal for Parent-Teacher Teams outlined a bounded, gendered definition of paraprofessional labor. It included suggestions for tasks such as "contribute to enrichment activities by utilizing her special talents," "alert the teacher to the special needs of individual children," "give special encouragement and aid to the non-English speaking child," and "be a source of affection and security to the children."[27] The women who did this work fulfilled these roles, but they also expanded on them, leading efforts to affirm students' language, culture, and experiences. At PS 207, Azalee Evans developed the first African American history curriculum.[28] In all PTT schools, paras served as translators for students and created bilingual materials for them and their parents.[29] As an assessment of the program's first year asserted, "The addition of a parent in the classroom benefits the children as much as the teacher and parent involved" because such a worker could "relate to children whose environment she shares."[30]

During the most contentious years in the history of public schooling in New York City, Parent-Teacher Teams garnered rave reviews. After a trial summer program in 1967, one teacher declared, "I can't wait to have a parent in my room." A parent replied, "I used to be so afraid of the school. Now I know it is a friendly place."[31] In February 1969, a PTT principal told reporters that the program "worked beautifully," a view echoed citywide.[32] In May 1968, the UFT released a survey of over 200 teachers, nearly all of whom loved these new workers. One noted the value of having a bilingual adult in the classroom, and another explained that she had been "so much more successful because of her [para's] assistance, especially reaching out to parents."[33] The survey also reached 230 paras, of whom only 4 reported negative experiences. Their responses revealed strong commitments to local children and the goal of "establish[ing] a closer relation between parents and schools." Paras also asserted their need for prompt pay and living wages, and hoped the Board of Education would make good on the promise of teacher training.[34]

The UFT's report revealed emerging solidarity between classroom workers. Paras and teachers brought mutual suspicions into their classrooms, but the time they spent together generated goodwill among those who shared the challenges of working women. As one PTT teacher explained, working with paras had taught her that "parents want the same thing that I want—each is looking out for the welfare of the child."[35] A Bronx activist later recalled that this first generation of paras had "made themselves essential" to students, parents, and teachers. In doing so, they laid the groundwork for a citywide campaign to secure their jobs.[36]

Securing Para Jobs with Unionization
and Community Organizing

When the UFT's report on paraprofessional educators appeared on May 20, 1968, no one was paying attention. Nine days earlier, the Ocean Hill-Brownsville administrator Rhody McCoy had transferred eighteen white teachers out of his district, igniting a conflict between the largely white, middle-class UFT and Black and Puerto Rican community organizers that had been gathering fuel for a decade. By the fall, the union was out on strike and parent organizers in Harlem were sleeping in their schools to keep them open. Paraprofessional programs came of age as New York City's school system came apart.[37]

During the 1968 strikes, many paras crossed picket lines to teach, particularly in the three "demonstration districts," which included Harlem's IS 201 complex. Preston Wilcox asked the trainees of the Women's Talent Corps to do so, and many volunteered to work in these schools when their own were closed. Other paras stayed out in solidarity with the teachers they worked alongside.[38] Those who did stay out frequently staffed "freedom schools" hosted by churches and community centers. On either side of the picket line, paras did the work of education for neighborhood children (and their parents, who desperately needed child care). The experience made a powerful impression on paras. As several WTC trainees told Laura Pires afterward, their work during the strikes had simultaneously convinced them of the importance of their positions and raised fears that "experimental" paraprofessional programs, like those housed in the demonstration districts, could be shuttered at any moment.[39]

Although paraprofessional educators had expressed interest in unionizing before the strikes, the UFT's scorched-earth attack on community control seemed to foreclose the possibility of any further partnership. In addition, the strikes badly divided the UFT's membership. Richard Parrish published a searing critique of his union subtitled "Blow to Education, Boon to Racism," in which he denounced the strikes and urged teachers to depose the leadership in favor of a "genuine partnership between the UFT and the black and poor communities." Parrish added, from experience, "unless Black and Puerto Rican people have a chance to get on the staff, to have job training and to develop as their white counterparts, they will never be able to hold their heads up and work" in either schools or the union.[40] Other opposition groups that emerged during 1968, including Teachers for Community Control, likewise supported the empowerment of paraprofessionals.[41]

The UFT's president Albert Shanker publicly excoriated anyone who crossed picket lines in 1968. However, facing pressure from his union's left flank and public perceptions of his union as a racist organization, and with clear evidence that paras sought the benefits of unionization, Shanker embraced them. At the recommendation of Bayard Rustin and A. Philip Randolph, two of the only Black leaders to support the UFT during the strikes, Shanker put Velma Murphy Hill in charge of renewing the campaign. Hill, a Chicago-born protégé of Rustin, had cut her teeth in New York on the Congress of Racial Equality's campaign to desegregate construction work at the State University of New York's Downstate Medical Center in 1963.[42] Like Rustin, she believed that integrated workplaces and public job creation were central to the future of the freedom struggle.[43]

An election was set for June 1969 between the UFT and the American Federation of State, County and Municipal Employees (AFSCME) DC 37, which was considered a far more progressive union. Hill and her team worked hard to define the UFT as an educator's union with "the experience and strength to obtain professional pay and status" for paras.[44] A report in the Baltimore Afro-American shared a different perspective, quoting the Harlem para Carolyn Frazier as saying, "I'm going to the highest bidder." Responding to this, the WTC faculty member Robert Jackson explained, "The paraprofessionals ideologically prefer DC 37, but from a practical standpoint, they feel that the UFT has more muscle."[45] These comments highlighted a tension in the campaign: although it seemed clear that the UFT was better positioned to secure community-based educational work, this was the union that had just crushed the city's boldest experiment in community control of schools. Given the vast disparities of power between working-class women and the largest local teacher's union in the country, several historians have argued that paraprofessional unionization amounted to little more than co-optation by the UFT leadership. If this was the case, paras were remarkably clear-eyed about it.[46]

In June, just enough paraprofessional educators chose the "school union" to give the UFT a fifty-three-vote victory (out of roughly 3,800 cast). Years later, two Bronx leaders who had fought the UFT during the 1968 strikes voiced approval of the vote, citing the importance of "institutionalizing" para jobs. They also supported bringing Black and Latinx voices into the UFT to make it more responsive to communities.[47] Paraprofessional educators had put their faith in the "union of professionals" (as the UFT described itself) to provide them with professional status without undermining their commitments to community-based educational work.

However, the Board of Education refused to bargain, daring paras to strike. Administrators believed the UFT's white rank and file would never walk out in support of paras, and that if the union did strike, the Black and Puerto Rican communities who had fought for local hiring would turn on paras and support the board in breaking their union. In response, paras and their union waged a novel two-front campaign in neighborhoods and union halls.

As strike rumors circulated in the spring of 1970, community organizations called meetings in disbelief. One HARYOU-ACT notice expressed a common fear, warning that "efforts are being made by the United Federation of Teachers to remove these workers from community control."[48] Paras, led by Velma Murphy Hill, attended these meetings. Although they met with "very hostile" crowds, they "got to tell their side of the story," promising to continue their community-based work and asking for help in securing their jobs.[49]

Paras also took to the press. In an article titled "Paraprofessionals Seek Parent Support," in the *New York Amsterdam News*, the Harlem para Bessy Canty hoped that "parents [would] understand their plight and support the education aides by keeping their children out of school." The paper also interviewed Congressman James Scheuer, the sponsor of "New Careers" legislation, who was unequivocally supportive. "We intended this program to provide a ladder from unemployment to paraprofessionalism and on up to professional employment status," Scheuer explained. "As the program is currently run, the paraprofessionals are being employed on an hourly basis with no job security, no sick leave, no vacation and effectively no chance for upgrading."[50] East Harlem's *El Diario* also covered the contract struggle, noting that Puerto Ricans at home would be shocked to learn of the low wages paid to paras by New York City schools.[51]

While these conversations were taking place in Harlem and East Harlem, the UFT conducted "one of the most intensive internal education campaigns in its history" to convince teachers to support paraprofessionals.

It relied on the voices of teachers who worked with paras.[52] Eloise Davis, a teacher at PS 108 in Harlem, told the *New York Amsterdam News*, "Parapro-fessionals need and deserve better salaries and benefits."[53] Armed with letters, testimonials, and even a one-act play, teachers from Harlem, the South Bronx, and Central Brooklyn traveled the five boroughs to convince their colleagues to support the contract struggle.[54] The board had gambled that teachers would never walk out with paraprofessionals—known to have crossed picket lines in 1968—but at Madison Square Garden in June 1970, teachers voted to strike alongside paras if necessary.

This two-front campaign forced the board to the table that summer. By the fall, paras had won a 140 percent wage increase, health care, and paid time off for teacher training. The *New York Amsterdam News*, which had excoriated Bayard Rustin for his support of the UFT in 1968, published an op-ed by Rustin titled "Triumph of the Paraprofessionals." Rustin described the contract as "one of the finest examples of self-determination by the poor."[55] As this phrasing suggested, the paras' campaign was not an endorsement of the UFT's leadership. It was an act of self-determination to secure their jobs and legitimate their labor.

Advancing Community-Based Education, 1970–1976

The new decade brought new challenges for community-based educators, but their contract proved a source of empowerment at first. Paras continued their work while taking on new leadership roles in schools and neighborhoods, attending college through their "career ladder" program, and organizing both for and against the UFT's leadership team. Leaders across the political spectrum also worked to take the "paraprofessional movement" national.

Paraprofessional educators in Harlem returned to a rapidly changing school environment in September 1970 on account of the partial decentralization of the city's school system.[56] Whereas the Central Board of Education retained control over most of the budget and faculty hiring, it transferred management of the Title I funds that supported paraprofessional jobs and hiring decisions about these jobs to thirty-one new Community School Boards. Although sensible on its face, this decision actually centralized paraprofessional programs and undermined smaller units of organization including the PTT clusters and the IS 201 community complex.

The uneven decentralization of funds also created incentives for school board members to tear up existing programs, either to put their own visions into practice or to consolidate power and patronage. District 3 (formerly District 5) in Southern Harlem and District 4 in East Harlem preserved many successful programs, but turnover and political infighting in Central Harlem's District 5 frequently undermined paraprofessional hiring and labor.[57]

Despite these challenges, Harlem paras continued working for educational equity and community empowerment in their schools and communities, aided by new opportunities for advancement. Georgina Carlo, who had started work in 1967 as a guidance assistant without a high school diploma, earned her GED (general equivalency diploma) and became a college adviser at East Harlem's Benjamin Franklin High School.[58] Her fellow WTC trainee Mercedes Figueroa "organized an anti-narcotics campaign with her neighbors" at IS 201.[59] In 1969, District 4's Community Education Center had launched a program, staffed primarily by paras, to provide materials on Puerto Rican history and culture to classrooms. With continued funding from District 4, the program evolved into El Museo del Barrio.[60] Even in District 5, where Superintendent Luther Seabrook blasted the district's "patronage" hiring in 1975, a "Reading Through Drama" program won praise from evaluators.[61] Staffed by paras, the program demonstrated that "students learn best through the process of interaction and communication."[62]

Frank Riessman used practices developed in Harlem to create a Career Opportunities Program (COP) that employed and trained nearly fifteen thousand paraprofessional educators across the nation in the 1970s.[63] In Harlem, the COP supported paras who worked for Youth Tutoring Youth, a program that trained middle and high school students as reading tutors for younger children, seeking the "double thrust of enriching the young 'teacher' as well as the student who has tuned out the message of the structured classroom."[64] At ten schools and public housing community centers in Harlem, paraprofessionals and teachers ran this program, which espoused the goal of involving "parents, indigenous teachers and paraprofessional personnel who have a stake in the community and an emotional investment in the progress of their children."[65] Reviewing the program in 1972, the on-site director, Edward Grant, noted the critical role of paras. They helped select and pair tutors and students, and the fact that paras were "able to empathize" with these students allowed them to "make the tutor aware of the things in his experience which can be used to teach others."[66] A decade after HARYOU responded to "social work colonialism" with "maximum feasible participation," unionized paraprofessional educators carried this work forward.[67]

Many Harlem paras became students themselves. Their contract created a Paraprofessional-Teacher Education Program (PTEP) at the City University of New York (CUNY), which educated approximately six thousand paraprofessionals each semester from 1972 through 1976.[68] Only a small percentage of paras became teachers; the process took six years, and only about two thousand paras had earned teaching degrees by the time the program was shuttered completely in the early 1980s.[69] Nonetheless, the program produced a significant influx of paid training into Harlem and East Harlem and contributed to the integration of the teaching corps.

Paras and their allies also believed educational opportunities inspired paras' children and students. "Children were proud of their mothers . . . and took a new interest in school work," noted one WTC report.[70] However, Velma Murphy Hill, who received regular letters asking for help enrolling in college, also observed that women attending school was not always easy on their families. She received many requests to "please talk to my husband, he doesn't want me to go to school."[71] Mercedes Figueroa told her supervisors that her work at IS 201 "raised real problems at home, for her husband was not prepared for his wife to take this sort of career woman, activist role."[72] In the face of deindustrialization and rising unemployment, opportunities for women threatened some men in Harlem families.

Radical Harlem activists looked warily on the process of professionalization. In 1973, Preston Wilcox wrote that professionalization was destroying community-based programs, turning "authentic, natural Black mothers into 'professional technicians,' unrelated to the Black community, comfortably subservient to the white community."[73] Nonetheless, Wilcox remained deeply committed to the goal of employing local residents in public schools. He came to the defense of paras whom District 3 barred from participating in PTAs in 1971, writing that "paraprofessionals, who are both 'poverty parents' and paid workers in schools are in a unique position to evaluate and monitor programs. Their experience and judgment could be valuable to other parent members."[74] Like Riessman, Wilcox took his vision of parent employment national, creating a "Parent Participation in Follow Through" program that hired "parent stimulators" to assert parent power at seventeen schools in eight states.[75]

Unionization provided new opportunities for working-class Black and Latina women to take on leadership roles in Harlem and beyond. The UFT paraprofessional chapter led voter registration drives at Harlem schools, hosted weekend conferences on political organizing led by Randolph and Rustin, and helped paras run for local school boards and church committees.[76] New York City paras also hit the road to replicate their successful campaign. Led by the tireless Hill, the American Federation of Teachers organized 100,000 paras by 1988.[77]

Not all paraprofessionals embraced the UFT's leadership. Some joined with the Teachers Action Caucus (TAC) and other rank-and-file opposition groups to demand a more substantive commitment to community empowerment from their union. The TAC called for the annualization of paraprofessional salaries beginning in 1972, asserting that "paraprofessionals are regular members and an integral part of the school staff . . . the services they perform are essential to the operation of schools."[78] Paras in the TAC challenged New York City's nascent school-to-prison pipeline and rejected the UFT's statements on school safety. When its union sought more security officers in schools in 1970, the TAC countered that the board should hire more community-based workers to address conflict between students and teachers.[79] In Harlem, the TAC supported a parent boycott in District 4 that demanded "more paraprofessionals," and it helped develop trainings for paras and teachers in small-group reading in District 3.[80]

By the time Winifred Tates gave her interview in 1976, paraprofessional educators could look back with pride on a decade of hard-won gains for their schools, communities, and children. Amid the increasingly uncertain political climate of the 1970s, they had reshaped the work of education and created thousands of jobs. However, the city's 1975 fiscal crisis presented new, existential challenges to their jobs and their work.

Defending Paraprofessional Programs

New York City's near-bankruptcy in 1975 wreaked havoc on public schools and "disproportionately affected" paraprofessional educators and other Black and Latinx workers, in the words of the deputy schools chancellor Bernard Gifford.[81] Harlem's paras and parents took to the streets in response. The PTAs of PS 76 and PS 144 blocked traffic at 125th Street and Adam Clayton Powell Jr. Boulevard in July, and PS 76's UFT chapter joined the protest after learning that their school would lose twenty-five of its forty-three paras. "This is a rip-off of Central Harlem," said Mrs. Ethel Hughes, the president of PS 144's PTA. "We are losing the most compared to other areas." The parent leader Annelle Munn added, "The budget cut is throwing a lot of us out of jobs."[82]

Despite these efforts, 5,970 paras, nearly two-thirds of the community-based workforce, had been laid off by the time schools opened in September.[83] Union and community support for paraprofessionals had proved complementary in the paras' 1970 contract campaign, but during the fiscal crisis, UFT seniority provisions put parents and teachers at odds with one another. In January 1976, Harlem parents described these UFT policies as the "destruction of parent power." If Black educators continued to lose jobs, the group argued, "the images that we have struggled so hard and so long to get for our children will be lost." The longtime Harlem activist Alice Kornegay noted, "White teachers failed us all these years, and in the last 10 years, Blacks have been coming in and doing the job."[84]

The fiscal crisis also gutted the career ladder program. In 1976, CUNY began charging tuition, and funds for paraprofessional training were eliminated from the Board of Education's budget. Cruelly, the board pushed paraprofessionals who planned to attend classes on summer stipends to apply for unemployment instead.[85] Having fought for years to win professional status as educators, paras now found themselves pushed back into the pool of out-of-work Harlemites. The UFT president Albert Shanker attacked the cuts, writing, "We are saving next to nothing, but we are denying the children the services of the paras, we are pushing far into the future the genuine integration of our schools staff, and we are once again needlessly placing people on the treadmill of poverty and welfare."[86] However, immersed in a battle to preserve teacher jobs, the UFT could not preserve the PTEP, even after paraprofessionals picketed union headquarters.[87]

After the immediate crisis, federal funds from the Comprehensive Employment and Training Act helped rehire many paras. However, the election of Ed Koch as mayor in 1977 presented a new political threat. On the campaign trail, Koch attacked community organizers in Harlem as "poverty pimps." Once in office, he targeted them for elimination. In the same budget that closed Harlem's Sydenham Hospital, Koch rejected annual salaries and pension benefits for paraprofessionals in the UFT's contract, recently adopted from the TAC's platform.[88] Despite pleas from his own schools chancellor, Koch argued that these measures were too expensive and would set a "dangerous" precedent for collective bargaining.[89]

Paras protested furiously. Velma Hill told the mayor, "You can't discriminate against one group." Shelvy Young, a paraprofessional on the Lower East Side, appeared in an advertisement titled "I Love New York, Mayor Koch. Why Doesn't New York Love Me?" A single mother of two, working full-time and attending school, Young's composed portrait in the *New York Amsterdam News* offered a staunch rebuke to Koch's rhetoric.[90] The paper authored an editorial in support of the paras and ran several articles on the fight.[91] After arbitration, Koch yielded a small regular summer stipend, but paraprofessionals did not receive pensions until 1983, and then, by an act of state government.[92]

Although paras managed to preserve their jobs, Koch's attacks set the tone for their marginalization as the 1980s wore on. The mayor deployed racism and sexism to redefine the work of education once again: paras were not educators but "welfare mothers," their jobs not work but patronage. The New York City schools chancellor Joel Klein would make similar arguments as he attempted to lay off hundreds of paras twenty-five years later.[93]

Nationally, Ronald Reagan and the Ninety-Seventh Congress radically restructured the Elementary and Secondary Education Act in 1982, moving the focus of funding away from community involvement and toward standards and testing. Reagan's administration disempowered community organizations and undermined public sector unionism, leaving paraprofessionals in Harlem with weakened allies. Shifting paradigms of educational reform that privileged elite outsider perspectives over local knowledge further challenged paraprofessional programs.

Local hiring in Harlem and East Harlem did not simply disappear in the late 1970s and early 1980s. In East Harlem, where stable school board politics and continued federal funding for bilingual education supported paras, their work continued apace. One 1985 study captured the effect of this funding differential on paraprofessional advancement; bilingual paraprofessionals were twice as likely to become teachers.[94]

After the rise of Koch and Reagan, community-based paras continued to provide instruction, guidance, and outreach in schools, and they do so to this day. However, the transformative potential that paras and their allies had envisioned for this work has been relegated to the margins of school policy and activism. The experiences of community-based educators in Harlem do not offer simple lessons, but their ideas, organizing strategies, and struggles against austerity have much to offer educators today who seek to make the work of education more holistic, communal, and equitable.

Notes

1. Evaluation of Winifred Tates, 1976, Archives of the Women's Talent Corps, folder 160 ("Student Interviews"), Metropolitan College of New York (hereafter MCNY).
2. Chapter 7 in this volume. See also Tamar W. Carroll, *Mobilizing New York: AIDS, Antipoverty, and Feminist Activism* (Chapel Hill: University of North Carolina Press, 2015).
3. Chapter 9 in this volume. See also Russell Rickford, *We Are an African People: Independent Education, Black Power, and the Radical Imagination* (New York: Oxford University Press, 2016).
4. Alan Gartner and Frank Riessman, "The Paraprofessional Movement in Perspective," *Personnel and Guidance Journal* 53, no. 4 (December 1974): 253–56.
5. Chapter 11 in this volume. See also Kim Phillips-Fein, *Fear City: New York City's Fiscal Crisis and the Rise of Austerity Politics* (New York: Metropolitan Books, 2017).
6. William P. Jones, *The March on Washington: Jobs, Freedom, and the Forgotten History of Civil Rights* (New York: W. W. Norton, 2014); Michael B. Katz and Mark J. Stern, "The New African-American Inequality" *Journal of American History* 92, no. 1 (June 2005): 75–108; Wendell Pritchett, *Brownsville, Brooklyn: Blacks, Jews, and the Changing Face of the Ghetto* (Chicago: University of Chicago Press, 2002); and Brian Purnell, *Fighting Jim Crow in the County of Kings: The Congress of Racial Equality in Brooklyn* (Lexington: University Press of Kentucky, 2013).
7. Annelise Orleck and Lisa Gayle Hazirjian, eds., *The War on Poverty: A New Grassroots History, 1964–1980* (Athens: University of Georgia Press, 2011), part 2, "Poor Mothers and the War on Poverty," and especially Adina Back, "'Parent Power': Evelina López Antonetty, the United Bronx Parents, and the War on Poverty," 184–208.
8. Christina Collins, *"Ethnically Qualified": Race, Merit, and the Selection of Urban Teachers, 1920–1980* (New York: Teachers College Press, 2011).
9. Carroll, *Mobilizing New York*; and Michael Woodsworth, *The Battle for Bed-Stuy: The Long War on Poverty in New York City* (Cambridge, Mass.: Harvard University Press, 2016).
10. "Negro Teachers Form a New Assn. to Aid Harlem Kids," *World-Telegram and Sun*, November 11, 1963, reel 1, Richard Parrish Papers (hereafter RPP), Schomburg Center for Research in Black Culture, New York Public Library (hereafter Schomburg).
11. "A Proposal to Establish After School Study Centers in the Central Harlem Area and to Develop New Approaches in the Area of Remediation, Academic Instruction, Guidance, and the Training of Teachers," reel 3, RPP.
12. Meeting, Minutes, April 5, 1963, PS 192, Manhattan, United Federation of Teachers Records (hereafter UFTR), box 115, folder 3, Tamiment Library and Robert F. Wagner Labor Archives, New York University (hereafter Tamiment).
13. HARYOU, *Youth in the Ghetto: A Study of the Consequences of Powerlessness and a Blueprint for Change* (New York: HARYOU, 1964); Laura Pires-Hester, interview with the author, March 9, 2015. On indigeneity as a category for mobilization and analysis in Black communities, see Rickford, *We Are an African People* and Christopher Emdin, *For White Folks Who Teach in the Hood . . . and the Rest of Y'all, Too: Reality Pedagogy and Urban Education* (Boston: Beacon Press, 2016).

14. Arthur Pearl and Frank Riessman, *New Careers for the Poor: The Non-Professional in Human Services* (New York: Free Press, 1965).

15. Preston Wilcox, "The Controversy at IS 201: One View and a Proposal," *Urban Review*, July 1966, Preston Wilcox Papers, box 24, folder 2, Schomburg.

16. "Views," Harlem Parents Committee, April 1966 and September 1967, UFTR, box 87, folder 25; and McGeorge Bundy, ed., *Reconnection for Learning: A Community School System for New York City Schools* (New York: Mayor's Advisory Panel on Decentralization of New York City Schools, 1967), accessed via ERIC, June 10, 2019, https://eric.ed.gov/?id=ED013287.

17. On the WTC's history, see Grace G. Roosevelt, *Creating a College That Works: Audrey Cohen and Metropolitan College of New York* (Albany: State University of New York Press, 2015).

18. Henry M. Brickell et al., *An In-Depth Study of Paraprofessionals in District Decentralized ESEA Title I : And New York State Urban Education Projects in the New York City Schools* (New York: Institute for Educational Development, 1971).

19. By 1967, HARYOU had merged with Associated Community Teams, and became known as HARYOU-ACT.

20. "Progress Report 6, March–April 1967," folder 12, MCNY.

21. "1968 Progress Report," folder 15, MCNY.

22. "Progress Report 5, January–February 1967," folder 11, MCNY.

23. Nancy Naples, *Grassroots Warriors: Activist Mothering, Community Work, and the War on Poverty* (New York: Routledge, 1998), 2–10. Naples builds on the concept of "othermothering" explored by of Patricia Hill Collins in *Black Feminist Thought: Knowledge, Consciousness and the Politics of Empowerment* (London: Routledge, 2000). See also Orleck and Hazirjian, *War on Poverty*.

24. Stephanie Gilmore, ed., *Feminist Coalitions: Historical Perspectives on Second-Wave Feminism in the United States* (Chicago: University of Illinois Press, 2008). In New York, see Carroll, *Mobilizing New York* and Roberta Gold, *When Tenants Claimed the City: The Struggle for Citizenship in New York City Housing* (Chicago: University of Illinois Press, 2014).

25. Collins, *Black Feminist Thought*; Naples, *Grassroots Warriors*; and Crystal Sanders, *A Chance for Change: Head Start and Mississippi's Black Freedom Struggle* (Chapel Hill: University of North Carolina Press, 2016).

26. "District Preliminary Proposal, ESEA Title I Project," Morningside Area Alliance, series 3, box 55, folder 16, Parent Teacher Teams, Columbia University Archives (hereafter MAA).

27. "District Preliminary Proposal, ESEA Title I Project."

28. "Parents Go Back to School: As Teacher Assistants and TC Students," *TC Week*, February 7, 1969, MAA.

29. "Untitled Report, Spring 1968," MAA.

30. "Untitled Report, Spring 1968."

31. "Untitled Report, Spring 1968."

32. "Parents Go Back to School: As Teacher Assistants and TC Students."

33. Gladys Roth, "Auxiliary Educational Assistants in New York City Schools," Internal Report, May 20, 1968, UFTR, box 80, folder 11.

34. Roth, "Auxiliary Educational Assistants."

35. "District Preliminary Proposal, ESEA Title I Project."

36. Aurelia Greene, interview with the author, August 27, 2014.

37. Daniel Perlstein, *Justice, Justice: School Politics and the Eclipse of Liberalism* (New York: Peter Lang, 2004); Jerald E. Podair, *The Strike That Changed New York: Blacks, Whites, and the Ocean Hill-Brownsville Crisis* (New Haven, Conn.: Yale University Press, 2002); and Jonna

Perrillo, *Uncivil Rights: Teachers, Unions, and Race in the Battle for School Equity* (Chicago: University of Chicago Press, 2012).

38. Letter from Audrey Cohen to David Selden, March 10, 1969, UFTR, box 80, folder 14; and "Second Annual Report and Evaluation, 1967–68," MCNY, folder 2.

39. "Final Report, 1968," MCNY, folder 2.

40. Richard Parrish, "The New York City Teachers Strikes: Blow to Education, Boon to Racism," *Labor Today*, May 1969, reel 1, RPP.

41. "What Does Control Mean?" Teachers for Community Control Newsletter, December 1968, Anne Filardo Papers on Rank and File Activism in the American Federation of Teachers and in the United Federation of Teachers (TAM 141), Tamiment, box 1, folder 1B, (hereafter AFP).

42. Velma Murphy Hill, conversation with the author, April 10, 2014. On the SUNY Downstate Campaign, see Purnell, *Fighting Jim Crow.*

43. Velma Murphy Hill, interview with the author, November 7, 2011.

44. Flyer, June 1969, UFTR, box 155, folder 3.

45. "Unions Fight to Enlist NY's Teacher Aides," *Baltimore Afro-American*, December 27, 1969.

46. Collins, *"Ethnically Qualified"*; Diana D'Amico, "Claiming Profession: The Dynamic Struggle for Teacher Professionalism in the Twentieth Century" (PhD diss., New York University, 2010); and Sonia Song-Ha Lee, *Building a Latino Civil Rights Movement* (Chapel Hill: University of North Carolina Press, 2014).

47. Aurelia Greene, interview; Lorraine Montenegro, interview with the author, September 24, 2014.

48. "Emergency Meeting Called on School Employment." *New York Amsterdam News*, November 29, 1969.

49. Velma Murphy Hill, interview.

50. "Paraprofessionals Seek Parent Support," *New York Amsterdam News*, May 2, 1970.

51. Clipping from *El Diario*, June 15, 1970, UFTR, box 255, folder 2.

52. "Internal Report," 1974, UFTR, box 80, folder 13.

53. "Paraprofessionals Seek Parent Support."

54. Newsletter from UFT Chapter Chairman Lucy Shifrin, PS 189K, April 1970, UFTR, box 155, folder 6.

55. Bayard Rustin, "Triumph of the Paraprofessionals," *New York Amsterdam News*, August 22, 1970.

56. Heather Lewis, *New York City Public Schools from Brownsville to Bloomberg: Community Control and Its Legacy* (New York: Teachers College Press, 2013).

57. Heather Lewis, "'There Is No Board of Education for Harlem': The I.S. 201 Experimental District and Its Aftermath," presentation at the Educating Harlem conference, October 2014.

58. Student Interviews, MCNY, folder 160.

59. Student Interviews.

60. "CSB 3 v. BOE, 1970, Isaiah Robinson Files, Board of Education (BOE), series 378, box 12, folder 12; and El Museo Del Barrio, "History+Timeline," accessed August 4, 2016, http://www.elmuseo.org/wp-content/uploads/2014/02/Timeline.pdf.

61. "Audit of the District 5 ESEA Programs from 1975–77," Amelia H. Ashe Files, BOE, series 312, box 61, folder 13.

62. "Board of Trustees Community Report, District 5, 1976–1977," Bernard Gifford Papers, BOE, series 1202, box 4, folder CSD 5 1976–77.

63. George Kaplan, *From Aide to Teacher: The Story of the Career Opportunities Program* (Washington, D.C.: Government Printing Office, 1977).

64. "Youth Tutoring Youth Harlem—East Harlem," May 27, 1970, BOE, series 1101, box 14, folder 7.
65. "Youth Tutoring Youth," June 7, 1970, BOE, series 1101, box 15, folder 25.
66. "Proposal Draft for YTY," May 18, 1972, BOE, series 1101, box 15, folder 25.
67. Chapter 7 in this volume.
68. Isaiah Robinson Files, BOE, series 378, box 38, folder 18.
69. Collins, *Ethnically Qualified.*
70. "Final Report and Evaluation of the Women's Talent Corps New Careers Program," 1966–67, MCNY, folder 1.
71. UFT Oral History Collection (OH.009), box 1, folder Velma Hill, Tamiment (hereafter UFT OH).
72. Student Interviews, MCNY, folder 161.
73. "Competencies, Credentialing and the Child Development Associate Program or Maids, Miss Ann and Authentic Mothers," Schomburg, Preston Wilcox Papers (hereafter PWP), box 11, folder 17.
74. Memo, March 1971, PWP, box 30, folder 3.
75. "Continuation Proposal: Parents as Community Developers," PWP, box 30, folder 2; "The Role of the Local Stimulator," PWP, box 30, folder 1; and November 23, 1971, Fact Sheet for 9 Afram-Affiliated Sites 1971–72, PWP, box 30, folder 4.
76. Velma Murphy Hill, interview.
77. AFT PSRP Conference Speech, American Federation of Teachers Records, Office of the President Collection, Albert Shanker Papers, box 65, folder 61, Walter Reuther Library, Wayne State University.
78. "Support the Paraprofessionals," December 19, 1972, AFP, box 1, folder 6.
79. "TAC Position on Violence," TAC Newsletter, January 1970, AFP, box 1, folder 4.
80. "Viva El Boicot!" TAC Newsletter, December 4, 1972, AFP, box 1, folder 6; and "Let's Help Our Children Read Better," District 3 TAC, AFP, February 1, 1973, box 1, folder 6.
81. "Thousands of Blacks Facing Loss of Jobs," *New York Amsterdam News*, May 7, 1975. See also chapter 11 in this volume.
82. "Harlem Takes to the Streets in the Battle of the Budget," *New York Amsterdam News*, July 2, 1975.
83. "4500 Teachers to Be Laid Off in Month," *New York Times*, September 13, 1975.
84. "Harlem Parents and Educators Unite for Better Education," *New York Amsterdam News*, January 10, 1976.
85. Memo to Deputy Chancellor Bernard Gifford and BOE from Frank C. Arricale II, May 28, 1976, Amelia Ashe Files, series 312, box 45, folder 559 Paraprofessionals—Rules and Regulations, BOE.
86. "Where We Stand: Some Cuts Are More Stupid than Others" *New York Times*, September 19, 1976 (Shanker's "Where We Stand" column ran as a paid advertisement on Sundays).
87. School Board Loses Arbitration on Pact: It Is Told to Pay Paraprofessionals for Training Despite Program's Removal from City's Budget," *New York Times*, October 29, 1976.
88. "Koch's Budget Unit Urges Closing of 15 Schools, Higher Lunch Fees," *New York Times*, January 4, 1979. See also Jonathan Soffer, *Ed Koch and the Rebuilding of New York City* (New York: Columbia University Press, 2012).
89. January 4, 1979, Letter from Ed Koch to Frank Macchiarola, Stephen R. Aiello Files, series 311, box 15, folder 157, BOE.
90. "I Love New York, Mayor Koch," *New York Amsterdam News*, March 10, 1979.
91. "UFT Fights for Salaries," *New York Amsterdam News*, September 1, 1979.

92. "Cuomo Signs Pension Bills Opposed by Koch as Costly," *New York Times*, August 13, 1983.

93. Abby Goodnough, "Teacher's Unions Sues Klein, Claiming Bias in Layoffs of Aides," *New York Times*, May 6, 2003.

94. Gary D. Goldenback, "Teaching Career Aspirations of Monolingual and Bilingual Paraprofessionals in the New York City School System" (PhD diss, Hofstra University, 1985).

PART FOUR

Post–Civil Rights Setbacks and Structural Alternatives

CHAPTER 11

Harlem Schools in the Fiscal Crisis

KIM PHILLIPS-FEIN AND ESTHER CYNA

M any afternoons throughout the spring of 1976, cars and trucks driving across the thoroughfare of 125th Street in Harlem would have found their way blocked by crowds of protesters out for what might have seemed a surprising cause: the protection of neighborhood public schools that the city's government was threatening to close in order to resolve its ongoing fiscal crisis. One day in March, for example, more than one thousand people participated in a demonstration in support of the local schools.[1] On another occasion in April, students, parents, teachers, and school staff marched down the Manhattan artery, bearing signs reading "S.O.S." and "P.S. 144 must live." The demonstrators represented two Harlem elementary schools (Public School [PS] 144 and PS 113, both in District 3) that had been slated to shut down as the city made budget cuts to respond to the fiscal shortfall that had brought it to the edge of bankruptcy the previous year. Parents, teachers, students, and staff at the schools swore they would hold an action every single day until September, in order to stop their schools from closing.

They were right to be concerned. Many schools throughout New York City were threatened with closure in the mid-1970s, but ultimately Harlem would lose more schools than most other neighborhoods in Manhattan.[2] In the years after the fiscal crisis that began in 1975, the number of schools in Harlem dropped sharply. District 5—the educational district that consists primarily of Central Harlem—lost eight schools between 1974 and

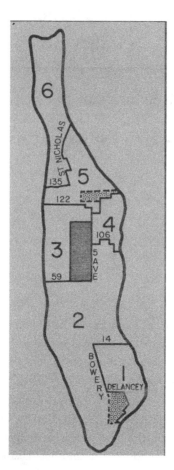

Figure 11.1 Boundaries of the newly created Community School Districts as of 1970.
Source: "Community School District System, Borough of Manhattan," NYCBOE,
Isaiah Robinson Papers, NYCBOE, MA.

1983, the largest decline of any of Manhattan's six districts (figure 11.1). By
comparison, only one school in District 3 closed over these years, and two
closed in District 1 and District 4 respectively; District 2 and District 6
each added one school, and the number of schools citywide actually grew
by five from 981 to 986. Seven of the District 5 schools that closed were
elementary schools, and one was a junior high school.[3]

The city's rationale for proposing the "consolidation" of schools was that
they were "underutilized," the number of children attending them having
declined sharply as families left the neighborhood. According to the Board
of Education, PS 144 was running with 513 students in a building con-

structed for 1,554, for a 33 percent utilization rate.[4] But these definitions of underutilization were not as clear-cut as they might have seemed. Although the city had a strong fiscal incentive to close schools, principals and parents contested the description of schools as underused. They argued that much more of the school space was regularly used than the Board of Education indicated and that the smaller school populations permitted smaller and more intimate classes. Moreover, they suggested that the charge overlooked the central role that these public buildings played in the neighborhood as afterschool centers and community hubs. Schools were not only for educating children—they were visible, public institutions that served as meeting places for various populations and they symbolized the broader commitment of the city to the neighborhood. As the chairperson for the parents' group that had formed to save the schools put it, public schools often provided the only "viable institution" in the neighborhood: "We don't have parks, gyms or recreational areas." In addition, the smaller population attending the schools in the 1970s in fact permitted some relief from the overcrowding that was otherwise the norm. "I can't understand why the Board would prefer to stuff 32 children into every classroom and force teachers to have to supervise them in ways more reminiscent of a prison than of a school," Bernice Johnson, the principal of PS 144, told the *New York Amsterdam News*.[5]

But there were deeper reasons still for the protests against school closures. The plans to close the schools generated such intense unrest because of the long-standing sense within the neighborhood that Board of Education officials—and the city and state politicians who were pressuring them during the fiscal crisis—knew little of the struggles of Harlem families or their schools. The protesters believed that the mandate for school closures reflected the dictates of administrators who were responding to budgetary pressures and for whom the schools of Harlem were merely an item on the budget line that could easily be crossed off. As one parent participant in the spring protests put it, "What people resent is that the decision is made to close the school arbitrarily by people who have never been here to see what kind of school it is. It makes people angry to have people making decisions who are so far removed."[6] Or as Principal Johnson said, "The Concerned Parents of P.S. 144 and P.S. 113 don't want these schools closed, and we expect to be out on the streets every day from now on."[7]

The New York fiscal crisis of the 1970s has long been recognized as a turning point for the city, a key moment when older traditions of liberal governance were scrapped in favor of a more market-oriented approach.[8] Beginning in the spring of 1975, the banks that were accustomed to financing the city government ceased to be willing to market the city's bonds and notes to investors across the country, citing the mounting debt load and growing expenses that they believed the city government was no longer able to repay. Although Mayor Abraham Beame protested that the banks were treating New York unfairly, that the city simply suffered from cash flow problems, and that it would never actually default, New York ceased to be able to obtain credit. Mayor Beame and Governor Hugh Carey went to Washington to request aid from President Gerald Ford. At first, this was not forthcoming, but at the end of the year, after New York State had essentially obtained control over the city's budget, Ford agreed to approve legislation that extended loans to New York contingent on the city's steps toward balancing its budget through steep budget cuts.

The causes of the fiscal crisis and the politics involved in its resolution have been the subject of vigorous historical debate, but the effect of the budget cuts on the daily lives of ordinary New Yorkers has received much less attention. Still less noted has been the vigorous protest with which many of these cuts were received. The city was roiled by intense division about whether, or to what extent, it was necessary to cut public services to cope with the crisis—and if so which ones should be prioritized. Over the next three years, the number of city workers was reduced by more than sixty thousand as city officials cut the budget under intense pressure from the state and federal governments. The political economy of access to education, knowledge, and culture quickly came to the forefront. Should the city fund these as generously as it had? The City University of New York (CUNY) came in for sharp criticism from President Gerald Ford and others on the right in national politics, who were troubled by New York's willingness to subsidize a tuition-free university that operated with "open admissions," guaranteeing access to higher education. There were proposals to consolidate and eliminate CUNY campuses and ultimately to begin charging tuition. Libraries (both branch libraries and the city's remarkable research libraries) were also threatened with cuts to services and even (in some cases) closure. To some extent, the tensions over the libraries and CUNY reflected ambivalence about the scope of New York's ambitions: should the city even attempt to run a public university system, or provide extensive library services?

But the crisis also had a profound effect on primary and secondary education, even though operating public schools was widely accepted as well within the normal purview of urban governance. The budget cuts fell with special force on the city's school system, affecting schools in middle-class and white districts as well as schools serving primarily poor, Black and Latinx children. These cuts were met with widespread protest throughout New York, even as the teachers, school workers, children, and families affected sought to adjust to the new reality of reduced funding. Suddenly, the central conflicts that had driven school politics during the 1960s and early 1970s—over community control and racial integration—were joined by a different struggle, focused on adequate funding for education. Throughout New York, parents, teachers and public school advocates found themselves forced to contend with budget cuts that slashed services in the schools and led the school board to propose closing schools.[9] The logic for these cuts and closures was enforced by the state agency (the Emergency Financial Control Board) that had been charged with monitoring the city budget and also by the federal government, which mandated cuts in return for fiscal aid. But the way the cuts would be implemented could not help but reflect choices made by the Board of Education—which schools could be treated as expendable, and which ones needed to be saved?

As the fiscal condition of the city bore down on individual schools, the result had the potential to be galvanizing. For neighborhood activists in Harlem, public schools had long represented an investment by the city in the literal future of the neighborhood. The schools were spaces in which people sought to imagine a more egalitarian society for their children and worked to instantiate and embody community values and racial pride. Children's academic accomplishments were publicized in local newspapers; graduations became occasions for celebration not only for parents and children but for the whole neighborhood. Cuts to the public schools, then, symbolized attacks by the city leadership on community institutions, on the idealism around community control of education that had flourished in the city during the 1960s and early 1970s and finally on the kinds of institutions that had the potential to link poor Harlemites with middle-class people within the neighborhood and the city as a whole. The city's budget contraction during the fiscal crisis caused great discontent in Harlem for many reasons, among them that African American city workers were far more likely to be laid off than white workers with more seniority as the city downsized, cutting off an important avenue to upward mobility. But its influence on education elicited an unusually powerful response. Many of the people who had been active in other forms of educational activism earlier in the twentieth century began to take up the issues raised by the fiscal crisis because they saw the problems of the neighborhood as intimately linked to the political economy of the city as a whole.[10]

In Harlem's District 3 and District 5, the public schools had long been the subject of intense community interest, engagement, and pride as well as frustration and criticism. Early in the 1970s, there was a great deal of energy around education and a sense of the ways that the public schools were failing to serve students as well as the possibilities that education offered for individual and communal uplift. The *New York Amsterdam News* carried regular reports on education in the neighborhood. The paper printed the names of all honors students at Central Harlem's District 5 schools in June 1975, reported on the winners of the Benjamin Banneker Mathematics Team Competition (in its second year in 1975), and described innovative school programs such as the Afro-American History Caravan (a mobile classroom that traveled throughout Districts 5 and 6 with the goal of educating African American students about "their history and culture") and the adult education classes provided by the Board of Education in the evenings.[11] Alternative schools such as Harlem Prep (a high school founded by private philanthropists with the goal of graduating high school dropouts and enabling them to gain college admission—admission to college was initially the criterion for graduation) also received regular coverage in the *Amsterdam News*.[12] "The salvation of our community, our city, our nation, our world is basically dependent on how well all adults educate the children to a responsible way of life," read one article reporting on St. Thomas Community School (an independent K–8 program).[13] Early in 1975, the *Amsterdam News* also ran an article by the public relations staff for District 5, claiming that it had "made considerable progress" toward resolving its long-standing problems: there were no more patronage or "no-show" jobs in the district, reading scores were climbing slightly, and active efforts were under way to improve the schools with federal funds for a math lab, bilingual programming, and antidrug efforts.[14]

Such recognition, praise, and tentative hopes for the schools coexisted with deep anxieties about their limitations as well as complaints and unhappiness about low test scores and the myriad barriers to student achievement. Often, parents were criticized for the problems of education in the neighborhood. The *New York Amsterdam News* regularly published letters from readers who castigated parents for failing to be more deeply involved with the schools.[15]

For a neighborhood so concerned with education, the fiscal crisis seemed a disaster. The budget cuts that followed the fiscal crisis affected the entire spectrum of city services, but they had an especially deep impact on education. The number of people employed by the Board of Education fell by almost 20 percent between 1975 and 1978, meaning that the schools employed thousands fewer teachers, not to mention guidance counselors and other support staff. Class sizes grew, art and extracurricular programs were cut back, basic maintenance and security were reduced, and the school day was shortened by ninety minutes. School crossing guards throughout the city were laid off. The budget for school athletics shrank by $1 million (from $2.5 million) with the result that twenty thousand fewer students could play and participate.[16]

The devastation was such that it met with a legislative response. In 1976, the state senators Leonard Stavisky and Roy Goodman (the latter a liberal Republican) proposed legislation that would bar the city from cutting education funding too rapidly as it sought to meet the terms of the fiscal crisis. Despite opposition from both Governor Hugh Carey and Mayor Abraham Beame (who argued that it would limit the city's ability to respond to the crisis), the legislation passed, and was then upheld by the legislature over Carey's veto.[17] But the cuts had already transformed the nature of the public schools in the city, making them schools of last resort for poor people, increasingly unattractive to middle-class families. One op-ed in the *New York Times*, written by a mother who had chosen to take her young daughter out of a public school and enroll her in a private one, bemoaned the changes: "New York is forcing middle-class children out of its schools and providing precious little education to those that remain."[18]

As soon as the depth of the fiscal crisis became evident and the likelihood of steep budget cuts clear, a strenuous community response began to build in Harlem. Education was not the only subject of concern. Neighborhood residents feared the loss of health institutions such as Sydenham Hospital, a historically African American hospital that earlier in the twentieth century had been one of the few places Black doctors could practice.[19] The Morningside Health Center, a neighborhood health center focused on women's health and prenatal care that served many young mothers in upper Manhattan, was threatened with closure.[20] Harlem Hospital announced in 1975 that it would close its School of Nursing.[21] All these cuts affected a population that had been in need of more health services before the fiscal crisis had even begun. In an announcement of a series of forums on the effect of the fiscal crisis on African American and Latinx New Yorkers, State Assemblyman Albert Vann articulated the problem well: "No one has really dealt with communities such as ours which were suffering from a lack of services before the fiscal crisis."[22]

There was a widespread sense that the threatened cuts should be met with forceful political resistance. African American legislators and community group leaders organized a voter registration drive for late August 1975 in an attempt to add 100,000 Black New Yorkers to the rolls in order to provide a form of "neighborhood protection from closing schools, firing teachers, closing hospitals, massive lay-offs and the curtailment of vital community services," as the *New York Amsterdam News* put it.[23] Many in Harlem were concerned that Black workers would be the first laid off from their jobs with the city government (jobs that had only recently become more secure avenues to middle-class status) because they had less seniority in union positions. The sense that the effects of the budget cuts would be felt most profoundly by poor African American and Latinx communities was augmented by the suggestion of Roger Starr, the city's deputy housing administrator, that New York should pursue a policy of "planned shrinkage"—strategically targeting its cuts to parts of the city that it would simply cease to fund or care for, essentially to let go. Neighborhoods that were losing population should no longer have subway service, fire protection, health care, and schools, which would eventually stimulate more people still to leave altogether. Starr's comments were met with outrage from city and state legislators and decried by others in the Beame administration. The city never formally adopted such a policy; instead, Starr left his position in city government. But from the perspective of affected communities, Starr's writing crystallized what many believed was the city's underlying attitude—a logic of neglect and disregard. "Fiscal Cuts—Or Racial Cuts?" asked one *New York Amsterdam News* editorial headline, criticizing the proposal to close several campuses in the CUNY system that served predominantly nonwhite students, including Hostos Community College in the South Bronx, and to turn other four-year colleges (such as Medgar Evers College in Brooklyn) into two-year schools.[24]

For all these varied concerns, fears about the effects of the fiscal crisis focused especially on schools. As soon as the magnitude of the cuts became clear in the summer of 1975, Deputy Chancellor Bernard Gifford warned that the school layoffs mandated by Mayor Beame would "fall disproportionately upon the shoulders of Blacks and Puerto Ricans." The *New York Amsterdam News* called on the United Federation of Teachers (UFT) and the city to adopt "a plan for all of us" that would avoid any pattern of discriminatory layoffs, especially in education—urging the UFT to give up on cost-of-living increases in order to reduce the number of teachers who had to lose their jobs. (This was a position the UFT would reject, instead choosing to prioritize teacher salaries.)[25] Such anxieties about the effects of cuts on minority teachers were justified. The federal Civil Rights Office of the Department of Health, Education and Welfare issued a 1976 report criticizing New York's Board of Education for its racially discriminatory practices—which had resulted in one of the lowest proportions of minority teachers in the country, only about 14 percent even after ten years of concerted effort to hire more African American teachers. This proportion did not decrease in the years after the crisis, as Gifford feared. But any progress that had taken place slowed to a standstill.[26]

In addition to the anxiety that the teaching staff of schools would become whiter as Black and Latinx teachers lost their jobs, parents were also afraid that the cuts would endanger the quality of education for students in schools that already had to grapple with many challenges. They quickly organized to meet the cuts with protests. Along with representatives of community groups, parents started the Harlem and East Harlem Coalition to Prevent the Closing of Schools.[27] Early in July 1975, the parent-teacher associations from PS 76 on West 121st Street and PS 144 on West 122nd Street organized protests that blocked traffic on 125th Street to protest the loss of paraprofessionals, teachers, and especially corrective reading and math teachers at their schools. Some prekindergarten and kindergarten classes would be eliminated entirely. Class sizes would increase to as many as forty-nine students with one teacher and no assistants. All these cuts took place against the backdrop of existing deprivation: as the head of the Parent-Teacher Association (PTA) at 144 said, "Our children are at least two years behind and we are losing the remedial reading program."[28]

Protests continued as the cuts went into effect. In the fall of 1976, students at the Frederick Douglass School (Intermediate School [IS] 10, a middle school located at Seventh Avenue and 149th Street) boycotted the school when they found that twelve teachers had been laid off with no replacements, leaving ten classrooms with no teachers at all in subjects such as social studies, English, science, and math, which students needed in order to pass the upcoming Regents exams.[29] Wadleigh Intermediate School in the early 1970s held an annual Black Solidarity Day on November 1, a one-day boycott of school by students, teachers, and staff, in recognition of "unity, love, peace and our common desire for a better community in which to live." In 1976, the president of the Parent-Teacher Association called for Black Solidarity Day to be dedicated as a "day of mourning" for "the death of public education in New York City, brought about by crippling budget cuts and layoffs." Such efforts were not the work of a fringe group of parents. The principal, Elfreda S. Wright, approved the action.[30]

Whatever effects such demonstrations may have had in particular cases, they were not adequate to prevent or slow the cuts across the board. District 3, for example, lost about 19 percent of its tax levy budget between 1975 and 1977. This meant that the number of elementary school teachers fell from 644 to 432, and junior high school teachers declined from 295 to 224.[31] The situation that prevailed in many public schools after such cuts was bleak—even more so than before the fiscal crisis. In March 1976, Board of Education officials visited one District 5 school—PS 123, a K–5 elementary school on West 140th Street—and described some of the difficulties. The school, with about 800 students, all of whom qualified for free lunch, had lost about half of its teaching staff over the fiscal crisis, going from 60 in 1974–75 to 30 in 1975–76. The number of paraprofessionals had declined from 11 to 7, a guidance counselor was present only one day a week, and there was one assistant principal in addition to the acting principal. The principal—who had served at the school for four years—believed that teachers were being excessed from "ghetto areas" and reassigned to more affluent ones. In their notes on the visit, the Board of Education representatives described "a general pattern of chaos" in the building near dismissal time, as children roamed the halls with little supervision, roughhousing and playing in ways that appeared dangerous—in front of a broken stained glass window, for example. There was no playground, and the principal had little interest in trying to take students to one in the neighborhood, saying they played too much already. Most depressing of all was the low morale. Although the principal blamed a "lack of responsibility" on the part of either teachers or students, he had little sense of anything that might improve the situation. He seemed, the observers noted, "most despondent over the progress of the children in his school," and he feared that they would not be able to overcome "a system which is stacked against them."[32]

Although the school cuts did impact middle-class schools as well as those serving poor people, many of the programs most affected were those that involved those most desperately in need. For example, the city wanted to close the five schools that it had operated for high school girls who became pregnant, which had served as a supportive space for students who were otherwise at greater-than-usual risk of leaving school altogether. "While we recognize that cuts have to be made, the total dismantling of such a program is a crime for it leaves 2,000 students out on the streets making them an even greater burden on society," one irate reader wrote to the *New York Amsterdam News*.[33] (Four teenagers organized a protest at City Hall, standing with their backs to television cameras. In 1978, the schools received funding extensions enabling them to remain open.)[34] Adult education centers also lost much of their funding—cuts that were borne especially by poor Black and Latinx neighborhoods, where the centers were less likely to be able to access alternative sources of money.[35] In some cases, the city had been supporting the schools with its most financially risky decisions, such as borrowing through the capital budget to pay for vocational schools or textbooks. Once this source of funding disappeared as the city cleaned up its accounting, it was far from clear where the money could be made up.

For some parents, the dangers to the public school system and the effect that budget cuts would have on the quality of education seemed sufficiently grave that they grew pessimistic about the chances that public education could offer their children. They began to press for alternatives, especially in the form of vouchers giving them state funds that could be transferred to private schools or new independent schools founded by concerned parents. By the fall of 1975, the Harlem Parents Union—a group representing parents with children in Districts 4, 5, 7, and 9—began to petition the state for school vouchers to enable them to send their children to private schools or to found new parent-run schools as alternatives to the public system. Parents with children in failing schools should be able to gain the funds that would go to those schools and seek out other routes to education. Some families kept their children home from school to boycott the "educational deprivation for Black and Spanish-speaking children in New York City," as a letter from the Citizens Committee for Effective Education (another parent-run organization) read.[36] People in the neighborhood looked to Brooklyn, where the Timothy Baptist Church opened its own school as an alternative to the public schools because of the latter's "failure" to provide "care, respect and quality education" for African American students.[37] Black parents on the Lower East Side who opened a private school also received positive mention.

But for other parents, the crisis became a chance to try to defend the public system, drawing on the long traditions within the neighborhood of fighting for better school buildings and improved education in general. This emerged most dramatically when schools were threatened not just with cutbacks, but with closure. The logic behind closing schools was simple. The population of Harlem was declining over the 1970s, and as a result the Board of Education argued that the neighborhood no longer needed as many schools. The board claimed that taken as a whole District 5 was failing to use 8,008 seats on the elementary school level and 2,537 on the middle school level. Its buildings were regularly not filled to capacity, or even close—they often enrolled less than half the students they could fit.[38] The answer, as the board saw it, was to close and consolidate Harlem's schools. Yet despite the widespread awareness of the many problems with the schools—problems only exacerbated by the funding cuts—neighborhood residents were still deeply troubled about plans that involved school closings or consolidation. This issue resonated with long-standing struggles over keeping schools within the neighborhood open, going back to the earlier conflicts over Wadleigh High School for Girls, which had been threatened with closure during the 1930s and then turned into a coeducational junior high school, thus depriving the neighborhood of its lone high school.

Street protests were one means by which to protect the schools. Filing appeals regarding school closures was another. The Community School Board (CSB) for Harlem's District 5 was a troubled institution, wracked with internal conflicts and rife with charges of nepotism and political patronage. However, it also briefly emerged in the mid-1970s as a protector of the schools in the district that were threatened with closure. In the summer of 1976, as the Board of Education sought to bring the budget into balance through school consolidation, the CSB filed a series of legal appeals of the board's decisions to close schools.

One of the most intense of these conflicts dealt with the board's decision to close Junior High School (JHS) 120—an alternative, unzoned junior high school with 665 children, operating in a building with a capacity of 1,515. JHS 120 had been one of the Harlem junior high schools that parents in the neighborhood had boycotted in 1958, saying that conditions at the school were substandard and refusing to send their children there. When the Board of Education brought the parents to court for keeping their children home, Judge Justine Polier instead charged the city with failing to provide the city's African American children with an adequate education.[39]

In 1976, however, parents sought to protect the very existence of JHS 120. The board wanted to close the school, saying that it was too underenrolled to keep open and that a new junior high school was set to open in the district anyway, which would further reduce the school population. In its appeal, the CSB argued that the school had special qualities that justified keeping it open. The school had excelled in a borough-wide mathematics competition. It had a unique curriculum focused on math and science. Most of all, the "financial and emotional hardships imposed upon children and parents of changing teachers, schools and locations could prove devastating."[40] The PTA for JHS 120 sent an additional letter, emphasizing that the school had a special math and science orientation, that sixty-three students had recently gained admission to specialized high schools that had entrance exams, and, in a reference to the unzoned nature of the school, which meant that parents had to specifically seek it out, observing that "parents chose this school for their children because of the special emphasis on mathematics and science." Speaking of her ambitions for the school, the president of the PTA wrote of her dream "to make Junior High School 120 an educational showcase, an 'Ivy League' junior high school within the geographic boundaries of Harlem."[41] Students at JHS 120 joined the fight, protesting and blocking traffic outside of their school in September 1976.[42]

Rather than close JHS 120, the Community School Board proposed closing an elementary school, PS 79, which had only 171 students. These students could be moved to JHS 120, which would then house two schools, one elementary and one middle school, helping the building to be more fully utilized.[43] (It should be noted that the parents at PS 79 strongly objected to this idea, and their PTA contacted the board as well to say that they had not been part of any discussions about closing the school.)[44]

The Board of Education was skeptical of the Community School Board's appeals. "I am in total agreement with your statement that the original decision to close these schools was correct and that the local board has yielded to political pressure in appealing," one Board of Education member wrote to Isaiah Robinson, the president of the board (and himself formerly a Harlem parent activist).[45] Although in other circumstances "smaller programs, more space for support services and special projects" might be priorities of the board as well as parents and Community School Boards, the fiscal crisis made this impossible. The Appeal Board of the Board of Education rejected the petition: "The school system now is faced with extensive and irrevocable cutbacks which necessitate economies in essential services."[46] The Community School Board continued to appeal the closure of JHS 120, attempting to bring a petition in New York State Supreme Court to challenge the closure. This, however, was also dismissed: the court ruled that the board had the power and the right to make the decision to close the school and that there was no justification for abrogating that in this instance.[47] In the end, JHS 120 was closed.

Community School Board 5 also clashed with the central board regarding its school guards. The board had ordered the district to lay off its school guards as it sought to comply with the budget reductions. Layoffs of guards were especially contentious—the *New York Amsterdam News* had reported on rising crime in the city's schools following the reduction in the number of guards.[48] District 5 refused to fire the nineteen guards employed by the district, and sought to reorganize funds in order to keep them on staff. The Board of Education wrote to the district superintendent, Luther Seabrook, to threaten the school district with "criminal liability" for failing to comply with the Emergency Financial Control Act.[49] "May I remind you that we have cut our services to children far beyond comparable cuts in other districts," Seabrook responded, arguing that the guards were necessary to maintain the safety of staff, students, and faculty.[50] He proposed other methods of saving money, including closing the District Office altogether during the month of July.[51] The board rejected this idea. Ultimately, angry that the local board had tried to keep hiring guards despite the directive to lay them off, the board attempted to freeze payments to the guards for work they had already done, although they relented on this position under pressure from the guards union.[52]

The tense relationships between the District 5 Community School Board and the central Board of Education came to a head when the latter decided to suspend the local school board. There were intense divisions within the

CSB (centered, in part, on the Board of Education's dismissal of Seabrook, a very popular African American superintendent, in the late spring of 1976, a decision that led to a widespread outcry in the neighborhood culminating in the occupation of the CSB offices by supporters of Seabrook) as well as many allegations of overall disorganization, malfeasance, and poor administration.[53] However, the fiscal crisis and the difficulty that CSB 5 faced in complying with the new mandates also played a role in the suspension. In July 1976, Deputy Chancellor Gifford recommended this course of action, warning that the CSB was projected to overspend its tax levy budget by $400,000, and that even as the central Board of Education ordered the school districts to reduce expenditures, the CSB had ordered the superintendent for District 5 to "'immediately rehire [terminated] neighborhood workers.'" Citing "fiscal responsibility" and the "legal mandate" of the Community School Board to carry out the policies of the Board of Education, Gifford recommended that the entire CSB be suspended and replaced "until such time as it is clear that the required fiscal controls and stability are firmly established in the district."[54] In October 1976, Chancellor Irving Anker followed through on the threat, citing the failure of the CSB to "excess" sufficient numbers of teachers (the school district had continued to employ about fifty teachers it was supposed to lay off) as evidence of the failure of the CSB to "comply with its duties under law."[55] The board members appealed, but to no avail. CSB 5 was undeniably plagued by long-standing fiscal and organizational problems, but the conflict is also notable because of the context of retrenchment that ultimately justified the takeover.

The fiscal crisis of the 1970s raised a host of new difficulties for Harlem's schools. In a neighborhood already short on resources and already facing such extensive needs, the fiscal crisis meant further cutbacks and greater instability in neighborhood institutions that had previously been unable to fully deliver on their promises. The result was the decline of any confidence whatsoever in public schools. Even when threatened cuts were rescinded, the experience taught that it was difficult to rely on public institutions. Before the fiscal crisis, educational activism in Harlem had often focused on issues of racial justice in the public schools, as well as the relationship between the central Board of Education and the quest of the neighborhood for greater community control. The fiscal crisis revealed a different aspect of this politics, as critics of the public schools were suddenly forced to defend their very existence. The myriad protests to keep Harlem schools from closing helped to determine which schools could be closed, but it did not address the larger problem of the lack of resources. As a result, the mobilization within the neighborhood—like much activism during the fiscal crisis moment—was limited: it could protest closures and cuts, but the questions about racial equality and local democracy that had animated Harlem's schools earlier in the century were unable to occupy the same space. The result, in some cases, was declining faith in the potential of the public system, which helped pave the way for the rise of charter schools.

However, the community school boards (despite their flaws) and the rich history of school-related protests in the neighborhood also helped to mobilize opposition to budget cuts during the fiscal crisis. The people who blocked traffic on 125th Street in the spring of 1976 did so out of an insistent faith that the schools and children of Harlem were not hopeless and should not be abandoned, that there remained much within them worthy of salvage and transformation.

Notes

1. George Goodman Jr., "Planned Closing of P.S. 144 Protested," *New York Times*, March 12, 1976, 37.
2. Some reports suggested that the city was planning at the outset to close about fifty schools. "Schools Proposed for Consolidation," Amelia Ashe Papers, box 82, folder 24–8, "School Closing Procedures," Board of Education Papers, Municipal Archives (hereafter AAP). It is difficult to identify a master list of all schools that the city initially planned to close during the 1970s, and newspaper reports conflict as well; what is striking is how many of the schools that ultimately did close were Harlem schools.
3. Community and High Schools Profiles, 1974–1975; and Community and High Schools Profiles, 1983–1984. These reports are available at the City Library.
4. Community and High Schools Profiles, 1974–1975; and Community and High Schools Profiles, 1983–1984.
5. Carlos V. Ortiz, "School Protesters Block Harlem Traffic," *New York Amsterdam News*, April 3, 1976, A10; and Robert Collazo, "PS 113 Vow to Keep School Open," *New York Amsterdam News*, February 14, 1976, C9.
6. Goodman, "Planned Closing of P.S. 144 Protested."
7. Ortiz, "School Protesters Block Harlem Traffic"; and Collazo, "PS 113 Vow to Keep School Open."
8. Analysis throughout this article draws on coauthor Kim Phillips-Fein's book on the fiscal crisis, *Fear City: New York's Fiscal Crisis and the Rise of Austerity Politics* (New York: Metropolitan Books, 2017). For earlier scholarship on the fiscal crisis, see, for example, Martin Shefter, *Political Crisis/Fiscal Crisis: The Collapse and Revival of New York City* (New York: Basic Books, 1985); Ester Fuchs, *Mayors and Money: Fiscal Policy in New York*

and *Chicago* (Chicago: University of Chicago Press, 1992); Raymond Horton and Charles Brecher with Robert A. Cropf and Dean Michael Mead, *Power Failure: New York City Power and Politics Since 1960* (New York: Oxford University Press, 1993); and John Mollenkopf, *A Phoenix in the Ashes: The Rise and Fall of the Koch Coalition in New York City Politics* (Princeton, N.J.: Princeton University Press, 1994). Joshua A. Freeman, *Working Class New York: Life and Labor Since World War II* (New York: New Press, 2000), 256–90, remains the best single chapter ("The Fiscal Crisis") on the politics of the fiscal crisis; and William Tabb, *The Long Default: New York City and the Urban Fiscal Crisis* (New York: Monthly Review Press, 1982) provides a survey of the budget cuts. Little has been written specifically on the schools in the fiscal crisis, other than Lynne A. Weikart, "Decision Making and the Impact of Those Decisions During New York City's Fiscal Crisis in the Public Schools, 1975–77" (PhD diss., Columbia University, 1984).

9. Farnsworth Fowle, "East Harlem School Facing End," *New York Times*, June 15, 1976, 40. According to this article, the number of schools to be closed was thirty-seven, for savings of $5 million.

10. Although scholars of education have recognized the narrowed budgets that urban districts faced in the 1960s and 1970s, many have treated these as the product of falling property tax bases via deindustrialization, and weakening will to support public education alongside rising student need. See, for example, the treatments of the 1960s and 1970s in classic works of urban educational history, including David Tyack, *The One Best System: A History of American Urban Education* (Cambridge, Mass.: Harvard University Press, 1974); and Jeffrey Mirel, *The Rise and Fall of an Urban School System: Detroit* (Ann Arbor: University of Michigan Press, 1988). This chapter goes beyond these more general treatments to interrogate the ways that political organizing and the distribution of political power determined how city budget conditions would shape education policy choices.

11. "June Is Graduation Time When Scholastic Honors Are Being Passed Out," *New York Amsterdam News*, June 25, 1975, C11; "School District 5 Math Team Winners," *New York Amsterdam News*, March 8, 1976, B8; "Harlem Classroom on Wheels," *New York Amsterdam News*, March 8, 1976, A5; and "New Kind of Success Story . . ." *New York Amsterdam News*, May 7, 1975, B8.

12. Harlem Prep affiliated with the Board of Education in 1974. For more on its history, see Barry M. Goldenberg, "The Story of Harlem Prep: Cultivating a Community School in New York City," Gotham: A Blog for Scholars, August 2, 2016, http://www .gothamcenter.org/blog/the-story-of-harlem-prep-cultivating-a-community-school -in-new-york-city.

13. "Parents, Teachers Work Together at St. Thomas Community School," *New York Amsterdam News*, November 12, 1976, B8.

14. Public Relations Staff, District 5, "District 5 Moves Forward," *New York Amsterdam News*, February 22, 1975, B3. That this article was by a District 5 staff member may be a reason to treat its claims with skepticism, but the decision of the paper to print it reflects the intense desire in the community to see improvement in District 5.

15. "Letter of Week," *New York Amsterdam News*, March 22, 1975, A4.

16. "City School Athletic Cuts Hurt Blacks," *New York Amsterdam News*, September 5, 1975, B1.

17. Robert W. Bailey, *The Crisis Regime: The MAC, the EFCB, and the Political Impact of the New York City Financial Crisis* (Albany: State University of New York Press, 1985), 100–103. See also Phillips-Fein, *Fear City*, 220–223.

18. Betsy Haggerty, "Kate Isn't in P.S. 87: Here's Why," *New York Times*, October 19, 1976, 39.

19. J. Zamgba Browne, "Harlemites Vow to Keep Sydenham Open," *New York Amsterdam News*, April 3, 1976, A1.

20. "Morningside Health Center in Jeopardy of Closing: Funds to Stop," *New York Amsterdam News*, March 1, 1975, C12.

21. Victor O. Koroji, "Harlem Hospital School of Nursing Facing Shutdown," *New York Amsterdam News*, July 23, 1975, A1.

22. "Set Community Forums on NYC Fiscal Crisis," *New York Amsterdam News*, January 10, 1976, B2.

23. "Political Group Formed to Register 100,000 Blacks," *New York Amsterdam News*, August 6, 1975, A1.

24. "Fiscal Cuts—Or Racial Cuts?" *New York Amsterdam News*, February 28, 1976, A4.

25. "Thousands of Blacks Facing Loss of Jobs," *New York Amsterdam News*, May 7, 1975, A1. See also "A Fair Solution," *New York Amsterdam News*, September 4, 1976, A4.

26. Weikart, "Decision Making," 167.

27. John O'Neill of the Community Development Agency at the Human Resources Administration to Bernard Gifford, May 5, 1976, Bernard Gifford Papers (hereafter BGP), series 1201, box 2, folder "CSD 5, 1975–1976," Board of Education of the City of New York Collection, Municipal Archives of the City of New York (BOE MA).

28. Simon Anekwe, "Harlem Takes to the Streets in the Battle of the Budget," *New York Amsterdam News*, July 2, 1975, A7.

29. Simon Anekwe, "Threaten School Boycott at IS 10," *New York Amsterdam News*, October 16, 1976, A1.

30. Wadleigh High School Collection, box 4, file 10, Schomburg Center for Research in Black Culture, New York Public Library.

31. Weikart, "Decision Making," 190. Weikert looked closely at three CSDs, District 3 being one of them.

32. "Notes on School Visit—March 4, 1976," Visited by Amelia Ashe—Bob Hanlon—School: P.S. 123, at CSB 5, AAP, box 61, folder 11.

33. Ruby S. Hill, "Schools for Pregnant Girls," *New York Amsterdam News*, September 23, 1976, A4.

34. Edward Ranzal, "Schools Closing, Pregnant Girls Stage a Protest," *New York Times*, October 16, 1976, 29; and David Vidal, "Extension Granted 5 Special Schools for Pregnant Girls," *New York Times*, January 22, 1977, 20.

35. Ralph R. Reuter to Stephen Aiello, February 21, 1978, Stephen R. Aiello Files, box 1, folder 2, "Adult Education, 1978–1979," New York City Municipal Archives. Reuter was the chairman of the advisory council of the Office of Continuing Education. In this letter to the president of the Board of Education, he reported that many centers in poor neighborhoods had been closed down—in Harlem, Bedford-Stuyvesant, the South Bronx—but wealthier centers had been kept open.

36. Simon Anekwe, "Black Parents Seek State Funds for Private Schools," *New York Amsterdam News*, October 8, 1975, 20.

37. J. Zamgba Browne, "Church Takes Lead in Education: Opens an Alternative School," *New York Amsterdam News*, December 4, 1976, A11.

38. Board of Education of the City of New York in the Matter of the Appeal of Community School Board No. 5, AAP, box 83, folder 25A.

39. See Adina Back, "Exposing the 'Whole Segregation Myth': The Harlem Nine and New York City's Desegregation Battles," in *Freedom North: Black Freedom Struggles Outside the South, 1940–1980*, ed. Jeanne Theoharis and Kozomi Woodard (New York: Palgrave Macmillan, 2003), 65–93.

40. Delia Ortiz to Harold Siegel, May 14, 1976, AAP, box 82, folder 251.

41. From Mrs. Delores Green, P.T.A. President, May 3, 1976, AAP, box 82, folder 251. The version of the letter in the Ashe papers is addressed to Charles Gadsen, but the letter appears to have been Xeroxed and was likely sent to several different officials.

42. "Harlem School Fight," *New York Amsterdam News*, September 25, 1976, C12.

43. Delia Ortiz to Amelia Ashe, June 22, 1976, AAP, box 82, folder 251.

44. The Parents Association of PS 79 Manhattan, John Haigley-Bey, President, to Amelia Ashe, June 24, 1976, AAP, box 82, folder 251.

45. Amelia Ashe to Isaiah Robinson, June 18, 1976, AAP, box 82, folder 251.

46. In the Matter of the Appeal of Community School Board 5 from the Actions of the Chancellor in Regard to the Closing of J-120-M, AAP, box 82, folder 251.

47. Memorandum of the Supreme Court of Kings County, in the matter of the *Application of Delores Green vs. Board of Education of the City of New York et al.*, September 24, 1976, AAP, box 82, folder 251.

48. Les Mathews, "Guards Are Laid Off, Crime Rate Increases," *New York Amsterdam News*, March 27, 1976, A12.

49. Alfredo Mathew to Luther Seabrook and the Chairman and Members of CSB 5, April 5, 1976, BGP, box 1202, folder CSD 5, 1975–1976.

50. Luther Seabrook to Bernard Gifford, April 26, 1976, BGP, box 2, folder CSD 5, 1975–1976. Seabrook wrote Gifford after the checks to pay the guards were held up at the Board of Education. "I do not seek confrontation; I do not seek special favors," he wrote. "I do expect equitable treatment, regardless of the 'alleged' powerlessness of my community. Please see that those checks are not held up on April 28th."

51. Luther Seabrook to Irving Anker, March 22, 1976, BGP, box 2, folder CSD 5, 1975–1976, BOE MA.

52. Frank Scarpinato to Irving Anker, April 28, 1975, BGP, box 2, folder CSD 5, 1975–1976.

53. For some discussion of the many other issues in CSB 5, and the board's response to them, see letter from the CSB Board members to Bernard Gifford, June 30, 1976, AAP, box 61, folder 12. This letter is not signed but it appears to be from CSB 5 board members, following a meeting with Gifford. Also worth noting is a letter from February 1976 signed by half the school board, appealing to Anker to take action against the other half; see John Davis, Louise Gaithner, Charles Gadsen, and John Hicks to Irving Anker, February 2, 1976, BGP, box 2, folder CSD 5, 1975–1976. Finally, see the letter from Marjorie Lewis, Charles Gadsen, Delia Ortiz, and Bernice Bolar to the Board of Education, November 8, 1976, appealing the suspension, AAP, box 61, folder 12.

54. Bernard Gifford to the members of Community School Board 5, July 20, 1976, AAP, box 61, folder 12.

55. Irving Anker to the members of Community School Board 5, October 26, 1976, AAP, box 61, folder 12.

CHAPTER 12

Pursuing "Real Power to Parents"

Babette Edwards's Activism from Community Control to Charter Schools

BRITTNEY LEWER

The longtime educational activist Babette Edwards defies easy characterization. In 1966, she fervently supported the push for community control in Harlem. As a Harlem resident and parent to two young boys, Edwards joined Milton Galamison, David Spencer, and other civil rights leaders to demand community control of Harlem schools. She invited Stokely Carmichael, at that time the face of the Black Power movement, to show support for parents at Harlem's Intermediate School (IS) 201, as they demanded a greater say in how the new community-controlled complex would be governed. Less than ten years later, Edwards shifted away from the idea of community control within state-run schools and instead pushed for vouchers that would provide funds for low-income Harlem students to attend private schools. Edwards's fellow voucher proponents included conservative white politicians like Rosemary Gunning—infamous for leading white mothers in Queens on an anti-integration march in 1964. Edwards would continue to cultivate dynamic and perhaps counterintuitive alliances in pursuit of a quality education for Black and Latinx students.[1]

Babette Edwards's career as a reformer illuminates the goals, roadblocks, and compromises that Harlem parents and activists navigated in pursuit of an excellent education for their children and reveals the connections between seemingly distinct education reform efforts. Edwards doggedly pursued academically rigorous schooling that would be accountable to parents.

Although she thought that well-informed parents and school leadership free from "interest groups" such as the New York City Board of Education and the United Federation of Teachers (UFT) would support effective education, Edwards's preferred mechanisms for realizing these conditions changed widely over her career. Disappointed with a community-control experiment that she felt failed to live up to its name, Edwards backed tuition vouchers and later supported charter schools as ways around the city's entrenched educational bureaucracy. She saw vouchers and charter schools as community control over schooling, not merely neoclassical economics. This chapter argues that Edwards juggled a sense of responsibility to Harlem youth with a deep pessimism about the city's willingness and ability to serve those children through public schools. Her reform efforts demonstrated she had faith that informed parents could ensure high-quality education for their children, and thereby usher in system-wide educational improvements in Harlem.[2]

IS 201 and Community Control

Babette Edwards was born and educated in New York City. She attended George Washington High School in Washington Heights. Edwards rarely spoke about her own education, though she wrote that her experiences as a student gave her direct knowledge of the "cumbersomeness" of the city's educational bureaucracy. She instead claimed that her neighbors prompted her first school-based activism. Neighbors who saw Edwards interact with the management at the housing complex where she resided asked her for help advocating for their children at Harlem's nearby Public School (PS) 80. Edwards remembered PS 80 as a bleak and dismissive space. She recalled incidents in which a teacher struck a student's face so hard that the student came home with a welt, and another incident in which the principal brushed off a mother's concerns by claiming that no third-grader should be expected to know how to read. By the time Edwards's two sons were old enough to attend school, "I was pretty much disgusted with what I saw . . . [and] I wasn't going to sit back and let my own children be treated in that manner."[3]

Edwards became involved with broader educational activism during the 1964 school boycotts against segregation in New York City schools. She performed various tasks for the Harlem Parents Committee, which organized the boycotts. Edwards became active in parent groups at PS 161, where her sons attended school through the mid-1960s. She praised the fact that parents enjoyed some oversight of the curriculum and school governance, though she later lamented the school's low reading scores. Edwards's involvement snowballed. By the end of 1966, she had marched overnight in single-digit temperatures to demand integrated schools, had agitated for the proposed IS 201 to become a community-controlled venture, and had been arrested for sitting in at the Board of Education headquarters alongside the more widely known educational activists Milton Galamison and Ellen Lurie.[4]

Edwards became a major player in the fight for community control at IS 201 (which is detailed in chapters 8 and 9 of this volume). She joined the IS 201 negotiating team, and later served as a community representative to its governing board. She pushed for meaningful community decision making over school personnel and finances. Anything less than true decision-making power was merely the "illusion of control." She called out "middle-class do-gooders who have allowed the Board of Education to keep them in an *advisory* status and who themselves have kept communities ignorant" by accepting leadership in name only. Edwards routinely contacted parent groups, Board of Education officials, and local media outlets to demand what she viewed as legitimate community control.[5]

Edwards's commitment to this robustly democratic version of community control led to her disappointment with the brief community-control period at IS 201, and her frustration only grew as New York City replaced community control with decentralization. Even while IS 201 remained technically independent of a decentralized school district, Edwards grew tired of internal attempts to quash parent participation at the complex. After four years on the governing board of IS 201, Edwards resigned in 1971.[6]

Her resignation letter, coauthored with fellow parent-activist Hannah Brockington, reaffirmed her vision of community control and scolded those who did not share it. The letter began, "For the last fifteen years we have fought those people who have deliberately crippled our children. Now in 1971 we are still fighting the same fight, only conditions are worse, because the cripplers in the past (largely white) have now been joined by destructive opportunist education pimps (largely black), who prey on the Harlem community, sucking [its] life's blood, the community's future, which is embodied in their children." Edwards and Brockington accused IS 201's principals and teachers of betraying Harlem students by siding with the

Board of Education and majority-white unions over Black students. These educators thought of Harlem schools "not as a place where children learn" but as a stepping-stone in their own careers, Edwards and Brockington alleged.[7]

The pair blamed a lack of achievement at the school complex on these Black professionals who, in their eyes, treated Black parents and children with the same contempt as did their white counterparts. Edwards and Brockington proclaimed that Black educators showed a "perverted allegiance" to the city's central Board of Education. Brockington and Edwards's resignation letter made clear that not every educator fit this description, though they alleged that prioritizing professional allegiances over duties to Black children and their families was common practice. Edwards and Brockington expressed frustration with parents who sided with school leaders, saving their praise for those parents who "realiz[ed] that when all is said and done, they are the only true protectors of their children."[8]

Edwards's skepticism of "professionalism" traced back to the earliest days of IS 201. She associated the term with the Board of Education's early efforts against community control. Edwards wrote that during the initial fight for Black leadership at IS 201 in the mid-1960s, "professionalism was an enemy ideology, . . . a euphemism used to describe the interests of people who ran an abominable school system" that excluded Black leaders and undervalued Black students. She continued to distrust "professionalism" as a justification for shifting control of the school to employees over parents—even at IS 201, where many of the school's leaders and teachers were also Black.[9]

Edwards's antiprofessional stance raised some controversy. As her resignation letter alluded, she had butted heads with other parents at IS 201, not to mention with teachers and principals. Many disagreed with her assertion that Black professionals bore responsibility for IS 201's shortcomings. Her fellow IS 201 governing board member Charles Wilson pointed to state interference, as well as overt opposition from unions, politicians, and whites who benefited from the existing school system, as the main obstacles to effective community control. The IS 201 principal Ronald Evans criticized the "defeatism" of those who blamed the demise of the community-control experiment on Black educators. But Edwards believed that meaningful reform would come only when parents could hold educators accountable. In the 1970s, she embraced vouchers as a tool that might enable Black and Latinx parents to do just that.[10]

Edwards lay the groundwork for expanding parent involvement in schools through the Harlem Parents Union. Originally a splinter group from within the Harlem Parents Committee, the Harlem Parents Union separated in 1970 and soon incorporated as its own nonprofit group with Edwards at the helm. The organization tutored Harlem schoolchildren, advocated for students at the individual and community level, and "challenge[d] the widespread notion that home conditions are responsible for poor academic achievement in isolated minority communities." It also sponsored workshops and conferences for parents, including a 1973 conference on Consumers and Public Education that would prefigure Edwards's own framing of parents as "consumers" of education. Edwards wrote in a 1977 anthology on school choice that parents should be the drivers of their children's education, but principals and teachers often stifled them. She lamented that school employees stamped out any sustained effort by parents to interrogate the curriculum or the teachers. The surest way up was out, Edwards suggested.[11]

Edwards first requested vouchers for Harlem students in February 1975. Petitioning the state commissioner of education on behalf of students in Central Harlem, Edwards's letter—and a half dozen that would follow—emphasized the burdens that substandard schools wrought on poor families of color. Though nearly 90 percent of students in Central Harlem schools had scored below grade level on the latest citywide literacy tests, their families had no recourse. Edwards wrote that while families in "rich, white communities" enjoyed higher-quality public schools and the ability to send their children to private schools of their choosing, families in "poor Black and Puerto Rican areas" had no choice but to subject their children to ineffective schooling. Without an education that justified their required presence in schools, "the children here are literally incarcerated." Doubtful of the city school system's ability and will to change, Edwards demanded that the state provide poor families an escape hatch: school vouchers. She wagered that credits toward private-school tuition, tutors, or new community-run schools would give parents a measure of real decision-making power over their children's education. A sluggish response from the commissioner's office prompted Edwards to ask, "How much more do we have to suffer before you respond to our predicament and make up your mind to do your duty as a public servant?"[12]

In September 1975, seven families answered Edwards's question by withdrawing their children from the local public schools. All seven families belonged to the Harlem Parents Union, though some hailed from the Bronx and Brooklyn. The parents charged the local schools with failing to meet the burden of an adequate education. By withdrawing their children, they risked a summons to family court for violating compulsory attendance law. The *New York Amsterdam News* and the *New York Times* reported on the boycotting families, identifying Babette Edwards as their spokesperson. Edwards and the Harlem Parents Union negotiated with city Board of Education representatives and State Commission on Education leaders on the parents' behalf. The Harlem Parents Union provided tutorial instruction to eleven boycotting students for a full school year. From nine in the morning until three in the afternoon, volunteers provided personalized tutoring at the group's Harlem Parents School-Community Neighborhood Center.[13]

Edwards had been inspired in part by the 1958 boycott organized by the "Harlem Nine" to protest segregation and unequal conditions in three Harlem junior high schools. She had worked with some of the boycotting mothers at IS 201, and she even sent updates about the new boycott to Judge Justine Wise Polier, who had been a sympathetic ear when the Harlem Nine boycotters came before the courts for attendance law violations.[14]

Yet Edwards had not initially pursued a remedy through the courts. She sought state-sponsored vouchers and negotiated with state and local officials who might acquiesce. These conversations often came to dead-ends, with state officials directing her to the local District 5 school board and the city's Board of Education. Only after the *New York Amsterdam News* broke the boycott story did a low-level state official respond. He wrote that Edwards's complaints about student illiteracy and a hostile school environment did not demonstrate "clear-cut evidence of a violation of the law," and thus the State Education Department would not intervene. Meanwhile, the local superintendent offered the boycotting students intradistrict transfers to four Central Harlem schools. Edwards rejected the offer, noting that two of the schools' literacy rates were worse than those at a school a student was actively boycotting, and none cracked the top 50 percent in the city's own rankings. Shuffling students from one failing school to another was not an option. Only vouchers would enable parents to make consequential choices and allow students access to meaningful education, whether through private schooling (including the possibility of a school run by the

Harlem Parents Union), supplemental tutoring, or the ability to enroll in a higher-achieving public school district.[15]

Several historians trace the first serious interest in vouchers to the economist Milton Friedman, who advocated for capitalist principles of competition to improve U.S. schooling. In practice, however, vouchers were first tested in the South immediately after *Brown v. Board of Education*. Louisiana employed vouchers to evade desegregation before federal courts struck down these discriminatory voucher plans. Edwards focused on vouchers not as past instruments of racial discrimination, but as liberatory tools for marginalized students. She followed the work of Christopher Jencks, who called for voucher programs for low-income students in New York and elsewhere in 1966. Edwards's records contain numerous articles from early voucher advocates such as Milton Friedman, Francis Overlan, and Benjamin Foster Jr. She corresponded with each, and even brought Foster and Friedman to Harlem to speak about the benefits of a voucher system (in 1973 and 1977, respectively).[16]

In addition to spreading the voucher idea to Harlem parents, these academics introduced Edwards to potential allies in a national fight for vouchers. Francis Overlan of the Education Voucher Project at Harvard University introduced Edwards to the New York State Federation of Catholic Parents, a group that supported vouchers for parochial schooling. Overlan believed that Edwards and Catholic voucher supporters could join forces, though Edwards represented "a different constituency with at least in part a different set of concerns." These Catholic connections helped to propel Edwards to the national stage. One Catholic parent group circulated Babette Edwards's 1975 pro-voucher speech in print. Most significantly, Edwards briefly joined the Center for Educational Freedom, which brought her to the respective Democratic and Republican platform hearings in 1976. Their alliance was short-lived. The historian Jim Carl notes that the Center for Educational Freedom shared Edwards's belief that legislation would be the most promising route to vouchers, but rarely seemed to "make the jump from vouchers in support of parochial schools to vouchers in support of urban students." Still, the group provided a substantially larger platform for Edwards's message.[17]

When Edwards first began campaigning for vouchers in 1975, they were virtually untested outside of the South, where they served to maintain segregation. By the mid-1970s, vouchers had gained little momentum, despite some support from small-government conservatives, groups of African

American parents in Boston and Milwaukee, policy advocates such as Jencks and Overlan, and Catholic-school supporters. Several districts investigated, then rejected, potential voucher programs in the early 1970s, perhaps due to vouchers' associations with segregationism and privatization. Edwards's advocacy told a different story, casting vouchers as a way for low-income students of color to escape failing education systems, and she put a voice and face to the fledgling pro-voucher movement.[18]

Edwards began direct appeals to policy makers and legislators. In the fall of 1975 through the summer of 1976, Edwards delivered a pro-voucher plea before politicians and policy makers in New York State as well as before the New York State Board of Regents, the State Legislative Forum, and both major party platform hearings in 1976.[19]

Edwards's most widely circulated address on vouchers lambasted the failure of New York City to educate Black and Latinx children. Edwards spoke on behalf of the Harlem Parents Union and the more recently formed voucher-advocacy group Citizens Committee for Effective Education. Beyond these two groups, however, Edwards claimed to represent Black and Latinx parents more broadly. Edwards spoke in the first-person plural throughout her statement, referring to a school system that had "wreaked havoc among us" Black and Latinx families. She addressed policy makers as "you," a comparatively white, affluent, and influential audience.[20]

Reminding her audience of the school system's history as a force of mobility for European immigrants, Edwards emphasized the great economic and social costs of a failing contemporary educational system for Black and Latinx children. Not only did the state waste money on ineffective schools, she argued, it "robbed" children of millions of hours of their time and millions of dollars in lost income. Edwards demanded recognition and empathy for Black and Latinx families. "When you are the victim," she pled, "when it is your children who are unenlightened, unemployed or unemployable, the criminal, the junkie, disillusioned, defeated before they even begin to live, then you see the problem in a different light." Middle-class parents could remove their children from failing schools with ease, but those of lesser means found themselves without options. "We are forced to be parties to these crimes, merely because we have no other means of educating our children," Edwards lamented. Although Edwards believed that education should be a public right, she rejected the notion that the New York City public school system was fulfilling its public obligations. The city neglected Black and Latinx children in particular, she alleged. With so low a bar, how could any educational alternatives possibly do worse?[21]

In her speech and the copies that circulated, Edwards embraced capitalism and pitched vouchers as a natural extension of fundamentally U.S. ideals. Edwards described vouchers as "American as apple pie." She pointed to the GI Bill, Medicare, food stamps, and existing textbook reimbursements as analogous "voucher systems," whereby state funding followed individual consumers into private markets. Edwards borrowed here from the charter proponent Francis Overlan of the Education Voucher Program, who had previously drawn parallels to the GI Bill. Vouchers were not a radical departure from a tradition of public schooling, but rather the realization of a tendency toward empowering individuals in pursuit of public goods.[22]

Edwards ended her statement by highlighting the consequences faced by low-income parents who refused to subject their students to a failing public system. They would risk prosecution under the compulsory education law. Though Edwards did not mention the Harlem Parents Union's boycott directly, she emphasized the consequences that she and other parents were willing to endure to pursue better options for their children. Educational options mattered, imminently and intimately. Vouchers were a "simple piece of paper" that could instantly create new options for thousands of students.[23]

Pushing vouchers into existence legislatively, Edwards and the Harlem Parents Union drafted legislation for the state's first voucher program. State Senator Joseph Galiber, a Democrat from the Bronx, sponsored the bill. Senate Bill 5314 would allow four districts—including Harlem's District 5—to create a demonstration voucher program and permitted parents in these districts to choose a public or private school in which to enroll their children. Vouchers equivalent to or more than the district's average per pupil cost would follow each student, with additional funds allocated for "disadvantaged children." But the monetary value of base and compensatory vouchers was to be determined later, as was the definition of a "disadvantaged child." Though the bill failed, its presence suggested the Harlem Parents Union's potential to influence legislative debates about education and to frame debates around how to treat students from disparate backgrounds fairly.[24]

Also lobbying for voucher schools that year was Rosemary Gunning, a former state assemblywoman and infamous leader of New York City's 1964 "white boycott" against integration. Gunning drafted an alternate voucher bill just before Galiber's bill was submitted to the Senate Committee on Finance in March 1977. Gunning's draft bill offered a standard voucher amount to all pupils in a district, but allowed it to be supplemented with family funds or private donations. Middle-income families could make up the difference between the state voucher and pricier private tuition, granting them access to a larger array of private institutions. Lower-income families who could not afford the gap between a voucher and tuition would again find themselves priced out of private institutions, rendering the voucher a less-effective tool of equalization than the Harlem Parents Union intended. The biggest difference between the Galiber-Harlem Parents Union bill and Gunning's, however, was that Gunning did not specify which New York City districts would be eligible to participate in the voucher program. Gunning hailed from Ridgewood, Queens, and advocated school choice for white families. The Harlem Parents Union made sure that, if their version passed, *Harlem* parents would have access to the program. Edwards and Gunning's alignment on vouchers as a means of circumventing the existing public school system obscured their disparate motivations for doing so, and it prefigured the similarly strange alliances that would emerge in national school choice fights during the last decades of the twentieth century.[25]

Nothing came of either proposed voucher bill. (A state-run, publicly funded voucher program would not come to fruition until Milwaukee's School Choice Plan in 1990. Milwaukee's voucher program would open with extensive backing from Howard Fuller, another community-control activist turned voucher activist, and a coalition of Black school reformers and conservative white politicians.) New York City would not see a large-scale voucher demonstration until the 1990s, and even that was privately funded. With the legislative defeat in New York, waning federal support for vouchers, and unfavorable reactions from voters in New England, the Harlem Parents Union gradually backed away from lobbying for vouchers. They instead worked to facilitate interdistrict transfers and private school scholarships that would allow students to leave Harlem.[26]

Certainly, not all Harlem educational activists shared Edwards's enthusiasm for vouchers. Luther Seabrook, the superintendent of Harlem's District 5, thought Edwards's decision to embrace vouchers meant abandoning public schools. Edwards responded that vouchers would provide accountability. Black and Puerto Rican representation on community school boards under decentralization had not fixed the underlying school system, she said, and it was "foolishness" to hope that the New York City Board of Education would change of its own accord. Having to compete for families and their dollars might incentivize the public schools to improve, she thought. Seabrook suggested that withdrawing from the public schools might leave those schools and the children attending them in an even worse state. Edwards conceded that was true, but countered that she felt compelled both to retreat from public schools and to fight for them. Edwards described the fight for reform of the public schools alone as a "losing battle." She described city schools as "failure factories" and questioned how anyone could, in good conscience, "hold a child in a Harlem school."[27]

Choice and Charter Schools

School voucher proposals gained little traction in New York City or State, but Harlem became a focal point in efforts for school choice in the form of charter schools. The latter phase of Edwards's activism for increased parent choice as a way to improve schooling brought her to charter schools during years in which New York's charter landscape both led and helped shape the national conversation.

Babette Edwards continued her work with the Harlem Parents Union and its Harlem Tutorial Project and served hundreds of students annually. In the early 1990s, the Tutorial Project created a Parent Information and Training Center, formalizing the Harlem Parents Union's commitment to helping parents navigate their children's educational options and participate in local school governance. Edwards brokered partnerships with local universities to procure volunteer tutors and to bring computers and the internet to Harlem schools and education centers. She continued to advocate for students directly, navigating Board of Education bureaucracy and local media to shame the Board of Education into providing textbooks for students in a Harlem school that had no textbooks throughout the 1991–92 school year.[28]

Edwards's advocacy extended to school choice within the public school system as well. After District 4 experimented with school choice in East Harlem, Chancellor Joseph Fernandez proposed increased school choice across zones and districts throughout the city. It was a modest proposal, reliant on vacant rather than reserved seats, but it was a symbolically important move toward choice, and Edwards expressed support. She insinuated that the chancellor's plan was too conservative, insofar as it did not extend choice to private institutions, but nevertheless she endorsed it as a major step forward.[29]

Despite her support for Fernandez's school choice proposal, Edwards had doubts about the city's small and alternative school efforts of the 1980s and 1990s. The small schools created in District 4's school choice effort of the 1970s and 1980s spawned many other small schools across the city, aided by infusions of philanthropic funds in the mid-1990s and again in the 2000s. Edwards remained skeptical, though, claiming that the Board of Education "tend[ed] to sabotage its own alternative programs." She maintained her consistent criticism of the United Federation of Teachers as an impediment to reform as well, arguing that union members prioritized salaries over students. She felt the long shadow cast over Black and Latinx communities' relationship with the UFT by the bitter battle over IS 201 and the community control districts in 1968.[30]

Scholars have noted that voucher programs, choice-based alternative schools, and charter schools share key ideological underpinnings, particularly the belief that increasing educational choice is good either on its own merits or because the pressures of competition will spur all schools to improve. Many historians tie the origins of charter schools to magnet schools, where families could elect to enroll in schools still governed by local school districts. These authors hold that magnet schools initially aimed to spur desegregation by attracting students to specialized programs and that their popularity increased exponentially when federal funds for magnet schools became available in 1984. In New York City, District 4's small alternative schools were one variation on this theme. For some, charter schools extended the ideas of voluntary enrollment, mission-based schooling, and autonomy in school governance beyond what was possible in alternative schools operating within the conventional school district.[31]

Although charters soon became aligned with antiunion activism, early versions of the charter school idea took shape within union circles. The Minnesota teachers union leader Ray Budde is often credited with coining the term, and the UFT president Al Shanker with spreading the idea. Under Budde's model, charter schools meant greater authority to teachers and administrators so that they could innovate, free from heavy regulation and district oversight. Shanker publicized the movement beginning in 1988. (Ironically, both major national teachers unions would later oppose charter schools, particularly over exemptions from collective bargaining agreements and doubts over charters' effects on educational attainment.) Edwards's voluminous clippings contain little about early charter school discussions, when unions were key advocates.[32]

Charter schools slowly gained momentum in New York State. After two failed attempts in 1997, the state legislature passed a charter school bill in December 1998. Governor George Pataki ushered the bill into law by "effectively [holding] the state legislature hostage," threatening to veto a hefty raise for legislators if they did not move the needle on charter school legislation.[33]

The resulting Charter School Act of 1998 promised to realize several of the goals that Babette Edwards had articulated for decades. According to the law, charter schools would aim to increase student learning by encouraging innovation, expanding parent and student choice, and shifting to outcomes-based accountability for schools. Charter schools would receive state funds but would "operate independently of existing schools and school districts." In addition to autonomy from local school districts, charter schools with 250 students or fewer in their first year were to be exempted from the collective bargaining agreements between districts and teachers unions. This arrangement gave charter school boards of trustees much greater authority over personnel decisions. Charter schools thus combined the public funding and relative autonomy that Edwards had named as crucial for meaningful reform during the days of IS 201 and voucher campaigns.[34]

Although Edwards had been an early leader in voucher advocacy in New York, she was a relative latecomer to the charter school effort in the state. She soon focused on helping parents become informed consumers in an increasingly choice-based educational system. The Harlem Parents Union's Tutorial Center invited experts from around the state to speak with Harlem parents about the promises and pitfalls of charter schools. The speaker lineups tipped heavily in favor of charter schools, as did Edwards. Just weeks after the charter bill had become law, Edwards and the Parent Information Center pitched an expanded Educational Alternatives Information Center that would be a hub for parents, and jointly run with Teachers College. The center would combat the "misleading propaganda from special interest groups, e.g. the United Federation of Teachers, the New York City Board of Education, etc." Edwards envisioned voucher and charter options as a one-two punch against ineffective education. They removed New York

City schoolchildren from the auspices of the UFT and the Board of Education.[35]

In 2000, Edwards moved to seize on the new charter school movement more directly—by starting a charter school of her own. Edwards had begun drafting plans for a school in Central Harlem in the mid-1990s, hoping that federal block grants and state education dollars would fund a school within an autonomous Central Harlem school district. When that funding did not materialize, framing the school as a charter allowed plans to move forward. Edwards penned the first letters about starting a charter school in 2000, calling on local leaders and politicians to support her effort. It would be called the Harlem Parents Charter School, she announced, and would act as "a safe, nurturing oasis" for students in Central Harlem.[36]

Edwards's initial description of her planned school focused on the role of parents as key partners in the future school's development and on "academic excellence" as the school's central pillar. An organizational chart for the school's proposed leadership structure depicted the Board of Trustees as equal partners with a Community Advisory Board, which would include the Harlem Parents Union as a "founding partner." Although Edwards claimed that the school would aim "to help all youngsters in Harlem achieve their full potential," she conceded that (like many other charters and alternative schools opening in New York City at that time) the school would need to start small.[37]

Logistical details about the proposed school shifted over the next two years, but the focus on parents and "academic excellence" remained rock steady. In 2002, Edwards convened a new group, the Harlem Education Roundtable, to develop her idea into a full charter school proposal. With the Harlem Education Roundtable at the helm, the Harlem Parents Union would play a diminished role in the school. The school's name changed, too, from the "Harlem Parents Charter School" to the tongue-tying "Harlem Education Roundtable Academy for Excellence in Education" to the almost acronymous "HEART Charter School."[38]

By the fall of 2002, things were looking up for the school. The recently elected mayor Michael Bloomberg had won unprecedented control over the city's schools, replacing the more than century-old Board of Education with a new Department of Education led by a chancellor selected by the mayor. Bloomberg and his first chancellor, the attorney Joel Klein, put the city's resources behind charter school and small public school development. The chancellor awarded a $50,000 grant to the Harlem Parents Union to develop a school plan. The proposed school attracted support from many activists who had been key collaborators on Edwards's earlier efforts. Lola Langley, who had withdrawn her son from Harlem's public schools alongside Edwards twenty-five years earlier, acted as treasurer for the Harlem Education Roundtable and was named as a board member for the charter school. Hannah Brockington, who had served on (and quit) IS 201's governing board with Edwards, wrote in support of the school, as did several community partners. Edwards's long history gave her a wide and deep base of community support on which to draw in imagining a homegrown charter school.[39]

Edwards's planning built up strong momentum, and she selected an experienced Harlem District 5 educator as "headmistress/CEO." Momentum quickly reversed, however, as struggles over consulting fees complicated the already challenging work of preparing an extensive state application, which asked more than sixty questions about the school's goals, leaders, and logistics. According to planning documents submitted in 2003, the HEART Charter School aspired to solve the educational crisis by setting high academic standards and giving Harlem families "a real choice" in their schooling, a small-scale realization of the educational goals Edwards had been fighting for over the past thirty-five years. The school aimed to span kindergarten through twelfth grade, starting with kindergarten through second grade and expanding upward by one grade annually. The proposed launch scaled back slightly from Edwards's original vision to an inaugural class of 250 pupils—the maximum number of students that would allow the school to operate without a unionized teaching faculty.[40]

The school's academic plan included boilerplate goals—meeting existing state standards and providing students "a strong foundation" in reading, mathematics, science, social studies, and the arts. The school's charter application used the same language of accountability that Edwards had been using for thirty years, promising to show quantitative results (now measured by state tests).[41]

Compared to her earlier work on community control at IS 201, Edwards's charter school said much less about parents as a part of school governance. A draft application referred to parents as key to the school's development, going so far as to rate them as the most important partner in the school's design, but the application gave the role of teachers more specific attention. The school's extended mission statement called for teachers to be respectful, responsive, and collaborative regarding students' needs and learning. Parents were only mentioned insofar as they were to be "actively involved in the process"—but how or with what authority was not specified. The school specified measures through which it would demonstrate accountability to parents—frequency of parent-teacher conferences, "the degree to which parents demonstrate a knowledge" of their children's academic interests, even "the level and frequency of parent complaints regarding all aspects of School operations." And parents would be involved in seminars and workshops about the school's goals. But Edwards's earlier emphasis on parents as school decision makers had faded, and was replaced by an emphasis on the choice parents made to enroll their child in the school and on the academic outcomes the school would achieve.[42]

The HEART Charter team sought resources from the Walton Family Foundation for a $10,000 startup grant. Walton, with the wealth of the Wal-Mart (now Walmart) empire to draw on, had awarded over $30 million to charter schools in less than a decade. Walton did not support the HEART Charter, and plans for the school came to a standstill. The State University of New York (SUNY), one of the state's charter-granting bodies, received Edwards's application in fall 2004. While SUNY recorded the application as "withdrawn," Edwards recalled that it was rejected by Chancellor Klein. Because the Harlem Education Roundtable championed parents, Edwards explained, "Klein could not stand us." She understood the rejection as "purely political" and noted that it "thoroughly de-energized" the roundtable's efforts.[43]

By 2007, Harlem housed fifteen charter schools, most of which now belong to multischool charter management organizations. Early media coverage of the city's charter schools emphasized how students at charters outperformed their peers at traditional public schools, even as some community members wondered whether this success came at the direct expense of traditional public schools. Increased academic performance as measured by the newly reorganized Board of Education—a formula that included student scores on state tests and attendance rates—indicated charters' success.[44]

The Harlem Children's Zone and its Promise Academy charter drew intense media attention. As the *New York Times* reported, the Harlem Children Zone founder Geoffrey Canada appealed to both liberals and conservatives by "pouring money into schools" and "directly taking on the problems of inadequate parenting." The Promise Academy's "no excuses" style, with its emphasis on intensity and highly disciplined behavior, was shared by other Harlem charter operators as well, and remains at the core of debates over the means and ends of schooling.[45]

Neither the "no excuses" model nor intervention into parenting practices had been part of Edwards's vision for school choice, but in many ways her work had set the stage for the predominance of parent choice in Harlem. Edwards's thinking about the role of parents in education had evolved, from a commitment to parents as participants in democratic governance of schools, to a conception of parents as informed consumers in a choice-based educational marketplace. Yet by the early 2000s, decisions about the shape of charter schooling made far from Harlem now left no place for Edwards's own community-specific vision of parent choice and quality education.

Edwards's long career suggests a painfully perpetual quest for effective education for low-income and Black and Latinx children, and for granting their parents a meaningful say in their schooling. Her work provides a window into the possibilities and limitations of in-school reform in Harlem during the latter decades of the twentieth century. Thousands of parents and students directly benefited from the Harlem Parents Union's workshops for parents and tutorial programs for students from the 1970s through 2003. But its efforts to bring widespread school choice and school governance to parents in support of robust community control were less successful. School choice options remained modest and dictated in large part by figures outside of Harlem. In her doctoral dissertation, completed in the midst of her pro-voucher advocacy in 1977, Edwards wrote that any successful education reform would require three crucial characteristics: it would have to "put real power into the hands of parents," grant parents a measure of choice for their children's schooling, and provide incentives for the public education system to improve. Edwards's willingness to deploy diverse strategies and to build issue-based partnerships with unlikely allies demonstrates the dexterity with which she navigated existing political systems in pursuit of these goals. Questions of how best to make schools responsive to parents and how to bring about meaningful school improvements guided Babette Edwards's half century of educational activism, and they remain vital but unresolved questions for education reformers today.[46]

Notes

1. "Parents Stage Tear-In at Board of Education," *New York Amsterdam News*, March 19, 1966, 25; Sonia Song-Ha Lee, *Building a Latino Civil Rights Movement: Puerto Ricans, African Americans, and the Pursuit of Racial Justice in New York City* (Chapel Hill:

University of North Carolina Press, 2016), 176; and Matthew Delmont, *Why Busing Failed: Race, Media, and the National Resistance to School Desegregation* (Oakland: University of California Press, 2016), 46.

2. For a sample of the myriad routes parents and educational reformers pursued to provide Black children a quality education in the later decades of the twentieth century, see Elizabeth Todd-Breland, *A Political Education: Black Politics and Education Reform in Chicago since the 1960s* (Chapel Hill: University of North Carolina Press, 2018); Michelle A. Purdy, *Transforming the Elite: Black Students and the Desegregation of Private Schools* (Chapel Hill: University of North Carolina Press, 2018); Ansley T. Erickson, *Making the Unequal Metropolis: School Desegregation and Its Limits* (Chicago: University of Chicago Press, 2017); Russell Rickford, *We Are an African People: Independent Education, Black Power, and the Radical Imagination* (New York: Oxford University Press, 2016); and Jack Dougherty, *More than One Struggle: The Evolution of Black School Reform in Milwaukee* (Chapel Hill: University of North Carolina Press, 2004).

3. E. Babette Edwards, "Responses to Application Questions 1, 2, & 3," n.d., box 18, folder 18, Babette Edwards Education Reform in Harlem Collection, Schomburg Center for Research in Black Culture, New York Public Library (hereafter BEERHC); and Babette Edwards, interview with Luther Seabrook, March 1977, box 17, folder 10, BEERHC.

4. Babette Edwards, interview with Luther Seabrook, March 1977, box 17, folder 10, BEERHC; Harlem Parents School-Community Neighborhood Center, Grant Application [likely to Whitney Foundation], n.d. [likely 1977], box 20, folder 15, BEERHC; "Here Is List of Vigil Keepers: Walking Around the Clock in Racial Harmony!" *New York Amsterdam News*, January 23, 1965, 1; Sara Slack, "Warn of More 201 Trouble," *New York Amsterdam News*, October 15, 1966, 1; and "Galamison and 11 Seized in Sit-In at School Board," *New York Times*, December 22, 1966, 1.

5. Negotiating Team of I.S. 201, press release, October 3, 1966, box 8, folder 8, BEERHC; E. Babette Edwards, "Additional Letters: Board of Ed," *New York Amsterdam News*, June 10, 1967, 17; Sara Slack, "Sutton Says Give IS Board a Chance," *New York Amsterdam News*, February 24, 1968, 1; E. Babette Edwards, "District Lines, Election Procedures, and Governing Boards," March 13, 1969, box 39, folder 5 (Writings, Interviews and Speaking Engagements), BEERHC; and Babette Edwards and Preston Wilcox, "What Happened to Community Control?" *New York Amsterdam News*, December 11, 1971, A7.

6. Harlem Parents Union, press release, April 8, 1971, box 5, folder 8, BEERHC.

7. Babette Edwards and Hannah Brockington to Dave [Spencer], February 5, 1971, box 5, folder 3, BEERHC.

8. Babette Edwards and Hannah Brockington to Dave [Spencer].

9. Edythe Babette Edwards, "A Review and Analysis of Three Educational Strategies for Positive Change in the Public School System of the City of New York," 56, 1977, box 39, folder 2, BEERHC.

10. Emile Milne, "IS 201 & Decentralization: Trouble—But Still Alive," *New York Post*, May 18, 1971; Charles Wilson, "School Problems Show We're in Deep Trouble," *New York Amsterdam News*, December 11, 1971, A7; Ronald Evans, "Lessons Gained in the Struggle," *New York Amsterdam News*, December 11, 1971, A7; and Babette Edwards and Preston Wilcox, "What Happened to Community Control?" *New York Amsterdam News*, December 11, 1971, A7.

11. Annie Stein to "To Whom It May Concern," February 11, 1975, box 39, folder 3, BEERHC; E. Babette Edwards, "Why a Harlem Parents Union?" in *Parents, Teachers, and Children: Prospects for Choice in American Education*, ed. James S. Coleman et al.

(San Francisco: Institute for Contemporary Studies, 1977), 60; "Consumers and Public Education Conference Report," 1973, box 15, folder 6, BEERHC; Edwards, "Why a Harlem Parents Union?," 60, 61, 63; and E. Babette Edwards to Steve Williams, April 15, 1996, box 15, folder 1, BEERHC.

12. E. Babette Edwards to Ewald B. Nyquist, February 10, 1975, box 22, folder 16, BEERHC; Sterling S. Keyes to E. Babette Edwards, March 25, 1975, box 20, folder 15, BEERHC; and E. Babette Edwards to Ewald B. Nyquist, August 21, 1975, box 24, folder 4, BEERHC.

13. WNBC-TV, Transcript of Editorial on Quality Education, November 9, 1976, box 14, folder 2, BEERHC; Harlem Parents School-Community Neighborhood Center, Grant Application [to Whitney Foundation?], [1977?], box 20, folder 15, BEERHC; Harlem Parents Union, Inc., Press Release re: Parents Boycotting Failing Public Schools in New York City, January 19, 1976, box 20, folder 15, BEERHC; Simon Anekwe, "Black Parents Seek State Funds for Private Schools," New York Amsterdam News, October 8, 1975, C9; "Boycotting Parents Want Funds Used for Private Schools," New York Times, January 22, 1976, 74; E. Babette Edwards to Irving Anker, September 13, 1976, box 14, folder 9, BEERHC; Thomas A. Johnson, "7 Parents Defying Schools by Setting Up Their Own," New York Times, November 2, 1976; and Joseph W. Horry, Summary Report on alternative schooling, June 16, 1977, box 17, folder 5, BEERHC.

14. Adina Back, "Exposing the 'Whole Segregation Myth': The Harlem Nine and New York City's School Desegregation Battles," in Freedom North: Black Freedom Struggles Outside the South, 1940–1980, ed. Jeanne Theoharis and Komozi Woodard (New York: Palgrave Macmillan, 2003), 65–93; and Justine Wise Polier to Babette Edwards, December 2, 1975, box 14, folder 2, BEERHC.

15. Babette Edwards, interview with Luther Seabrook, March 1977, box 17, folder 10, BEERHC; Anthony E. Terino to E. Babette Edwards, October 10, 1975, box 24, folder 4, BEERHC; Simon Anekwe, "Black Parents Seek State Funds for Private Schools," New York Amsterdam News, October 8, 1975, C9; E. Babette Edwards to Alfredo Matthew Jr., February 5, 1976, box 20, folder 15, BEERHC; Harlem Parents School-Community Neighborhood Center, Grant Application [to Whitney Foundation?], [1977?], box 20, folder 15, BEERHC; and "Positions of the Citizens Committee for Effective Education on Various Questions," [1975], box 24, folder 5, BEERHC.

16. Jim Carl, Freedom of Choice: Vouchers in American Education (Santa Barbara, Calif.: Praeger, 2011), 16, 24; Lisa Stulberg, Race, Schools, and Hope: African Americans and School Choice After Brown (New York: Teachers College Press, 2008), 81–86; S. Francis Overlan, "Regulated Compensatory Voucher Plan," April 1973, box 13, folder 19, BEERHC; Benjamin Foster Jr., "The Case for Vouchers," May–June 1973, box 22, folder 16, BEERHC; Milton Friedman, "The Role of Government in Education,"1962, box 22, folder 16, BEERHC; E. Babette Edwards to Benjamin Foster Jr., October 11, 1973, box 14, folder 1, BEERHC; and "How to Put Learning Back Into the Classroom," lecture flyer, September 15, 1977, box 18, folder 5, BEERHC.

17. S. Francis Overlan to E. Babette Edwards, February 26, 1975, box 14, folder 1, BEERHC; E. Babette Edwards, "Speech to the New York State Board of Regents," September 10, 1975, box 18, folder 5, BEERHC; and Carl, Freedom of Choice, 99.

18. Stulberg, Race, Schools, and Hope, 70–82; and Dougherty, More than One Struggle, 115–16.

19. E. Babette Edwards, Resume, 1976, box 39, folder 5 Writings, Interviews and Speaking Engagements, BEERHC; Edward F. Spiers, Request for Appearance at 1976 Republican National Convention Committee on Resolutions (Platform), box 14, folder 2, BEERHC; Edward F. Spiers to E. Babette Edwards, May 6, 1976, box 14, folder 2,

BEERHC; and E. Babette Edwards, "Statement to the Democratic Party Platform Committee," May 20, 1976, box 23, folder 1, BEERHC.

20. E. Babette Edwards, "Speech to the New York State Board of Regents," September 10, 1975, box 18, folder 5, BEERHC.

21. Edwards, "Speech to the New York State Board of Regents."

22. Babette Edwards, "Speech to the New York State Board of Regents"; and S. Francis Overlan, "Regulated Compensatory Voucher Plan," April 1973, box 22, folder 16, BEERHC.

23. Edwards, "Speech to the New York State Board of Regents."

24. E. Babette Edwards and Joseph W. Horry Jr., "Interim Report—August and September 1977," October 19, 1977, box 17, folder 5, BEERHC; E. Babette Edwards and Joseph W. Horry Jr., "Interim Report—July 1977," August 11, 1977, box 17, folder 5, BEERHC; Mae A. D'Agostino to Babette Edwards, February 2, 1976, box 22, folder 16, BEERHC; and An Act to Create a [Voucher] Demonstration Program, New York S. 5314, 182nd Congress (1977).

25. Delmont, Why Busing Failed, 47–48; Rosemary R. Gunning to "Dear Friends," March 12, 1977, box 23, folder 1, BEERHC; An Act to Create a [Voucher] Demonstration Program; Douglas Martin, "Rosemary R. Gunning, 92, Foe of School Busing," New York Times, October 7, 1997; and Rickford, We Are an African People, 259–61.

26. Dougherty, More than One Struggle, 180–93; William G. Howell and Paul E. Peterson, Education Gap: Vouchers and Urban Schools (Washington, D.C.: Brookings Institution Press, 2005), 34–35; Denis P. Doyle to Babette Edwards, March 29, 1976, box 14, folder 2, BEERHC; Harlem Parents School-Community Neighborhood Center, "A. Student Services," n.d., box 20, folder 18, BEERHC; E. Babette Edwards and Joseph W. Horry Jr., "Interim Report—August and September 1977," October 19, 1977, box 17, folder 5, BEERHC; and Joseph W. Horry, Summary Report on alternative schooling, June 16, 1977, box 17, folder 5, BEERHC.

27. Babette Edwards, interview with Luther Seabrook, March 1977, box 17, folder 10, BEERHC.

28. E. Babette Edwards to William Lynch, February 28, 1995, box 22, folder 6, BEERHC; Harlem Parents Union, Inc., "Proposal to Expand Our Existing Parent Training and Information Center," n.d., box 23, folder 1, BEERHC; "Walton Foundation Grant Application," May 22, 2003, box 26, folder 2, BEERHC; "Agency Interim Report, School Year 1983–1984," [1984?], box 22, folder 6, BEERHC; "Proposal to Establish the Harlem Parents Institute," February 22, 2002, box 22, folder 13, BEERHC; and Sheryl McCarthy, "Other Kind of School Violence," January 12, 1994, box 39, folder 5 (Writings, Interviews and Speaking Engagements), BEERHC.

29. E. Babette Edwards, "Future Directions in Obtaining Effective Education," New York Amsterdam News, January 19, 1980, 11; Joel Handler, Down from Bureaucracy: The Ambiguity of Privatization and Empowerment (Princeton, N.J.: Princeton University Press, 2001), 187; and E. Babette Edwards to H. Carl McCall, December 2, 1992, box 4, folder 4, BEERHC. For more on small schools in New York City, see also Deborah Meier, The Power of Their Ideas: Lessons for America from a Small School in Harlem (Boston: Beacon Press, 1992); and Heather Lewis, New York City Public Schools from Brownsville to Bloomberg: Community Control and Its Legacy (New York: Teachers College Press, 2015), 120–37.

30. Howard Bloom and Rebecca Unterman, "Sustained Progress: Findings About the Effectiveness and Operation of Small Public High Schools of Choice in New York City," New York, MDRC, 2013, accessed July 26, 2018, https://www.mdrc.org/publication/sustained-progress; E. Babette Edwards to Isaiah Robinson, April 26,

1972, box 22, folder 15, BEERHC; "Schools Called Anti-Parents," *New York Amsterdam News*, April 22, 1972, A1; and Leah Fritz, "A Look at the Schools," February 1973, box 39, folder 5 (Writings, Interviews and Speaking Engagements), BEERHC. For histories of the animosity caused by the 1968 UFT strikes, see Jerald E. Podair, *The Strike That Changed New York: Blacks, Whites, and the Ocean Hill-Brownsville Crisis* (New Haven, Conn.: Yale University Press, 2008); Daniel H. Perlstein, *Justice, Justice: School Politics and the Eclipse of Liberalism* (New York: Peter Lang, 2004); Lewis, *New York City Public Schools*; and Jonna Perrillo, *Uncivil Rights: Teachers, Unions, and Race in the Battle for School Equity* (Chicago: University of Chicago Press, 2012).

31. Paul E. Peterson and David E. Campbell, "A New Direction in Public Education?" in *Charters, Vouchers, and Public Education*, ed. Peterson and Campbell (Washington, D.C.: Brookings Institution Press, 2001), 5–6, 9; and Handler, *Down from Bureaucracy*, 186–87.

32. Joseph Murphy and Catherine Dunn Shiffman, *Understanding and Assessing the Charter School Movement* (New York: Teachers College Press, 2002), 22–26, 36–38. For more on the origins of charter schools, see Ray Budde, *Education by Charter: Restructuring School Districts* (Andover, Mass.: Regional Laboratory for Educational Improvement of the Northeast and Islands, 1988).

33. Senate Bills 3252 and 5433, of February and June 1997, were virtually identical to the successful Senate Bill 2850. Lance D. Fusarelli, *The Political Dynamics of School Choice: Negotiating Contested Terrain* (New York: Pan Macmillan, 2003), 95. For contemporary debates over charter schools, see Iris C. Rothberg and Joshua L. Glazer, eds., *Choosing Charters: Better Schools or More Segregation?* (New York: Teachers College Press, 2018); and Eve L. Ewing, *Ghosts in the Schoolyard: Racism and School Closings on Chicago's South Side* (Chicago: University of Chicago Press, 2018).

34. New York Charter Schools Act of 1998, N.Y. Consolidated Laws: Education, §§ 2850–57; and E. Babette Edwards, interview with Luther Seabrook, March 1977, box 17, folder 10, BEERHC.

35. E. Babette Edwards to Richard Hoke, July 3, 1998, box 15, folder 1, BEERHC; Harlem Parents Union and the Center for Educational Outreach and Innovation, "All the Information You Should Know About Public Charter Schools" flyer, May 1999, box 13, folder 19, BEERHC; and E. Babette Edwards to Verne Oliver, January 12, 1998, box 15, folder 1, BEERHC.

36. E. Babette Edwards to Peter Cookson, November 24, 1998, box 18, folder 20, BEERHC; Dr. Roscoe C. Brown Jr., "A Proposal for Establishment of a Harlem Independent School District," May 18, 1994, box 24, folder 22, BEERHC; Veronica Holly, conversation with the author, May 1, 2018; E. Babette Edwards to David Patterson, July 24, 2000, box 15, folder 1, BEERHC; E. Babette Edwards to Calvin Butts, July 24, 2000, box 15, folder 1, BEERHC; E. Babette Edwards to Herman Badillo, July 24, 2000, box 15, folder 1, BEERHC; and E. Babette Edwards to William Perkins, July 24, 2000, box 15, folder 2, BEERHC.

37. E. Babette Edwards to David Patterson, July 24, 2000, box 15, folder 1, BEERHC; and "Envisioned Organizational Structure, Harlem Parents Charter School," September 2000, box 13, folder 19, BEERHC.

38. "Part II Question 1," n.d. [likely 2003], box 26, folder 3, BEERHC; E. Babette Edwards to David Patterson, July 24, 2000, box 15, folder 1, BEERHC; Michele Cahill to E. Babette Edwards, December 11, 2002, box 25, folder 10, BEERHC; and Peter W. Cookson Jr. to Babette Edwards, January 17, 2003, box 25, folder 9, BEERHC.

39. Michele Cahill to E. Babette Edwards, December 11, 2002, box 25, folder 10, BEERHC; "The Harlem Round Table Academy of Excellence," November 20, 2002,

box 25, folder 9, BEERHC; Edythe Babette Edwards, "A Review and Analysis of Three Educational Strategies for Positive Change in the Public School System of the City of New York," 1977, box 39, folder 2, BEERHC; Harlem Education Roundtable, Form 990-EZ, 2004, accessed February 18, 2019, http://www.guidestar.org /FinDocuments/2004/731/678/2004-731678165-01ce37f0-Z.pdf; and Hannah Brockington to E. Babette Edwards, December 4, 2002, box 25, folder 9, BEERHC. For more on the recentralization of the New York City Board of Education, see Lewis, *New York City Public Schools*, 137–41.

40. Sarah Kershaw, "State Regents Battle Schools Chief's Hiring," *New York Times*, December 15, 1995; Regina L. Smith to Marie L. Taylor, February 24, 2003, box 26, folder 2, BEERHC; Mary C. Bounds, *A Light Shines in Harlem: New York's First Charter School and the Movement It Led* (Chicago: Lawrence Hill Books, 2014), 52–53; and "Walton Foundation Grant Application," May 22, 2003, box 26, folder 2, BEERHC.

41. "Walton Foundation Grant Application," May 22, 2003, box 26, folder 2, BEERHC; and Perrillo, *Uncivil Rights*, 157.

42. "Walton Foundation Grant Application," May 22, 2003, box 26, folder 2, BEERHC.

43. "Charter Schools: Challenges and Opportunities," *Philanthropy Magazine*, January/February 2003, accessed February 26, 2018, http://www.philanthropyroundtable .org/topic/excellence_in_philanthropy/charter_schools_challenges_and _opportunities; John F. Kirtley and John Walton, "Annual Meeting Highlights: Salute to Effective Education Philanthropy," *Philanthropy Magazine*, January/February 2003, accessed February 26, 2018, http://www.philanthropyroundtable.org /topic/excellence_in_philanthropy/annual_meeting_highlights_salute_to _effective_education_philanthropy; Ralph Rossi II to Joel Klein, October 18, 2004, New York State Education Department Charter School Unit, Charter School Denied/Withdrawn Applications, box 6 (acc. 20196-07), folder labeled "Heart Charter School Correspondence," New York State Archives, Albany (hereafter NYSED Charter); James Merriman IV to Joel Klein, November 30, 2004, NYSED Charter; and Babette Edwards, phone conversation with the author, May 28, 2019. Notes in the author's possession.

44. USNY and the State Education Department, *Annual Report [. . .] on the Status of Charter Schools in New York State 2007–08*, October 2009, accessed February 16, 2019, http:// www.p12.nysed.gov/psc/documents/07-088-3-09.pdf; and Jennifer Medina, "Charter Schools Outshine Others as They Receive Their First Report Cards," *New York Times*, December 20, 2007, B8.

45. Paul Tough, "The Harlem Project," *New York Times*, June 20, 2004; and A. Chris Torres and Joanne W. Golann, "NEPC Review: *Charter Schools and the Achievement Gap*," (Boulder, Colo.: National Education Policy Center, 2018), accessed February 17, 2019, https://nepc.colorado.edu/thinktank/review-no-excuses.

46. Edythe Babette Edwards, "A Review and Analysis of Three Educational Strategies for Positive Change in the Public School System of the City of New York," 63, 1977, box 39, folder 2, BEERHC.

CHAPTER 13

Teaching Harlem

*Black Teachers and the Changing Educational Landscape
of Twenty-First-Century Central Harlem*

BETHANY L. ROGERS AND TERRENDA C. WHITE

W
ho taught in Harlem? What did the presence, or absence, of
Black teachers in this historically Black community mean
for teachers, schools, and students? Teaching has long occupied a special place in the history of African American communities, as the
discussion of Harlem Renaissance artists who were also teachers helps show
in chapter 1 of this volume. Despite theoretically objective notions of
teacher "quality," teachers' identities—who they are, what attributes they
bring to bear, and how those factors are perceived to support students' opportunities to learn—have mattered a great deal historically as well as
today. In an era in which there were few Black teachers in New York City
or Harlem, Black teachers were key figures and activists at Wadleigh High
School (see chapter 3 of this volume). Black (and white) teachers used the
structure of the union to further activism, as described in chapters 4 and 6
of this volume. Just as the nature of teaching is central to schooling, understanding teaching is fundamental to a deeper understanding of Harlem's
educational history. The questions of who taught and who should teach
animated debates over community control in the 1960s, reflected both
compliance and resistance to central school district mandates in the 1980s,
and took on new meaning in early twenty-first-century Harlem, given an
educational landscape with a large and growing number of charter schools.

Starting in 1966, New York state or city authorities collected statistics
documenting the "racial/ethnic profiles" of New York City teachers.[1]

Examining these data for Central Harlem between 1972 and 2015 reveals that in 1972, in a city where Black teachers had been severely underrepresented as compared to the majority Black and Latinx student population, nearly half of Central Harlem's teachers were Black. This proportion grew to a high point of 70 percent in the year 2000 and then began a precipitous decline, so that by 2015, only about 45 percent of the area's teachers were Black.

This chapter seeks to document these trends and identify some of the social and political forces, competing visions of schooling, and transformative events of the time that shaped Harlem's teaching force during this period. Contextualized within this longer historical trajectory, the chapter also ponders what it has meant to some Black teachers to teach within the new educational landscape of twenty-first-century Harlem. The ebb and flow of Black teachers in Central Harlem reveal differing definitions of teacher quality, which variously prioritized race, culture, or credentials; tensions between teacher agency and the systemic ghettoization of Black teachers; and the evolving struggle of a community to access educational opportunity for their children. This account is not definitive, but it is an initial effort to trace who taught in Harlem, suggest meaningful continuities and disruptions across Harlem's educational past and present, and raise questions that invite further research.

In the period from 1972 to 1999, the proportion of Black teachers rose, and between 2000 and 2015, it declined.[2] These periods span the 1969 decentralization of New York City schools and the reconsolidation of the system (under Mayor Michael Bloomberg in 2002), governance changes that reshaped the city's educational system and reconfigured the way Harlem was defined as an educational unit in the larger city. These were also periods of educational change: the persistent quest on the part of Harlemites for educational opportunity and self-determination, including through community control and charter schools, and national and local shifts in ideas about teacher quality and teacher preparation, licensing, and assignment. These narratives intersect in the story of Harlem's teachers, and they have resonance as well for the larger history of Black teachers in northern urban communities in the post–civil rights period.

Regarding the geographic scope of this inquiry, Harlem is divided into three different local school districts within New York City—Districts 3, 4, and 5—effectively turning Harlem into "Harlems"[3] (see chapter 11, figure 11.1 in this volume). In this chapter, we concentrate on the story of

Central Harlem's District 5. Unlike District 3, which loops into the Upper West Side of Manhattan to incorporate white, affluent blocks, or District 4, which contains a large Latinx presence, District 5 has long been known as a primarily Black or African American community (though that has changed over the past several decades, part of the larger story of transformation in regard to who teaches in Harlem).

Scholars of African American history have long placed educators at the center of their narratives, as far back as W. E. B. Du Bois's depiction of reconstruction schools in *The Souls of Black Folk*, given the bond between schooling and hopes for racial progress.[4] Over the past thirty years historians have produced a rich scholarly accounting of African American teachers who taught in segregated Black schools in the Jim Crow and post–*Brown v. Board of Education* South. These histories variously explore Black teachers' beliefs about and intentions for teaching,[5] their pedagogical approaches and the quality of their teaching,[6] and the status these teachers held in their communities.[7] Much of this literature suggests that "engaged, caring faculties," along with powerful parental investment and community support, characterized the best versions of segregated African American schools.[8] Such accounts further establish themes of "connectedness" on the part of Black teachers to their community as well as a sense of obligation, as relatively socially privileged individuals within struggling communities, to racial uplift.[9] Many Black teachers held high expectations for their students, going above and beyond the confines of the classroom to support them, and taking responsibility not only for academic instruction but also for students' "life success—and for the long term success of the African American people."[10]

The history of Black teachers who taught in the urban north in the post–civil rights period has not been nearly as well-documented as that of southern Black teachers. A notable exception is the work of Christina Collins, *"Ethnically Qualified,"* which considers why the proportion of minority teachers in some urban centers remained so low during the postwar era, despite growing populations of students of color in American cities.[11] Collins draws on the particularly egregious example of New York City, where a pernicious "network of institutional racism" shaped the selection of teachers and resulted in a system in which, as late as 1975, only 13 percent of the city's teachers were not white, though the proportion of students of color had risen to 64 percent.[12] In exposing the ways that different stages in the New York City Board of Education (BOE) process for becoming an educator filtered out teachers of color, Collins makes an invaluable contribution regarding the metropolis as a whole, ultimately showing how the removal of such barriers over time led to growing representation of Black teachers.[13]

Collins documents a crucial macro story of Black teachers' struggles to gain purchase within the enmeshed system of accreditation, licensing, hiring, and advancement in the New York City public schools, but her account contains tantalizingly little evidence of what Black teachers themselves made of their experiences. From the sparse literature that exists about Black teachers in the post–*Brown* urban north, we can surmise that most of them continued to teach in segregated schools, and that many also persisted in their special commitment to their Black students and to making schooling a part of a larger liberation strategy, even if not all Black teachers understood their work and their students in the same ways.[14]

Aggregate urban stories about New York have obscured the unique and at times divergent accounts of particular communities, such as Harlem, within the larger metropolis. The racial and ethnic profile of Harlem teachers departs from that of New York City as a whole during the decentralization period, roughly 1969–2000. This chapter offers quantitative and qualitative views of Central Harlem's teacher population shifts from 1970 to 2015, with preliminary queries about the sources and meanings of these shifts.

Teachers in Harlem, 1972–2000

For as long as Black children remained segregated (by "law and custom"), teaching presented a significant professional opportunity for Blacks.[15] Thus, in the early part of the twentieth century, Black teachers in America overwhelmingly taught Black children in the segregated South.[16] By midcentury, approximately 82,000 African American teachers were teaching 2 million African American public school students, though major northern cities still had relatively few Black teachers in relation to their Black populations.[17] But the 1954 *Brown v. Board of Education* decision precipitated a dramatic decline in Black teachers: between 1954 and 1972, over 39,000 Black teachers lost their jobs in 17 southern states, and from 1970 to 1986, African American participation in the overall teaching force steadily waned.[18] Starting in the late 1980s, although the *number* of Black teachers

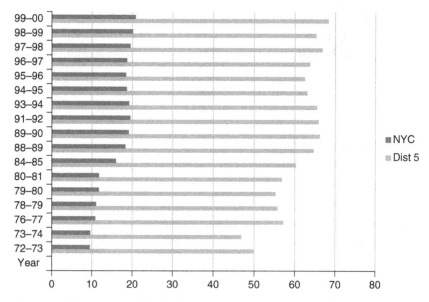

Figure 13.1 Proportions of Black educators in District 5 compared to NYC overall,
1972–2000.

Source: Data derived from a series of available annual reports, *Racial/Ethnic Distribution of Public School Students and Staff*, authored by the USNY and published by the NYSDOE as part of its Basic Educational Data System. Reports featured here through 1984–85 present data on *Public School Staff*, meaning all professional staff assigned full-time to one school, central office professional staff, and those assigned to more than one school; beginning with the 1988–89 report, we found an additional category that excluded central office staff, *Public Classroom Teachers*, which we used to chart the remaining years through 1999–2000.

actually increased (a factor of a growing national teaching corps), the actual proportion of Black teachers continued to shrink, dropping from 8.2 percent to 6.7 percent of the country's teaching force.[19]

Against this period of national decline, New York City looks quite different, at least between 1972 and 2000, when Black teachers increased from 9.5 percent to almost 21 percent of the teaching force. Harlem's District 5 also saw a trend upward in the proportion of Black teachers, though at a different order of magnitude. In 1972, half of the educators in District 5 were Black—a powerful preponderance compared to less than 10 percent citywide. That proportion grew to nearly 70 percent in District 5 by the year 2000 (figure 13.1).[20]

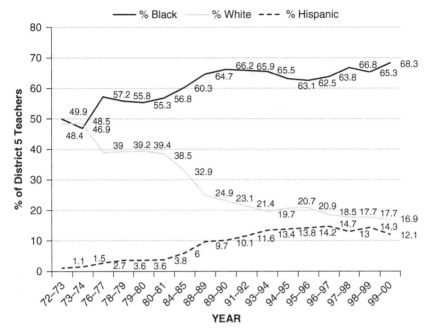

Figure 13.2 Racial/ethnic distribution of District 5 educators, 1972–2000.
Source: Data derived from a series of available annual reports, *Racial/Ethnic Distribution of Public School Students and Staff*, authored by the USNY and published by the NYSDOE as part of its Basic Educational Data System. Reports featured here through 1984–85 present data on *Public School Staff*, meaning all professional staff assigned full-time to one school, central office professional staff, and those assigned to more than one school; beginning with the 1988–89 report, we found an additional category that excluded central office staff, *Public Classroom Teachers*, which we used to chart the remaining years through 1999–2000.

As the share of Black teachers in District 5 grew, so did the ranks of those defined as Latinx teachers, from a tiny 1 percent representation in the early 1970s to 12 percent by 2000.[21] And as the proportions of District 5 Black and Latinx teachers expanded during these years, the fraction of District 5 white educators shrank correspondingly, from nearly 50 percent in 1972 to 17 percent by the year 2000. Within a city historically hostile to hiring Black teachers, they made up a growing majority of District 5's teaching force from the late 1970s through the end of the century (figure 13.2).

What factors interacted to cause this high proportion of Black teachers in District 5? Why did that proportion rise between 1972 and 2000? The answers to these questions depend in part on the persistent segregation of

Harlem's schools, the predilections of the city's white teachers, and the politics of hiring practices. More broadly, the phenomenon may also have been influenced by changing demographics, the dynamics of District 5's Community School Board, as well as the powerful demand on the part of parents for community control of the schools, which served to support and sustain more African American and Latinx teachers.

Exclusion, Segregation, and Teacher Hiring

Over the past several decades, New York State has earned the dubious honor of being the state with the highest degree of school segregation; according to researchers, the New York metropolitan area in particular reflects "persistent residential and educational segregation" as well as a failure to develop viable desegregation plans for schools.[22] The high proportion of Black teachers in District 5 bears out a national historical pattern in which Black teachers are and have been concentrated in districts (or schools) that serve high proportions of students of color.[23] In New York City in particular, there has been a "strong tendency" over the twentieth century to assign teachers according to "their ethnic and racial match" with students.[24] In the early 1970s, when only 10 percent of all New York City teachers were Black, only about 20 percent of New York City's total populace was Black.[25] At the same time, District 5's community population was 85 percent Black, and the district contained a much higher proportion (nearly 50 percent) of Black teachers.[26]

This racial imbalance across the city was the result of both white educators' preferences and the city's hiring and assignment policies. Well before the decentralization period under consideration, many experienced teachers (the vast majority of whom were white) sought to avoid working in Harlem, citing "difficult" schools, often code for Black students living in poverty, but also indicative of poor conditions in the area's schools.[27] Through the early and mid-1960s, the teachers' union successfully fought mandatory transfers of experienced teachers to schools serving low-income students despite evidence of continued staffing inadequacies in such schools.[28] And United Federation of Teachers (UFT) lobbying helped to ensure that the 1969 decentralization law would preserve aspects of the centralized hiring system for teachers (a hedge against the splintering of union power): the Community School Boards (CSBs) were "most restricted in their authority over the hiring, promotion, transfer, and firing of teachers."[29]

Continued unequal teacher assignment patterns by race caught the attention of the U.S. Office of Civil Rights (OCR) in 1972 and, though never as incendiary an issue as student segregation, provoked a federal investigation.[30] Findings revealed that minority teachers were "grossly underrepresented" across the city, and that teachers of color were channeled to and "highly concentrated" in minority schools.[31] Both Black and white educators roundly condemned the Board of Education's 1977 remedy, in which teachers of color would select their teaching assignments from one list of schools, and white teachers would choose from another, each list designed to contrast with the teachers' racial identification. Teachers' dismay suggested not only white teachers' discomfort in being assigned to Black schools. More broadly, it meant that a "statistical approach to addressing education equity" failed to address the desire on the part of many Black teachers to "go where you are needed," as opposed to counting as just "another Black face," and further ignored Black parents' calls for more teachers who looked like them.[32]

Even with intervention from the OCR, race-matching patterns of teacher assignment seem to have persisted, occurring "not only as a result of past practice," but well into the 1980s.[33] In fact, the pattern the OCR sought to remedy—race matching of teachers and students—came to be seen as desirable by many Black teachers, parents, and community members, revealing the tension between an ideal of providing Black role models for Black students and the ideal of a more desegregated distribution of faculty across the city.[34]

In the decades following the OCR agreement, Board of Education policy called for licensed teachers to be randomly assigned to schools from the board's central office, as a means of ensuring teacher diversity and filling hard-to-staff positions across the city.[35] Principals had the right to refuse up to two candidates, but were then obligated to hire the third. Beneath this official system, however, Collins maintains that "insider knowledge" and connections remained an important factor in acquiring desirable placements, and not only in the 1960s and 1970s.[36] Studies conducted in the late 1980s and mid-1990s also support this contention, indicating that many teachers were actually hired by principals through a much more informal process "through someone they knew in a school or district or because they were already known to the school through their experience as a student teacher, para[professional], or substitute teacher."[37] Principals realized that if they hired unlicensed teachers through an informal network, they could gain a far greater say in who they hired than if they followed the formal process through the central office.

According to one researcher, teachers of color fared poorly in this system, because they lacked contacts in these informal networks.[38] Indeed, Eulene Iniss, who worked as a principal in District 5 at one point in her career, described encountering "a lot of nepotism, and a lot of discrimination," in the Board of Education hierarchy.[39] But some educators of color suggested otherwise. Barbara Wilson-Brooks, who was a student at District 5's Public School (PS) 133 in the late 1960s, remembered that a lot of the individuals who worked in the schools "as paraprofessionals . . . teachers, or teachers' aides" lived in the community, implying membership in a local network.[40] (Nick Juravich agrees that paraprofessionals came from the local community, though he notes that teachers were less likely to; see chapter 10 in this volume.) A District 4 teacher in East Harlem recalled that she got her job in the late 1980s because "I knew somebody. . . . And then . . . they liked me so much that they made ways for me to stay in the community to teach."[41] Although only speculation, it seems plausible that, as in other teacher job markets across the city, District 5 principals found ways to hire adults—paras and teachers—who belonged to a common informal network within the community and shared important beliefs about how Harlem students should be educated.

While hiring on the basis of personal connections may have helped to bind the community and the school, the practice was complicated by the widespread employment of uncredentialed teachers, a chronic issue in Harlem. Such teachers may well have brought critical knowledge of the community to bear, but they lacked the formal qualifications meant to certify their ability to teach. For example, the East Harlem teacher who found her job through personal contacts also acknowledged feeling "bad," as she had no teaching degree—only a BA in psychology—or experience when she was hired.[42] But she was hardly alone. Of those who started teaching in New York City in 1988, for example, a staggering 88 percent began as temporary per diem substitutes (TPDs). Some of those new teachers had completed programs of teacher preparation and were awaiting approval for certification, but more than three-quarters of them were "'emergency' TPDs," with little or no training.[43]

Prior research makes a convincing argument for the "substantial sorting of teachers across schools" in which high proportions of those uncertified and inexperienced teachers taught in districts with high percentages of minority students and teachers of color.[44] The implications are stark: although children of color may encounter greater numbers of teachers of color, they are also less likely to have fully certified and experienced teachers. For some, these overlaps may suggest an unfortunate and simplistic association between teachers of color and educational problems in urban schools. The reality is more complex: there likely were some incompetent teachers in District 5, as in other districts, but credentialing has not always operated as an accurate proxy for teacher quality either. Indeed, principals in District 5 likely held competing perceptions of what counted as "quality," which included not only licensure but also identity and belonging in the community, for example, which may have informed hiring decisions. Taken together, these competing perceptions suggest that the dichotomy of credentialed versus uncredentialed teachers, although valid, misses key areas of value that mattered within the community and may have helped produce hiring and retention of Black teachers in Harlem at a greater pace than in other parts of New York City.

Decentralization, the Fiscal Crisis, and Parent Dissatisfaction

Battles over community control, which culminated in the citywide 1968 teachers' strike precipitated by events in Brooklyn's Ocean Hill-Brownsville demonstration district, ultimately led to the passage of the 1969 decentralization legislation that divided Harlem into Districts 3, 4, and 5. Though not necessarily reflected in the letter of the law, community control activists had achieved some success in promoting the importance of hiring more teachers of color in schools serving students of color. Decentralization itself did not necessarily cause the increase of Black teachers in District 5. But concurrent with the enactment of decentralization, explicit consideration of race had become part of hiring, whether in the guise of OCR's efforts to even out citywide imbalances or under the auspices of a local school principal's efforts to hire more African American and Latinx teachers in the belief that more teachers of color would better the education of students of color.[45]

Decentralization was a troubled time in Central Harlem's District 5. Reflecting on those first years of decentralization, Bernard R. Gifford, the chancellor at the time, suggested that the Community School Board in District 5 was "beset by troubles," including "tangled affairs and mismanagement," from the outset.[46] Yet, as the education historian Heather Lewis points out, the rollout of decentralization occurred against the backdrop of fiscal austerity, a prelude to the full-blown fiscal crisis of the mid-1970s as discussed by Kim Phillips-Fein and Esther Cyna (chapter 11 of this volume). The economic woes of the time severely inhibited the implementation of all reforms for education and equity, but the fiscal crisis profoundly altered the teaching force. Cutbacks on the part of the city forced teacher layoffs: elementary schools lost 21 percent of their faculties over two years, and junior high and high schools cut 16 percent of their teachers. Novice teachers were let go first, so that by 1977, 85 percent of the teaching workforce had over five years of experience, an increase of more than 15 percent from 1975.[47] These years align with a slight downturn—about 2 percent—in the proportion of Black teachers in District 5 that occurred between 1977 and 1980; it is plausible that many of the laid-off teachers in District 5 were Black and, on average, less senior in the system and thus more vulnerable to layoffs.[48]

Beyond the retrenchments associated with the fiscal crisis, troubles associated with the District 5 Community School Board also took their toll on "educational quality and staff morale" in the schools.[49] Rapid turnover of superintendents and political infighting on the District 5 CSB made for difficult working conditions and poorly performing schools. And although the community appreciated the presence of Black teachers, many parents' frustrations with the quality of Harlem's schools centered on teachers, some of whom they accused of being insensitive, abusive, or unwilling to educate Harlem children. The belief that District 5 served as a "dumping ground" for ineffective or otherwise objectionable teachers haunted these years. In one 1974 case, parents at PS 46 forced out and then protested the reinstatement of four teachers they believed were incompetent or not qualified. Two of the teachers were rumored to have used corporal punishment; all four (three of whom were white, one of whom was Black) had received unsatisfactory ratings from the principal.[50] As a *New York Times* account reported, "One woman [from the community] asserted that P.S. 46 had been turned into a receiving center for teachers rejected elsewhere, and she said angrily: 'Send the garbage to Canarsie,'" a white working class community in Brooklyn.[51] Conversely, two years later, parents and students at Intermediate School (IS) 10 protested the removal of nine popular teachers, who were dismissed (part of the financial cutbacks during the fiscal crisis) to make room for teachers with greater seniority, and the subsequent failure of those teachers' replacements to show up at the school.[52] By 1984, District 5 (along with other districts serving New York City's poorest neighborhoods) faced a severe teacher shortage. The superintendent of District 5 at the time, Luther Seabrook, called the situation a "disaster," declaring that "these kids are getting ripped off twice—once because they're perceived as being in a school district incapable of properly educating them, and secondly because they're incapable of being served by qualified teachers."[53]

Between the years of 1972 and 2000, Harlem's District 5 presented a stark contrast to the overall demographics of the New York City teaching force. At a time when Black teachers made up less than 10 percent of teachers in the city, they composed nearly half of District 5's educators—a proportion that would increase to nearly 70 percent by the year 2000. Many factors appear to have played a role. The city continued to facilitate a segregated system, in which white teachers (aided by the UFT) found ways to opt out of teaching in Black communities like Harlem. Meanwhile, although decentralization failed to provide Community School Boards with the authority to hire teachers, local principals across the city flouted the formal centralized system of teacher assignment in favor of informal hires. In District 5, this workaround afforded the hiring of a greater number of Black teachers—and may have driven the growth of Black teachers in Harlem during the decentralization years—but it accompanied the hiring of many uncertified teachers. And finally, although hiring more Black teachers was a goal for many activist efforts in New York as well as elsewhere from the 1960s onward, during these years, District 5 exhibited both high numbers of Black teachers and continued dissatisfaction on the part of some parents regarding school and teacher quality.

Teachers in Twenty-First-Century Harlem

Between 1972 and 2000, District 5 saw both a greater plurality of Black teachers than was found across the city and a steady upward trend in the proportion of Black teachers, but the year 2000 marked an acute turning point. The presence of Black teachers in District 5 began a sharp decline:

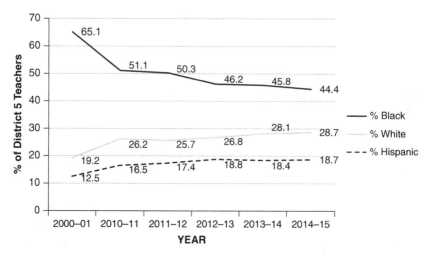

Figure 13.3 Racial/ethnic distribution of District 5 educators, 2000–2015.
Source: Information regarding the racial and ethnic profile of teachers in Harlem between 2000 and 2015 comes from NYCIBO Public School Teacher Data, which was provided by Ray Domanico, the director at the time, upon request, September 22, 2016.

over the subsequent fifteen years, the proportion of Black teachers fell by a third, and the concomitant proportions of White, Latinx, and Asian teachers grew (figure 13.3).[54]

This decline in Central Harlem may reflect a limitation of the data: the state does not collect information about charter school faculty in the same way it does about district school teachers. Charter schools have grown rapidly in Harlem, with approximately twenty-two operating there as of 2013–2014.[55] As charters grew, Board of Education schools held a shrinking share of the school market. A shrinking population of Black teachers now taught in a smaller number of district schools and were part of a smaller pool of BOE teachers in Harlem. District 5's teaching population declined from 1,023 in 2000 to 984 in 2015.[56] Were Black teachers leaving District 5 in general, or were they leaving district schools for charter schools? Although the latter is certainly possible, the declining portion of Black teachers in District 5 between 2000 and 2015 is not an outlier. According to New York City Independent Budget Office data, the proportion of Black teachers in New York City overall declined by several percentage points between 2000 and 2012, from 21 percent to 19 percent, within a teacher workforce that shrank by about 5 percent, representing a drop of nearly

15 percent in the share of Black teachers in New York City.[57] (Although the decline has occurred across schools, Black educators remain more heavily concentrated in high-poverty schools such as those in Harlem). This pattern has been replicated in other large urban districts such as Cleveland, and in cities with large charter school sectors, such as New Orleans.[58]

What led to this decline in the proportion of Black teachers in District 5 in the twenty-first century? Several factors, including substantial changes in New York State's laws regarding teacher credentialing and hiring requirements as well as innovations in the city's educational policy—which led to district school closures and the emergence of a concentrated charter school market—influenced the presence of Black educators in District 5. Interviews with Black educators offer on-the-ground perspectives regarding the choices of Black teachers and the meanings they attached to their work in District 5 during the first fifteen years of this century.

Changes in the Pipeline: Teacher Credentialing and Hiring Policy

The twenty-first century brought sweeping changes to public education across the country, including a mix of centralized accountability mandates by the federal government and decentralized governance structures at state and local levels, many designed to shift control of major aspects of public schools to external groups. Likewise, an array of somewhat contradictory federal and state policies aimed to ratchet up the quality of teachers through tightening requirements and standards in some cases and loosening or even circumventing them in others. The passage of charter legislation, which allowed for new pathways into the classroom, offers an example of "loosening." But New York State also tightened requirements. In 2001, the New York State Regents and Commissioner Richard Mills developed a "comprehensive plan to improve teaching" that involved raising standards for teacher education programs and certification.[59] These elevated standards, combined with Mills's successful suit against the New York Board of Education to require a certified teacher in every classroom of the state's failing schools, directly challenged and ultimately changed the city's standard practice of hiring uncertified teachers.[60] Over the subsequent decade and a half, New York City, including Harlem's District 5, saw a consistent increase in permanently certified teachers, and concomitant decrease in the employment of teachers with temporary and provisional certification.[61] Researchers found that the teacher qualifications gap that had characterized New York City schools declined appreciably in just the first five years of the new policies. Simultaneous to the "virtual elimination of newly hired uncertified teachers" was "an influx of teachers with strong academic backgrounds from alternative certification programs." There was also some sleight of hand, as some teachers on alternative routes to become certified were given waivers to teach.[62]

The influx of teachers in alternate route programs signifies a second, significant break with the past. New pathways to the classroom, such as Teach For America and the New York City Teaching Fellows, drew a new population of teachers, many from outside the community, into Harlem schools.[63] The proportion of new teachers who entered District 5 from alternate pathways has varied—in 2012–13, nearly half of the new hires in the district came from alternate paths, including the New York City Teaching Fellows, but only slightly over 30 percent of the 2014–15 new hires arrived by way of alternate routes—though such paths nevertheless represent a relatively substantial share of teachers hired into district schools.[64]

Alternate pathways to teaching grew alongside the expansion of charter schools. Nationwide, charter schools report higher proportions of teachers of color compared to district schools (27 percent and 16 percent, respectively).[65] Urban charter schools, however, when compared to existing workforce patterns, report lower shares of new teacher hires who are Black, despite enrolling much higher proportions of Black students than district schools.[66] Therefore, urban charter schools in cities such as New York yield wider representation gaps between Black students and teachers compared to district schools.[67] For example, in 2012, New York City's charter sector had a representation gap between Black students and teachers that was four times higher than the district sector (36.9 percent and 9.2 percent, respectively).[68]

Several other pipeline issues may have affected the presence of Black teachers in Harlem. Between 2002 and 2012, influenced in part by the No Child Left Behind legislation (which called for a "qualified" teacher in every classroom by 2006), state-level praxis exams and the National Teacher Exam became "increasingly important in teacher selection in New York City," as well as in other urban districts that depended on federal funding.[69] The ethnic difference in passing rates on such assessments has been well documented, and suggests that the tests operated as an obstacle for teachers of color.[70] In addition, the 1970 Open Admissions policy of City

University of New York (the source of the lion's share of New York City's teachers) had helped the city to grow its proportion of minority teachers in the 1970s and 1980s by guaranteeing entry to almost all New York City graduates and providing an affordable path to teaching. But the introduction of tuition (courtesy of the 1975 fiscal crisis), as well as tightening admissions, new curricular requirements, and rising tuitions—trends begun in the 1980s but accelerated after the year 2000—undercut the numbers of eligible Black and Latinx candidates.[71]

The decline of Black teachers may be more than a pipeline issue, however. Scholars have pointed out that retention is critical, and is a problem particularly for teachers of color.[72] Nationally, minority teachers are hired at a higher proportional rate than other teachers, but they are also leaving the profession at higher rates than other teachers, both voluntarily and involuntarily.[73] In 2012, for example, the rate of involuntary turnover was much higher for Black teachers than for all other teachers, a phenomenon directly related to "school closings in urban districts due both to declining enrollments and sanctions" (the latter targeted to underperforming schools); Black teachers who choose to leave ("voluntary leavers") often do so out of dissatisfaction with job conditions, rather than (as with non-Black teachers) personal or family reasons.[74]

Local data show that a growing proportion of recent new hires in District 5 are Black teachers: in 2010, only 18 percent of new teachers hired in District 5 were Black; by 2014, 30 percent were.[75] But of all new teachers hired in 2011, less than 50 percent were still teaching in District 5 four years later. About a quarter of those teachers who left went to teaching positions elsewhere in New York City, and the remaining quarter represented those who were no longer employed by the New York City Department of Education. If Harlem follows national trends, Black teachers may well have turned over in the district at greater rates than other demographics, contributing to their declining share of the teaching force there.

Changes in Educational Policy: Charters and Choice

The particular struggles changed over time, but Harlem residents maintained a strong, if often thwarted, desire for access to high-quality education for their children. Looking at the last few decades of the twentieth century, it becomes clear that New York City public schools' continued apathy (or even resistance) toward responding to the community's demands helped sustain the activism for educational self-determination that emerged in the 1960s and ultimately laid the groundwork for many twenty-first-century developments. In part a result of this activism, as demonstrated through the story of Babette Edwards (see chapter 11 in this volume), school choice and the development and expansion of charter schools fundamentally transformed the educational landscape of District 5 and reshaped its teaching force.

In New York City, where Mayor Michael Bloomberg achieved mayoral control of the schools in 2002, new policies sought to standardize curricula and other practices across schools, while others devolved control to individual school sites in return for outcomes-focused accountability. The Bloomberg administration's policies showed a preference for market-based reforms expressly designed to foster choice and competition between schools, and school choice and charter schools emerged as two central strategies of the Bloomberg era. Under the tenure of the Bloomberg appointee Chancellor Joel Klein, and in the wake of New York's 1998 law authorizing charter schools, market reformers who had long abhorred educational bureaucracy could finally restructure the financial, organizational, and human resource parameters of the city's public schools. But charter schools also drew an enthusiastic audience from among parents and community groups in disenfranchised communities, where the struggle to access better educational options for their children carried into the twenty-first century. Activists such as Babette Edwards turned to charters to create public schools better aligned with the educational values of the community. Harlem went on to become a chief base for charter expansion, accounting for nearly two-thirds of Manhattan's charter schools in the subsequent decade.[76]

Although there is a lack of centralized data about charter school teachers, including their racial composition, in New York, some evidence suggests that the nascent sector suffered from an underrepresentation of teachers of color, particularly Black teachers, that was more severe than in district schools.[77] However, we know little about whether Black teachers were more prevalent in Harlem's charter schools than in charters in other areas of the city; in other words, it is not clear whether charters were replicating the uneven distributions of teachers found in district schools, and whether Harlem charters followed or diverged from other charter schools in the city, state, or country.

Studies featuring interviews with teachers in charter schools in Harlem suggest that early charters may have been havens for Black teachers, particularly those interested in establishing long-desired alternative educational environments.[78] For example, the African American teachers Derek Andrews and Marvin Humphrey began their careers in one of Harlem's first charter schools, which were founded by community-based organizations with parents and teachers on the boards of trustees.[79] Recalling his decision to work in a small stand-alone charter school in 2000, Humphrey described a longing for a sense of community, "I'm from Harlem. I was born in Harlem. I went to school in Harlem. I love this community, and I love the rapport I have with people in the community."[80] Humphrey's charter school was housed in a building funded by a community-based organization. The school sought to provide a flexible learning environment for students, promoted a keen awareness of cultural heritage, used project-based learning, and leveraged community resources, such as parks or museums, for educational experiences.

Humphrey's school was emblematic of early Harlem charter schools. However, a new wave of charter schools would soon emerge, with different curricular priorities. In 2007, legislators passed an amendment that raised the initial limit on the number of charters that could operate in New York from 100 to 200. In 2010, in an effort to secure federal grants from President Barack Obama's Race to the Top initiative, legislators again lifted the cap, approving authorizations for more than 200 additional charters and ushering in a second phase of charter expansion. With the new caps, charter authorizers anticipated more than 400 charter schools, with approximately 136 already in operation in the city by 2012, primarily located in three neighborhoods: Harlem, Central Brooklyn, and the South Bronx.[81]

At this new scale, both the sponsoring organizations and the curricular emphasis of many charters changed. By 2008 this new crop of charters showed up in Harlem. These were schools founded by high-profile national charter management organizations (CMOs), which coordinated operations and curricular programming in multiple schools from central offices in the city by way of regional managers and prominent executives.[82] Harlem became a particularly intensive site of charter expansion. Manhattan contained six community school districts with approximately fifty-nine charter schools in operation in 2012–13; those districts encompassing Harlem housed the largest share of those charters (approximately forty-four), with Central Harlem alone accommodating the greatest saturation (approximately twenty-two charters).[83] Stand-alone charters tied to community groups, such has Humphrey's school, came to represent a minority of the charter population, as nearly two-thirds of all the Harlem charters were managed by CMOs in 2013–14; in fact, just three CMOs managed approximately half of all charter schools in the neighborhood.[84]

Charter expansion coincided with high-stakes accountability mandates, which included interventionist "turnaround" efforts to improve low-performing schools. Such efforts resulted in the closing of scores of district schools across the city. Since 2002, 140 out of roughly 1,800 New York City schools were closed, especially in epicenters of charter saturation such as Harlem. In similar situations in New Orleans and other cities, district school closures helped depress Black teacher employment, as these teachers fared less well in the expanding charter sector.[85]

The teacher recruitment pool for CMO charters was also distinct: many teachers came from out of state via alternative teacher certification programs, such as Teach For America, and expressed short-term interests in teaching, with an eye toward business, law, leadership, or social entrepreneurship in the longer run. Teachers in CMO charters were rarely unionized and worked as at-will employees, setting the stage for top-down decision making by leaders and tenuous relationships between CMO managers and teachers.[86] Shawn Lewis, an African American male teacher who taught in one of Harlem's charter schools, struggled with CMO managers and private donors: "The idea from donors was that 'we are giving your school all of this money, so where are our results?' But when money came, the quality of instruction became diluted. . . . It was suddenly about *quick*, short results."[87] Lewis eventually left his CMO charter for a stand-alone charter school, which he described as a better match for his ideas about teaching and learning: "My [old charter school] wasn't really about developing the whole child. They were about 'results.' That's it."[88]

Several CMO charters in Harlem had some of the highest teacher turnover rates in the city and state. Turnover for all teachers (district and charter) in the state was 11 percent in 2015–16, but 24 percent of District 5 (district and charter) teachers turned over from 2015–16 to 2016–17. The rise in the number of charter schools in District 5 likely exacerbated the district's already high turnover rate, as nearly all charter schools reported turnover rates above the state average in 2015–16. One large CMO, in particular, had three schools in District 5 with turnover rates that doubled the district's average in 2015–16, including Success Academy 2 (56 percent turnover), Success Academy 4 (48 percent turnover), and Success Academy 5 (65 percent turnover).[89]

Some Black educators in Harlem, however, were drawn to its new charter sector, particularly those who had worked in district schools and experienced years of overcrowding and inadequate resources. Theresa Sanders, for example, is an African American teacher who left her district school—where "just to get a ream of paper was gold!"—to work as a third-grade teacher in one of Harlem's largest chains of CMO charters; as she recalled, "The materials alone were enough to leave my district school."[90] Sanders's experience is not farfetched. According to studies of national CMOs, many organizations enjoy significant private investment, yielding upward of $5,700 in additional per pupil spending (on average). In Sanders's charter school, private donations likely pushed total funding beyond 30 percent of average per pupil funding in the city's district schools.[91] Despite the largesse, however, Sanders described the same kind of struggles that Lewis identified, including a lack of autonomy and decision-making authority about how to teach, particularly in the face of powerful donors and a largely white cadre of central managers: "I mean it's not that many of us [Blacks] in the CMO. I could probably count on one hand how many Black people there are. . . . And they [CMO managers] go about this whole bullying tactic with teachers. Managers try to bully teachers into doing what they [the managers] want . . . but they should want people to do things because they [people] see the value in it, not because they [managers] tell us to do it."[92] Limited by weak teacher protections (CMO teachers are usually at-will workers and rarely have tenure or belong to unions with a collective bargaining agreement), Theresa Sanders ultimately left her charter school in Harlem to seek work in schools where working conditions, as she described, were less rigid and hierarchical.

Unlike Sanders, some educators in Harlem's new charter sector left their schools involuntarily. Anthony Charles, an African American teacher who worked as a math coach in a CMO charter school in District 5, noted that he was "let go" (a nonrenewal of his teaching contract) unexpectedly in the summer before his fourth year with the school. "I worked for that CMO for three and half years, and my dismissal took two minutes."[93] Charles attributed his layoff to philosophical differences between teachers, leaders, and managers: "The school had a great reputation and many of our board members were famous millionaires and billionaires, but they operated from a business standpoint. So they were only looking at children's test scores or results, and to them teachers were either getting results or not getting results."[94] After his termination, Charles questioned the results-driven strategies of those who managed the new schools in Harlem, expressing particular concerns about their apparent indifference to broad social and cultural curricula and their influence on students in Harlem: "Educators are not supposed to make students feel as though historically their people don't function on the level as another group of people within the same nation. We shouldn't make some groups feel inferior . . . but kids in Harlem are in just that sort of predicament."[95]

In the first decade and a half of the twenty-first century, changes in credentialing and hiring requirements, the steady closure of district schools, the spread of market-driven charters managed by private groups, and the visions of education espoused by many of those charters fundamentally influenced who taught in Harlem. Taken together, these reforms affected teachers differently, depending on teachers' preparation pathway, philosophies of teaching, and beliefs about the educational needs of Black and Latinx children and children in Harlem, as well as the blunt force of powerful groups with unprecedented autonomy to shape teachers' classroom practices and hire or fire teachers accordingly. Ultimately, compared to earlier trends, education reforms in the twenty-first century adversely affected the recruitment and retention of Black teachers in Harlem, and white teachers rebounded in number and proportion in the same period. In particular, the expansion of CMO charter schools with hierarchical working conditions, weak labor protections, alternative teacher preparation programs that rely on out-of-state hires, and an indifference to culturally inclusive curricula all presented clear challenges for Black teachers, many of whom may have nurtured more locally rooted, historically informed visions of education in Harlem. Though community-based visions emerged in some early charters in Harlem, these visions (and the teachers who enlisted to carry out these plans) were peripheral by 2015, as entrepreneurs, managerial elites, and philanthropists took charge of Harlem's new educational landscape and its new pool of teachers.

The changing racial and ethnic profile of teachers in Harlem between the late 1960s and 2015 was indelibly shaped by race, policy, and larger social forces, but also by competing ideals of teacher quality and educational opportunity and, finally, by Black teachers' own commitments, philosophies of education and educational equity, and social networks. Harlem's social location as a community historically segregated and circumscribed by in-equities in resources, yet also emboldened by struggles for political power and cultural representation, gave rise to both opportunities and constraints. Over time, the teaching force in Harlem has reflected an unequal distri-bution of teachers with formal qualifications. Yet the Harlem teaching force has also included a self-conscious cadre of teachers with social justice com-mitments and alternative visions for a culturally inclusive learning envi-ronment; and it has encompassed a critical mass of community members called to participate through their local social networks.

From the postwar period through the twentieth century, white teachers balked at Harlem teaching assignments, and racism still narrowed the path-ways to teacher preparation and certification for Black teachers. The result was a near-chronic teacher shortage. Consequently, as early as the mid-1950s, "a greater proportion of substitutes" was hired in Harlem than in "the more favored parts of the city."[96] The 1955 report, *The Status of the Public School Education of Negro and Puerto Rican Children in the City*, gave language and salience to this discrepancy, and helped to introduce "teacher quality" as a form of inequity between Black and white schools.[97] The call for better teachers in Harlem between the 1940s and early 1960s generally associated "quality" with training, licensing, experience, or "special qualifications."[98] The later 1960s and 1970s, however, saw increasing demands for a different form of quality, in the form of Black and Latinx teachers who could provide role models for children of color.[99] Layoffs of the 1970s complicated these demands, delivering a far more senior teaching force in Harlem, but at the expense of less experienced teachers of color who lost their jobs. By the early 1990s, with little appreciable improvement in District 5's performance, critics suggested that hiring minority teachers was not a panacea and that "quality" was more elusive than the experience, academic credentials, and licensing privileged by the New York City Board of Education, on the one hand, or simplistic race matching, on the other.[100] Quality might include a "talent for identifying with Black children," or a sensitivity to the "lan-guage and values of Black children" and, as former Brooklyn superinten-dent Jerome Harris asserted, this quality may "come in all colors."[101]

The lack of consensus around what criteria define teacher quality con-tinues to devil the education profession. Meanwhile, Harlem has become a poster child for new conceptualizations of teacher and educational quality. Our data show that the introduction of new players and variables beginning in the twenty-first century essentially altered who teaches in Harlem. But these innovations—the stricter credentialing requirements, alternate routes to teaching, new models of school governance, and different working conditions inside schools as well as curricular and pedagogical priorities tied to accountability and market-based competition charter schools—served to restructure definitions of teacher quality as well. Indeed, alternate routes and charter schools have contributed to new forms of credentialism: today, for example, many charter schools in Harlem recruit teachers who may not have fulfilled formal teacher preparation requirements, but who do well on the standardized competency tests and are oriented toward raising student achievement (as measured by standardized tests). Yet such recruits are usually short-lived—they leave teaching after only a few years—and are expensive to the district in terms of churn. Moreover, most of these teachers are not only outsiders to the community and its culture, they are also novices, and thus re-create the persistent problem of concentrated inexperienced teachers in District 5.

Demographic changes among those who taught in Central Harlem, along with debates about teacher quality, played out against the tumultuous backdrop of the community control movement, decentralization, and mayoral control. They occurred in tandem with the city's struggle over time to adjust its teacher assignment policies to comply with federal mandates from the Office of Civil Rights, to fulfill local community desires for more teachers of color, and to meet increased state requirements in the twenty-first century. And they have run alongside the introduction of new forms of schooling and means of procuring teachers, which have taken hold most firmly as ways of educating poor children of color. Yet despite all the change and innovation, one outcome that has remained elusive through these years is the development of a stable, diverse, cadre of teachers who are well-prepared to teach District 5 students.

Notes

1. According to one report, "The collection of racial/ethnic data on the school population of New York State was initiated in 1961 with a census of public elementary schools. Since 1966 such information has been collected annually from all public elementary and secondary schools and is now a part of the Department's Basic Educational Data System. The information is used within the Education Department to provide a longitudinal record of school integration throughout the state. See University of the State of New York (hereafter USNY), *Racial/Ethnic Distribution of Public School Students and Staff, 1972–1973* (Albany, N.Y.: State Education Department Information Center on

Education, 1973). These reports furnished data for the years from 1972 to 2000 featured in this chapter. Information regarding the racial and ethnic profile of teachers in Harlem between 2000 and 2015 comes from New York City Independent Budget Office (hereafter NYCIBO) Public School Teacher Data, which was provided by Ray Domanico, the director at the time, upon request, September 22, 2016.

2. The earliest report we located that broke out racial/ethnic profile data by Community School Districts in New York City refers to the 1972–73 school year. We could not locate a complete version of the 1971–72 document; and the 1970–71 report provided only aggregated racial/ethnic profile data for all of New York City.

3. An unpopular legislative compromise between community control advocates and forces of centralization, the law established thirty-two community school districts in New York City, each with its own elected school board, though the central Board of Education maintained important authority, including the hiring of teachers. See Heather Lewis, *New York City Public Schools from Brownsville to Bloomberg: Community Control and Its Legacy* (New York: Teachers College Press, 2013).

4. W. E. B. DuBois, *The Souls of Black Folk* (New York: Oxford University Press, 2007 [1903]).

5. Michael Fultz, "African American Teachers in the South, 1890–1940: Powerlessness and the Ironies of Expectations and Protests," *History of Education Quarterly* 35 (1995): 401–22; Ronald Butchart, *Schooling the Freed People: Teaching, Learning, and the Struggle for Black Freedom, 1861–1876* (Chapel Hill: University of North Carolina Press, 2010); and Sonya Ramsey, *Reading, Writing, and Segregation: A Century of Black Women Teachers in Nashville* (Urbana: University of Illinois Press, 2008).

6. Michele Foster, *Black Teachers on Teaching* (New York: New Press, 1997); Vanessa Siddle Walker, *Their Highest Potential: An African American School Community in the Segregated South* (Chapel Hill: University of North Carolina Press, 1996); Michael Fultz, "Teacher Training and African American Education in the South," *Journal of Negro Education* 64 (1995): 196–210; David Cecelski, *Along Freedom Road: Hyde County, North Carolina and the Fate of Black Schools in the South* (Chapel Hill: University of North Carolina Press, 1994); Adam Fairclough, *A Class of Their Own: Black Teachers in the Segregated South* (Cambridge, Mass.: Harvard University Press, 2007); Linda Perkins, "The History of Blacks in Teaching: Growth and Decline Within the Profession," in *American Teachers: Histories of a Profession at Work*, ed. Donald Warren (New York: Macmillan, 1989), 344–69; and Davidson Douglas, *Jim Crow Moves North: The Battle Over Northern School Segregation, 1865–1954* (New York: Cambridge University Press, 2005).

7. Stephanie Shaw, *What a Woman Ought to Be and to Do: Black Professional Women Workers During the Jim Crow Era* (Chicago: University of Chicago Press, 1996); Ramsey, *Reading, Writing, and Segregation*.

8. Melanie Acosta, Michele Foster, and Diedre Houchen, "'Why Seek the Living Among the Dead?' African American Pedagogical Excellence: Exemplar Practice for Teacher Education," *Journal of Teacher Education* (March 2018), accessed March 20, 2018, https://doi-org.proxy.library.csi.cuny.edu/10.1177/0022487118761881.

9. Foster, "Constancy, Connectedness, and Constraints," 1991; Vanessa Siddle Walker, "Valued Segregated Schools for African American Children in the South, 1963–1969: A Review of Common Themes and Characteristics," *Review of Educational Research* 70 (2000): 253–70; and Fairclough, *Class of Their Own*. See also Shaw, *What a Woman Ought to Be*, 218.

10. Judith Kafka, "In Search of a Grand Narrative: The Turbulent History of Teaching," in *Handbook of Research on Teaching*, ed. Drew Gitomer and Courtney Bell (Washington, D.C.: American Educational Research Association, 2016), 85.

11. Generally, the proportion of Black teachers in urban centers was and is higher than the proportion of Black teachers nationally. Christina Collins, *"Ethnically Qualified": Race, Merit, and the Selection of Urban Teachers, 1920–1980* (New York: Teachers College Press, 2011), 7.

12. Collins, *"Ethnically Qualified,"* 4, 7.

13. New York's increase was contrary to national trends, but in line with what was happening in other urban areas. USNY, *Racial/Ethnic Distribution, 1972–73,* 73; USNY, *Racial/Ethnic Distribution of Public School Students and Staff, 1999–2000* (Albany, N.Y.: Office of Information, Reporting and Technology Services, 2001), 70; and Collins, *"Ethnically Qualified,"* 178.

14. See, for example, Lewis, *New York City Public Schools,* 104, 106; and Dionne Danns, *Something Better for Our Children: Black Organization in the Chicago Public Schools, 1963–1971* (New York: Routledge, 2002). It is also worth noting that these schools were not segregated by law, but by generations of public policy choices that had the same effect. Regarding multiple perspectives of Black teachers, see Daniel Perlstein, *Justice, Justice: School Politics and the Eclipse of Liberalism* (New York: Peter Lang, 2004); for the emergence of class divisions, see Kafka, "In Search of a Grand Narrative"; Foster, *Black Teachers*; and Jean Anyon, *Ghetto Schooling: A Political Economy of Urban Educational Reform* (New York: Teachers College Press, 1997).

15. Jacqueline Jordan Irvine, "An Analysis of the Problem of Disappearing Black Educators," *Elementary School Journal* 88 (May 1988): 504; D. Coursen, *Women and Minorities in Administration* (Arlington, VA: National Association of Elementary School Principals, 1975); and Foster, *Black Teachers.*

16. Linda C. Tillman, "Unintended Consequences? The Impact of the *Brown v. Board of Education* Decision on the Employment Status of Black Educators," *Education and Urban Society* 36 (May 2004): 282; and Foster, *Black Teachers.*

17. Tillman, "Unintended Consequences?," 286; M. J. Hudson and B. J. Holmes, "Missing Teachers, Impaired Communities: The Unanticipated Consequences of *Brown v. Board of Education* on the African American Teaching Force at the Precollegiate Level," *Journal of Negro Education* 63 (1994): 388–93; and Jack Dougherty, "'That's When We Were Marching for Jobs': Black Teachers and the Early Civil Rights Movement in Milwaukee," *History of Education Quarterly* 38 (Summer 1998): 121–41.

18. Samuel B. Ethridge, "Impact of the 1954 *Brown vs. Topeka Board of Education* Decision on Black Educators," *Negro Educational Review* 30 (October 1979): 217–32; National Education Association, *Status of the American Public School Teacher, 1985–86* (Washington, D.C.: National Education Association, 1987); and Sabrina Hope King, "The Limited Presence of African-American Teachers," *Review of Educational Research* 63 (Summer 1993): 124–25.

19. Richard M. Ingersoll, Elizabeth Merrill, Daniel Stuckey, and Gregory Collins, "Seven Trends: The Transformation of the Teaching Force—Updated October 2018," *CPRE Research Reports,* accessed January 30, 2019, https://repository.upenn.edu/cpre _researchreports/108. The trend for Black teacher representation differs from that of minority teachers (Black, Hispanic, Asian and Pacific Islander, American Indian, and multiracial), which grew from 12 percent in 1987 to 17 percent of the teaching force in 2012. See Albert Shanker Institute, *The State of Teacher Diversity in American Education* (Washington, D.C.: Albert Shanker Institute, 2015), 2.

20. These numbers refer to elementary and middle school teachers: not only did District 5 have no high schools, high schools in New York City belonged to a separate district altogether.

21. The state-defined categories for teachers' racial/ethnic identities are problematic in terms of how those identities were defined and how the definitions changed over the years. Available reports from the early 1970s included categories of Black; Spanish surnamed American; American Indian and Oriental; and Other. (Other in this case was meant to include the default of white.) By the 1976–1977 report and going forward, these categories had changed to Black (not Hispanic origin); Hispanic; American Indian, Alaskan Native, Asian or Pacific Islander; and White (not Hispanic origin), which quite likely would have resulted in categorization of some individuals that differed from where they would have been slotted in earlier reports.

22. Gary Orfield, quoted in Susanna W. Pflaum and Theodore Abramson, "Teacher Assignment, Hiring and Preparation: Minority Teachers in New York City," *Urban Review* 22 (March 1990): 19. See Gary Orfield (with F. Monfort and R. George), *School Segregation in the 1980s: Trends in the States and Metropolitan Areas* (Chicago: National School Desegregation Project, 1987); and John Kucsera with Gary Orfield, *New York State's Extreme School Segregation: Inequality, Inaction and a Damaged Future* (Los Angeles: The Civil Rights Project/Proyecto Derechos Civiles, 2014).

23. Tillman, "(Un)intended Consequences?"; and Erica Frankenberg, "The Segregation of American Teachers," *Education Policy Analysis Archives* 17 (January 2008), accessed September 13, 2017, http://epaa.asu.edu/epaa/v17n1/.

24. Pflaum and Abramson, "Teacher Assignment," 21.

25. U.S. Census Bureau, Race (SE:T12), 1970. Prepared by Social Explorer, accessed September 26, 2017, https://www.socialexplorer.com/tables/RC1970/R12193272.

26. Steven Manson, Jonathan Schroeder, David Van Riper, and Steven Ruggles, *IPUMS National Historical Geographic Information System: Version 12.0* [Database] (Minneapolis: University of Minnesota, 2017), http://doi.org/10.18128/D050.V12.0. Prepared by John Fleming, August 4, 2017.

27. Collins, *"Ethnically Qualified,"* 106–7.

28. See Lewis, *New York City Public Schools,* 19.

29. Lewis, 57–59. Before decentralization, the UFT sought to consolidate its power by resisting central board authority over teachers' work; however, after 1969, the UFT preferred to situate control over key functions such as hiring within the central board. Albert Shanker, the UFT president, argued for this configuration to protect against the influence of patronage or racial, ethnic, or religious bias on hiring, and to ensure an "equitable distribution of teachers" among city schools; not incidentally, this arrangement also helped to preserve union power to bargain with a single entity rather than the local districts. The Community School Boards did gain one measure of flexibility through the law: they were permitted to hire candidates who passed the National Teacher Exam rather than the city's exams to teach in low-performing elementary and middle schools. See Collins, *"Ethnically Qualified,"* 121.

30. See Michael Rebell and A. R. Block, *Equity and Education: Federal Civil Rights Enforcement in the New York City School System* (Princeton, N.J.: Princeton University Press, 1985).

31. Jonna Perrillo, *Uncivil Rights: Teachers, Unions, and Race in the Battle for School Equity* (Chicago: University of Chicago Press, 2012), 160.

32. Perrillo, *Uncivil Rights,* 162.

33. Pflaum and Abramson, "Teacher Assignment," 29.

34. This tension is documented in research that promotes the importance of Black teachers for Black students as well as literature that advocates fairer distribution of teachers of

color. See J. A. Grissom and C. Redding, "Discretion and Disproportionality: Explaining the Underrepresentation of High Achieving Students of Color in Gifted Programs," *AERA Open* 2 (2016): 1–25; C. A. Lindsay and C. M. D. Hart, "Teacher Race and School Discipline: Are Students Suspended Less Often When They Have a Teacher of the Same Race?" *Education Next* 17 (2017): 1–6; as well as, for instance, Rebell and Block, *Equity and Education*, 1985.

35. Donna Tapper, *Swimming Upstream: The First-Year Experiences of Teachers Working in New York City Public Schools* (New York: Educational Priorities Panel, 1995), 1. The author argues that neither of those functions—getting teachers into hard-to-staff schools and ensuring teacher diversity—was served by the centralized system.

36. Collins, *"Ethnically Qualified,"* 121.

37. Tapper, *Swimming Upstream*, 1.

38. Tapper, 1.

39. Interview with Eulene Iniss, conducted by Terrenda White, March 20, 2015.

40. Barbara Wilson-Brooks, "Barbara Wilson-Brooks Oral History," conducted within the Harlem Education History Project, harlemeducationhistory.library.columbia.edu.

41. Louise Burwell, "Louise Burwell Oral History," conducted within the Harlem Education History Project, harlemeducationhistory.library.columbia.edu.

42. Burwell, "Louise Burwell Oral History."

43. Pflaum and Abramson, "Teacher Assignment," 26.

44. Donald Boyd, Hamilton Lankford, Susanna Loeb, Jonah Rockoff, and James Wyckoff, "The Narrowing Gap in New York City Teacher Qualifications and Its Implications for Student Achievement in High-Poverty Schools," *Journal of Policy Analysis and Management* 27 (2008): 793.

45. Collins, *"Ethnically Qualified,"* 135.

46. Leonard Buder, "Schools See Hope for District Five," *New York Times*, December 26, 1974.

47. Lewis, *New York City Public Schools*, 74.

48. USNY, *Racial/Ethnic Distribution of Public School Students and Staff, 1976–1977* (Albany, N.Y.: State Education Department Information Center on Education, 1977); USNY, *Racial/Ethnic Distribution of Public School Students and Staff, 1978–1979* (Albany, N.Y.: State Education Department Information Center on Education, 1979); USNY, *Racial/Ethnic Distribution of Public School Students and Staff, 1979–1980* (Albany, N.Y.: State Education Department Information Center on Education, 1980); and USNY, *Racial/Ethnic Distribution of Public School Students and Staff, 1980–1981* (Albany, N.Y.: State Education Department Information Center on Education, 1981).

49. "School War Holdout," *New York Times* editorial, November 21, 1978.

50. Leonard Buder, "4 Teachers Return to Jobs Despite Parents' Protests," *New York Times*, October 18, 1974.

51. Leonard Buder, "Parent Protest in Harlem Keeps 1,000 Out of School," *New York Times*, October 19, 1974.

52. Lena Williams, "Harlem School Boycott Threatened," *New York Times*, October 13, 1976.

53. Joyce Purnick, "City's Poor Districts Are Hit Hard by a Severe Shortage of Teachers," *New York Times*, February 29, 1984.

54. NYCIBO, Office Public School Teacher Data, provided by Ray Domanico upon request, September 22, 2016.

55. NYCIBO, School Indicators for New York City Charter Schools, 2013–14 School Year, New York, July 2015, 6, accessed June 12, 2019, https://ibo.nyc.ny.us/iboreports

/school-indicators-for-new-york-city-charter-schools-2013-2014-school-year-july
-2015.pdf.

56. NYCIBO, Office Public School Teacher Data.

57. NYCIBO, "Demographics and Work Experience: A Statistical Portrait of New York
    City's Public School Teachers," *Schools Brief* (May 2014): 3–4.

58. Albert Shanker Institute, *State of Teacher Diversity*, 2. These data refer to the combined
    sectors of charter and district school teachers.

59. Nicholas Michelli, "The Politics of Teacher Education: Lessons from New York City,"
    Journal of Teacher Education 56 (May/June 2005): 236.

60. Michelli, "Politics of Teacher Education," 237.

61. New York State Department of Education, "Basic Educational Data System (BEDS)
    Personnel Master File (PMF) Statistical Runs," generated by Lauren Fellers, using
    PMF Standard Statistical Runs, 2001–2016, accessed January 24, 2017, http://www.p12
    .nysed.gov/irs/pmf/.

62. Boyd et al., "Narrowing Gap," 815.

63. Teach For America (started in 1989) and the New York City Teaching Fellows
    (started in 2000) are alternate route programs that sought to place graduates of elite
    institutions of higher education (Teach For America) or professionals from other
    fields (New York City Teaching Fellows) into classrooms quickly, circumventing the
    traditional certification process.

64. NYCIBO, Public School Teacher Data.

65. National Center for Education Statistics, Characteristics of Public and Private Elemen-
    tary and Secondary School Teachers in the United States: Results From the 2011–12
    Schools and Staffing Survey, 2013, accessed June 12, 2019, https://nces.ed.gov/pubs2013
    /2013314.pdf.

66. Center for Research on Education Outcomes, *Charter School Growth and Replication*,
    2013, accessed September 16, 2014, https://credo.stanford.edu/research-reports.html; E.
    Frankenberg, G. Siegel-Hawley, and J. Wang, *Choice Without Equity: Charter School Seg-
    regation and the Need for Civil Rights Standards* (Los Angeles: Civil Rights Project/
    Proyecto Derechos Civiles, 2010).

67. Albert Shanker Institute, *State of Teacher Diversity*.

68. Albert Shanker Institute.

69. Collins, *"Ethnically Qualified,"* 179.

70. Freeman A. Hrabowski III and Mavis G. Sanders, "Increasing Racial Diversity in the
    Teacher Workforce: One University's Approach," *Thought and Action* (Winter 2015):
    101–16.

71. Collins, *"Ethnically Qualified,"* 178. See also David E. Lavin and David Hyllegard,
    Changing the Odds: Open Admissions and the Life Chances of the Disadvantaged (New Ha-
    ven, Conn.: Yale University Press, 1996); and Michael Fabricant and Stephen Brier,
    Austerity Blues: Fighting for the Soul of Public Higher Education (Baltimore: Johns Hopkins
    University Press, 2016).

72. Richard Ingersoll and H. May, "Recruitment, Retention and the Minority Teacher
    Shortage," *Consortium for Policy Research in Education*, CPRE Research Report #RR-
    69, 2011; Desiree Carver-Thomas and Linda Darling-Hammond, *Teacher Turnover:
    Why It Matters and What We Can Do About It* (Palo Alto, Calif.: Learning Policy In-
    stitute, 2017), 20–23; and Albert Shanker Institute, *State of Teacher Diversity*.

73. Albert Shanker Institute, *State of Teacher Diversity*, 2.

74. Carver-Thomas and Darling-Hammond, "Recruitment," 23.

75. NYCIBO, Public School Teacher Data.

76. Of the forty-five charter schools in Manhattan in 2013–14, thirty were located in the Harlem neighborhood (including CSDs 3, 4, and 5). NYCIBO, School Indicators, 38
77. Albert Shanker Institute, *State of Teacher Diversity*.
78. Terrenda Corisa White, "Culture, Power, and Pedagogy in Market-Driven Times: Embedded Case Studies of Teaching in Four Charter Schools in Harlem, NY" (PhD Diss., Columbia University, 2014).
79. These teachers' names as well as those of all subsequent teachers who describe their experiences in Harlem's charter sector are pseudonyms.
80. Interview with Marvin Humphrey, conducted by Terrenda White, January 9, 2013.
81. New York City Charter School Center, *Charter School Facts 2012–13*, New York Department of Education, 2012, accessed February 28, 2019, http://www.nyccharterschools .org/sites/default/files/resources/charter_school_facts_082912.pdf.
82. NYC Charter School Center, *The State of the Charter Sector* (New York: NYC Department of Education, 2012), accessed February 28, 2019, http://www.nyccharterschools .org/sites/default/files/resources/state-of-the-sector-2012.pdf.
83. NYCIBO, School Indicators, 38.
84. Center for Research on Education Outcomes, *Charter School Growth and Replication* (Stanford, Calif.: CREDO, 2013), accessed September 16, 2014, https://credo.stanford .edu/research-reports.html.
85. Albert Shanker Institute, *State of Teacher Diversity*, 19.
86. J. Golann, "The Paradox of Success at a No-Excuses School," *Sociology of Education* 88 (2015): 103–19; M. Q. McShane and J. Hatfield, "Measuring Diversity in Charter School Offerings," July 2015, American Enterprise Institute, accessed July 28, 2015, http://www.aei.org/wp-content/uploads/2015/07/Measuring-Diversity-in-Charter -School-Offerings.pdf.
87. Interview with Shawn Lewis, conducted by Terrenda White, July 26 2013.
88. Interview with Shawn Lewis.
89. New York State Education Department, New York School Report Card, 2015–16, Success Academy Charter School Harlem 2, accessed June 12, 2019, https://data.nysed .gov/reportcard.php?instid=800000061092&year=2016&createreport=1&teacherqual =1&teacherturnover=1; Success Academy Charter School Harlem 4, accessed June 12, 2019, https://data.nysed.gov/reportcard.php?instid=800000061093&year=2016&create report=1&teacherqual=1&teacherturnover=1; Success Academy Charter School Harlem 5, accessed June 12, 2019, https://data.nysed.gov/reportcard.php?instid =800000067671&year=2016&createreport=1&teacherqual=1&teacherturnover=1.
90. Interview with Theresa Sanders, conducted by Terrenda White, July 26, 2013.
91. For example, based on the data about KIPP charter schools and their revenue, we estimate that per pupil expenditure in Harlem's CMO schools was nearly $23,000, about 30 percent more than district per pupil funding in 2013.
92. Interview with Shawn Lewis.
93. Interview with Anthony Charles, conducted by Terrenda White, January 10, 2013.
94. Interview with Anthony Charles.
95. Interview with Anthony Charles.
96. Benjamin Fine, "New Policy Asked on Teacher Posts," *New York Times*, December 6, 1956.
97. Public Education Association, *The Status of the Public School Education of Negro and Puerto Rican Children in the City* (New York: Public Education Association of New York City, October 1955); and Perillo, *Uncivil Rights*, 86.
98. Kenneth Clark, *Dark Ghetto: Dilemmas of Social Power* (New York: Harper and Row, 1965), 138.

99. Collins, *"Ethnically Qualified,"* 98, 124; and Resolution by District 5, n.d. after June 1968, United Federation of Teachers–Subject, box 17, F476, cited in Collins, 124.

100. Joseph Berger, "Pessimism in Air as Schools Try Affirmative Action," *New York Times*, February 27, 1990; and Joseph Berger, "McCall Will Push for More Minority Teachers," *New York Times*, June 28, 1991.

101. Berger, "Pessimism in Air."

Conclusion

ERNEST MORRELL AND ANSLEY T. ERICKSON

Across our thirteen chapters, we recount the persistent dignified struggle of familiar and new actors in Harlem's educational landscape, in the face of relentless structural opposition.

Just as the struggle to learn and to teach has been a feature of four hundred years of African diasporic history in North America, educational activism has been consistently present since African Americans and Afro-Caribbeans first migrated to Harlem in the twentieth century. Daniel Perlstein puts Black educators at the center of New Negro intellectual life as he situates Gertrude Ayer and Mildred Johnson's Black progressive educational visions and practice in the New Negro understandings of race, education, and modern life expressed in celebrated literary works that helped define the Harlem Renaissance. Thomas Harbison contends that during the Great Depression, parents and community members in Harlem vocally opposed a restrictive curriculum that administrators thought appropriate for the growing presence of Black southern and West Indian students in the 1920s and 1930s, arguing it was yet another form of discrimination and injustice. Lisa Rabin and Craig Kridel place the Teachers Union's Harlem Committee at the center of a critical media pedagogy that used film in high school classrooms to promote dialogue around issues of race and justice.

Jonna Perrillo reveals a lesser-known side of the poet Langston Hughes: as an author of African and African American history texts for children. Clarence Taylor engages parents and community members who were willing

[328]

to take on the Teachers Union when they felt there was more concern being given to job security than to the pedagogical needs of their children. Ansley Erickson explores an early 1960s program, initiated by Kenneth Clark and his colleagues, in which Harlem youth ages fourteen to twenty-one became researchers and agents of change in their community. Russell Rickford explores the many ways that activists attempted to translate Black Power into subversive and transformational educational practices in formal and alternative autonomous educational spaces. Nick Juravich explicates the dignity and agency of local mothers who served as paraprofessionals in the Harlem schools bringing literacy and culturally responsive curriculum into the schools that served their children. Kim Phillips-Fein and Esther Cyna encounter the determination of local residents to combat the inhumane austerity measures that the city meted out during its infamous fiscal crisis in the early 1970s. Brittney Lewer shares the work of Babette Edwards, an early advocate for vouchers and ultimately charter schools in Harlem.

It becomes difficult to say anything collective about these efforts. They involved diverse actors with different viewpoints over different eras with different degrees of success, defined in various ways. What unites them is their persistence, their unabashed agency in the face of often overwhelming odds, and their collective belief that the children of Harlem were worth more and deserved better from their schools, and from their city and country. The local human energy and intellect fervently devoted to improved educational opportunities for Harlem's school children over this eighty-year period simply cannot be overstated. Nor should it be overlooked. Contrary to the narrative of continued and persistent urban decline there have been key "victories" and successes throughout; ongoing struggle is a better frame for the relationship between oppressive structural contexts and collective local praxis for change.

We have endeavored to introduce new historical actors and to trace the ways that women, working-class people, and young people have been key figures in the fight for equitable schooling in Harlem. On the Harlem education stage we name as actors school administrators, artists, young people, church leaders, social workers, architects, librarians, mothers, union organizers, activists, Black Power leaders, university professors, and journalists, among others.

Our chapter authors bring to the forefront variations, tensions, and debates within advocacy movements across these eras. There is no single Harlem movement; no one approach to educational change. Our chapters repeatedly highlight the diversity within the "movement" in their conscious attempts to pluralize Black Harlem in the historical educational narrative. Rickford speaks to the divergences within the Black Power framework as he articulates that no single ideology shaped the terrain of alternative education in Harlem. Lewer shows conscientious Black public intellectuals on both sides of the voucher debate in the 1970s.

Despite this resistance, imperialist and structuralist-racist policies and practices persist at the peril of African American communities in Harlem. Oppression continues to grow and adapt in response to powerful community resistance. Kimberley Johnson illuminates the multiple forms of structural segregation in Harlem that precipitated the decline and closing of Wadleigh High School. Juravich presents the working-class women of color who choose the United Federation of Teachers—a victory—but not without hierarchy. Phillips-Fein and Cyna's analysis of the mid-1970s fiscal crisis reveals that as the city began to suffer financially it turned first and most violently to those who were most vulnerable. Harlem, they argue, faced more school closures than almost any other neighborhood in the city; Lewer situates Babette Edwards's transition to voucher advocacy in her disgust with an entrenched educational bureaucracy that increased her skepticism about the city's willingness and ability to serve Harlem's children through public schools. And Bethany L. Rogers and Terrenda C. White highlight the effects of a reconfigured Harlem educational landscape on teachers of color in Harlem, where the population fell from a high of 70 percent in 2000 to 45 percent in 2015. In each era we find this dialectical tension between local community agency and oppressive educational structures in an unequal city. This is the real story.

On Positions

Although sometimes scholars stand silently while letting their work speak for itself, there is a certain danger in positioning ourselves as invisible scribes without location or values or presence. We are acutely conscious of our positionalities as authors located in Harlem (if you extend the contested border to the west of Morningside Park), as scholars working under the banner of a privileged institution, which has been at times a quiet bystander, at times an unwelcome intervener, and at times a well-meaning, even dutiful partner in urban transformation—but always privileged. We are penning a historic narrative of schooling and resistance while in the employ of an institution that has sometimes been the cause or the object of resistance by the neighborhood we study and write about. We chose not to devote a chapter to Columbia's story because much of it falls outside of our focus on K–12 schooling, but we could not end this volume without acknowledging our presence and the presence of Columbia as an actor at key moments in the decades we do cover.

In 1968 the Student's Afro-American Society at Columbia University sided with Black residents in Harlem to prevent the university from building a gymnasium in Morningside Park. Stefan Bradley's *Harlem v. Columbia University* explores the role of Black Power ideology in fomenting resistance from within the university to the imperialist project of the institution. In this case the students exist as hybrid actors—part of the university and part of the community.[1] It is difficult to say that Columbia speaks with one mind at all times, but it is also clear that the administration stood firmly on the side of claiming the space of Harlem for its own use without reciprocation or collaboration with its neighbors east of Morningside Drive. These moments are not forgotten by a community whose view of campus is generally from the outside, through iron fences and security gates as well as barriers of cost and procedure. And even when not fighting over land, where has Columbia stood when the residents of Harlem have risen up against the city and the city's school system? Do Columbia's frequent silences speak of complicity or merely indifference? Is there a real distinction between the two? What legitimate access have Harlem's grade school and secondary students had to the academic arsenal of the university? What landmark scholarship has been focused on transforming the educational conditions of Harlem's schools? And how can the largest (and some say the best) college of education in the world have, as its backyard, a school system that frequently disappoints its residents? This was not the terrain of our book, and we may not be the scholars to write it. But we hope that the full scope of the university's relationship to Harlem and its schools will gain the robust investigation it deserves.

Columbia has also existed as an economic engine, as a developer of land and an architectural force across the decades. LaDale Winling explores the role of Columbia University along with many of its Ivy League partners in generating growth and development during the mid-twentieth century.[2] Winling identifies the tensions that frequently existed with local grassroots organizations when universities that were often flush with federal money imposed their will on communities for good and ill. This was not at all a zero-sum game. Winling argues that university expansion and the production of knowledge often occurred at the expense of local neighbors in communities such as Harlem. Similarly, Michael Carriere argues that the well-meaning post–World War II expansion and redevelopment initiatives of campuses such as Columbia often employed war metaphors (i.e., war on blight) and positioned the university as "liberating" the surrounding community and, at the same time, local citizens felt themselves to be combating colonial expansion.[3]

Future Work

There is more work to do. The silences or absences within or between our chapters point to work that later scholars can and should take up.

We do not directly address the role of churches in activism and organizing, parent action in earlier periods, or questions about space (beyond Gutman's account of IS 201). Beyond The Modern School discussed in chapter 1, not much in our volume deals with the role of Catholic or other nonpublic schools in early and mid-twentieth-century Harlem. We lack a larger discussion of the material conditions of Harlem, primarily its persistent poverty. Although their roots in local educational activism are explored in chapter 12, we have not offered a full accounting of charter schools, especially Harlem-based influential models such as the Harlem Children's Zone, which is now well into its third decade.

Our volume does not wrestle with gentrification as a real estate development endeavor and manifestation of racial capitalism as well as a set of demographic and cultural shifts. Future historians will need to address this, especially in considering how the fragmentation of the Harlem educational landscape into schools of choice—and then into schools of choice under public and private management—may have been intertwined with gentrification.

Although we emphasize the presence of women and women's leadership, much is left to do to understand the way that gender mattered. This is a potentially fruitful line of inquiry not only for educational activism but also for the experience of schooling in Harlem for Black and Latinx communities. How did schooling relate to or become part of the gendered policing of Black and brown students in public space? How did the gendered realities of the carceral and social welfare states shape student and school experience? In the century after Mildred Johnson, Babette Edwards, and Gertrude Ayer pioneered Black women's school leadership, how does gender figure in the leadership of schools in a changing Harlem?

We recognize a need to stitch the story of schooling into the story of mass incarceration in the United States, especially in a highly policed area such as Harlem, which was one geographic center of the drug trade as well.[4] This volume intentionally focuses on formal schooling, but rich opportunities remain for the study of educational spaces outside of school. Rickford's exploration of alternative and community education efforts and Erickson's investigation of HARYOU point to some examples of spaces that could be examined, but much more needs to be done. Part of rooting out still-dominant deficit perspectives of Black and Latinx communities involves recognizing the presence of learning in many community locations, not only in schools.

In the late twentieth and early twenty-first centuries, immigration helped change Harlem, in particular with the arrival of growing West African communities. We need more scholarship on the experience of these communities with schooling and the interactions between different diasporic communities in Harlem's school hallways and classrooms. We need to know much more about Harlem's educational movements in the 1980s and 1990s in general. This includes a robust historical analysis of the early years of the Harlem Children's Zone and the early days of the charter school movement in Harlem. We call, in general, for *more* nondeficit stories. We need more gender-focused accounts. We need more narratives told from the so-called margins. We need more research that strives to locate and explicate moments of persistence, resistance, and occasional triumphs, not just decline. We need more Harlem-focused scholarship that explores the myriad ways that the city's educational and political-economic structures counteract organized community action.

And surely the educational moments that we do study will merit further research in the future. In this book, we have different—not contradictory, but different—takes on Intermediate School (IS) 201. Rickford and Lewer each emphasize the quest for autonomy in decision making and the disappointments of not receiving it fully. By contrast, Marta Gutman recognizes these limits but wants to shine light on what was accomplished by the school's leadership—as professionals, in their commitment to Black history, and affirming pedagogy. IS 201 is thus a reminder that multiple stories often come out of the same sites and moments, and that scholarship evolves and grows over time.

Michel-Rolph Trouillot examines the silences of the archives and their influence on the production, the making of history.[5] We simply cannot study what just is not there. Part of the work of future historians of urban education in the twentieth century entails cultivating and curating the archives we need to better ensure the telling of the narratives that need to be told. In the ongoing Harlem Education History Project at Teachers College, we have been involved in efforts to make digital copies of yearbooks, photos, and artifacts of resistance and to record oral histories that capture the everyday lives of students and their families.[6] The technologies exist for us to archive the words of the actual participants in Harlem's educational life, and a greater effort needs to be made to preserve the educational experiences of students, paraprofessionals, teachers, principals, parents, and community advocates. There is no good reason for these voices to be absent in our historical conversations. In her major work of literary criticism, Toni Morrison discusses the missing Africanist presence in American literary theory.[7] She defines her critical task as one of presencing, of revelation. We see a parallel role for the community of urban educational historians.

Beyond History

Bob Marley claims that "If you know your history, then you would know where you coming from."[8] Why do the educators, school leaders, and policy makers of the present need to seriously regard the educational history of Harlem? What can be learned from a close examination of the past? We began this work in hopes that we would speak to historians and nonhistorians alike. We conclude our joint work with a few points of consideration.

Critical historical work should challenge us to renarrativize the past as we act in the present. History is a contested terrain and, as contemporary educators, we need to tell ourselves more robust, divergent, and complicated stories about how communities have responded to educational conditions in the past. In her 2009 TED Talk, the Nigerian novelist Chimamanda Ngozi Adichie warns of the danger of a single story.[9] She cautions that the danger of stereotypes is not that they are untrue, but that they are incomplete. She speaks most directly of fiction, but the same can be said for historical narratives. Easy understandings of how communities and schools work need to be challenged. Narratives of perpetual decline need to be consistently challenged. Narratives that ignore agency and resistance need to be challenged. Narratives that silence need to be challenged. And narratives about what schooling is and what schooling means need to be made more complicated and more nuanced. The idea that Harlem is like every other urban neighborhood or that there is a single, simple story of urban education needs to be challenged. Good work should broaden our perspective. It should force us off the simple story. It should increase our appetite for more information about the peculiarities of contexts. It should encourage us to look for tensions, contradictions, and counterdiscourses. Mostly, though, we should feel urged to contemplate more humane and humanizing narratives of our predecessors. We hope to have given a human face (or faces) to education, resistance, and persistence in Harlem. We also hope that our readers who work within educational systems feel license to end the "tinkering toward utopia" that has been so much school reform over the last century.[10] Bold moves to dismantle systemic oppression in constant dialogue with local stakeholders is the only conscionable way forward.

Collectively we need a more robust understanding of the sacrifices that parents and families make for their children and their fundamental beliefs and hopes in education to forge different futures. Urban educational history helps to disrupt the myths that parents and communities do not care about the education of their children. As Harbison shows, families risked everything to leave the South in search of an increase in educational opportunity, among other things. From their arrival in the early decades of the twentieth century, these families never stopped advocating despite the sometimes overwhelming odds against them. The persistence and the boldness of their hope remain undertold in traditional historical narratives of urban schooling; but we need to call out that hope when and where we see it in the present and we need to link to this past.

In his work Ernest Morrell has seen the powerful effect of introducing contemporary youth advocates to the youth cultural workers of the past.[11] In many ways the work of HARYOU is a precursor to recent movements such as Youth Participatory Action Research (YPAR), and the proponents of YPAR would do well to engage the story of HARYOU.

The field needs a better understanding of the ways that teachers have advocated inside and outside of classrooms in curricular interventions such as the Human Relations Film Series and the organizing efforts of the Harlem Committee. As we write these words, teachers are striking all across the country in search of better lives for themselves and the students they serve. Morrell and Jeff Duncan-Andrade have identified that increasing numbers of educators in city schools are turning to critical pedagogy and culturally responsive teaching to create humane learning spaces where children are affirmed in local cultural identities while they develop academic competencies.[12] Harlem's teacher leaders as well as the visions Harlem parents pushed them toward offer inspiration in these efforts.

Future scholarship must recognize the agency and solicit the voices of everyday workers from nondominant communities, particularly from Black youth and women. One common task is to educate ourselves on the contributions of the frequently marginalized, and to be humbled and bolstered by the persistence of the struggle for educational justice. Finally, we need to remain vigilant in documenting the long trail of undeniable and intentional neglect from a pervasive inequitable system. As the HARYOU authors put it in 1964, "Given a history of criminal educational neglect, the children of Harlem deserve no less than the highest level of education that human intelligence can devise."[13] As constant as the boldness and spirit of the Harlemites past and present are, so too is the constancy of neglect, obfuscation, and subterfuge and the denial of basic rights. The structures remain and so the work must continue, and as long as the injustices persist, so must we.

Notes

1. Stefan M. Bradley, *Harlem v. Columbia University: Black Student Power in the Late 1960s* (Urbana: University of Illinois Press, 2009).
2. LaDale C. Winling, *Building the Ivory Tower: Universities and Metropolitan Development in the Twentieth Century* (Philadelphia: University of Pennsylvania Press, 2017), 103–6.
3. Micheal Carriere, "Fighting the War Against Blight: Columbia University, Morningside Heights, Inc., and Counterinsurgent Urban Renewal," *Journal of Urban Planning* 10, no. 1 (2011): 5–29.
4. Although released too late for full incorportaion into this volume, Carl Suddler's *Presumed Criminal: Black Youth and the Justice System in Post-War New York* (New York: New York University Press, 2019) provides an important step in this direction.
5. Michel-Rolph Trouillot, *Silencing the Past: Power and the Production of History* (Boston: Beacon Press, 2015).
6. Harlem Education History Project at Teachers College, harlemeducationhistory.library.columbia.edu.
7. Toni Morrison, *Playing in the Dark: Whiteness and the Literary Imagination* (New York: Vintage, 1993), 3–14.

8. "Buffalo Soldiers," by Bob Marley and Noel "King Sporty" Williams, recorded by Bob Marley and the Wailers, track 2 on *Confrontation*, Island Records, 1983.

9. Chimamanda Ngozi Adichie, "The Danger of a Single Story," filmed July 2009 in Oxford, TED video, 18:43, https://www.ted.com/talks/chimamanda_adichie_the _danger_of_a_single_story.

10. David Tyack and Larry Cuban, *Tinkering Toward Utopia: A Century of Public School Reform* (Cambridge, Mass.: Harvard University Press, 1995).

11. Ernest Morrell, *Critical Literacy and Urban Youth: Pedagogies of Access, Dissent, and Liberation* (New York: Routledge, 2008).

12. Jeff Duncan-Andrade and Ernest Morrell, *The Art of Critical Pedagogy: Moving from Theory to Practice in Urban Schools* (New York: Peter Lang, 2008).

13. HARYOU, *Youth in the Ghetto: A Study of the Consequences of Powerlessness and a Blueprint for Change* (New York: HARYOU, 1964), 423.

Contributors

ESTHER CYNA is a PhD candidate in the Program in History and Education at Teachers College, Columbia University. Her research examines the recent history of school finance reform in North Carolina.

ANSLEY T. ERICKSON is an associate professor of history and education at Teachers College, Columbia University, codirector of the Harlem Education History Project, and a former public school teacher in Harlem. She is the author of *Making the Unequal Metropolis: School Desegregation and Its Limits* (University of Chicago Press, 2016).

MARTA GUTMAN is an architectural and urban historian who has written extensively about public architecture for city children. Her new book, *Just Space: Architecture, Education, and Inequality in Postwar Urban America* (University of Texas Press, forthcoming), developed from her research for this book.

THOMAS HARBISON is an instructional designer and multimedia specialist at the Borough of Manhattan Community College (City University of New York). He also serves as managing editor of the *Radical History Review*, a journal published three times a year by Duke University Press.

KIMBERLEY JOHNSON is a professor of social and cultural analysis at New York University. She studies the intersections of race, space, politics, and policy in cities and, more broadly, the United States. She is the author of numerous publications including two books.

NICK JURAVICH is an assistant professor of public history and labor history at the University of Massachusetts Boston. His first book is *The Work of Education: Community-Based Educators in Schools, Communities, and the Labor Movement* (University of Illinois Press, forthcoming).

CRAIG KRIDEL is the E. S. Gambrell Professor Emeritus of Educational Studies and Curator Emeritus of the Museum of Education at the University of South Carolina. His current research focuses on education during the Jim Crow era, and he has recently self-published *Becoming an African American Progressive Educator: Narratives from 1940s Black Progressive High Schools.*

BRITTNEY LEWER is a doctoral candidate in the History of Education Program at New York University, currently writing a dissertation about parents' activism in New York City after 1970. In addition to research in urban history, she is devoted to supporting meaningful history education in high schools and colleges.

ERNEST MORRELL is the Coyle Professor of Literacy Education and Director of the Center for Literacy Education at the University of Notre Dame. He was formerly the Macy Professor of English Education and director of the Institute for Urban and Minority Education at Teachers College, Columbia University.

DANIEL PERLSTEIN is a historian and chair of the Critical Studies of Race, Class, and Gender Program at the University of California-Berkeley's Graduate School of Education. His writings explore schooling and popular culture, teacher unionism, and the educational ideals and activities of the African American freedom struggle.

JONNA PERRILLO is an education historian and associate professor of English education at the University of Texas at El Paso. She is the author of *Uncivil Rights: Teachers, Unions, and Race in the Battle for School Equity* (University of Chicago, 2012) and is currently completing a manuscript on the history of immigration and education inequality in borderland schools.

KIM PHILLIPS-FEIN is an associate professor in the Gallatin School of Individualized Study and the History Department of the College of Arts and Sciences at New York University. She is the author of *Fear City: New York's Fiscal Crisis and the Rise of Austerity Politics* (Metropolitan Books, 2017) and *Invisible Hands: The Businessmen's Crusade Against the New Deal* (W. W. Norton, 2009).

LISA RABIN is an associate professor of Spanish at George Mason University, where she teaches film and media studies in Spanish. Her research on historical film audiences has been published in *Illuminace: Journal for Film Theory, History, and Aesthetics, The Velvet Light Trap,* and *Film History: An International Journal.*

RUSSELL RICKFORD, an associate professor of history at Cornell University, specializes in African American political culture after World War II, with a focus on Black Power, transnationalism, and the Black Radical Tradition. His recent book, *We Are an African People: Independent Education, Black Power, and the Radical Imagination* (Oxford University Press, 2016), examines the African American movement to create autonomous, Pan Africanist educational institutions in the 1960s and 1970s, and he teaches and writes in both scholarly and popular contexts about African American philosophies of education, citizenship, and social belonging in transnational contexts.

BETHANY L. ROGERS is an associate professor at the College of Staten Island, City University of New York (CUNY), in the educational studies department; she holds an appointment at the CUNY Graduate Center in the doctoral program in urban education; and she currently serves as a state director for the Teaching Fellowships Program at the Woodrow Wilson National Fellowship Foundation. As an education historian, her research focuses on the history of teachers, urban education, and school reform, and the connection of those histories to contemporary policy.

CLARENCE TAYLOR is professor emeritus of history at Baruch College, City University of New York. He is the author of multiple books on racism, religion, and civil rights in the twentieth-century United States including, most recently, *Fight the Power: African Americans and the Long History of Police Brutality in New York City* (New York University Press, 2018).

TERRENDA C. WHITE is an assistant professor of education foundations, policy, and practice at the University of Colorado Boulder. She is a former public school teacher, and she studies contemporary educational policies and their effects on racially diverse communities, including students and teachers of color.

Index

Abyssinian Baptist Church, 18, 88,
143–44, 166
activist mothering, 239
activists, 142, 155, 164, 167, 261, 329; and
African anti-colonial movements,
129; Black history campaigns of, 3;
and Board of Education mock trial,
143; and boycotts, 3, 184, 222;
children as, 4; and civil rights, 187;
and Cold War, 20; and community
change, 203; and community
control, 222, 307; and Harlem Nine,
281; and Harlem Renaissance, 33, 49;
and higher education, 5; and
integration, 95, 141; and IS 201, 188;
and liberation consciousness, 212,
219; at Mount Addis Ababa, 227; and
paraprofessionals, 246, 252; parents
as, 171, 219; and pedagogy, 211; and
racism, 34; and school-building
conditions, 153; and school vouchers,
285; and segregation, 91–93, 148;
students as, 4, 107; and teachers as, 17,

104, 141, 154, 298; and teacher
training, 3; and tracking, 84, 85; and
varied ideologies of, 4, 61; and women
as, 4, 9. *See also* Edwards, Babette
Adler, Felix, 45
adolescents, 7, 169, 171
Africa, 128
African American. *See* Black people;
West Indian immigrants
African American freedom movement,
211
African American history. *See* Black
history
African Bazaar, 213
African-Hispanic History and Cultural
Institute, 223
African history. *See* Black history
African Jazz Art Society, 213
African resistance, 128
Afro Arts Cultural Center, 228
All Souls Church, 195
alternative education, 211, 222
American Federation of Labor, 149

American Indian, 119
American Institute of Architects, 194, 196
American Museum of Natural History, 203
Amsterdam News, 64, 67, 244, 263, 264, 270, 281; and Gertrude Ayer, 42; and progressive education, 42
Andrews, Derek, 315
Anker, Irving, 271
anticolonialism, 212
anti-imperialists, 216
antipoverty programs, 234
Antonetty, Evelina, 199
Arabic, 215
architects, 183, 186, 188, 190, 193–95, 198; African American, 190, 203; and cost of energy, concern for, 195; and Educational Facilities Laboratories (EFL), 192; and Harlem appreciation for, 196; and parent appreciation for, 196; radical, 203. *See also* Curtis and Davis
Architects Renewal Committee in Harlem (ARCH), 203
architecture, 4, 28, 187, 190, 201, 203; and activism, 222; and African style of, 196; and Educational Facilities Laboratories, 192; and European style of, 196; and modern style of, 28; Native American style of, 196; polarization caused by, 183, 186; and Wadleigh High School, 79. *See also* Curtis and Davis
architecture historian, 188
Architecture in the Neighborhoods, 203
architecture school, 192
Armstrong, Louis, 119
arts, the, 176, 201, 216, 290
Aspinal, Eddie Mrs., 66
Associated Community Teams, 167

Atlanta, 7
Atlanta Daily World, 41
Atlanta University, 42
Autobiography of an Ex-Colored Man, The, 35
autonomous development. *See* self-determination
Ayer, Gertrude: and Adam Clayton Powell Jr., 42; and administrative career of, 43; and Black humanity, 44; and Black women teachers, responsibility of, 44; and discrimination, 43; and double oppression of Black women, 43–44; and education of, 42; and family background of, 42; and Harlem Renaissance, celebration announcing, 42; Henry Street Settlement, 42; and James Baldwin, 31; married-women teacher ban, 43; and New Negro consciousness, 42; and New York Urban League (NUL), 43; and *People's Voice*, 42; and the *Pittsburgh Courier*, 31; and principalship, 43; and progressive education, 31, 32, 44; and teaching career of, 42; and Tuskegee, 43

Baker, Ella, 49, 142
Baker, Houston, Jr., 33
Balboa, 119
Baldwin, James, 2, 49, 139, 199, 201
Bambara, Toni Cade, 48
Baraka, Amiri, 178, 216
Beame, Abraham, 263
beatings, 18
Benjamin Franklin High School, 5, 245; and film in curriculum, 17, 105, 107, 109, 114
bilingual education, 199, 223, 249
biography, 128

Black, Derrick, 200

Black artists, 34

Black Arts, 10, 217

Black Arts Theatre/School (BARTS), 178, 216, 217

Black consciousness, 211, 217

Black doctors, 263

Black history, 14, 104, 125, 175, 177, 201, 214, 217, 228, 300; absence of teaching, 17, 18, 174, 216; activist campaigns for, 2, 3, 186; and African independence, 128; and African resistance, 128; benefit to other ethnicities, 147; and early African civilization, 128; and Ethiopian society, 128; *The First Book of Negroes*, 122; and Harlem Committee teaching of, 109, 112; and HARYOU teaching of, 165, 171, 174; and IS 201 teaching of, 199; and Modern School teaching of, 48; and Nation of Islam teaching of, 215; and roots of teaching, 4; and teachers study of, 148; and teaching of, 128, 216, 240; and youth-led teaching of, 170

Black intellectuals, 34; and Ethical Culture School, 45

Black nationalism: Audley "Queen Mother" Moore, 226; and Black Arts Repertory Theatre/School (BARTS), 216; and Congress of Racial Equality (CORE), 218; and education, 211, 213; and the Nation of Islam, 215; and and West Harlem Liberation School (WHLS), 220

Black Panther Party, 186, 217

Black people, 1, 2; and achievement, 119, 122; and development of Harlem, 1, 2; and the Diaspora, 120; and discrimination, 143; and Ethical Culture School, 45; and excellence,

48; and exploitation, 212; hostility against, 2; and identity, 34, 49, 226, 228; and National Memorial Bookstore, 214; and participation in U.S. life, 34, 50; reflected in curriculum, 3, 104, 133; and segregation, 26; soldiers, 2; and youth, 176, 179

Black population, 56

Black Power, 141, 200, 211, 217; and transforming education, 21, 211, 329

Black Solidarity Day, 266

Black studies, 199, 223

Black teachers: and Black students, proportion to, 148; and *Brown v. Board of Education,* 310; and charter schools, 210, 312, 314, 315; and Community School District 5, 304, 308–10, 311, 312, 313; and connectedness to community, 300; and culture of poverty concept, 139; and decentralization, 307, 309; discrimination against, 45, 67, 81, 139, 300–301, 319; and ghettoization of, 299; and Harlem, presence in, 312, 313, 318; and high expectations of, 300; and history of, 24, 299, 300; and integration, 100; and job losses, 301; and legislation, 312; and Manhattan, 12, 139, 298; and New York City, 304, 310–11; and the North, 301; and numbers of, 299, 300, 301–2, 313; and parent dissatisfaction with, 309; and parity with white teachers, 110; and pedagogy of, 36; and retention of, 307; as role models, 305; and school assignments of, 305; and the South, 301; and students of color, proportion to, 300, 304; teaching force, proportion in, 302–3; and

Black teachers (*continued*)
turnover of, 313; and twenty-first
century Harlem, 299, 318; and
underrepresentation of, 299; and
Wadleigh, 90
Bloomberg, Michael, 299
Blumenfield, Adrian, 194
Board of Education Commission on
Integration, 141
Bogart, Humphrey, 103
Bond, Max J., 203
Bontemps, Arna, 35
Boston Redevelopment Authority, 194
Brockington, Hannah, 290
Bronx, the, 19
Brooklyn, 7, 10, 188, 244, 264, 268, 307;
Canarsie, 308; and charter schools,
315; and deindustrialization, 18; and
Harlem Parents Union, 281
Brooklyn Eagle, 123
Brotherhood of Sleeping Car Porters,
144
Brownie's Book, The, 40
Brown v. Board of Education, 164; and
New York City, 71n1, 141, 149; and
Wadleigh, 78
Buder, Leonard, 195
Bulkley, William L., 57, 59
Bundy, McGeorge, 198
Burroughs, W. J. Mrs., 66
Bushwick High School, 41
Byrne, Margaret C., 90, 91, 93

Campbell, James E., 222
Canada, Geoffrey, 4
Cane, 35, 38, 39
capital, 2
Career Opportunities Program, 245
Carey, Hugh, 263
Carlo, Georgina, 245
Carmichael, Stokely, 186

Catholic schools. *See* parochial schools
Catskills, 227
Center for Urban Education, 199
Central Harlem, 5, 17, 77, 126, 289; and
demonstration district, 21
charter management organizations, 316.
See also charter schools
Charter School Act, 288
charter schools, 332; and Babette
Edwards, 277, 286, 288, 314, 329;
and Black teachers, 310, 315, 316;
charter management organizations
(CMOs), 316, 318; and closings of
district schools, 316; and collective
bargaining agreements, 288; and
community control, 299; and
community groups, 316; and
curriculums of, 315; and enthusiasm
for, 314; and funding of, 288, 291,
316; and George Pataki, 288; and
Harlem, large concentration of, 23,
291, 298, 310, 314, 315, 316, 333; and
Harlem Education Roundtable
Academy for Excellence in Education
(HEART) charter team, 291; and
Harlem Parent's Union, 288;
ideologies of, 287; and legislation,
288; and Manhattan, 315; and
market-based reform, 314; and media
coverage, 291; and origins of, 287;
and oversight of, 287; and rise of,
272, 288, 312; and school choice, 286;
and School District 5, 316; and
self-determination, 299; and student
performance, 291, 316; studies of,
315; and teacher quality, 319–20; and
teacher recruitment, 316; and
teachers of color, 312; and teacher
turnover, 316; and Teach For
America, 316; and unions, 316
Chicago, 194

"The Children Speak: Art from I.S. 201," 203
Christ, 128
citizenship, 128
Citron, Alice, 112, 147, 154
City University of New York, 264
civil rights, 128; and New York City, 71n8
civil rights history, 9
Clark, Kenneth, 4, 20, 55, 329; and Adam Clayton Powell Jr., 166–67; and *Brown v. Board of Education*, 171; and "culture of poverty," 163; and integration activism, 171; and segregation, 149
Clark, Mamie, 4
Clarke, John Henrik, 165, 175–76
class divisions, 19
Cogen, Charles, 148–49
Cold War, 19, 20, 186
Coleman, Charles, 161. *See also* HARYOU
Colonial Park, 5. *See also* Jackie Robinson Park
Commissioner's Plan for New York City, 1
Commission on Integration, 141, 149, 152
Committee on Delinquency, 146
communism, 4, 10, 121
Communist Party, 17, 86, 140, 154
community-based hiring, 234
community control, 3, 9, 224
Community Council on Housing, 173
community education, 211
Community Education Center, 223
community rights, 8
Community School Board 5, and Board of Education, 269, 270–71; and decentralization, 307, 309; and difficulties experienced by, 271,

307–8; and internal dynamics of, 304; and New York City fiscal crisis, 270; and school closings, 269
community school boards, 244, 272, 285, 304
compensatory education, 4
Congress of Racial Equality (CORE), 186, 219; and community control, 21; and new high school, 22
Cooper Junior High School (JHS), 120. *See also* James Fenimore Cooper Junior High School
correctional facilities, 194
Crisis, 40, 41
Crosswaith, Frank, 61, 144
Crowder, Lillie, 190, 196
Cruse, Harold, 216
Cuban Missile Crisis, 193
Cullen, Countee, 41, 49, 65, 68, 123
Cultural Fair, 193
culture of poverty, 6, 139, 163, 236, 239
Cummings, Blondell, 201
CUNY. *See* City University of New York
curriculum, 14, 17, 222; and Black history, 240; and Black students, 64; and educational advocates, 17; and immigrant curriculum, 15, 57; and migrant curriculum, 15, 57; Schomburg Complex innovations with, 223; and tracking, 84; using film in, 104
Curtis, Nathaniel, 186. *See also* Curtis and Davis
Curtis and Davis, 183–98; and best practices, 190; and IS 201 architecture, 188, 190, 194, 196, 201; and National AIA First Honor Award, 193; and unethical practices, 193
Cyna, Esther, 23, 308, 329

dance, 45, 46, 47, 123; and HARYOU, 165, 176, 177, 178; and IS 201, 203, 223

Darby, Michael, 200

Davis, Anthony Q., 186. *See also* Curtis and Davis

Davis, Eloise, 244

Dead End, 103

deindustrialization, 6, 19, 246, 273n10

De Jongh, James, 33

demonstration districts, 198, 200, 224, 241

de Porres, Martin, 119

Depression, the. *See* Great Depression

DePriest, Oscar, 83

Detroit, 6, 11, 219, 273n10

Dewey, John, 33, 45

disinvestment. *See* divestment

District 5, 245, 262, 268, 306; and the *Amsterdam News*, 262–63; and Babette Edwards, 281, 285; and Black teachers, proportion of, 302–5, 308, 309; and the Board of Education, 270; and charter schools, 31; and community hiring, 306; and community population of, 304; and decentralization, 307; and geographic boundaries of, 299–300; and increase in teachers, 307; and loss of teachers, 266, 310–11; and Luther Seabrook, 285; and new teachers, proportion of, 312–13; and New York City fiscal crisis, 266, 270; and paraprofessionals, 245; and Parent-Teacher Teams (PTT), 239; and performance of, 320; and school closures, 257–59, 268; and teacher quality, 307, 308, 320; and teacher shortages, 309; and teachers of color, proportion of, 24; and teacher turnover, 316; and transformations, 314; and voucher program, 284

divestment, 6, 7, 18, 23, 173

Douglas, Ann, 33

Dowery, Mary, 203

drivers, 2

drugs, 19

Du Bois, W. E. B., 34, 37, 40, 41, 48, 49; and Booker T. Washington, 59; and celebration announcing Harlem Renaissance, 42

East Elmhurst, 19

Eastern District High School, 41

East Harlem, 4, 17; and demonstration district, 21

East Harlem Demonstration District, 222

East Harlem Triangle, 203

East Harlem Union for Equal Achievement, 188

economic exploitation, 2

economic revitalization, 2

education activists. *See* activists

educational bureaucracy, 7, 277, 314, 330

educational facilities: and Alice Kornegay, 191; condition of, 8, 66, 80, 85, 94, 143; and cutbacks, 23; and the Harlem Nine, 183; lack of sufficient, 1, 7, 8, 60, 66, 68, 69, 70, 149; and the South, 21, 186; and West Harlem Liberation School, 220

Educational Facilities Laboratory, 192, 203

educational struggle, 3, 4

educational success, 8, 81

Edwards, Babette, 190, 211, 222, 224; and charter schools, 289–90, 314; and community control, 24, 276; and David Spencer, 276; and Harlem Parents Union, 281; and housing, 277; IS 201, 281, 287; and Milton Galamison, 276; as reformer, 276;

and Stokely Carmichael, 276; and
support of vouchers, 329, 330
E. J. Kress, 64–65
Elementary and Secondary Education
Act, 249
Ellington, Duke, 122
Ellington, Ruth Dorothea, 83, 89
Ellison, Ralph, 32
El Museo del Barrio, 245
Eloise Moore College of African
Studies, 227
Emergency Financial Control Act, 270
employment discrimination, 2
Erickson, Ansley, 20, 329
Ethical Culture School: and Black
students, 41, 45; and Teacher
Training Program, 45. See also
Mildred Johnson
Ethiopian society, 128
European immigrants, 1
Evans, Ann Crary, 198, 199
Evans, Azalee, 240
Evans, Ronald, 198, 279

Faison, George, 177
Fauset, Jessie, 35, 41, 42, 49
federal policy makers, 4
Ferguson, Herman, 201
Fieldston School, 45. See also Mildred
Johnson
Figueroa, Mercedes, 245, 246
film studies, 4, 104, 112
Fire!!, 41
First Book of Negroes, The, 18, 119–20,
121–23, 124–34, 135n9. See also
Hughes, Langston
Fisk, 40
Florida, 119
Ford Foundation, 198. See also
demonstration districts
Fortune, Thomas T., 59

Frank, Waldo, 36, 38
Frazier, E. Franklin, 49, 66
Freedom Day, 184
freedom schools, 22, 23, 176, 216,
237, 241
Friends of Harlem CORE, 219
Frost, Robert, 62, 63

Galamison, Milton Rev., 184
Gallagher, Buell G., 149
Garvey, Marcus, 2, 42, 213. See also
Garveyites
Garveyites, 4. See also Garvey, Marcus
Gattegno approach, 199
gentrification, 2
Germany, 62
Girl Friends, 48
Girls' High School, 93
Gluck, Julius, 68–9
Goodman, Roy, 263
Graham, Mary C., 93
Grandassa fashion shows, 213
Granger, Lester, 144
Gray, Jesse, 173
Great Depression, 2, 8
Great Migrations, 2, 3, 77
Greenberg, Cheryl, 8
Gunning, Rosemary, 276, 285
Gurdjieff, George Ivanovich, 38, 39
Gutman, Marta, 21, 22, 120, 222, 333

Hall, James, C. 48
Handy, W. C., 119
Harbison, Thomas, 15, 43, 77, 123,
328, 335
Harlem: and Black people, 1; as Black
space, 2; and the Depression, 2; as
symbol, 2; and development of, 1,
7, 8; and diversity, 4; educational
influence of, 4; educational
innovation, 22; and educational

Harlem (*continued*)
struggle, 3, 4; effect of white
suburbanization, on, 2; and European
people, 1; and Jewish people, 1; as
mecca of New Negro, 14; population
of, 16; and protests, 2, 3, 7; and
rebellions in, 228; and shifting
boundaries, 5; and teacher training
for mothers, 3; and white people, 2;
and working-class people, 8
Harlem Education History Project,
334
Harlem Education Roundtable Academy
for Excellence in Education
(HEART), 289
Harlem History Club, 41
Harlem Hospital, 264
Harlem Hospital School of Nursing,
264
Harlem Merchants Association, 65
Harlem Nine, 281
Harlem Parents Charter School, 289;
activist support of, 290. *See also*
Edwards, Babette
Harlem Parents Union, 281, 289
Harlem Prep, 262
Harlem Renaissance, 2, 14, 31, 32, 34,
38, 41, 298; and Augusta Baker, 125;
and celebration announcing, 42;
and Countee Cullen, 123; and
historian interests, 13; and Langston
Hughes, 120, 123, 131; and literary
works, 328; and the Long Harlem
Renaissance, 49; and Mildred
Johnson, 44–45; and power of, 3;
and progressive education, 33, 36;
and radical organizing, 49. *See also*
Ayer, Gertrude; Cullen, Countee;
Du Bois, W. E. B.; Fauset, Jessie;
Hughes, Langston; Johnson, James
Weldon; Johnson, Mildred; Larsen,
Nella; Locke, Alain; New Negro
Movement
Harlem Repertory Theatre, 223
Harlem State Office Building, 211,
228
Harlem Youth Opportunities
Unlimited. *See* HARYOU
Harris, Jerome, 319
Harvard University, 42
HARYOU (Harlem Youth
Opportunities Unlimited), 161–79;
and Adam Clayton Powell Jr.,
166–67; and African American social
workers, 166; and the arts, 176–8;
and Associated Community Teams,
167; and audio recordings, 166,
168; and Black history, 165, 170, 174;
and Brenda McCoy, 178; and
community advancement, 165; and
community control, 21; and
curriculum, 165; and focus on
injustice, 165; and funding of, 161, 164,
167, 179n1; and Dunlevy-Milbank
Center, 174; and duration of, 166;
and George Faison, 177; and Harlem
Neighborhood Association, 168; and
HARYOU Associates, 162, 168, 169,
170–71; Heritage Program, 174;
Higher Horizons Program, 172; and
James Conant Bryant, 176; and John
Henrik Clarke, 165, 172–73, 174–76;
and Kenneth Clark, 20, 161, 162, 163,
166, 168, 171–72, 173, 178; and
Kenneth Marshall, 176, 178; and Larry
Houston, 172; and Laura Pires, 172;
Leadership Training Workshop, 165,
171, 173, 174; and Livingston Wingate,
176; and Malcolm X, 171, 172; and
Mildred Bond, 172; and nurturing,
168, 179; offices at Harlem YMCA,
161, 168; and parents, 171; and political

controversy, 22; and Ronald Drayton, 174–75; and Saltus and Coleman, 161, 162, 163, 164, 166, 165, 168, 178; and research, 168; and Sherron Jackson, 172, 178; and social sciences, 166; and St. Philip's Church, 174; and student ethnographic fieldwork, 168–69; and student roles, 21; and Summer programs, 176; and War on Poverty, 178; and women, 165; and youth experts, 20–21; and youth program development, 163–64, 170–71; and youth research participation, 163–64, 165, 169, 170–71

Haskins, Jim, 195

Hennessey, John F., 194

Hercules, Dellora, 199

heroin, 19. *See also* drugs

Higginbotham, Evelyn Brooks, 33

higher education, 5

high schools, 78; academic, 138; architecture of, 79; and Black boys, 84, 189; and building of, 22, 203; and Countee Cullen, 41; and educational justice, 17; enrollment in, 94; as flagship for Black people, 83; and Gertrude Ayer, 42; and Jessie Fauset, 41; and Leora King, 48; and Nella Larsen, 40; and philanthropists, 262; and specialized, 138, 199, 269; and State Office Building protests, 22, 225–26; and status of attending, 7; and teacher cutbacks, 308; vocational, 69; Wadleigh, 14, 16, 77–95; and zoning of, 83, 84, 93

Hill, Velma Murphy, 246

Hispanic, 200. *See also* Latinx people; Puerto Rican people

historians, 4; and foci of study, 6

Hollis, 19

Hollywood, 104

Horowitz, Irving Louis, 79

housing, 8, 12, 14, 65; and Babette Edwards, 277; and discrimination, 2, 61; and Leadership Training Workshop, 171, 177–78; and Metropolitan Life, 16; and public housing, 103, 163, 245; and school zones, 12; and segregation, 12, 16, 78, 110, 113, 141; struggles for, 2, 11, 60, 107; substandard, 11, 20, 93, 94, 107, 145, 147

Houston, Charles Hamilton, 144

Howard University Law School, 144

Huggins, Nathan, 32, 49, 80

Huggins, Willis, 41

Hughes, Langston, 17, 41, 199; as author of children's history texts, 18, 328

Hult, Eugene F., 192

humanity, 2, 14, 34

Human Relations Film Series, 104

Humphrey, Marvin, 315

Hurston, Zora Neale, 38, 199

Hutchinson, George, 33, 39, 40

Imes, William Lloyd, Mrs., 91

immigrants: from Anglophone Caribbean, 5; Afro-Caribbean, 56; European, 6, 57, 283; and Nella Larsen, 40; West Indian, 2, 57, 77

Innis, Eulene, 306

integration, 80, 81, 82, 93, 152, 261; and Albert Shanker, 248; and debates regarding, 78, 84; and HARYOU, 172; and IS 201, 183, 184, 210; and parents, 187; and Queens, 276, 285; and report on, 320n1; and the Teachers Guild, 151; and teaching force, 141, 246; and United Federation of Teachers (UFT), 248; and Wadleigh High School, 78, 95; and war effort, 111

Intermediate School (IS) 55, 188
Intermediate School (IS) 201, 8–9, 332,
    333, 352; and African-Hispanic
    History and Culture Institute, 223; as
    air raid shelter, 188, 193; and
    anti-narcotics campaign, 245; and
    architecture, 21, 183–98; and
    architecture effect on children, 196,
    197, 200, 201; and the arts, 201, 203;
    and Babette Edwards, 188, 222, 224,
    278–79, 281, 287, 290; and Black
    Power, 201; and Black studies, 223;
    building of, 188, 211, 222; and
    community control, 184, 186, 198,
    211, 222, 224, 237; and community
    education, 198–99; and Community
    Education Center, 223; and David
    Spencer, 224; and demonstration
    district, 21, 186, 224; and
    experimentation, 203, 224; and Ford
    Foundation, 186; and governing
    board, 24, 198, 201, 222, 223, 224,
    290; and Herman Ferguson, 201; as
    middle school, 21; and Preston
    Wilcox, 198–9; and Puerto Rican
    Studies, 223; and Ron Evans, 279;
    and segregation, 184, 187, 198, 201,
    203; and specialized high schools,
    199; and summer tutoring, 199
IS 201 Complex. See Schomburg
    Complex

Jack and Jill, 48
Jackie Robinson Park, 5
Jackman, Harold, 41
Jackson, Sherron, 172
Jacoby, Helmut, 188
jail, 1
James Fenimore Cooper Junior High
    School (JHS) 120, 17, 112, 125
jazz, 14

Jazz Age, 2
Jewish people, 1, 45
Jim Crow, 2, 34, 58, 143
Johns (Mrs.), 92
Johnson, Georgia Douglas, 37
Johnson, James Weldon, 14, 34, 35, 38;
    and celebration announcing Harlem
    Renaissance, 42
Johnson, Kimberley, 16, 330
Johnson, Mildred, 44–48, 328; and
    Ethical Culture School, 45; and
    Fieldston School, 46; and parents
    of, 45; and progressive education, 31,
    32, 44
Johnson, Thelma, 237
Jones, Leroi. See Baraka, Amiri
Julliard, 177
Junior High School (JHS) 136, 1
Juravich, Nick, 22, 306, 329, 330

Keliher, Alice, 104
Kilgore, Thomas, 48
King, Jonathan, 194
King, Leora, 48–49
King, Martin Luther, Jr., 201
King, Shannon, 8, 60
Kingsley, Sidney, 103
Kiswahili, 228
Klein, Joel, 314
Koch, Edward, 248
Kochiyama, Yuri, 216
Kornegay, Alice, 186
Kridel, Craig, 17, 328
Kweli, 199, 223

LaGuardia, Fiorello, 65, 67
Lamothe, Daphne, 34
Lane, Layle, 42, 49
Langley, Lola, 290
Lanning, Helen, 41
Larsen, Nella, 36, 38, 40

Latinx people, 5, 22, 139, 140, 141, 156;
and Babette Edwards, 276, 279, 283,
292; and Board of Education hiring
of, 147; and City University of New
York (CUNY), 313; and community
control, 3; and community education,
333; and contributions to U.S. culture,
109; fiscal crisis, 247, 264; and IS 201,
199; and IS 201 architecture, 195–96;
and loss of teaching jobs, 265; and
school districts, 300; and segregation,
113, 143; and student population of,
299; and teachers, 151–52, 318; as
teachers, 24, 303–4, 307, 310, 319; and
Teachers Guild, 141, 145, 150, 151,
153, 155; and Teachers Union, 143,
147, 150, 154; and United Federation
of Teachers (UFT), 155, 243, 287; and
women educators, 332. *See also*
Puerto Rican people
Latinx teachers, 24, 265, 303–4, 307,
310, 319
Lawrence, Margaret Morgan, 80, 88
Leadership Training Workshop, 171,
177–8. *See also* HARYOU
Lefebvre, Henri, 21, 203
Lehman, Herbert, 65
Lenox Community Center, 13
Levittown, 19
Lewer, Brittney, 23, 276, 329, 330
Lewis, David Levering, 32
Lewis, Heather, 308
Lewis, Oscar, 163
Liberation School, 216, 221
liberation schools, 211
librarians, 1
library, 222
"Lift Ev'ry Voice and Sing," 48
Lightfoot, Sara Lawrence, 80
Lincoln Hospital, 40
Lindsay, John, 198

Lisser, Stanley, 186
literary renaissance. *See* Harlem
Renaissance
literature, 2, 14
Locke, Alain, 14, 34, 35, 38, 49–50; as
adult-education teacher, 41; and
editing Progressive Educational
Association publication, 41; and
Harlem Renaissance, 42; and
humanity, 34; and riot, 65
Logue, Edward, 194
London, Norman, 125, 154
Louis, Joe, 122
Louisiana: New Iberia, 226; New
Orleans, 190, 193, 194
Lurie, Ellen, 278
lynching, 17

Macgowan, Kenneth, 38
Madison Square Garden, 244
Malcolm X, 2, 171, 201, 216;
assassination of, 211; and Queen
Mother Moore, 226
Mallory, Mae, 186
Marcantonio, Vito, 107, 144
March on Washington, 169
married-women teacher ban, 43. *See also*
Ayer, Gertrude
Marshall, James, 68
Marshall, Kenneth, 166, 176. *See also*
HARYOU
McCann, William R., 65
McCoy, Rhody, 241
McDougal, Cornelius, 42
McGruder, Kevin, 8
McKay, Claude, 199
Medgar Evers College, 264
medical facilities, 225
Meier, Deborah, 4
Met Life. *See* Metropolitan Life
Metropolitan Life, 16

Michael, Dorothy, 95

Michaux, Lewis, 214

Mickenberg, Julia, 128

middle-class, 4, 18, 19–20, 163, 168; and
HARYOU Associates, 169, 263

militancy, 211, 217

Mitchell, Lucy Sprague, 47

modernity, 42, 43

Modern School, The, 17, 46, 48. *See also*
Johnson, Mildred

Monteyne, David, 188

Montgomery, Alabama, 164

Moore, Audley "Queen Mother," 211,
226, 228; and summer program, 22

Moore, Richard B., 214

Morgan, Margaret, 80, 88

Morningside Health Center, 263

Morrell, Ernest, 335, 336

Morris High School, 93

Mount Addis Ababa, 227. *See also*
Moore, Audley "Queen Mother"

Moynihan, Daniel Patrick, 139

music, 2, 203

Myers, Walter Dean, 20

Nassau County, 18–19

Nation, The, 65, 147

National Association for the
Advancement of Colored People
(NAACP), 40, 48, 58, 61; and
release of LaGuardia commission
report, 67

National Black Theatre, 228

National Memorial Bookstore, 214, 215.
See also Michaux, Lewis

National Urban League (NUL), 48,
59, 144

Nation of Islam, 22, 213, 215

Native Son, 148

Naumburg, Margaret, 38

Neal, Larry, 214

Negro assimilationism, 213

Negro Experimental Theatre, 41

Negro Labor Committee, 144

Negro people. *See* Black people

Negro Revolution, 212

"Negro Speaks of Rivers, The," 128

New Negro Movement, 14, 31, 32, 33,
34, 49; and art, 38; and *Cane,* 36, 38,
39; and centrality of Black educators,
29; and construction of identity, 35,
121; and education, 38; and Gertrude
Ayer, 42; and Harlem, 41; and
luminaries as teachers, 42; and
Quicksand, 36, 39; and shaping of
landmark novels, 36; and societal
visions, 50; and Sugar Hill, 41; and
white progressive education, 35, 42.
See also Locke, Alain

New York Age, 61

New York Chapter of the American
Institute of Architects, 194

New York City: and heroin, 19; and
housing market, 12; and investment
in schools, 7; and married teacher
ban, 43

New York City Board of Education,
262; and adequate education, denial
of, 155; and Advisory Committee on
School Construction, 203; and
anticommunist campaigns of, 140,
155; and Audio-Visual Committee
of, 109; and Audley "Queen
Mother" Moore, 227; and *Brown v.
Board of Education,* 85, 141, 148–49,
164, 183; and citizen participation
with, 187; Committee on Buildings
and Sites, 190; and community
concerns, 144; and community
control, responses to, 224; and
Congress of Racial Equality
(CORE), 217; and decentralization,

187; and early emphasis of, 15; and employment, rates of, 263; and fiscal crisis, 266; and Gustav Shoenchen, 142; and Harlem Committee, 68; and Harlem Youth Opportunities Unlimited (HARYOU), 235, 237; and integration, 77, 141, 184, 192; involuntary transfer plan, 141; and IS 201, 190, 222; IS 201 architecture, 190, 193, 196; IS 201 siting, 191, 198; Isaiah Robinson, 198; and juvenile delinquency, 14; married-women teacher ban, 43; and multicultural curriculum, 109; and open enrollment, 183; and the Organization of African American Unity (OAAU), 216; and overcrowding, 66; and paraprofessionals, 234, 238, 240, 243, 244, 248; and parents, 186, 219, 237; and Preston Wilcox, 238; and principal, mock trial of, 17–8, 86, 88, 143–44; and racial discrimination, 265; and school closures, 258–59, 261, 268; and school districts, 84; and schools, building of, 154, 155, 191, 192, 203; and Teachers Guild, 143, 155; and teacher transfer plan, 152–54; and Teachers Union (TU), 126, 140, 141; and textbooks, 125–32; and urban school seminars, 194; and Wadleigh High School, 16, 77; and Women's Talent Corps (WTC), 238; and the Young Lords, 221; and zoning, 78, 83

New York City fiscal crisis, 22; causes of, 260; and community response, 23, 263, 329; and CUNY tuition, 313; effect on Black people, 261, 264; effect on education, 8, 263, 265–71, 308–9; effect on Latinx people, 264;

effect on teachers, 308–9; and healthcare, 263–4; and legislation, 263; and market economy, 259–60; and most vulnerable, 330; and paraprofessionals, 235, 247–50; and protests against, 257, 272; and school closures, 257, 271

New York City Municipal Archives, 190

New York Teachers Guild, 142; critical of Harlem activists, 142, 143; critical of Teachers Union, 142, 143; nightlife, 2

New York Teaching Fellows, 312

New York Times, 195, 263, 281, 308

New York Urban League, 60

Northside Center for Child Development, 55

OAAU Liberation School, 222

Obama, Barack, 4

Ocean Hill-Brownsville, 71n1, 141, 188

Office of Civil Defense, 193

Office of School Facilities Planning, 192

oppression, 2, 14

Organization of African American Unity (OAAU), 216. *See also* Malcolm X

O'Shea, William, 59

Osofsky, Gilbert, 7, 32, 79, 85

Our School, 228

overcrowding, 3, 7, 8, 16, 60; and 1970s, 259; and building of new school, 191; and campaigns against, 3; and decreasing student class time, 66; and elementary and junior high schools, 112; and Harlem, 317; and Queens, 94; and Wadleigh, 85

Oxford, 48

Pan-Africanism, 2, 4, 226
Pan-Africanists, 228
paraprofessionals, 234–49, 329; and
    Harlem innovation, 22, 23; and
    support of United Federation of
    Teachers, 22; and teacher solidarity
    with, 244; and unionization
Parent Information Center, 288
Parent-Teacher Teams, 239, 240
parochial schools, 195
Parrish, Richard, 237
Pataki, George, 288
pedagogy, 4, 10, 211; and anti-racism,
    111; and architecture, 192, 196;
    and Black teachers, 36; and child
    centered, 199; and community
    endeavors, 211; and critical education,
    336; critical media education, 328;
    and culturally affirming, 334, 336;
    and Ethical Culture school, 41, 45;
    and experimentation, 199; and
    Harlem Renaissance, 68; and IS 201,
    199; and John Henrik Clarke, 175;
    and Mildred Johnson, 45; and
    progressive education, 35, 40;
    student directed, 47
people of African descent. See African
    Americans; Black people; West
    Indian immigrants
People's Voice, 146
Perillo, Jonna, 18, 110, 328
Perlstein, Daniel, 2, 4, 14, 15, 120–21,
    150, 328
Permanent Committee for Better
    Schools, 92, 142
Permanent Committee on Harlem
    Schools, 142
Peterson, Dorothy, 38, 41
Phillips-Fein, Kim, 23, 308, 329, 330
Picket, Charles J., 69
Pittsburgh Courier, 64

planned shrinkage, 264
poetry, 14
police, 2, 64, 87; and brutality, 65; and
    juvenile crime, 147; and killing, 167;
    and uprising, 65
policing, 8, 60, 333
political organizing, 8, 165, 247. See also
    activists
political representation, barriers to, 2
political science, 4
Ports, Suki, 186
poverty, 63, 68, 103, 147, 163; and
    educational challenges, 8, 16, 90, 304;
    and effect on Harlem, 8, 19, 67, 332;
    and government programs to
    mitigate, 179, 216, 222, 235, 237; and
    Jean Toomer remarks, 37; statistics
    of, 20; and urban school systems, 6.
    See also culture of poverty; War on
    Poverty
Powell, Adam Clayton, Jr., 18, 144; and
    political differences with Kenneth
    Clark, 166–67; support of Harlem
    Committee petition, 68
progressive education, 14, 31–32, 35, 36,
    42, 43, 105; and Gertrude Ayer, 44,
    326; and Mildred Johnson, 328;
    versus human relations programs,
    106. See also Ayer, Gertrude; Harlem
    Renaissance; Johnson, Mildred; New
    Negro Movement
Progressive Education Association, 41
Progressive Education Association
    Commission on Human Relations,
    104, 105
Promise Zones. See Canada, Geoffrey
protest movements, 71n1
Public School (PS) 5, 18
Public School (PS) 22, 62
Public School (PS) 50, 62
Public School (PS) 108, 244

Public School (PS) 109, 62
Public School (PS) 125, 219
Public School (PS) 133, 198–200, 306
Public School (PS) 207, 240
Puerto Rican people, 122; identity
    and, 228; teacher training for
    mothers, 3
Puerto Rican studies, 223
Puerto Rico, 5, 77

Queens, 19. See also East Elmhurst;
    Hollis; St. Albans
Quicksand, 36, 39

Rabin, Lisa, 17, 328
racial consciousness. See Black
    consciousness
racial hierarchies, 128
racial pride, 211
racism, 2, 33, 129
racist textbooks, 112
radicalization, 212
Randolph, Philip A., 43, 61, 144
Rankin (Dr.), 90
Ray, Charles B., 80
Reagan, Ronald, 249
recreational facilities, 58
Reid De, Ira A., 42
reparations, 226
Republic of New Africa, 227
Rhodes Scholar, 34
Rickford, Russell: and Black Power, 21,
    329, 330, 120; and community
    control, 9; and IS 201, 201; and
    school autonomy, 333
Riessman, Frank, 245
riots. See uprisings
Rivera, Lino, 64
Riverdale, 45
Robeson, Benjamin C., 90
Robeson, Paul, 45

Robinson, Isiah, 203, 270
Robinson, John, 65
Rogers, Bethany L., 24, 42, 330
Rooney, Walter, 194
Rosenwald Fund, 132
Ross, Jacob, 57, 58, 64, 68
Rustin, Bayard, 236

Sallid, Otis, 177
Saltus, Ford, 161. See also HARYOU
San Francisco, 7
Schlockow, Oswald, 62–4, 84
Schoenchen, Gustav, 18
Schomburg collection library, 4
Schomburg Complex, 198, 222, 223,
    241, 244
school construction, 154
school facilities, 85
school guards, 270
school resources, 3
school vouchers, 285
Schuyler, George, 63–64, 80, 84
Seabrook, Luther, 270–71, 285, 309
segregation, 12, 23, 77, 84, 108, 172; and
    advocacy against, 141; and Black
    elites, 81; and Black teachers, 81, 148;
    and boycotts against, 212, 277; and
    Brooklyn, 7; and Brown v. Board of
    Education, 148, 150, 183; and Congress
    of Racial Equality (CORE), 218; and
    David Spencer, 186; and education,
    78; and employment, 141; and
    George Schuyler, 64, 84; and Harlem,
    7, 23, 183, 191, 304; and Harlem
    Committee film series, 110–11; and
    the Harlem Nine, 183, 281; housing,
    12, 78, 81, 84, 92, 103, 114, 162,
    304; IS 201, 21, 184, 187, 203, 221;
    and Jean Toomer, 37; and juvenile
    delinquency, 113, 114, 145; and labor,
    57, 146; and Mae Mallory, 183;

segregation (*continued*)
and migrants, 11, 12; multiple forms of, 77, 330; and New York outlawing of, 80; and New York State, 304; and Oscar Schlockow, 84; patterns of, 9, 141; and policies supporting, 3; and pre-Great Migration I, 80; and school vouchers, 282–3; and teacher assignment, 305; and tracking, 66, 146; and union support of, 146; and Viola Waddy, 183; and Wadleigh, 77, 83–85, 91, 93, 95; and Washington, 37; and W. E. B. Du Bois, 37; and Youthbuilders, 113; and zoning, 16, 20, 61, 92–93, 95
self-determination, 2, 234
Seltzer, Morris, 154
Shabazz, Betty, 201
Shanker, Albert, 248
Slack, Sara, 46
slavery, 57, 120, 121, 128, 226
small-school approach, 4
Smith College, 199
Snitow, Virginia L., 147
socialism, 121, 150, 226
Society of Ethical Culture, 45
sociology, 4, 6
the South, 2, 3
South Carolina, 57
Spanish, 199, 223, 228
Sparta Agricultural and Industrial Institute, 37
speakers' corner, 1
specialized high schools, 199
Spence, Eulalie, 41
Spence, Lucile, 82, 90
Spencer, David, 211, 224
St. Albans, 19
Stanford-Binet, 58
Starr, Roger, 31
Stavisky, Leonard, 263

street grid, 1, 4
street speakers, 2
Student Nonviolent Coordinating Committee (SNCC), 186
suburbanization, 6, 18, 131
Sugar Hill, 41
Sun Ra, 216
Supreme Court, 149
Sydenham Hospital, 263

Tates, Winifred, 234
Taylor, Clarence, 19, 71n1, 127, 328
Teachers College: and communities of color, 7, 141, 145, 150, 155, 304–12, 320; and teacher qualifications, 239, 288, 334. *See also* Black teachers; Latinx teachers
Teachers Guild, 18
teachers of color, 306; and charter schools, 312, 314; and community desire for, 320; and District 5, 24; and filtering of, 301, 305, 307; and Harlem transformation, 330; and job losses, 319; and National Teacher Exam, 312; and retention of, 313; and urban schools, 3, 307
teacher's strike of 1968, 21, 22, 141
Teachers Union, 138–56; and Board of Education, 127; and Communist Party, 17, 19; and community control, 224; and community empowerment, 127; and Fiorello LaGuardia commission, 65; and Harlem Committee of, 17, 103–15, 125, 132, 328; labor, 8, 14; and Langston Hughes, 125; and mandatory transfer, 304; Negro History Week publication, 125; and Nella Larsen, 40; and protests, 67; and opposition to charter schools, 287–8; and organizing, 2; and school

improvement, 19; and segregation, 57, 146; and Teachers Union, 17–20, 22, 24, 62, 67, 104, 108, 109, 110; and textbooks, 125–6

Teachers Union Institute, 104, 109. *See also* activists

Teach For America, 312

tenant organizing, 2

tenant rights, 226

Tenderloin district, 57

Testamark, Helen, 186

theater, 203

Third World, 223

Thomy Lafon Elementary School, 193

Thurman, Wallace, 38

Tildsley, John L., 86, 89

Time magazine, 193

Timothy Baptist Church, 268

Toomer, Jean, 36, 37, 38, 39, 40

Truth, Sojourner, 214

Tubman, Harriet, 119, 214

Tuskegee, 39, 40, 43

unemployment, 218, 221, 243, 246; and discrimination, 114, 144; and Great Depression, 8, 60, 110; rates of, 147

unemployment insurance, 248

United Bronx Parents, 199

United Federation of Teachers (UFT): and collective bargaining rights, 19; and paraprofessionals solidarity, 22; and women of color, 330

Universal Association of Ethiopian Women, 227

University of Sankore, 128

upper class, 168

uprisings, 85, 211

urban crisis, 4, 228

urban education: Harlem trajectory of, 3–4, 7; and historians, 334; history of, 335; and neglect, 16

urban school systems: and Black community, 3; and budgets, 273n10; and South, 6; structure of, 6

U.S. Southwest, 119

Vann, Albert, 264

Van Vechten, Carl, 45

Vietnam War, 188

Villard, Oswald Garrison, 65, 66

Violenes, Cecilia, 92, 93

vocational classes, 66

Wadleigh High School for Girls, 14, 16, 77–95; and African American enrollment, 82, 86; as all-Black school, 78; and architecture of, 79; and Black teachers, 82; Black urban girls, 78; and Board of Education, 77, 84, 85, 87, 89, 90, 91, 92, 93, 94; and closure of, 77, 92, 93, 94, 95; and community population, 82; and construction history of, 79; and curriculum, 84, 90, 91; and declining enrollment, 90, 91, 92; and discrimination, 80; and downtown location, 79; and Fiorello LaGuardia, 91; and Harlem Parents Association, 86; and Harlem riot, 85; and identification as Negro School, 90, 91, 92; and integration, 78, 82, 113; and John L. Tildsley, 86, 87, 88; and landmark status, 79; and Lucile Spence, 82, 90; and Margaret C. Byrne, 91; and Margaret Morgan Lawrence, 80; Mayor's Committee on Unity, 91; and *The Owl*, 79; and Permanent Committee for Better Schools, 86, 92; and plan for relocation, 87, 88, 89; and protection of white girls, 79; and racist tracking, 16; and renovation of, 95; and Ruth

Wadleigh High School for Girls (*continued*)
Dorothea Ellington, 83, 89; and school
populations, 8; and segregation, 83,
84, 93, 94; and supportive academic
environment, 80; transformed to
junior high school, 95; and the Upper
West Side, 79; and urban north Civil
Rights movement, 78; and vocational
courses for Black people, 16, 84, 89;
and West Indian enrollment, 82, 86;
and white hostility to Black people,
78, 82, 85, 86; and white refusal to
send daughters to, 90; and white
withdrawal, 90; and zoning rules,
83–4, 89, 92
Walmart, 291
Walton Family Foundation, 291
War on Poverty, 20, 161, 162, 164, 167;
and HARYOU, 178
Washington, Booker T., 57, 59, 119
West Harlem Liberation School, 21, 219
West Indian immigrants, 2, 5, 15, 77, 82,
86, 328
White, Terrenda C., 24, 330
White, Walter, 121, 131
white people: and bigotry, 39; and the
closure of Wadleigh High School for
Girls, 16; and discrimination, 12, 13;
and divestment, 6, 7; as educators, 15;
and enforcing educational inequities,
64, 81; and gentrification, 2; and
Gertrude Ayer, 42; and Harlem
early development, 1, 11, 79; and
Harlem Renaissance, 34, 45; Harlem
school population, 61; and Harlem
uprising, 65; and homeownership,
6, 12; and IS 201, 9; and Jean
Toomer, 36, 38; as landlords, 12; and
leaving Harlem, 12, 56; and Mildred
Johnson, 47; and Nella Larsen, 40;
and power in Harlem, 2; and

progressive education, 2, 14, 19,
32, 35, 37, 47; and psychological
development of Black children, 40;
and racist fear, 12; and racist tracking,
84; schools in early New York, 80;
as social scientists, 6; and state power,
6; and suburbanization, 2, 18; as
teachers, 17, 19, 86; and teachers
union, 22; and teaching force, 22;
and underfunding of Black schools,
12; and unemployment rate versus
Black rate, 60; and violence, 12, 36;
Wadleigh population, 16, 77, 79, 80,
85; and Wadleigh, preservation of
school status, 86; Wadleigh, resistance
sending daughters to, 82, 83; and
wealth, 6; and white flight, 18–9, 57;
and white supremacy, 24, 64, 175; and
women's wages versus Black women,
43; World War I, 11. *See also*
Wadleigh High School for Girls
Wilcox, Preston, 190, 203, 211, 246; and
IS 201, 196, 198–99, 203, 237, 241
Willis, Benjamin, 194
Wilson-Brooks, Barbara, 199, 200, 306
Women's Talent Corps, 241
working-class people, 8, 132, 330
World War II, 3, 18, 19
Wright, Elfreda S., 266
Wright, Richard, 49, 91, 148

Yale University, 198
Yoruba, 228
Yoruba Temple, 213
Young Lords, 221
youth, 1, 2, 4, 20. *See also* HARYOU
Youthbuilders, 113
YWCA, 48

Zoning Resolution of 1961, 195
Zuni, 119

CPSIA information can be obtained
at www.ICGtesting.com
Printed in the USA
JSHW031101180721
16988JS00001B/1